INTERVIEWING IN CONTEXT

Interviewing
in Context

GERALD L. WILSON
University of South Alabama

H. LLOYD GOODALL, Jr.
University of Utah

McGRAW-HILL, INC.

New York St. Louis San Francisco Auckland Bogotá
Caracas Hamburg Lisbon London Madrid Mexico Milan
Montreal New Delhi Paris San Juan São Paulo Singapore
Sydney Tokyo Toronto

INTERVIEWING IN CONTEXT

2 3 4 5 6 7 8 9 0 DOC DOC 9 5 4 3 2 1

ISBN 0-07-070858-4

This book was set in Times Roman by the College Composition Unit
in cooperation with Ruttle Shaw & Wetherill, Inc.
The editors were Hilary Jackson and Scott Amerman;
the production supervisor was Denise L. Puryear.
The photo editor was Debra P. Hershkowitz.
R. R. Donnelley & Sons Company was printer and binder.

Library of Congress Cataloging-in-Publication Data

Wilson, Gerald L., (date).
    Interviewing in context / Gerald L. Wilson, H. Lloyd Goodall, Jr.
    —[1st ed.]
        p.   cm.
    Includes bibliographical references and index.
    ISBN 0-07-070858-4
    1. Interviews—Authorship.   2. Interviewing.   I. Goodall, H.
Lloyd.   II. Title.
PN171.I66W55   1991
158′.39—dc20
                                                      90-6653

ABOUT THE
AUTHORS

Gerald L. Wilson is Associate Professor of Communication and Coordinator of Graduate Study at the University of South Alabama where he teaches courses in organizational communication. He received his B.S. from Bowling Green State University, his M.A. from Miami University, and his Ph.D from the University of Wisconsin—Madison. Professor Wilson is an active consultant to business and industry, working over the past 10 years with such organizations as RCA Corporation, Jefferson National Life Insurance Company, Scott Paper Company, and International Paper Company.

Professor Wilson has authored numerous articles for journals as well as papers for professional meetings. He is co-author of five books about communication. His most recent books are *Communicating in Business and Professional Settings,* 3d ed. (McGraw-Hill, 1991), and *Groups in Context: Participation and Leadership in Small Groups,* 2d ed. (McGraw-Hill, 1990).

H. Lloyd Goodall, Jr., is Associate Professor of Communication at the University of Utah. In addition to teaching courses in organizational communication, cultural studies, and ethnography, he is the author or co-author of 10 other books and over 50 articles and papers. His most recent scholarly books featuring interviewing processes are *Casing a Promised Land: The Autobiography of an Organizational Detective as Cultural Ethnographer* (1989) and *Living in the Rock 'n' Roll Mystery: Reading Context, Self, and Others as Clues* (1991). His co-curricular interests include investigative work, rock music, and archaeology.

We dedicate this book to
Sandra Goodall, Clarence and Martha Bray, and Ryan Stewart Wilson,
who enrich and sustain our lives.

CONTENTS

PREFACE

Our aim in writing *Interviewing in Context* was to develop a book for the growing number of undergraduate communication courses that address a variety of interviewing situations. What was needed, we thought, was a lively textbook that would be comprehensive, and that would blend current theory and research with practical skills and applications. We also wanted a book that was richly illustrated with real-life examples from a broad range of professional and organizational settings. We had become convinced, on the basis of our teaching, research, and consulting experiences, that such a book was much needed.

Interviewing in Context is designed to treat the main topics that are common to an interviewing course. To that end we conducted a survey of people who teach the course. We also made a careful analysis of materials used to teach the course—both textbooks and course outlines—in order to discover the list of topics that are covered most often. Beyond this, we asked fourteen people who regularly teach the interviewing course to review our manuscript at various stages. We believe our book responds well to the needs of those teaching the interviewing course. Although we believe our organizational motif makes good sense, each of the organizational and professional context chapters is self-contained so that an instructor may assign reading in whatever order he or she may like.

In all of our work on this book, we have tried to keep the student reader in mind, repeatedly asking ourselves: What does the student need to know about this concept? Can we provide a real example of that idea? Will the reader be able to relate to this example? What learning aids can we provide to make the learning experience more complete?

We believe interviews to be an important part of a person's personal and professional life. All of us give and collect information on a daily basis through interviews, which is how we learn much of what we know about our world. Interviews are essential tools for clarifying our understanding of the expectations of our coworkers, friends, and bosses. We also use interviews to secure employment, understand how we are doing on the job, and manage performance difficulties. In addition, when we are ill, we use interviews to inform the health care professional. When problem solving is required, we use interviews, too. And, of course, interviews are central to professionals who engage in marketing, public relations, organizational development, journalism, health care, and sales. Being a skillful interviewer is central to personal and professional success.

FEATURES

Interviewing in Context presents a balanced approach—a blend of theory and practical application. We believe this approach is useful because it maintains intellectual integrity while showing students how to apply the ideas to interviews in real-life contexts. With this objective in mind, we have written a text that is well grounded in both classic and contemporary research, and that is also richly illustrated with real-life examples.

The title *Interviewing in Context* suggests our vision for the book. In writing this text we focused on what we believe is the key factor that enhances learning and makes it a more exciting and meaningful enterprise. Understanding the context that surrounds an interview and the requirements that it places on the participants is also central to being a successful interviewer or interviewee. Likewise, a book that is to successfully teach interviewing must do the same. Thus we focus on context and contextual factors—the physical, social-psychological, temporal, and cultural environment—in our presentation of interviewing.

Context is operative in the learning process. It is certainly possible to present concepts and ideas relatively apart from context. We think that when this happens, the learning process is hampered. On the other hand, when ideas are framed in a concrete, relatable circumstance, they are likely to be more fully understood. We believe that an interviewing textbook that is written to optimize learning must illustrate its ideas and discussion of principles with real-life examples presented in context. We have been especially careful to follow this principle.

Another important asset for a textbook, written with this goal in mind, is a writing style and content that students find engaging. It is neither too energetic nor too scholarly, but a blend of principles and practical applications that make the book interesting and engaging. We believe we achieve this aim.

Application and transfer of concepts to real-life situations is an important reason for teaching interviewing. Yet students do not find it easy to make the transition from classroom to personal interviewing experiences. We sought to address this issue by providing a substantial number of current real-life examples drawn from the many interviewing contexts students may encounter. Examples from business and industry, from government, from community situations, from educational situations, and from social and health care organizations have all been included. This feature suggests the broad applicability of the principles to a variety of situations, and ensures that the book will be a useful handbook for reference in the years to come.

SPECIAL FEATURES

When people engage in communication as responsible professionals, we believe they agree to conform to what is considered ethical and responsible behavior. Ethics is an important issue for all of us and of much concern to society. In planning this book, we concluded that it would be essential to integrate treatment of ethical concerns. Thus we began in Chapter 1 with a discussion of ethics as both an interpersonal and an organizational issue. Then, in each of the six chapters where interviews in organizational and professional contexts are presented, application of ethical concerns is addressed.

We also believe that a book about interviewing is more useful to students if it provides them with methods for addressing problems they might encounter, both now and in the future. Often, as time passes, the specifics of concepts and their application fade from memory. Thus, this book is designed so that it can serve as a useful reference to the professional and to students when they enter their chosen professions. The applications we have described do not change much over time. The suggestions we have made for effective interviewing will hold up well in years to come, as they have over the past twenty years of our experience. In order to provide easy access to these suggestions, a troubleshooting guide is provided toward the end of this text. This guide indexes interviewing problems by posing questions the readers might ask, and then refers to places in the text where those questions are answered. This troubleshooting guide and the complete index of authors and topics guarantee access to the substantive and practical materials of this book.

LEARNING AIDS

This book is designed to be a useful teaching and learning device. It includes not only carefully developed illustrations throughout, but also clear statements of learning objectives for each chapter, clear summaries of the material in each chapter, suggestions for further reading, and a glossary of important terms. The book also includes interviews for evaluation and discussion as well as suggestions for practice assignments at the end of each chapter.

Each chapter begins with a list of *objectives* that point to the most important themes in that chapter. Our effort has been to make the intent of our book, chapter by chapter, as clear as possible to our readers. *Key terms* are italicized and defined as they are presented. *Chapter summaries* at the end of each chapter recast the important ideas of the chapter into general statements that should leave no doubt in the reader's mind about what the key ideas are. *Interviews for analysis* provide an opportunity for a class to analyze an interview for applications of the principles they have been studying.

Over the years we have found that classroom discussion and understanding of the materials presented in these chapters is facilitated by certain *discussion questions* and *experiences*. We include the questions and experiences we have found most helpful at the end of each chapter. There, too, is found a carefully selected *recommended readings* list. Our aim in suggesting these materials is to identify the best, and in some cases most influential, works available in communication and interviewing literature. We think students should be made aware of the benchmarks in a discipline. We also think less well known works, when they are especially relevant, should be brought to readers' attention, and so some of those works are mentioned, too.

ORGANIZATION OF THE BOOK

Part 1: Preliminary Considerations

This book is organized in deductive fashion. Part 1, "Preliminary Considerations," which consists of Chapters 1 and 2, introduces basic ideas related to communication and the interviewing process, and provides a basic conceptual foundation for the rest of the book.

Part 2: Basic Considerations: Foundations for Communication in Interviews

The second section of this book encompasses three chapters that present information about basic interview development. We begin, in Chapter 3, with a discussion of basic interview structure and issues related to it. Then, in Chapters 4 and 5, we provide a thorough explanation of the questioning process. Chapter 4 provides an understanding of questions while Chapter 5 discusses effective usage.

Part 3: Organizational Contexts

Interviewing serves two basic purposes at the organizational level: bringing people into the organization and conveying an assessment of their performance. This part of the book addresses these issues in Chapters 6 and 7, selection interviewing, and Chapter 8, "The Performance Appraisal Interview."

Part 4: Professional Contexts

The final section looks at how a professional person will use interviewing in carrying out her or his work. Chapters 9 and 10 look at interviewing situations in which data is being gathered. First, in-depth information gathering is considered, then the survey interview. These techniques are applicable to a variety of circumstances, ranging from creating a feature story to collecting data regarding reasons for separating from a group or organization. Next, in Chapter 11, the problem-solving interview is considered. Here, the professional person may be handling a work problem or counseling regarding a client problem. Finally, in Chapter 12, the persuasive interview is investigated. This interview is designed to present a proposal, whether it be to a boss or to a client.

RESOURCES FOR INSTRUCTORS

An *Instructor's Manual* is available to aid instructors in their teaching. It will provide sample syllabi and assignments as well as materials for evaluating mastery of the text.

ACKNOWLEDGMENTS

The following individuals have provided excellent suggestions as we revised this manuscript: Marcia Benjamin-Leiter, Manchester College; Patrice Buzzanell, Marquette University; Kenneth Cissna, University of South Florida; Robert Greenstreet, East Central University; Lisa Newman, University of Cincinnati; Norman Perrill, Arizona State University; Terry Pickett, Iowa State University; James Quisenberry, Morehead State University; Steve Ralston, Iowa State University; Diane Reid, Indiana University Southeast; Beulah Rohrlich, Syracuse University; Elizabeth Rygh, University of Northern Iowa; Frances Sayers, University of Southern Maine; and David Walker, Middle Tennessee State University. We are grateful, and we take this opportunity to express our sincere thanks to them.

The following have responded to our survey about their interviewing courses: Stephen Blatt, University of Dayton; Warren Burns, University of Maine, Orono; Phillip Clampitt, University of Wisconsin, Green Bay; Suzanne Hagen, University of Wisconsin, River Falls; Robert Heath, Oral Roberts University; David Hopcroft, Quinebaug Valley Community College; Jo Keller, Manchester College; Paul King, Texas Christian University; Jerry Martin, Muskingum College; Norman Perrill, Arizona State University; Loyd Pettegrew, University of South Florida; Beulah Rohrlich, Syracuse University; W. Robert Sampson, University of Wisconsin, Eau Claire; and Ralph Webb, Purdue University. We are grateful to them.

Authors write manuscripts, which are then turned into books by extraordinarily able, dedicated people employed by the publishing company. We especially want to thank our editors, Roth Wilkofsky, Hilary Jackson, Scott Amerman, and Kathleen Domineg, who contributed their exceptional expertise and knowledge to this project.

Gerald L. Wilson
H. Lloyd Goodall, Jr.

INTERVIEWING IN CONTEXT

Preliminary Considerations

CHAPTER 1

AN INTRODUCTION TO INTERVIEWING

OBJECTIVES

After reading this chapter you should be able to:

Explain the seven basic ideas inherent in the study of
   communication.
Provide a definition of interviewing.
Provide a definition of context.
Explain how the concept of culture applies to interviewing
   in contexts.
Discuss the types of interviews commonly encountered in
   professional and social life.
Suggest how interviewing can have an impact on your life.
Develop ethical guidelines for interviewing.
Prepare a set of objectives to guide your study of
   interviewing in contexts.

Dorothy Quinn, a counselor at a northwestern university, is awaiting the arrival of an undergraduate student who wants to talk with her. The student, Hannah, is a nineteen-year-old freshman in her first term of school. She was a good high school student, and she is enjoying college, but she is very concerned about her anxiety regarding test taking. She has decided to ask for help.

Dr. Quinn begins the interview:

Dr. Quinn: Good morning, Hannah. I am Dr. Quinn. I understand that this is your first term at the university. How do you like being with us?

Hannah: I really enjoy school. I've made lots of good friends and have a great roommate. She and I have a lot in common. I even found out that we both took karate lessons a couple of years ago.

Dr. Quinn: It sounds like you are really comfortable with the move from high school to college.

Hannah: It's really been great! But I'm a little scared about doing well. My mom and dad are counting on me, and I got some really low grades on my midterms. I've never had such bad grades before. I'm really nervous about finals.

Dr. Quinn: I see. Your high school grades were good, but you find that you are not doing so well on college tests?

Hannah: That's it.

Dr. Quinn: Let's talk more about this test-taking situation. Tell me about the last test you took.

In the regional office of a large paper-making company, Benjamin Wolfe is waiting for a job interview with Eric Duncan, a department manager. Ben has prepared for this interview and feels confident about his abilities. Although he had not anticipated this wait, it has given him time to mull over some questions. How should he greet Mr. Duncan? What, if anything, should he say about starting late? What unexpected questions might be asked? Will Mr. Duncan give him the opportunity to find out what he wants to know about the company? What kind of man is this Mr. Duncan, anyway? When will they get started?

Every day millions of people take part in counseling interviews, job interviews, informational interviews, sales interviews, problem-solving interviews, appraisal interviews, and survey interviews. Because interviews take place so frequently, we often rely on what we have learned by the trial and error of going through the process. Perhaps you have taught yourself a great deal about interviewing through this method. But, if you think back to recent experiences you have had with interviews, you will probably agree that you could have been more effective. The old saying that "practice makes perfect" does not always hold. It is possible to practice some unwise habits. Practice can make perfect, but only when that practice is informed by careful study and the following of good models.

Interviewing is a particularly important skill because all professional fields require it. Interviewing is used daily, both formally and informally, to collect information, get jobs, hire capable people, sell ideas and products, learn from performance appraisal, and solve problems.

Our purpose in writing this book is to introduce you to the basic principles of interviewing and show you how they can be used effectively in each of the above contexts. Our goal for you is to move far beyond what you have been able to learn from trial and error. Interviewing is a form of interpersonal communication, and as such, it involves all the essential ingredients or components of the communication process.

COMMUNICATION: THE SEVEN BASIC COMPONENTS

In the study of science you learn that there is an important vocabulary of concepts that includes words such as *cell, mitosis, gravity, matter,* and *energy.* The purpose of learning the definitions of these words is to give you the fundamentals of the language of science, a language that will help you to understand your world.

The same is true for the study of communication. In this section we will explore the seven basic components of the communication process; all these basic elements are part of an effective interview.

To begin, think of what communication between two persons "looks like." If you were to draw a picture of it, what would that picture include? Of course, the picture would include at least two people, the communicators, whom we will call a *source/encoder* and a *receiver/decoder.* There would have to be some way of labeling the communication they exchange—we will call communication that expresses an idea the *message*. The exchange is more than transmission of a message, there is a response to the message that we will call *feedback*. And, of course, the messages and feedback pass between the source and receiver through something we call *channels*. You would also want to include some way to depict interruptions, interference with the message or feedback, what we will call *noise*. Finally, there should be some way of naming the context for the exchange of messages, or what we will term the *situation*. These are the basic components of the communication process: (1) source/encoder, (2) channels, (3) message, (4) receiver/decoder, (5) feedback, (6) noise, and (7) situation. Perhaps, if you had actually sketched out these ideas, they would resemble the drawing in Figure 1.1.

Source/Encoder and Receiver/Decoder

A source/encoder is the person who initiates the interaction. This person starts the exchange of information. A receiver/decoder is the person who receives and interprets the meanings of the messages sent by the source.

Figuring out precisely how this works in actuality is more complicated than it initially appears. Consider the case of Bob and Ellen:

> Bob and Ellen have been going together for about a year. They would describe their relationship as relatively serious. Ellen has been out of town on a week-long break. Before she left, they both had made a tentative commitment to spend the weekend at the beach upon her return. Bob has been eagerly looking forward to this time together and intends to make the final plans. Ellen has a problem. She left an important project undone, so she now needs to use the weekend in order to complete it.

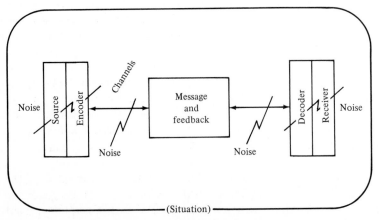

Figure 1.1   Model of the communication process.

Bob enters Ellen's apartment and begins by commenting on the new print she has on her wall. She tells him that she picked it up on her trip to California. For another few minutes they talk about California. Then there is a long pause, and Bob sees it as an opportunity to begin his discussion about their weekend at the beach. He begins, but is quickly interrupted by Ellen, who sees his shift in topic to be the perfect opening for her discussion of her uncompleted project.

Who has initiated this interaction? Obviously, the answer is Bob. After all, he was the one who came to Ellen and began the communication—first, about the new print, then about their plans for the weekend. However, it is also clear that Ellen had a specific purpose in mind, and she seized the first opportunity she had to pursue it. Both Bob and Ellen were potential sources of this interaction; however, Bob is labeled the source at this point because he was the one who actually started the conversation.

What this scene shows is the difficulty of assigning source/encoder status to one person in an interaction that, by definition, includes two people, both of whom have motives for talk. Topics change rapidly as conversation flows, and soon it becomes difficult to locate the source. This scene points out how quickly source/encoder status change. Once Bob is interrupted by Ellen, who wants to talk about her need to commit time to her project, we might say he becomes a receiver/encoder and she attains source/encoder status because she is initiating a new topic and sending the message. As the interaction continues, source/encoder status shifts between them as each one seizes an opportunity to send a message to the other and the other listens.

While the terms *encoder* and *decoder* may sound like engineering concepts (in fact, they are), they are useful in our study of human communication. They point out the relationship between *encoded meaning* versus *decoded meaning*. There is no such thing as a direct transfer of meaning from source to receiver. Meaning is *negotiated* as the source and receiver talk back and forth as they work to clarify meaning and achieve understanding. But the process is not precise, so the meaning we convey may not be exactly the meaning we intend. And further, the meaning the receiver attributes to the message may be a misinterpretation. The responsibility for exchanging the intended message rests on both the sender and the receiver. Figure 1.2 depicts one way of understanding this relationship.

In the figure we have drawn a narrative map of Ellen's and Bob's thoughts. These are the sum totals of what each individual was thinking about—the motives for their talk and the information that they planned to share.

We have also depicted what they actually said under the label "conveyed meaning." Notice that there are fewer words, and they are generally of a far more abstract nature. These are the verbal "shorthands" they used in the encoding and decoding process. For the source/encoder, the inten-

Bob   # Ellen

Thoughts	Conveyed Meanings	Thoughts
I'm glad she's back! Now we can talk about our weekend. Why does she look so uptight? Nice print! Looks cheap, though. Should I bring up how tense she looks? I guess I'll just ignore how she looks. She's probably just tired.	Nice print, Ellen! ⟶ ⟵ I picked it up in California.	How am I going to tell him about the project? Maybe the subject of the weekend will come up. Will Bob be angry? Oh, he finally noticed my print. I picked it up in California. It's really cheap. I wonder if he'll notice?

Figure 1.2   Narrative map of Bob and Ellen's thoughts.

tions are converted into brief statements that for the speaker convey the intended meanings. However, the receiver/decoder must again convert these words into meanings.

For the source/encoder and receiver/decoder there is no guarantee that what is intended will be adequately communicated; nor is there any guarantee that what is communicated will be adequately understood. Encoding and decoding are terms that represent the complex process of figuring out how to say what we mean and how to understand what someone else means. Later in this book we will provide techniques to help you develop these skills within interviews.

Messages and Feedback

A *message* is whatever ideas are conveyed by the verbal and nonverbal behavior of a source. *Feedback* is the verbal and nonverbal behavior of a receiver directed back to the source in reaction to the content of the message. Because source and receiver status change frequently during an interview, so does message and feedback status. Let's return to Ellen and Bob to illustrate this idea.

Bob has just been interrupted by Ellen, something he absolutely can't stand. So, he provides feedback regarding her interrupting behavior. He stops her in mid-sentence:

Bob: You know, Ellen, I don't like it when you interrupt me.

She continues her sentence:

Ellen: ...so what I need to know is what you think about———?

She pauses, squints, and says:

Ellen: What did you say?

Bob: I said I don't like it when you interrupt me. It's like saying that what I'm talking about isn't important.

Ellen: I'm sorry, Bob. I was just preoccupied with this project. You know I have to make a presentation on it and I'm worried because I'm behind schedule.

Bob: I know you're worried about the project, but I don't think that's a good reason to interrupt me. I'd like to finish my idea, and then I'll listen.

Ellen: I'm just afraid I won't meet the deadlines.

Bob: I know it's going to be difficult to meet the deadline. But, you know I can help. And I'm willing to help.

Ellen: Tell me about your ideas for this weekend.

We interrupt Bob and Ellen at this point in their interaction. We can see that deciding what we want to call a message and what we want to call feedback can be difficult. What is the message here? What is Bob conveying to Ellen—that he wants to talk about the weekend or that her behavior toward him is impolite? And what about Ellen? Is her feedback that she is worried about the deadlines, or that she doesn't pay attention to Bob when he talks?

Conceptually a *message* is verbal and nonverbal information used to accomplish a purpose, and *feedback* is verbal and nonverbal behavior directed back to a source from a receiver about the message. However, as we have just shown in Bob and Ellen's communication, we must know who initiated the particular message in order to discover the source. Beyond this, it is often correct to say that there are multiple messages, each of which might produce feedback.

Channels and Noise

A *message* is the idea or combination of ideas expressed by the source. It is created by the arrangement of symbols that are meaningful to the source/encoder and interpreted by the receiver/decoder. *Channels* are the medium through which the message is sent. Thus, channels may be aural channels (such as speech sounds, music, pausing, phrasing, and so on) or visual channels (such as gestures and facial expressions). We transmit and receive messages with the aid of our five senses, which represent the variety of communication channels illustrated in our model.

It is generally more correct to refer to channel*s*, rather than channel, when we talk about transmitting a message. You will rarely communicate through only one channel. Consider Susan, a sales representative, conducting a persuasive interview. She will be careful to pick the right words. But she will also try to maintain direct eye contact, raise the volume of her voice when appropriate, and perhaps use her voice to give a sense of urgency. She is using multiple channels to enhance the reception of her message.

Often we will experience interference in the channels, which disrupts our ability to receive a message. This interference is called *noise*. Noise can be located externally or internally to the participants in the communication exchange.

External noise is *physical noise*. Some stimulus, external to us, interferes with our ability to fully receive a message. The interference may be caused by sounds such as the passing of jets, trains, or cars; the scraping of chairs; or the movement of people in an adjacent hallway. The distraction may be visual, too. Perhaps the light is too bright or too dim, or something is obstructing our view of the person with whom we are communicating. The distraction might be another environmental factor, too, such as heat or the discomfort of our chair. Almost anything in our environment might become noise.

Sources of internal noise also are many. You might be experiencing *physiological noise* if you are hungry or not feeling well. Or perhaps you are experiencing some kind of *psychological noise*. Perhaps you have an important meeting to make and an interview is going longer than it should. You might be preoccupied with thoughts about how you will explain your lateness instead of focusing fully on the interview. Perhaps relational factors are creating psychological noise. You may have had negative experiences with a person you must interview and you can't get those out of your mind. Perhaps your boss is using a tone of voice that is saying, "Don't forget that I *am in charge*." Sometimes psychological noise is related to semantic factors. One interviewer we know calls adult men "boys"; many of his interviewees are distracted by this expression, which they find old-fashioned. The message can at least temporarily be lost in this semantic noise.

Situation

Situation, for our purposes, refers to the physical and psychological environment that surrounds an interview. You can think of it as a boundary formed by (1) physical setting, (2) the goals of a specific communication episode, and (3) the outcomes and actual exchanges. Suppose, for example, that you decide to ask your boss for a raise. You might describe the general situation as follows: I am going to talk to my boss in her office at 2 o'clock on Friday. I want to be seen as a competent employee who is deserving of being rewarded. I will ask for a 5 percent raise and expect to get it. I expect the communication exchange to be pleasant.

The importance of thinking about communication as being situational lies in the concept of talk. Some communication scholars believe that talk is a strategic response we make to a situation.[1] Our talk is "*given* to a situation," it is a response to some problem, idea, or circumstance. We don't talk about just anything; instead, we tend to confine our talk to the situation in which we find ourselves, and we restrict our talk to whatever rules or standards seem to be appropriate to a given situation. For example, if a friend of ours approaches us with a problem, we will focus the talk on that problem. We may even have an agenda of our own, but we will put it aside because the situation requires us to focus on our friend and his or her problem.

Our communication thus usually occurs within a situation. By defining any situation in general terms first, then in specific ones (in this book, interviews, specifically an employment interview, a performance appraisal interview, a counseling interview, and so on) we bring to the situation a set of expectations that is useful both for developing and evaluating it. We will see in subsequent chapters where we discuss interviewing standards in detail that each interview situation involves situationally derived expectations on the part of the participants. They use these expectations to evaluate their own, and each other's, effectiveness.

We have discussed seven basic components of the communication process: source/encoder, channels, message, receiver/decoder, feedback, noise, and situation. Understanding these components is important because they serve as a foundation for communication language and as a basis for our study of interviewing; each component exists in the interview situation.

INTERVIEWING DEFINED

An interview is *a communication process in which two or more people interact within a relational context by asking and answering questions designed to achieve a specific purpose.*

A Communication Process

As you have just learned, a communication process refers to an exchange of talk that can be described by seven key elements.

The term *communication process* was introduced by David Berlo in 1960. As he used it, *process* was simply intended to mean *a phenomena that occurs over time and changes with time as it occurs.* The adjective *communication* implied any speech act, such as talking with a stranger, exchanging information in a group, or making a public speech. Therefore, Berlo's meaning for communication process was any speech act that develops meanings over time and changes those meanings with the passage of time. Today we accept this view of process as readily as we accept the laws of physics.

Interaction within Relational Contexts

The phrase "in which two or more persons interact within a relational context" defines boundaries. For example, most interviews are conducted in dyads. A *dyad* is defined as two people. But, occasionally, people do conduct group interviews, so more than two people can be involved. To *interact* is to exchange both verbal and nonverbal messages. *Relational context* is defined by the formal and informal roles that the participants assume.

In an interview, two people are in the process of exchanging verbal and nonverbal messages, each person performing the role described by his or her position in a group or organization: a shop foreman discussing manufacturing plans with a worker, a lawyer interviewing a potential client about a case, a manager talking about a raise with a computer operator, or a journalist interviewing a mayor. In addition, informal roles, such as the role of a friend, will have impact on the exchange.

Within the context of the interview, interaction takes on three important characteristics. First, it tends to be rule-governed. This means that whatever standards exist within the culture for the exchange of talk between members, whether it be organizational or societal, will be in force. Rules may govern how superiors and subordinates should be addressed, who has "control" over the situation, and what information ought to be included in answers. If the relationships within the organization or profession consist of loosely coupled co-equals, such as salespeople in a department store or a journalist and community leader, different rules probably will be in effect.

Second, the interaction in interviews tends to be polite and goal-directed. By *polite* we mean that interruptions, name-calling, use of coarse language, and failure to cooperate are seldom appropriate. By *goal-directed* we mean that the questions asked and the answers received should correspond to the purpose and scope of the interview.

Third, the interaction in interviews adheres to certain legal requirements. Within interviews, laws govern against articulating biases and prejudices against women and minorities, abusing people's civil rights, and other violations of legal standards.

The concept of relational context is important to the study of interviewing because it helps us understand how interpersonal relationships can influence any kind of talk. For example, two individuals who dislike each other but have to work cooperatively are more likely to show superiority, attempts to deceive, or harm in an interview than are persons who like and respect each other.

Two special characteristics of the relational context need our consideration. First, formal roles take precedence over informal roles in talk exchanged during interviews. This means that although two people have a personal relationship beyond the interview setting, during formal interviews the formal role tends to become more important. This does not mean that the informal relationship ceases to exist, merely that it should be of secondary concern.

Second, the relational context of an interview should not alter the group or organizational roles enacted during the course of the interview. This means, simply, that the person in charge of conducting the interview should remain in charge. Clearly, this is different than the relational context between two friends having dinner, where "who is in charge" in most cases is not an issue, or between colleagues sharing informal talk on a more equal basis.

Questions and Answers to Achieve a Specific Purpose

The substance of all interviews is questions and answers. As you will learn in subsequent chapters, the ability to phrase a question is important because it determines the way in which that question will be answered. You will also learn that there are several types of questions, each one designed to gain a particular kind of response.

Answers are only truly useful when they provide information that helps the interviewer reach the specific purpose. Interviews can have a variety of purposes—from gaining information to solving a problem—and there is a great deal of skill involved in understanding your purpose clearly enough to guide your selection of appropriate questions. Without a clear purpose, the interview may drift and most likely will produce information of little value to either participant.

Thus far, we have said that interviewing is a form of interpersonal communication, and as such, involves all the essential ingredients or components of the communication process. In interviews this process has a specific purpose and more formal roles and boundaries than in informal exchanges of "talk."

INTERVIEWS IN CONTEXT

You often hear the remark by a person who believes that he or she is being misunderstood, "You're taking my statement out of context." This person (the source) is complaining that the listener did not consider or understand important information when interpreting the message. Joseph DeVito has defined *context of communication* as "the physical, social-psychological, and temporal environment in which communication takes place and which exerts influence on the form and content of communication."[2] In essence, DeVito is saying that we should take a wide view of what surrounds a communication event—the physical setting, the social makeup of those people communicating, their mental state, and the point in time in which they are communicating—to understand what constitutes its context.

Both of these understandings of context supply useful ideas. The commonsense definition of context suggests that the meaning of a particular communication is best understood in terms of the context. DeVito adds to our understanding by suggesting that we need to look to the physical, social-psychological, and temporal environment to see how it influences the form and content of communication. So, the context of a selection interview, for example, might be:

> A placement center at a large midwestern university, with a 22-year-old communication major, nervous because this is his first interview, and a 50-year-old veteran interviewer from a major industry, on Friday afternoon at three o'clock.

The time of day, inexperience, and nervous state of the interviewee will undoubtedly influence the event. So, too, will the long experience the interviewer has with the process. The participants' understanding of what constitutes a selection interview will help them understand and interpret the event. So the context both influences and gives meaning to the communication event, and we are to look to the physical, social-psychological, and temporal environment to aid our understanding.

Context is also important to our understanding of the principles and practices of interviewing. When studying interviewing, we will want to view context in two basic ways: generic and particular. A *generic* aspect of context refers to a factor that is present across all interviews, such as the roles connected with a particular kind of interview. Within the context of a problem-solving interview, for example, we can identify the generic roles that the participants are likely to assume, perhaps counselor and client.

However, each problem-solving interview will have unique characteristics such as the physical setting, psychological states, cultural setting, and the like. Such concrete details are called the *particular* aspect of context. These details allow us to "place" the interview and thus give a basis for viewing and understanding it. One aspect of the particular context that requires further explanation is culture. We turn to that important topic now.

The Cultural Context

Communication is culturally dependent. We use the term *culture* to mean both the general culture of a particular group of people (for example, American culture, Italian culture, Indian culture) and the culture of a particular organization (for example, "the way we do things here"). Webster's dictionary has defined culture as "the integrated pattern of human behavior that includes thought, speech, action, and artifacts and depends upon man's capacity for transmitting knowledge to succeeding generations." This definition suggests that the prominent features of a society—its thought, speech, and action—are related to communication.

Cultural dependency suggests two important ideas. First, *our understanding of appropriateness and inappropriateness is derived from cultural standards*. In some cultures, such as some federal governmental agencies, jokes are considered inappropriate. People who tell jokes are revealing a character flaw—they are insufficiently serious. In other cultures—such as the public speaking club Toastmasters International, for example—the ability to tell a joke is an essential skill. Rules of etiquette and appropriateness need to be understood in order for people to manage themselves in a particular organizational culture.

Second, *our understanding of relationships, and the communication in them, is derived from our culture.* Cultures develop their own standards for behavior. So the organizations or groups within which an interview takes place do the same—they develop standards that regulate relationships among people of differing status and power. Behavioral standards develop in regard to interviewing behavior, too. These standards govern such things as the way the interview will proceed, the issues that can be discussed, and the way conflict may be managed. The cultural standards you learn in one setting may be quite different from those you will need to know in another.

The various aspects that make up an organization's culture directly influence the communication that takes place within it. For example, it might be more acceptable for a job candidate to engage in joking and small talk in an interview for a sales position in the private sector than to do so in an interview with a federal governmental agency. Both the interviewer and interviewee need to be aware of specific contexts—both generic and particular aspects, including the cultural setting—because they will be effecting the interaction.

The idea of context, the wide view of it, has thus far been described as being that which surrounds an interview: the physical, social-psychological, temporal, and cultural environment. Knowledge of these elements, it has been argued, is important for your understanding of the interview as a communication event and your degree of competency in interview situations. A great deal more about this important idea will be said in upcoming chapters. With this in mind, let's turn to identifying some common kinds of interviews that occur across a variety of contexts.

TYPES OF INTERVIEWS

Our discussion here of interview types is an introduction to how different types of interviews serve different purposes. Subsequent chapters will explore in greater detail how the communication process helps interview participants accomplish those specific purposes and build relationships. The six general purposes of interviewing are: selection of employees or members of a group, appraisal of performance, in-depth information gathering, collection of survey-type information, problem solving, and persuasion.

Selection

Many students enroll in an interviewing class because of their apprehensions about selection interviews. This type of interview is conducted to make a decision about the interviewee's membership in some program, group, or organization. Most people will participate in several selection interviews throughout their life as new job opportunities become available and career decisions are made.

The selection interview shares common characteristics with other interviews. It consists of at least two people exchanging information through the use of questions and answers. Here, however, the similarities end. The selection interview is a special context because it has a singular purpose—to make a decision about admission to a group, program, or job. Because of its "either/or" decision outcome, the selection interview tends to a highly planned, narrowly purposeful activity that separates it from all other interviewing types and formats.

Performance Appraisal

One of the most essential skills an employee of any company will ever have, regardless of position, occupation, or profession, is the skill of performance appraisal interviewing. This is because the performance appraisal is a tool commonly used by organizations to ferret out productive from less productive employees, and it is a major tool used to determine raises and promotions. In short, it is likely to be the method by which you and your work will be evaluated in any organization.

The performance appraisal interview is the end product of an organizational process known as "the review cycle." This cycle generally begins with formal and informal information gathering about employees by supervisors or managers responsible for doing the interview. This is followed by a formal written performance appraisal that becomes the basis for communication during the interview. Unlike selection interviews, performance appraisal interviews seldom involve "either/or" decisions (that is, either retention or dismissal), because those decisions have generally already been made. Instead, the performance appraisal interview tends to focus on encouraging the employee to perform at a satisfactory level and discussing performance difficulties. As many authorities have pointed out, the performance appraisal becomes the chief communication mechanism by which organizations either improve or fail.[3]

Performance appraisal skills transfer to any interpersonal settings where evaluations of attitudes, values, beliefs, and behavior are at issue. Beyond this, these skills are useful in circumstances in which a person is called upon to help others solve personal problems.

In-Depth Information Gathering

The in-depth information gathering interview provides the broadest possible range of purposes and relational possibilities. It is used by newspaper and television reporters, radio personalities, academic researchers, popular authors, technical writers, advertising and marketing specialists, actors and directors, and organizational consultants and trainers.

Broadly defined, the in-depth information gathering interview is basically designed *to acquire information about a subject, process, or person.* It consists of at least two people—an interviewer and interviewee—and is characterized by the asking and answering of both planned and spontaneous questions. When it is accomplished competently, it has the smooth flow of informal, intelligent conversation.

No doubt you have witnessed such an interview as conducted by nationally known celebrities such as Barbara Walters or Ted Koppel, but the everyday work of newspapers, magazines, biographers, radio and television talk shows, and businesses depends on the same sort of interview. The purpose of the interview is to acquire information, but to accomplish that purpose requires using the raw materials of communication to build a relationship capable of inducing that information.

One of the attractive features of mastering the in-depth information-gathering interview is that the skills developed are useful in a variety of situations you will encounter. You undoubtedly use this kind of interview in both the acquaintance process and to periodically update what you know about those around you—new acquaintances, family members, friends, and colleagues. Another frequent use is to collect information about issues important to you. You surely have talked with people about career choices and possible employment opportunities. And, too, most of us have investigated the features of major purchases. Learning how to ask questions during this type of interview is a skill that you can practice every day in a variety of settings.

Survey

Have you ever been stopped while entering a store by a person conducting a survey? If you have, chances are good that you experienced firsthand what it is like to be interviewed in this context. The skill of collecting survey data, such as buying habits, attitudes toward a new zoning policy, or thoughts and feelings about a national problem, is a very specialized one. The characteristics of a survey interview are essentially similar to an in-depth information-gathering interview. There are at least two people—an interviewer and an interviewee—who exchange information based on questions and answers. However, the survey interview differs from an in-depth information-gathering interview in two important respects. First, it generally lasts for a shorter length of time. Second, it is usually accompanied by a paper-and-pencil instrument for recording responses to brief preplanned, pretested questions.

Learning the skills of survey interviewing is important in many ways. If you plan to pursue a career in marketing, advertising, public relations, or politics, these skills will form a valuable part of your practical education because they will be integral aspects of the job. Even if your career plans do not include these professions, the skills acquired through a study of survey interviewing will still be important. They will help you become a better-informed consumer of survey data, and they will show you how to pursue data-based research that can be extremely useful in a variety of business and educational settings.

Problem-Solving

Interviews can be used to acquire information, but they can also be used to make a decision about a course of action. When the intent of the interviewer is to work through a difficulty with an interviewee, this is a problem-solving interview situation.

There are many different uses of problem-solving interviews. For example, counselors use them to help employees overcome work and personal problems. Nonprofit agencies use them to acquire funding for programs, and health care agencies use them to handle patient and client problems effectively. Managers use them to prevent problems from interrupting work and to help employees meet deadlines. In each of these contexts, however, problem-solving interviews involve similar plans of action, similar lines of questioning, and similar ways to evaluate progress.

Skills acquired in problem-solving interviews have many applications, both at work and in the home. They tend to be useful as reasoning and motivating tools, as ways to overcome conflict, and as ways to negotiate desirable outcomes. The ability to solve problems, after all, is one of the contemporary hallmarks of a well-educated, communicatively competent individual.

Persuasion

The persuasive interview takes place in a context in which the interviewer consciously seeks to exert influence over the interviewee. The interviewer asks questions and creates messages that are meant to lead the interviewee to think, feel, and/or act in a particular way.

One of the most common persuasive interviews involves selling a specific product. Over six million people in the United States are engaged in a sales occupation. But, beyond selling products, many of us sell ideas. We persuade our bosses to do things that we think will make our work more productive. We persuade friends, parents, children, and colleagues to help us with our projects. Recruiters persuade candidates to take jobs. Health care professionals persuade their patients and clients to follow prescribed advice. Our world is filled with opportunities for persuasive interviews.

Ethics and Responsibility in Interviewing

When people engage in communication as responsible professionals, they agree to conform to what is considered ethical and responsible behavior. Ethics is an important issue for all of us and of much concern to our society.

From the time of the Watergate scandal to the present day, concern about ethics seems to be rising in our country. *Time* seemed to be trying to capture the thoughts of the average American when editors picked the question, "What Ever Happened to Ethics?," to introduce their cover story in May of 1987.[4] *Time* went on to report that over 100 members of the Reagan administration had ethical or legal charges leveled against them. Of course, that same number had not been indicted on the charges.

Further evidence of this skepticism appeared just two months earlier in *U. S. News & World Report* from a survey it conducted in conjunction with the Cable News Network.[5] One finding was that more than half of the persons surveyed believed people to be less honest than they were ten years earlier. Seven out of every ten of those surveyed were dissatisfied with the current state of honesty as they perceived it. This leads us to conclude that we all, as responsible members of our society, ought to take time to examine what it means to be ethical in our business and professional lives, whether we be an interviewer or interviewee or, for that matter, a participant in any communication exchange.

Recall that interviews are interpersonal events that occur within professional or organizational settings. They serve as a basis for organizing our consideration of ethical issues.

INTERPERSONAL ETHICS

If you think about interpersonal communication events as dialogues, you are likely to communicate ethically. Charles T. Brown and Paul Keller[6] developed this idea of dialogue in their book, *From Monologue to Dialogue*. A *dialogue* is a communication event in which each participant sees herself or himself as both speaker and listener. Dialogue can be characterized in two ways: fundamentally empathic and fundamentally authentic.

Empathy suggests an attempt to identify with the other's experiences, feelings, and problems, and to affirm the other's self-worth. Thus, to communicate ethically in an interpersonal event is to respect the other's right to a position, to think of the other person as worthy, and to encourage the other's free choice. *Authenticity* suggests an attempt to present oneself as direct, honest, and straightforward in communicating information and feelings. This is not to say that everything is communicated; it means that we communicate what is relevant and legitimate for us to communicate given the situation.

(Continued)

ORGANIZATIONAL ETHICS

Gary Kreps[7] presents three general criteria that are useful across organizational situations to promote communication competence. He has labeled these *honesty, avoiding harm,* and *justice.* Let's look at each of these.

1. *Organizational members should not intentionally deceive one another.*
 Very few of us would be willing to argue against this principle. Yet, knowing what it might mean is more difficult than we would suspect at first glance. Consider that most of us believe we know more about situations than the mere facts. We might even believe that telling the mere facts in an interview would mean deceiving the other person. Do we tell just the facts? Or, do we go beyond the facts and add our opinion which we believe to represent the truth? Do we present our opinion as opinion or do we present it as fact?

2. *Organizational members' communication should not purposely harm any other member of the organization or members of the organization's relevant environment.*
 This principle suggests that organizational members have the responsibility to assess harm that may befall others as a result of their communication. But what kind of assessment of harm are we talking about? Suppose a colleague steals from the organization and you are aware of the theft. Is it ethical for you to say nothing because what you say may lead to the person's termination? Most of us would think that we have a responsibility to tell the truth, particularly if asked. So we must assess which is worse: betraying our own ethical standards by hiding the truth or harming our fellow employee by telling the truth.

3. *Organizational members should be treated justly.*
 The perception of justice obviously varies from one context to another. For example, one organization may permit executives to drive their privately owned vehicles into the company motor pool for servicing. Another may not. Thus, a behavior that might normally be seen as unjust in one organization is considered just in another. Servicing the vehicle may be considered a fringe benefit of upper-level status. Justice often finds itself played out differently at various ranks within an organization too. So, to be ethical, we must make a judgment about what is just within the context of the specific organization, based on corporate standards or rules of behavior.

 These basic guidelines offered by Gary Kreps provide a good foundation for developing ethical standards for interviews and all communication in organizations. We will turn to the issue of ethics again when we discuss specific interview contexts.

WHY STUDY INTERVIEWING?

Perhaps you are wondering what benefits you might obtain from studying interviewing as a form of communication. Research reports suggest that interviewing is seen as a skill related to professional success.[8] In fact, Dan Curtis and his colleagues report that personnel directors in an ideal management profile ranked as second the ability to gather accurate information from others to make a decision[9]—an ability requiring both informational and survey interviewing skills.

Since interviewing has a major impact on our lives, the study of it can be significantly beneficial. Your understanding of interviewing can help you to be a more effective student and productive professional.

Students often interview fellow students and teachers for a variety of reasons. For example, when you are unsure of an assignment you will interview other students, and perhaps the instructor, in order to clarify your understanding. If you are considering a change of major, again, you may collect information through the interview. Beyond this, you will interview to secure employment.

Professionals all want to be employed in a satisfying job and want to be able to do that job well enough to merit advancement. We believe that studying interviewing will help accomplish these goals for the following reasons:

1. To gain employment requires an employment interview. A variety of studies have shown that the ability to communicate effectively during the job interview is especially important. In fact, some believe that it may be *more important* to the actual hiring decision than an applicant's school record, job-associated skills, or letters of recommendation.[10] Beyond gaining entry through the employment interview, organizational members play an important role in the selection and hiring processes. The ability to perform in this role makes an important contribution to the organization.

2. To maintain a job requires at least meeting or exceeding established performance standards set by an employer. Most companies require annual or semi-annual performance reviews that depend on interviews between supervisors and subordinates. The ability to communicate what we've accomplished, how we plan to improve, what feedback and training we need to help us improve, as well as to engage in problem-solving discussions of performance deficiencies will contribute significantly to the outcomes of those reviews.[11] As we advance in our organization, we may be expected to conduct performance appraisal interviews.

3. Job advancement is associated with job performance. It is also a fact of working life that how we fit into the culture of the organization, how well we are liked and respected by others, and how well we communicate within the contexts of formal and informal organizational relationships shapes the impressions of our work and the likelihood of promotion.[12]

4. Sometimes interviewing is a central part of the job. Journalists, researchers, and sales representatives, for example, must collect information and persuade people in order to carry out their job responsibilities. Thus, their ability to skillfully carry out an interview is crucial to being competent.

On the other hand, when interviewing is not a primary communication activity for a professional, it still plays a vital role. For example, nearly all professionals carry out research regarding possible career changes, problems they are experiencing, solutions they are proposing, and the like. The more skillful they are at interviewing the more likely they will be successful as professionals.

Broken down into more manageable units of study, these skills translate into how efficiently you ask and answer questions, how productively you deal with conflict, and how well you are able to manage your professional working relationships. To a large extent, all of these units of study comprise communication skills, and most of them are directly related to interviewing skills.

As you can see, there is a clear need to understand and be able to perform well in interviewing situations.

SUMMARY

The process of communication contains seven basic elements: (1) source/encoder, (2) receiver/decoder, (3) message, (4) feedback, (5) channels, (6) noise, and (7) situation. A source/encoder is the person who initiates the interaction. The receiver/decoder is the person who interprets the meanings associated with the behavior of the source. A message is what is conveyed by the verbal and nonverbal behavior of the source/encoder. Feedback is what is conveyed by the verbal and nonverbal behavior of the receiver/decoder in response to the source's message. Channels are the medium through which the message is sent. Noise is any interference in a message. This may be physical noise, relational noise, or semantic noise. Situation is the boundary that surrounds the communication; it defines the type of exchange.

Interviewing is a communication process where two or more people interact within a relational context by asking and answering questions designed to achieve a specific purpose. A communication process occurs over time, seemingly has no beginning or end, and is interpreted individually. Relational context is defined by formal and informal role relationships. In an interview, those involved are typically aware of their roles, sense relatively precise beginnings and endings, and have predetermined purposes. The interaction within an interview tends to be rule-governed, legally-governed, polite, and goal directed. Special characteristics of the relational context include: formal roles take precedence over informal roles and personal/external relationships should not alter hierarchical roles.

Context is a term used to describe the environment that surrounds the interview. It includes physical, social-psychological, and temporal aspects that both influence and give meaning to the interview. Generic aspects of context are present across interviews, while particular aspects of context pertain to the specific interview situation.

Every interview has a purpose that is sought by individuals within a set of relational definitions and rules and within a specific cultural situation. Communication is the means through which these are expressed. Purposes of interviews are: selection of members, appraisal of performance, collection of survey-type information, in-depth information gathering, problem-solving, and persuasion.

The substance of an average day in our lives is filled with talk and, within that, various kinds of interviewing. Interviewing helps us gain employment, meet our job requirements, meet our professional obligations and fit into the culture of our groups and organizations.

NOTES

[1]Kenneth Burke, *Language as Symbolic Action* (Berkeley: University of California Press, 1966); Lloyd F. Bitzer, "The Rhetorical Situation," *Philosophy and Rhetoric, 1* (1968), 1–14.

[2]Joseph A. DeVito, *The Communication Handbook: A Dictionary* (New York: Harper & Row, 1986), p. 79.

[3]H. Lloyd Goodall, Gerald L. Wilson, and Christopher L. Waagen, "The Performance Appraisal Interview: An Interpretive Assessment," *The Quarterly Journal of Speech, 72* (1986), 74–87.

[4]Walter Shapiro, "What's Wrong: Hypocrisy, Betrayal and Greed Unsettle the Nation's Soul," *Time,* May 25, 1987, 14–17.

[5]Merrill McLaughlin, Jeffery L. Sheler, and Gordon Witkin, "A Nation of Liars," *U. S. News & World Report,* February 23, 1987, 54–60.

[6]Charles T. Brown and Paul Keller, *From Monologue to Dialogue: An Exploration of Interpersonal Communication* (Englewood Cliffs, NJ: Prentice-Hall, 1979).

[7]Gary L. Kreps, *Organizational Communication,* 2d ed. (New York: Longman, 1989), pp. 248–254.

[8]June Smith, "An Examination of the Status of Organizational Communication Programs in Texas Colleges and Universities," (ERIC Document ED 221 904); Dan

B. Curtis, Jerry L. Winsor, and Ronald D. Stephens, "National Preferences in Business and Communication Education," *Communication Education 38,* 6–14.

[9]Curtis, Winsor, and Stephens, p. 12.

[10]F. M. Jablin, "Formal Organizational Structure," in F. M. Jablin et al. (eds.), *Handbook of Organizational Communication: An Interdisciplinary Perspective* (Newbury Park, CA: Save, 1987); H. Lloyd Goodall and Donna B. Goodall, "The Employment Interview: A Selective Review of the Literature with Implications for Communication," *Communication Quarterly, 30* (1982), 116–123.

[11]E. M. Eisenberg and M. Witten, "Reconsidering Openness in Organizational Communication," *Academy of Management Review, 12* (1987), 418–426; Goodall, Wilson, and Waagen, 1986.

[12]Goodall, Wilson, and Waagen, 1986; Michael E. Pacanowsky and Nick O'Donnell-Trujillo, "Organizational Communication as Cultural Performance," *Communication Monographs, 50* (1984), 126–147; R. M. Kantner, *Men and Women of the Corporation* (New York: Basic Books, 1977).

EXPERIENCES

1. Interview a person who holds the kind of job you might look for when you complete your degree. Determine what kinds of formal and informal interviewing this person does. How much time is spent in these interviewing activities?

2. Locate other textbooks on interviewing in the school library. Examine the definitions of interviewing from three of these, comparing and contrasting them to the one offered in this chapter. Now decide which definition you find most useful. Write a short essay that suggests what your favorite definition is, how it defers from others, and why you favor it.

3. Discuss in small groups the components of the communication model presented in this chapter until they are understood by each member of your group. Now construct a communication model that illustrates the communication process as your group sees it. Once you have developed a model, extend it to describe communication in an interview. Present this model of communication within the interview to the class. Compare your model to others that were presented.

4. Select a person in your class to meet. Spend five minutes getting to know each other. Now select a person to meet through an informational interview. Decide who will be the interviewer and who will be the interviewee. Conduct a five-minute interview. Then switch roles and repeat the interview process. Finally, as a class compare and contrast these two methods of getting to know a person.

5. Consider your experience in both formal and informal interviews. Take a sheet of paper and list your strengths and weaknesses as an interviewer and interviewee. Based on what you have written, list several goals you will adopt for the term in order to improve in areas you judge as weaknesses. Give the paper to your instructor, who will return it to you at the end of the term so that you can check your progress.

RECOMMENDED READINGS

Anderson, James A., *Communication Research: Issues and Methods* (New York: McGraw-Hill, 1987), especially Chapter 12: "Participant Observation: Creating the Research Text."

Arnett, Ronald, "The Status of Communication Ethics Scholarship in Speech Communication Journals from 1915 to 1985," *Central States Speech Journal, 38* (1987), 44–61.

Douglas, Jack D., *Creative Interviewing* (Beverly Hills, CA: Sage Publications, 1985).

Goodall, H. L., Jr., "A Theatre of Motives and 'The Meaningful Orders of Persons and Things' in One Organization's Culture," in James A. Anderson (ed.), *Communication Yearbook 13* (Newbury Park, CA: Sage Press, 1990), 69–94.

Smircich, Linda L., "Concepts of Culture and Organizational Analysis," *Administrative Science Quarterly, 28* (1983), 339–358.

CHAPTER 2

UNDERSTANDING CONTEXTUAL FACTORS

OBJECTIVES

After reading this chapter, you should be able to:

Explain the kinds of needs and images the interviewer and
and interviewee bring to an interview, giving examples
of how these might impact the interview.

Suggest how misunderstandings and disagreements might
occur in an interview due to verbal communication
behavior.

Give examples of how these nonverbal communication
behaviors might affect an interview: appearance,
gesture, posture, movement, touch, face and eye
behavior, vocalics, use of time, and physical
environment.

Provide definitions for *listening* and *responding* and discuss
suggestions for improving these communication
behaviors in interviews.

Explain the components of the listening process: sensing,
attending, understanding, and remembering.

Suggest how the various elements of the general and
specific situations can have impact on the interview.

Compare and contrast the directive and nondirective
approaches to interviewing, telling advantages and
disadvantages of each.

Chapter 1 defined interviewing and laid out the basics of the communication
process. Two primary purposes of communication in interviews were explained and illustrated—accomplishing tasks and developing relationships.
Finally, the basic types of interviews were introduced.

In this chapter, we go beyond these introductory issues to gain an in-
depth understanding of contextual factors. We will explain each element of
the context and illustrate why it is important and what impact it has on interviews. Contextual factors work together to achieve the goals for the particular interview. We begin by looking at the needs and images that the interviewer and interviewee bring to the interview. Then we move on to
consider their verbal and nonverbal communication behaviors, including listening and responding. Finally, we examine the situation and its effect on
the interview.

THE INTERVIEWER AND INTERVIEWEE

Both the interviewer and the interviewee bring to the interview personal needs and images of themselves and the other. Let's take a look at what these might be and how each has impact on the interview.

Needs

We suggested that interviews are conducted to achieve task and relational outcomes. This notion provides an obvious starting place for an examination of needs.

Most certainly, the interviewer and interviewee hope to gain information related to their individual goals. For example, the journalist wants to obtain information to contribute to a news broadcast or a feature article. The health care professional wants to gain information that will lead to a reliable diagnosis and treatment. The job applicant wants to know enough about the employer to make an informed decision about an offer of employment. Thus, there always are *task needs,* related to the goals for the interview.

Social needs are those related to benefits the person might receive from the social relationship between the interviewer and interviewee. These benefits for the most part involve personal satisfaction. For example, Phil's boss might express support and caring for him during a performance appraisal interview. This nurturing would meet a social need, perhaps esteem.

A number of scholars have considered ways of thinking about what personal satisfactions people desire in relationships. We find William Schutz's discussion of needs helpful and easy to understand.[1] Schutz suggests that people approach interpersonal relationships, such as those in interviews, seeking satisfaction of three needs: control, affection, and inclusion. Of course, the strength of these needs varies from person to person. In the area of control, for example, this means that two separate interviewers might want different amounts of control over a job applicant and the interview situation.

The *need for control* is the desire both to exercise power and authority and to have it exercised over us. In an interview this need is expressed in relation to two areas: control over the interview and control over the relationship.

A person's satisfaction with the interview, in part, relates to the ability to exercise the kind of control desired. Although both the interviewer and interviewee can control the interview, in most contexts the interviewer has the greatest opportunity to set some level of control because he or she generally asks most of the questions. For example, the interviewer may sense that the interviewee is having difficulty with questions that are general in nature and move to ask more specific questions.

On the other hand, the interviewee can control the interview if the interviewer allows that to happen. The interviewee may even ask directly for a more specific question by telling the interviewer that a question is not clear. Or perhaps the interviewee may exercise control by refusing to answer certain questions. Control is a matter of negotiation between the interviewer and interviewee. In some circumstances each party may be interested in producing a satisfactory outcome. Therefore, both the interviewer and interviewee will attempt to be sensitive to the other's need for control.

The *need for affection* is the desire to like and be liked by the other person in the interview. Liking is experienced through a close, personal relationship. Just as they do for the need for control, people experience the need for affection in varying degrees. The interviewer's desire for affection may be different from that of the interviewee. For example, a journalist may wish to keep an interview on an impersonal professional level, while the mayoral candidate she is interviewing may want it to be on a more personal level.

The purpose can also exert an influence on the affection each party expects. A selection interview, for example, may require less display of affection than a counseling interview. The expectation for the selection interview is that personal issues are not an area of questioning; the opposite is usually true of a counseling interview. Also, the degree of familiarity that the persons in an interview have with each other affects expectations for intimacy. When people know each other well, they are likely to talk of topics beyond the formal purpose of the interview.

The *need for inclusion* represents our willingness to participate in the interview as well as our willingness to allow the other to participate. Here, too, each individual who approaches an interview situation will have different levels of this need. A reporter might stop you on the street for a brief interview. You may not wish to take the time to talk, nor do you particularly care to let your views be known. The reporter, on the other hand, may need the opinion of somebody just like you. She may also have a deadline that makes it important that she get your interview. She has a strong need to include you; you have a low need to be included. Obviously, the incompatibility of needs might well present difficulties for the interviewer in this situation.

Images

How the interviewer and interviewee view themselves is another important element of interviewing contexts. The image the participants have of themselves, their sense of who they are, comes from their beliefs, values, and attitudes.[2] Beliefs represent people, places, and things. Values appraise people's beliefs, and attitudes guide their behavior toward those values. These components influence behavior in the interview. We can see how these work together to create an image by examining the following example.

Bryant is a pastor of a new church. Ten years ago, he organized the church with the help of thirteen families from other local churches. Today he leads a congregation of 1700 members, with a full-time staff of seven. Although Bryant is a humble man, he is undoubtedly proud of his church and its accomplishments. We might reasonably expect that he also has confidence in himself and his abilities. He is likely to see himself as a good communicator, given the kind of work he does and the success he has had. Bryant has agreed to an in-depth information-gathering interview for a local magazine that features successful people in the community.

Imagine now, if our speculation is correct, how Bryant's image of himself might influence this interview. He is a person who is used to taking charge. He might take charge of the interview. Perhaps his pride in the church will lead him to exaggerate or embellish his responses. Maybe he will convey information that he wants the reporter to use as the focus of her story. This could lead him to ignore, or perhaps twist, the reporter's questions to fit his goals for the interview.

Image of self can be a powerful influence on an interview. In some interviews, it may lead to control issues. In others, it may lead to nonparticipation. Managers and counselors understand that low self-concept can lead to lack of participation. In the case of Bryant, above, we looked at the interview in terms of influence exerted by the interviewee. Certainly, the interviewer can be equally influential. For example, the interviewer who is reserved might be viewed as cold and unfriendly, and this could cause an interviewee who had intended to participate fully to hold back. The interviewer who brings a confident image, on the other hand, might encourage the interviewee to cooperate enthusiastically.

A value system also provides a frame of reference through which we filter our experiences in the interview. The *frame of reference* acts much like a pair of sunglasses in that it colors the way we interpret whatever we are observing. Bryant, the pastor, has images of what people who write for the press are like. So, his frame of reference includes images and beliefs about those who might engage him in an interview. He knows this particular reporter; he brings impressions of her to the interview. Perhaps he has a friend who has complained about this person's inaccurate reporting. He will undoubtedly come to this interview with concern about how he will be quoted.

More data are gathered about the other person as the interview progresses. The professional manner of the reporter, for example, may convince Bryant that his friend must be mistaken. Such nonverbal cues as hairstyle, manner of dress, and posture affect his impression. In addition, the kinds of questions asked or the way they are phrased by the reporter may reveal this person's values, beliefs, and attitudes to Bryant. All these data are integrated into Bryant's frame of reference regarding reporters, and this reporter specifically.

THE COMMUNICATION BEHAVIORS

In Chapter 1, we introduced you to the notion that communication is interaction. Here we add that the interview process is a series of interactions designed to lead to the accomplishment of a specific purpose. What exactly do these interactions involve? Well, for one thing, interactions involve creating messages through words and actions—verbal and nonverbal behavior.

Interactions also involve the feedback behaviors of listening and responding. Effective interactions require an understanding of these basic elements in the communication process.

The Verbal Message

Clear expression is a central concern for those who interview. Misunderstandings, disagreements, and even conflict can occur when interviewers and interviewees do not express themselves clearly. The problem is that we imagine we are being clear even though we may not be. Since what we are saying makes sense to us, we expect our meaning to be clear to others. We think of our meaning as the "correct," and *only,* meaning. And if our meaning is the "correct" meaning, then chances are that the other person in the interview—a correct thinking person, too—will be thinking the "correct" meaning. Needless to say, this often is not the case.

Verbal misunderstandings can arise when one person's frame of reference doesn't coincide with that of the other, resulting in the use of terms that are unfamiliar or too complex. The interviewer may use a technical term that is not part of the interviewee's experience. Perhaps the interviewer is an attorney and uses the word *arraignment.* This is a legal term, and it well may be that the interviewee does not know what the word means (it means "to appear in court to answer an accusation").

Of course, as an interviewee, it would be wise to identify and define words used by professionals in a field as you are researching a topic for an interview. Beyond this, if this happens to you, ask the interviewer for the meaning of terms of which you are uncertain.

If, instead, you are the interviewer in this situation, be alert for an interviewee who is repeatedly asking for clarification or who looks at you with a puzzled expression. Remember that a less complex word is more likely to be understood in many contexts. For example, a police officer, interviewing a motorist, might say *speed up* instead of *accelerate.* An attorney might say *think* rather than *presume.* A physician could say *sore* rather than *inflamed.* A reporter might use the word *correct* rather than *rectify.* Be aware, though, that language that is seen as too simple can create a problem. It might be viewed as "talking down" if the other person is used to a higher-level and more complex vocabulary.

Verbal misunderstandings also can result when a word has a highly personal meaning attached to it. Words that are emotionally charged fall into this category. A supervisor might mention "counseling" to an employee during an appraisal interview. The interviewee might be thinking "psychiatric counseling," while all the supervisor had in mind was setting up another interview later for the purpose of talking over the employee's work problem.

The Nonverbal Message

Nonverbal interactions are a significant part of any interview. They provide very important information about the meaning of messages and how they are being received. Consider the information that an observant interviewer might collect about you as an interviewee. You might yawn, smile, glance at your watch, shuffle papers, speak at an unusually fast rate, stumble over words, be dressed too casually or too formally, fold your arms in front of you in a blocking gesture, or fail to maintain eye contact. Any of these nonverbal behaviors may communicate a message to the interviewer. And since they may, it is important to explore nonverbal communication within the contexts of interviews. We can do this by examining the following nonverbal codes and their uses: appearance, gesture and movement, touch, face and eye behavior, vocalics, time, and physical environment.

Appearance.   It is commonly believed that you can learn a great deal about a person by merely observing the person's appearance. People do, in fact, make judgments about others based upon their appearance.[3] People who are thought to be physically attractive are also seen as more personable, persuasive, interesting, confident, sociable, and outgoing than individuals who are not perceived as physically attractive. So physical appearance can have an impact on your perception of the other party in an interview and on you as well.

What do you make of this information if you are "sort of average"? Many people who are not beautiful are personable, confident, persuasive, sociable, outgoing, and more! So it seems reasonable to assume that physical attractiveness is not necessarily tied to physical beauty. Rather, it appears to be tied to a cultural norm. You can keep physically fit and well groomed. You can try to control your weight and make sure your clothes are clean and fresh, which constitutes a positive image.

With regard to dress, both interviewers and interviewees should generally adhere to the degree of formality called for in any particular context. If you are not familiar with the usual dress standard, ask someone who knows. Study the dress of those in the group or organization. Look for elements of dress these people share, and if it seems reasonable, follow their lead.

Gesture movement.   Gesture and movement help to regulate the flow of communication in interviews, and so it's important that you learn to let your body communicate. John E. Baird and A. Schubert[4] reported that leaders of groups gave more positive head nods than nonleaders and that they gestured more. Later Baird[5] demonstrated that this nonverbal participation is related to leadership emergence as well.

We think these data apply to the leadership of an interviewer too. Gestures of this type reinforce the listener's behavior and are likely to provide encouragement to participate. For example, an interviewer who wishes an interviewee to say more might signal this by a nod.

It is not possible to give specific suggestions about how to gesture. Yet, there is some general advice that makes good sense. It is good advice to say that you should relax, but not so much as to suggest inattentiveness. Also, pay attention to any gestures or movements that might distract. In particular, rattling papers and manipulating a pen or pencil are movements that fall into this category.

Touch. As a matter of social grace, most interviews will provide the opportunity for handshaking. When the opportunity presents itself, be sure you give a firm but not overly harsh handshake. Rarely will other touching behavior be appropriate, except as a show of support when the persons involved know each other fairly well. This kind of touch seems most likely in situations such as a counseling interview, where comforting the interviewee might be appropriate.

Face and eye behavior. The face exerts a special influence because facial cues are important indicators of a person's orientation. Dale Leathers draws these conclusions about facial expression from research literature.[6]

1. The face communicates *evaluative judgments*—good and bad— through pleasant and unpleasant expressions that suggest whether the communicator sees the current object of attention as good or bad.
2. The face communicates *interest or disinterest* in other people or the surrounding environment.
3. The face communicates *intensity* and, hence, the degree of involvement in a situation.
4. The face communicates the amount of *control* the individual has over his or her own expressions.
5. The face probably communicates a grasp of what the person is saying or a lack of *understanding*.

Eye contact usually produces less ambiguous messages than does facial expression. People make direct eye contact when they want to indicate they are open for communication and when they are soliciting feedback after making a statement.[7] People use eye contact to decrease distance psychologically, and sometimes to show hostility.[8] Constant eye contact makes other people nervous because it can be a sign of confronting behavior. But keep in mind that in our culture the listener maintains more eye contact than the speaker.

Vocalics. Characteristics such as aptitudes, interests, personality traits, ethnic background, education level, and anxiety can be inferred by listening to a person's voice. Some vocal factors are not easily controlled, but with effort you can control others. Careful attention to your articulation, rate of speaking, fluency, and volume may help you produce the kind of image you wish.

Be aware of what you are communicating with your voice. A choppy delivery of sentences, for example, may be viewed as not knowing what you want to say. Unless you have the opportunity to take a voice and articulation course, you will have to discover what needs you have in this area on your own. You might wish to tape-record yourself in a practice interview situation to discover what your voice may be saying about you. Perhaps, also, a friend will listen to you and provide help. If you hear vocal qualities or patterns you wish to change, additional work with a tape recorder often proves beneficial.

Use of time.   Two aspects of time are important in an interview. The first aspect relates to promptness. People draw important inferences from starting interviews on time or late. Time may mean money to the other party in the interview. People often take time away from their work to participate—and at considerable cost to their organization. Start at the designated time if you are in control. If you are the interviewee, arrange to be at the meeting place a few minutes early so that you don't delay the interview. Also, prepare for possible questions so that the interview will flow smoothly. Your use of time may be more than a matter of courtesy.

The second aspect related to time has to do with the length of an interview. When an interview goes on and on, people become uneasy and uncomfortable. People can maintain attention and a fairly high level of participation for about an hour. Be sensitive to this fact, as either the interviewer or interviewee.

Physical environment.   If you are the interviewer, think about how you will arrange the seating. Your choices about seating arrangement can enhance your effectiveness as an interviewer. First, consider distance between yourself and the interviewee. Three to four feet seems optimum for this kind of communication. Closer distances are generally reserved for intimate communication and, therefore, may make the interviewee uncomfortable. Greater distances may create an impersonal climate and cause the interviewee to feel less involved. Of course, it is difficult to give precise rules for distances.

Next, consider such variables as status, sex, cultural norms, furnishings, and intimacy of the relationship. All these will affect what is considered to be comfortable and appropriate in the interview. Status, for example, can be enhanced by an arrangement where the interviewer sits behind his or her desk or across the table from the interviewee. Status can be deemphasized when the interviewee sits in a chair that is at a right angle from the interviewer, such as around the corner of a table. Equality can be further emphasized—as is often done in informal interviews or in a counseling interview—by using a round table. This arrangement is especially useful if more than one other person is involved in the interview since it allows participants to see each other without someone having to sit at the head-of-the-table position.

In summary, verbal and nonverbal messages work together in the interview to convey the messages of the participants. Thus, attention to both is important.

Listening: Receiving, Interpreting, and Remembering the Message

The acts of receiving, interpreting, and remembering the message taken together constitute the *listening process.*[9] Listening is a critical skill in all interviewing contexts.

The listening process.   Because there are many things in every interviewing environment to stimulate our senses, we must work to focus our attention on the information that is of particular interest and importance to us. How can we do this? Our *frame of reference,* that is, our past experience with the topic, the other person, and even the particular context, allows us to make decisions about what is important for us. For example, in a counseling interview between Omar, a health care professional, and his client Marta, Omar brings to the interview an understanding of the particular problem from study and from other cases he has seen, a history in working previously with Marta, information about the current situation, and the like. Knowing these things allows Omar to make decisions about what is important from all the information provided by Marta.

A second step in the process of listening is interpreting the message. It requires that we organize the components of the message; assign meaning to them; compare and contrast what we think has been said with our experience with the topic, speaker, and context; and come to conclusions about what the message as a whole means. How would this apply to the case of Omar, the health care professional, and his client Marta? The various pieces of information related to the problem have to be organized and interpreted. Understanding cannot happen in isolation. Omar has to take into consideration what he knows about Marta, the topic, and the context.

Finally, we must *remember.* Remembering is a difficult task for many. But taking in a message, interpreting it, and then immediately forgetting it is *not* listening for us. For many interviewers, the solution to remembering what was said is to take notes or use a tape recorder.

Listening: Understanding and Evaluating

Listening can have two specific aims: understanding and evaluating. Listening for understanding requires paying careful attention to what is being said and asking follow-up questions if there is any doubt about the meaning of the message. Listening for evaluating focuses heavily on analyzing the meaning once you understand it. These two tasks of listening—understanding and evaluating—are more crucial in an interview than in a casual interpersonal encounter.

Listening in the interview.   Listening in an interview is more difficult than in casual interpersonal communication because the information being received is usually more complex. In addition most participants in interviews are receiving information in regard to a number of lines of questioning, while, at the same time, mentally preparing follow-up questions. This complexity requires the receiver to organize, interpret, and remember information that relates to several distinctly different aspects of the topic. Thus, listening in an interview requires a different kind of concentration than does casual interpersonal listening.

The listening task is usually different for an interviewer than it is for an interviewee. The interviewer must receive, organize, and interpret greater quantities of information than the interviewee. We do not mean to suggest, of course, that an interviewee may not have difficulty listening. (The interpreting part of the listening process may be especially difficult for the interviewee if the interviewer is not skillful in wording questions.) But here we focus on specific behaviors that allow an interviewer to be a more effective listener.

Listening to comprehend and evaluate. The ability to listen for comprehension and evaluation is an especially important skill in an interview. Here are some guidelines for listening to comprehend and evaluate:

1. *Be sure you know why you are asking each question.* It is important that you know what you want from the interview when you ask a question. Otherwise, you will not know how to evaluate the response. If necessary, write purpose statements as you plan the questions.

2. *Identify the significant content and ideas in what the person has said.* What is the person's main idea? What information or data are being used to elaborate on or support that idea?

3. *Ask a follow-up question if the information presented is not clear.* You could say, "I'm not sure I understand what...means. Can you say more?" Or perhaps you might say, "I'm puzzled by your statement.... Would you tell me a little more about it?"

4. *Identify any feelings that may accompany the content.* It is important that you try to identify any feelings being presented. Feelings can help you to understand the attitudes, values, and/or emotional state of the interviewee. Understanding these will help you understand more fully what the other person in the interview is experiencing and expressing.

5. *Ask yourself if the answer is complete.* Does it fully answer your question? Perhaps it has sidestepped the question. Or perhaps the question is incomplete because it lacks elaboration or supporting data.

6. *If the answer is not complete, ask one or more follow-up questions.* Of course, you must listen carefully to the answer and focus in on what is missing. Note here that preparation for the interview—so that you know what information you need to get from the interviewee—is vital in order for you to recognize that there are gaps in an answer.

7. *If your task is to evaluate the interviewee's responses, form your conclusion once the information is complete.* Working on an evaluation and conclusion before you have heard a complete thought can distract from listening. Hear the speaker out before you evaluate.

Feedback

Feedback is the observable response of a receiver to the message that has been communicated. It becomes a useful part of the communication event only if both the verbal and nonverbal responses are sensed and interpreted by the speaker. Subtle behavior such as lowered eyes, for example, might be missed. Yet this behavior could alert an interviewee to an interviewer's uneasiness (or vice versa).

Understanding what part of a particular message might be considered feedback, as we pointed out in Chapter 1, is a matter of perspective. For the interviewer, the interviewee's response to questions is not only an answer, but feedback. The interviewer, by taking in and processing the response, gains a sense of how the interviewee has received the question. Likewise, for the interviewee, the interviewer's response to the answer is feedback.

Feedback serves the general purpose of letting the source of a message know how it has been received. Feedback can suggest a variety of responses. It can confirm that the message has been *received* or *not received*. It can reveal that the message has been *understood* or *misunderstood*. Feedback also can suggest *qualitative information:* it can suggest how the message was received and, perhaps, the receiver's depth of understanding of the message; and it can suggest to what extent the receiver is able to identify with and empathize with the speaker and the message. In addition, it can provide information about *how the the relationship is being viewed* at the moment.

Not all feedback provides this kind of information. Yet a listener can consciously respond in a way that does provide it, by engaging in active listening. *Active listening* is a response in which the listener paraphrases the speaker's ideas and feelings. It is actually something a listener does *after* listening carefully. The interviewer or interviewee hears the listener's translation of what he or she has said and in doing so knows how well the other party understands the ideas and the feelings being communicated. This active listening response might then be followed by some indication of support and/or empathy toward the speaker if the context, perhaps a counseling interview, suggests it. Perhaps the listener will tell of a similar experience that he or she has had. Perhaps the listener will suggest that he or she cares.

The active listening and the display of empathy taken together send the speaker a signal about how the listener views the relationship. The fact that the listener cares enough to listen this fully often suggests that the listener values the speaker and the relationship. So this kind of response to the speaker can positively affect the climate of the interview.

Active listening may seem awkward to those who have never used it, but it is a technique that with practice will be easy to use. You can learn to use it skillfully by following these guidelines:

1. *Devote your full attention to the speaker.* The active listening response is not a follow-up question. Your task is processing and remembering the speaker's ideas. It is wise to resist the urge to think about a follow-up question. There will be time to concentrate on follow-up once you have given your active listening response.

2. *Focus on the main idea being presented, treating the minute details as important but secondary.* If the speaker's message is complex, it may not be possible for you to remember everything. It is especially important that you are able to feed back the main point or points. Work to remember these.

3. *Lead into the feedback with language that suggests you are giving your interpretation of what was said and felt.* You might say, "What I heard you say is...." Or you might indicate, "Let me see if I understand you. You said...?" Or perhaps, "I see. So you are saying...?"

4. *Try to remain nonevaluative in your response.* Most of the time in an interview you will not be trying to express your evaluation of the speaker's ideas. You will want to be friendly, but remain neutral, unless you have as your goal showing empathy. (The display of empathy, of course, may not be perceived as remaining neutral, but does usually help to create a positive, effective communication environment.)

5. *If strong feelings are being presented, feed them back, but try not to get caught up in the emotionalism of the moment.* It is very easy to lose control of the interaction when you get hooked emotionally. One outcome of getting caught up is focusing more and more on your own thoughts and on how you want to respond. Then you may stop listening.

6. *If you are unclear about part of the message, state your understanding of it and follow this with a question to clarify.* Begin your response with a statement of your understanding of the idea. It is generally more productive to state what you have received and interpreted so that the speaker knows what parts of the message you have understood. Then the speaker can tailor his or her subsequent message to what you did not understand.

7. *Finally, don't try to paraphrase everything the other person tells you.* Too much paraphrasing—recasting what the other person has said in your own words—can get in the way of the communication.

All of us can remember as a child teasing another person by repeating each idea that person presented. Eventually the other person grew angry because the repetitiveness grew annoying. So save active listening for the especially important or unusually complicated ideas being presented.

The details of providing follow-up responses are the subject of Chapters 4 and 5, "Understanding Questions" and "Using Questions." There we will discuss the kinds of follow-up questions you might wish to ask, and we will provide examples of each from a variety of interviewing contexts. Here we give you examples of how interviewers gave active listening responses.

A health care professional asked: "How did your weekend go?"

The interviewee responded: "My friend keeps inviting me to go drinking with the old gang. She knows that I have stopped drinking, but keeps asking me to go out with them to bars. I've told her politely that it's not for me. I wish she'd lay off."

The counselor responded: "So one of your friends keeps asking you to go drinking, even though you have told her that you don't drink any-more? You are angry with her when she ignores your needs?"

A journalist asked a member of a city council: "What is your position on signing the agreement for Mobile, Alabama, to become a sister city with the Soviet city, Rostov-on-Don?"

The city council member responded: "I'm personally in favor of such an agreement. There would be economic advantages for both cities. But some of the people in my district have called me, complaining about the idea."

The reporter responded: "Let me see if I understand you. You are personally in favor of the sister city plan because of its economic advantages, but are concerned about signing such an agreement because some of the voters in your district do not like the idea of such an arrangement with the Soviets?"

A manager asked an employee in a performance appraisal interview: "How would you describe your performance during the past several months?"

The saleswoman responded: "I think I've been doing a pretty good job. I've met my sales quota for two months and exceeded it in the third by 15 percent. I know that is off a bit from my previous quarter, but you know that I had two bouts with flu. You can see that the past month was quite good. So, I'd say that I'm doing a pretty good job."

The manager responded: "You are saying that you didn't do quite as well during this quarter as you did in the past one? But that you think you did pretty well when you take into account that you were sick? You seem a little worried about how I might respond to the fact that your performance, on the average, is off from your usual?''

Each of these interviewers gave an active listening response. They paraphrased the speakers' answer, vocally putting a question mark on their paraphrase. They also labeled and fed back the feelings they thought they were sensing. In each case, the interviewees had the opportunity to confirm, deny, or modify the interviewers' understanding of their answer.

THE SITUATION

The final component of the interviewing process is the situation. All interviews, like other kinds of communication, take place within a situation. A situation can be broken into two categories: general and specific.

General Situation

A *general situation* is, of course, the events that surround the interview in its given time in history. Political, economic, and cultural events of the time fall into this category. It is appropriate for the interviewer to ask if any events within the general situation may have an effect on the interview. It may be hard to imagine that these kinds of events might have an impact on an interview, but they can. Consider, for example, the difference that a weak economy might make in an employment interview to both the interviewer and interviewee. The weak economy may cause the interviewer to ask questions about the economy to test the interviewee's understanding of economics. The weak economy might also make research into and understanding of the organization's financial status a more critical part of the candidate's planning for the interview.

Specific Situation

The *specific situation* refers to the immediate events and circumstances that surround the interview. It includes the situational variables of purpose, approach, and setting.

Interview purpose.   The purpose of the interview can affect the expectations of the participants. Consider how the purpose might have impact on the climate. *Climate* is the atmosphere present in an interview. It is a function of the prevailing attitude that the interviewer and interviewee have about each other and the task as they are engaged in interaction. When the purpose is screening job candidates, we might find a politely formal climate. We would expect friendly, but somewhat reserved, behavior from both participants. On the other hand, if the purpose is counseling, we might expect to find a wider variety of climates. There may be hostility. There may be empathy and warmth. There is likely to be an opportunity for more of the participants' personalities to come out. We can't predict specific behaviors, but it is clear that the interviewer and interviewee are likely to have greater freedom of expression and control in a counseling interview than in other contexts. Or perhaps the purpose of the interview is persuasion. Here we might expect that an attempt will be made to build a friendly relationship based upon some perceived mutual interest. We'd also expect that the interviewer will take more control and do more of the talking than in the counseling interview. So it is important to take time to consider how the purpose might affect the expectations for the interview.

There are two general purposes for communication in interviews: (1) to accomplish tasks and (2) to create, maintain, or modify relationships. Let's examine these purposes in more detail.

Communication and the accomplishment of tasks. One way to think about communication is to think of it as a *tool*. Viewed this way, communication is an instrument that can be used to do something—to make things work, to fix problems, to accomplish tasks.

Let's consider the case of Catriona, a personnel supervisor for a manufacturing company. Catriona thinks of communication as a tool, and she uses it purposefully. When she talks about her job, she tends to focus on tasks that she has to accomplish. When asked how she plans to accomplish them, she reaches mentally for the tool of communication. She says she will arrange interviews to solve problems, conduct performance appraisal interviews with members of her department to maintain and increase productivity, and meet with a new employee to counsel regarding a drinking problem. Catriona is a goal-oriented individual, and from her point of view, communication is what allows her to accomplish goals.

Of course, not everyone thinks about work in precisely this manner, as some people are more goal-oriented than others. Some people think about communication as a tool, but like readers of exotic car magazines who never own such a car, they may not be able to use it purposefully. Other people are quite strategic and use communication exclusively as a tool to implement their strategies. Most of us fall somewhere in between these two extremes. We know communication can be thought of and used as a tool to help us accomplish tasks, but it also serves other purposes, specifically helping us to get along with and to enjoy the company of other people.

Communication as the material of relationships. A second way to think about communication is as a set of *raw materials* necessary in the building and maintaining of human relationships. Viewed this way, communication consists of words, silences, uses of time, thoughts, feelings, facial expressions, sensitivity to similarities and differences, body movements, mental and physical distances between people, gestures, and moods—the materials to weave the intricate fabrics of human involvement.

Communication is the substance of human relationships.[7] Talk—the raw material—is how people meet and greet each other, exchange information, ask questions, tell jokes, bargain for raises, make presentations, discuss feelings. However, communication is also how people argue, fight, fail to greet each other, misunderstand or misuse information, ask inappropriate questions, tell jokes in poor taste, and otherwise fail to make efficient and effective use of this raw material. Simply having the potential to communicate doesn't guarantee one's ability to use it *effectively* in every situation.

Consider the case of Mario, a television reporter who is thought of in his local community as a good communicator. This image has been created over the years through Mario's careful scripting of his "person-on-the-street" interviews. He labors for hours over each one, making sure that the appropriate quip, the right fast answer, the penetrating question, the concerned facial expressions are all in place. Off camera, there is another and very different story. Mario is basically a reticent individual, a person who does not feel comfortable communicating with others, particularly in one-to-one situations. His is the case of a person who has—or at least knows how to use—the raw materials of communication to build and maintain human relationships, but chooses not to use them when he isn't working.

We want you to think of communication during an interview as both a tool for accomplishing specific tasks and the raw material needed to develop a relationship. This means we want you to learn to use communication *purposefully* and to be sensitive to its *relational implications*. We will come back to these issues again and again to discuss them in specific contexts because they are an integral part of every communication.

General Approach

Interviews may take either a directive or nondirective approach to achieve a specific purpose. Sometimes an interviewer will choose to mix these two approaches within a single interview. A *directive approach* means that the interviewer begins by establishing the purpose of the interview and generally continues to control the interview by structuring and asking nearly all the questions. The intent here is for the interviewer to control, although sometimes an aggressive interviewee may take control away from the interviewer. A *nondirective approach,* in contrast, suggests that the interviewer turns over to the interviewee the control of the interview. For example, a supervisor, Naomi may perceive that the interviewee, Kenji, needs to vent some dissatisfaction in an appraisal interview before productive discussion can take place. Naomi, might begin with, "I sense that you may have some things you want to say to me, Kenji. Why don't you begin?"

In spite of the fact that the interviewee is allowed to control the interview, there was some reason that the interview has been called and that usually influences the direction the interview will take.

Typically the perceived purpose of an interview will affect whether a particular kind of direction will be seen as appropriate. Often a directive approach is used for in-depth probing, survey, employment/selection, and persuasive interviews. On the other hand, a nondirective approach is seen as useful in some counseling, performance appraisal, and problem-solving interviews.

Here are the two contrasting approaches used in an employment interview. We begin with the directive approach.

Interviewer: I see from your resume that you are a student at the University of Denver. How did you decide to go to school at Denver?

Interviewee: I was looking around for a school that had a good department of communication, and Denver had one. I was living in Denver at the time and had a good job. So because the program in communication was a good one and I could keep my job, I decided that going to school at Denver was a good choice for me.

Interviewer: Tell me what area of communication you chose as your focus?

Interviewee: The area of communication that interested me most was communication in business settings—particularly, organizational development and training.

Interviewer: Why did this area interest you so much?

Interviewee: My neighbor worked as a director of training and development for a large company. He talked frequently with me as I was growing up because his daughter and I hung around with each other. I liked him, and he sort of took an interest in what I was doing in school. He took me out to his plant a couple of times when I was in high school—just to show me around. I was interested in what he was doing. So I decided to look into organizational development as a career when I was looking for a major area of study. This kind of work does interest me, and I did find it challenging.

Now see how this same interview might have been conducted using a nondirective approach.

Interviewer: Tell me about your college experience.

Interviewee: Toward the end of my junior year of high school I was looking around for a college to attend. I looked at several, but was not ready to make a decision. Then I began talking to my friend's father about the kind of work he does. He works in organizational development and training. He even took me to his work to show me around. I liked him and what I saw, so I decided to look for a school that was good in the field.

I was living in Denver at the time, so I visited the University of Denver's department of communication. I liked the person I talked to, and so I asked my friend's father what he thought about that department and communication training for a career in the organizational development field. He was positive about it all.

I also wanted to keep my job, rather than look for a new one. I got along well with the people at work and was getting a lot of good experience. So I went to school at Denver and continued in my job. This has turned out to be a good choice for me.

I think my college work has trained me quite well for your position. In particular, I think that these courses...[the interviewee would continue on to complete this thought].

The differences between the two approaches are interesting. There are advantages and disadvantages to each. Charles Stewart and William Cash[10] have suggested these advantages and disadvantages of the directive approach:

DIRECTIVE APPROACH

Advantages	*Disadvantages*
1. It is easy to learn.	1. It is inflexible.
2. It takes less time.	2. It is limited in variety and depth of subject matter.
3. It can provide quantifiable data.	3. It limits the interviewer's range of techniques.
4. It can supplement other methods of data collection such as questionnaires and observations.	4. It often replaces more effective and efficient means of collecting data.
5. It can be replicated by controlling variables such as voice, facial expressions, and appearance.	5. The validity of the information may be questioned because of variables such as voice, facial expressions, and appearance.

Stewart and Cash[11] suggest these advantages and disadvantages of the nondirective approach:

NONDIRECTIVE APPROACH

Advantages	*Disadvantages*
1. It allows the interviewer to probe deeply into subject matter.	1. It is time-consuming.
2. It gives the interviewer greater flexibility.	2. It requires acute psychological insight and sensitivity.
3. It gives the interviewee greater freedom to give lengthy answers and to volunteer information.	3. It often generates unneeded information.
4. It tends to generate more information.	4. It tends to generate excessive information.
5. It allows the interviewer to adapt to each interview.	5. Adaptation to each interviewee may reduce replicability.

Setting.   All interviews take place within an environment that may have considerable effect on the outcome. We've discussed the physical environment from the standpoint of nonverbal messages earlier in this chapter. Here we will address the effect of the time of day and week, the location, and the events that surround the interview.

Time of day and week. The time of day and week can have a dramatic effect on the interview. For example, research into decisions made by recruiters shows that interviewing at the "wrong" time of day can decrease the chances of a favorable hiring decision.[12] Observations of people around us suggest that they have best times and worst times of the day and week. A perceptive interviewer or interviewee will consider time of day and week if he or she is able to know about that person's best times. An important interview might be scheduled to take advantage of one of this person's peak times.

The fact that researchers have been able to collect data about selection interview outcomes and time of day suggests that there are some common "down" times. These data indicate that for selection interviews these times are just before and and toward the end of the workday. Whether these are bad times for other interview contexts and purposes we cannot say for certain, but they might be. In addition, Monday mornings and Friday afternoons seem to be less productive times for many people. These may be times you would want to avoid scheduling an important interview.

Location. The location of an interview is another concern related to setting. Of course, some of the obvious considerations of location are noise level, privacy, and comfort factors such as lighting, temperature, and ventilation. You might also want a location where you can control interruptions. Interruptions can be very disruptive to the interview as they break concentration and can seriously impose upon the climate. If you interview in your office and a secretary is not available to intercept calls, you will want to move to a location where you will not be interrupted by the telephone.

Also try to determine if the interviewing space is free from outside distractions. Is there likely to be noise in the hall or in adjacent rooms? Will a secretary be typing a long document next door? Will there be secretaries or others coming and going? Are there visual distractions from a busy street outside? Any of these may make a location less than ideal.

Events that surround the interview. Sometimes particular events that surround an interview can have a significant effect on it. Look at the calendar to see if you are scheduling the interview close to some holiday. Traditionally, holiday seasons are not very productive times for interviews that convey some kind of bad news or have as their aim dealing with some problem. These times, on the other hand, may be good for scheduling interviews that are less upsetting or disruptive, as the participants may have less hectic schedules. You may wish to schedule sales, selection, or in-depth probing interviews for these times. If the interviewer is a counselor, then these times may be critical ones for helping the client cope. Holiday periods are often very lonely times for those who are in crisis situations.

Ask yourself if there are likely to be events in the person's work life that might distract from the interview. If the interview is in a work setting that you both share, you may be able to discover whether there are circumstances that might affect the person's ability to concentrate in the interview. Is this a period of heavy work loads? Is there a lot of pressure resulting from labor problems or safety problems? The work situation may make a difference in an interview with a particular employee.

Sometimes the interview situation in placement centers can be less than satisfactory. An interviewee may be forced to schedule back-to-back interviews. If the interviewee has had one or more interviews immediately preceding yours, he or she may be physically and emotionally exhausted. You may not be able to know when this is the case, but be aware that it occurs so that you can take it into account if you wish to do so.

SUMMARY

Understanding the contextual factors begins with a consideration of the participants. The interviewer and interviewee have needs that they hope to fulfill. In the task dimension, there are needs related to the goal of the interview. In addition, in the social dimension there is a need to experience a satisfying relationship. People also seek satisfaction of their needs for control, inclusion, and affection.

Both parties also bring to the interview images of themselves and the other person. The image we have of ourself comes from our beliefs, values, attitudes, and recognized abilities. Self-concept and a strong value system provide a frame of reference through which we filter our experiences of the interview. The frame of reference helps us interpret whatever we observe.

The interview process is a series of interactions designed to accomplish a specific purpose. These interactions are designed to create messages through verbal and nonverbal behavior. Misunderstandings, disagreements, and even conflict can occur when interviewers and interviewees do not express themselves clearly, have differing frames of reference or use words that are too complex, or use words with highly personal meanings.

Nonverbal interactions are a significant part of any interview. They provide very important information about the meaning of messages and how they are being received. Nonverbal codes include appearance, gesture and movement, touch, face and eye behavior, vocalics, time, and the physical environment.

Listening is a process that includes the acts of receiving, interpreting, and remembering the message. The ability to listen for comprehension and evaluation is especially important in the interviewing situation. Guidelines were offered for improvement of comprehension and evaluation.

Feedback is the observable response of a receiver to the message that has been communicated. Feedback might confirm that the message was received, not received, understood, or misunderstood. Feedback can also provide qualitative information about how the message was received and the relationship. A listener might respond with active listening by paraphrasing the speaker's ideas and feelings.

The final component of the interview process is situational context. A general situation is the events that surround the interview in its given time in history. Political, economic, and cultural events fall into this category. The specific situation refers to the immediate events and circumstances that surround the interview. Specific situation includes purpose, approach, and setting.

NOTES

[1] William C. Schutz, *The Interpersonal Underworld* (Reading, MA: Addison-Wesley Publishing Company, 1969).

[2] Gerald L. Wilson, Alan M. Hantz, and Michael S. Hanna, *Interpersonal Growth through Communication* (Dubuque, IA: Wm. C. Brown Publishers, 1988), p. 102.

[3] See Keith Gibbins, "Communication Aspects of Women's Clothes and the Relation to Fashionability," *British Journal of Social and Clinical Psychology, 8* (1964), 301–312; Ellen Berscheid and Elaine Walster, "Physical Attractiveness," in *Advances in Experimental Social Psychology,* vol. 7, Leonard Berkowitz (ed.), (New York: Academic Press, 1974); C. L. Kleinke, *First Impressions: The Psychology of Encountering Others* (Englewood Cliffs, NJ: Prentice-Hall, 1975).

[4] John E. Baird and A. Schubert, "Nonverbal Behavior and Leadership Emergence in Task-Oriented and Informal Group Discussion." Paper presented at the International Communication Association Annual Meeting, New Orleans, 1974.

[5] John E. Baird, Jr., "Some Nonverbal Elements of Leadership Emergence," *The Southern Speech Communication Journal, 42* (1977), 352–361.

[6] Dale G. Leathers, *Nonverbal Communication Systems* (Boston: Allyn and Bacon, 1976), pp. 33–34.

[7] James McCroskey, Carl Larson, and Mark Knapp, *An Introduction to Interpersonal Communication* (Englewood Cliffs, NJ: Prentice-Hall, 1971), pp. 110–114.

[8] Ralph V. Exline, "Explorations in the Process of Person Perception: Visual Interaction in Relation to Competition, Sex, and the Need for Affiliation," *Journal of Personality, 31* (1963), 1–20.

[9] Lyman K. Steil, Larry L. Barker, and Kittie W. Watson, *Effective Listening: Key to Your Success* (New York: Random House, 1983), pp. 20–29.

[10] Charles J. Stewart and William B. Cash, Jr., *Interviewing: Principles and Practices* (Dubuque, IA: Wm. C. Brown Publishers, 1988), p. 7.

[11]Stewart and Cash, pp. 7–8.

[12]Harvey D. Tschirgi and Jon M. Huegli, "Monitoring the Employment Interview," *Journal of College Placement* (Winter 1979), 39.

EXPERIENCES

1. Using an audiotape from a discussion, analyze the verbal interaction and identify any major dysfunctional language use. Suggest what might be done to improve language use for those instances that you identified as potential problems.

2. During an interview have observers ask the participants to "freeze" in place several times. Discuss what nonverbal cues seem to be given by the interviewer and interviewee. What kinds of messages do the participants seem to be conveying?

3. Ask dyads to conduct get-acquainted interviews in two contrasting settings. Report back to the class on the effect that setting had on the interviews.

4. Observe an interview to determine how the interviewer seeks to meet or fails to meet interviewee needs. How were inclusion, control, and affection needs met? How effective was each attempt to meet these needs? What might the interviewer do or say to meet these needs more effectively?

5. Prepare a 5-minute informational interview that includes at least three major lines of questioning. Interview a classmate, and at the conclusion of each line of questioning, summarize fully the ideas the interviewee presented. Then ask the interviewee for confirmation or clarification of your summary. Based on the results of the feedback you received, analyze your listening skill. What conclusions can you draw about your listening? What might be done to improve your listening?

RECOMMENDED READINGS

Goodall, H. L., Jr., *Casing a Promised Land: The Autobiography of an Organizational Detective as Cultural Ethnographer* (Carbondale, IL: Southern Illinois Press, 1989). See especially Chaps. 2–5.

Hickson, Mark L., and Don W. Stacks, *NVB: Nonverbal Communication Studies and Applications,* 2d ed. (Dubuque, IA: Wm. C. Brown Publishers, 1990).

Pettegrew, Lloyd S., "The Importance of Context in Applied Communication Research," *Southern Speech Communication Journal, 53* (1988), 331–338.

Stewart, John (ed.), *Bridges, Not Walls: A Book about Interpersonal Communication,* 5th ed. (New York: McGraw-Hill, Inc., 1990).

Wilson, Gerald L., Alan M. Hantz, and Michael S. Hanna, *Interpersonal Growth through Communication,* 2d ed. (Dubuque, IA: Wm. C. Brown Publishers, 1989).

Wolvin, Andrew, and Carolyn Gwynn Coakley, *Listening,* 3d ed. (Dubuque, IA.: Wm. C. Brown Publishers, 1988).

PART II

Basic Considerations: Foundations for Communication in Interviews

CHAPTER 3

DEVELOPING THE STRUCTURE OF THE INTERVIEW

OBJECTIVES

After reading this chapter, you should be able to:

Explain how the concept of structure can underscore the importance of tasks and relationships in an interview.

Develop interviewer goals for the beginning (opening) of an interview.

Discuss management strategies for contextual, topical, and relational elements of the beginning (opening) of an interview.

Develop a cogent pattern of questioning for an interview.

Discuss interviewer strategies for accomplishing the purpose of the interview through selection of an appropriate pattern of questioning.

Develop a strategy for conducting an interview.

Patricia, one of our interviewing students, returned from a job interview with a small, recently begun, high-technology firm. She was very enthusiastic about the company and was sold on its future. When one of us reminded her that she had been less than enthusiastic before the interview and had expressed serious concerns about the company, she responded:

> I know. But that was *before* I was interviewed. I admit that I had questions about whether or not the company was going to be able to pay its bills and what the future would hold for me there. But when I arrived, the woman doing the interviewing was ready for me. She made me feel welcome, showed me around the offices before the interview, and introduced me to some really sharp people. And her conduct of the interview was so professional! She began with a good description of the firm and what my responsibilities would be. We talked—and I mean really talked—about my qualifications and what working there would be like; and before the interview ended, she reviewed what we had gone over and told me when I could expect to hear from the company. If that interview is any indication of what the company is like, then I'm sure it is the place for me!

We were happy to hear such a bright report from one of our students. What stood out in her impression of this company was the way in which the interview was conducted. More precisely, it was the application of knowledge of contextual factors regarding *structuring* the interview that impressed Patricia, and led her to conclude that this company would be a good place to work.

Because some of our students have had the opposite experience—boring, unstructured, or even hostile interviews—we have learned over the years that how candidates perceive the job interview correlates directly with their impressions of the firm and with their decision about working there. What is true of the selection interview is, of course, true for other kinds of interviews. For this reason it is important to study the structure of an interview with the purpose of learning how to master it.

In this chapter, we address the structure of interviews. We explore how an interview should open, develop, and close. Within each of those divisions we present examples from the perspective of differing contextual factors: purpose and balance between task and relational concerns.

BEGINNING THE INTERVIEW

We know from organizational research that early experiences at work tend to shape later expectations and understandings.[1] And what has been shown to be true of the work experience can logically be extended to apply to most experiences. Thus, in interviews too, our initial experience shapes later expectations and understandings. It is important, then, that the first part of any interview be well structured. In addition, the interviewer must communicate effectively. These principles may seem obvious, but we have found that most students have given little thought to how to go about implementing them.

In this section we will discuss beginnings. We will talk about the goals of an opening, look at some examples of openings, and examine the goals in terms of task and relationship concerns.

Goals of the Opening

Organizational research studies[2] as well as practical experience show that there are three interrelated goals for the opening of an interview:

1. To make the interviewee feel welcomed and relaxed
2. To provide the interviewee with a sense of purpose
3. To preview some of the major topics to be covered during the interview

Let's examine each of these goals in greater detail.

First, it is important to make the interviewee feel welcomed and relaxed. There is more to this goal than simply being polite. We know that we perform better when we are not experiencing too much tension, and the opening of an interview should provide a climate that allows for maximum performance.

How is this goal accomplished? The answer to this question depends a great deal on the personalities of the individuals involved in the interview. However, in general, the ability of the interviewer to talk openly about a variety of topics related to the interview helps an interviewee feel comfortable and less threatened. Thus, it is advisable for the interviewer to be well versed in the subjects to be pursued.

Keep in mind also that nonverbal cues, such as a smile, a friendly facial expression, eye contact, a firm handshake, open gestures, and positive relational feedback, can set a positive, nonthreatening tone. Introduce yourself and greet the interviewee by name if possible. Relational communication is sometimes initiated by a polite inquiry such as, "How is it going today for you?"

Consider this statement, taken from another one of our interviewing students:

> How did he make me feel comfortable? Well, he introduced himself and greeted me warmly. He smiled in a polite way and talked easily about the company and my job description. He knew a lot about my background too, which made me feel like he was really interested in me. When we went into his office, he helped me feel relaxed and offered me coffee. I expressed interest in some pictures of his family, and so he showed them to me before the interview began. Overall I'd say it wasn't any one thing that he did to make me feel comfortable with him, but the whole impression he gave me of who he was and what he was doing.

We agree. Although techniques for making a person feel relaxed and comfortable are listed above, in the end it is the total impression left with the interviewee that counts. Be careful, however, not to spend too much time in small talk or be overly friendly or informal as these behaviors can create a negative impression.

How long should an opening be? There really is no established length, but as a general rule it should take no more than five minutes and usually will require less time.

The second major goal of an effective opening is to provide the interviewee with a sense of purpose and direction. This is primarily the responsibility of the interviewer, who should state what the purpose of the interview is early on, and try to provide any additional information relevant to that purpose. For instance, at the beginning of an employment interview the interviewer often will establish the purpose by describing the company and the job description and by explaining in general terms what type of employee is being sought. During an appraisal interview the supervisor should establish the purpose by explaining the policies concerning performance appraisals and by letting the interviewee know how the interview will proceed. During in-depth informational interviews, the interviewer should state the purpose clearly and directly soon after greetings have been exchanged and should clear up any questions about how the information will be used. And during survey and problem-solving interviews, the interviewer should state the purpose and then follow up with an explanation of the method that will be used to conduct the interview.

The third major goal of an opening should be to preview the main topics of the interview. This will help the interviewee see the direction of the interview.

Previews serve as markers for people and therefore should make use of numerical references (such as *first, second, third*) and key words that will be easily recalled (for example, *education, work experience, future goals*). It is also important to limit the number of markers in the preview to between two and four for easy recall.

Let's look at some examples of how interviewers fulfilled the three goals for openings (to make the interviewee feel welcomed and relaxed, to provide a sense of purpose, and to preview some of the major topics) in particular contexts.

Examples in Contexts:

Employment interview.   "Good morning, Ms. Wing. I'm Jaime Sanchez, the director of personnel for our company. I've been looking forward to meeting with you. Would you have a seat? How about a cup of coffee?

"Are you comfortable? Shall we begin? Good. Today what I want to do is talk with you about your educational preparation for this job, and then go into some detail about your career goals and aspirations relevant to this position and the objectives of our company. Does that sound all right with you?

"Good, then let's begin...."

Appraisal interview.   "Darryl, good to see you. I'm always encouraged when an employee shows up a little ahead of time for an appraisal. Shows enthusiasm, and that's always good. Come into my office, won't you?

"Would you like to review my written comments about your performance for a few minutes while I get a soft drink? That will give you some time to think through the items that we can then discuss in greater detail. Can I get you something to drink while I'm out? No? Okay, why don't you just sit down there and read the paperwork. I'll be back in about five minutes."

[The interviewer returns and offers a preview of the interview.]

Survey interview.   "Good afternoon. I'm Alice Tobacci, and today I'm conducting a survey on our new product Cheddar Tidbits. If you will participate in my survey, I'll be happy to give you a free sample of each one of these new products that we think you and your family will enjoy. Would you be willing to take a few minutes to sample our product and answer some questions about it?

"Good. Now what I will do is ask you a series of four questions after you taste our product. We want you to answer honestly and openly. You don't have to please; we really want your opinion. Our job is to get good, solid information from people just like you. Are you ready?"

Problem-solving interview.   "Good to see you again, Mrs. Jacobs. How are you feeling today? Is that foot still bothering you? That was a nasty fall, but it seems to be healing nicely.

"Today I want to talk with you about three programs we offer for the purpose of rebuilding and strengthening injured bones and muscles. What I will do is describe each of them, explain how they operate, and then answer any questions you might have about them. Okay? Good, let me begin...."

Persuasive interview.   "Good morning, Yuen. Do you have time for a cup of coffee? I have an idea to share with you.

"The department has been experiencing a problem over the past several months with misplacing personnel action folders. This can be a serious problem, as you know. I would like to work with you to develop procedures that will reduce loss of personnel action folders.

"Let me ask you a couple of questions concerning the problem, and then I'll present my suggestion."

The goals of an opening—to make the interviewee feel comfortable and relaxed, to provide a sense of purpose, and to preview major topics of the interview—are accomplished by planning and are mastered by experience. In our view they should also be accomplished in the order we have discussed them; however, the demands of individual interviews may call for modifications.

Let us now consider how what we have said relates to task and relationship concerns. Remember that communication in an interview should accomplish its task and contribute to the building or maintenance of a productive relationship.

Relationship Concerns

Both the interviewer and the interviewee may have topics to pursue during an interview.

However, in most cases the announcement of topics "belongs" to the interviewer. As noted before, during the beginning of an interview the interviewer should preview these topics to help both parties concentrate on the business that needs to be accomplished. The interviewer may say: "I want to pursue four major issues with you..." and briefly explain what those issues are. This statement helps the interviewee focus on the topics to be pursued during the interview, and to foresee how they may relate to each other. It also allows the interviewee to think ahead toward any questions he or she may want to raise with the interviewer about either the topics or how the information will be used.

To specify the topics for an interview is to accomplish both practical and expressive goals. On the practical side, it schedules the agenda for the interview, explaining what topics will be pursued and in what order they will be pursued. On the expressive side it helps relax the interviewee because the topics help define the areas to be discussed. This reduces the ambiguity of the setting and thus demonstrates concern for the other person.

Relationships in organizational settings consist of an interplay between two dimensions—the practical and the expressive.[4] The practical dimension is related to what we have described as the "task" component of relationships, or the ability of communication to get the job done. The expressive dimension is subtler. Viewed one way, it consists of a variety of nonverbal cues, such as facial expression, eye contact, and gestures and movements, that detail emotional and intuitive responses to an individual. Viewed another way, the expressive dimension consists of verbal statements about how an individual is responding to another individual as a person. Taken together, the practical and expressive dimensions of organizational relationships account for how individuals think and feel about each other, and how their behavior mirrors these thoughts and feelings.

During the opening of an interview, emotional levels tend to be high. The interviewer, conscious of an agenda and goal for the talk, may unconsciously send control messages to the interviewee. The interviewee, conscious of self-presentation and ambiguity, may unconsciously send corresponding messages to the interviewer. The result is often awkward. Both individuals are talking to each other, but neither one is engaged in communication. When the focus is on self and those involved are not being sensitive to the other's needs, the result is a failure to respond effectively. Christine's experience as an interviewer mirrors this problem during an informative interview with a NASA director:

> I was invited into the office to conduct the interview. I was nervous, because the interviewee was a very important individual in the nation's space program. As it turned out, he was nervous too. He had just spent an hour in a heated debate about funding and had forgotten that we were scheduled for an interview. To tell the truth, I don't remember a thing that happened until several minutes later, except this general feeling of uneasiness and awkwardness.

Christine's sentiments echo those of numerous others in similar situations. When we feel uneasy and are placed into a highly ambiguous situation, we tend to forget what transpires. Perhaps you've experienced this problem when meeting a stranger: you exchange names but a few minutes later realize that you don't remember the other person's name.

As you can imagine, this lack of relational focus—the ability to listen to the other individual and respond to what she or he is saying—is detrimental to a successful interview. The practical, or goal-oriented, aspects of the interview tend to lose out to the expressive, or emotional, aspects of the relationship, and the result is a failure to communicate and a loss of information.

To overcome this problem in the opening of the interview it is helpful to remember that the participants are there because of each other and that the objective is to get information from the other person. This is, of course, easier said than done. However, the more experience you gain in interviews with these practical and expressive characteristics in mind, the more you will be able to use them.

Now that we have described the beginning of an interview, we will go on to explore how an interview develops.

DEVELOPING THE PATTERN OF QUESTIONING

Although the opening of the interview establishes rapport between the participants and outlines the topics to be pursued, it is the development of the interview that fulfills the expectations of both parties. In this section we will describe three interrelated concerns for the development of questions during the body of an interview: (1) stating the purpose, (2) selecting a pattern of organization, and (3) determining what kind of structure is needed. Throughout this section we will be emphasizing the role of the interviewer because that is the person chiefly responsible for the management of the agenda.

Stating the Purpose

Most people will answer questions honestly, intelligently, and sincerely if you tell them why you are asking the questions. Thus in an interview, be sure to explain the purpose of your questions. As simple as this seems, it is perhaps the best advice we can give to you about developing questions for an interview. In support of this advice, listen to Mike:

> I was interviewed for a job at _____ . The interviewer told me that she was looking for an entry-level marketing person. Then she explained that she was going to talk about my education and my work experience, and then we would explore my goals for the future. This relaxed me because I had a sense of what to expect. I think it made me more willing to talk about my experiences too.

Mike's testimony suggests that how the interviewee perceives the intent of the interviewer can be very important in how much detail the interviewee will be willing to provide. When the interviewer is clear about his or her intent—by forthrightly telling why he or she wants to pursue certain topics and what uses will be made of the information—the interviewer will reduce the anxiety and apprehension that surrounds the interview.

A statement of purpose will orient the interviewer (and the interviewee) throughout the interview. It should be placed at the beginning of each major topic sequence, and it should include the following:

1. An explanation of why the topic is important to the interview
2. A brief statement about how the information will be used by the interviewer and the organization

Here are some illustrations of how these goals can be accomplished in different types of interviews.

Employment interview.   "Now we want to turn to the area of career goals and aspirations. As you probably know, we are interested in this sort of information because it helps us match what you might want to do with what we can do for you in terms of career growth. This does not mean that if your career goals are not in line with our expectations that we won't hire you. It means that we can explain to you some of the paths you might want to consider. Many times we have found that people are pleased to have that information."

Appraisal interview.   "Let's move on to the area of performance of job duties. As you can see, this category asks me to describe your duties, to rate your performance in them, and to rank you with other employees doing the same job in the firm. I need to know from you if this written description fits your understanding of your job. Okay?

   "I want to begin by talking with you about your duties. I have found in the past that the time we spend together will be more productive if we are clear about the assigned duties. Sometimes getting the job done goes beyond your job description. We will want to be aware of this if it is the case. This will allow us to think about your performance based on what you really do."

Survey interview.   "Now I want to ask you two questions about the reasons you purchased _____ instead of _____ . Before I ask them, though, I want to emphasize the importance of getting at the real reasons for your choice. Let me explain why this is important. In one of our regional tests we asked this question to over 700 people and found that only about 10 percent of them bought the product because of its packaging. So we figured that wasn't very important. However, we repeated the test later because our product wasn't improving its sales. This time we asked more detailed questions about packaging and found that it accounted for nearly 40 percent of the sales! Imagine that. So if there is a reason you have for buying one over the other and I don't list it, please tell me anyway. I need the information to do my job."

Problem-solving interview.   "Let's discuss how you want to solve this problem. I've outlined some treatment programs that are available to you free of cost, and I think I've given you a pretty good idea of what's involved in them. Now I'm going to ask the tough question: Which one do you feel you want to participate in? Before you answer it, though, I'd like you to know that choosing one program does not bar you from changing to another one at some future date.''

Persuasive interview.   ''I would like to make a proposal that will let you secure computer equipment on a rent-to-purchase plan. Let me begin by asking you a few questions about computer usage within the department. That information will allow us to talk more specifically about equipment that will meet your needs and cost.

Selecting a Pattern of Organization

Stating a purpose for each topic area is important because it explains how the information received will be evaluated. Equally important is the selection of a pattern of organization to guide the development of topics. In our experience we have found four basic patterns: topical, time, cause to effect, and problem solving.

1. *Topical Pattern.* This pattern is based on the assumption that an interviewer has more than one basic area of questioning that needs to be explored. This pattern must have a logical ordering and not too many topics if it is to be effective. We suggest you limit topics to five or fewer. The topical pattern would be a good choice, for example, for a journalist who wants to interview a stockbroker about the investment potential of a variety of over-the-counter stocks, as well as municipal bonds and commodities. It would allow the interviewer to categorize the topics according to their major headings—stocks, bonds, commodities—and pursue questioning under each topic.

    The topic pattern is also widely used in performance appraisal interviews. The supervisor normally has a list of topics (performance categories) to be pursued, such as attitude toward work, relationship with others, performance of established duties, and training needs. Because there are a variety of topics to be discussed, the topical pattern is appropriate.

2. *Time Pattern.* Chronology is important to a wide range of interviews, both as a general organizing device and as a way to pursue a subunit of questioning. Because chronology deals with time and time moves in a linear sequence, it allows the interviewer to organize topics to be pursued according to corresponding dates. So, for example, a person in a computer firm who wished to interview a development expert to obtain information for a technical document could use the time sequence to construct questions.

    As you might imagine, the time pattern is extremely useful in arranging the topics for an employment interview. This is because the employment interview might begin with a discussion of the applicant's high school education, then move on to early work experience, then take up college education, and so forth. Thus, the topics of the interview are arranged chronologically. And beyond this, each topic can be patterned in a chronological arrangement.

One of the major uses of the time sequence is as a subunit in topical, cause-to-effect, and problem-solving structures. Here again, any subject or line of questioning that lends itself to dates and times is appropriate for a chronology.

3. *Cause-to-Effect Pattern.* This structure is primarily used as a major sequencing structure in performance appraisal and problem-solving interviews, although it can find applications as a questioning subunit in informative and employment interviews. The principle is to discuss causes before effects and then to link causes to effects. Cause-to-effect ordering can also be used very effectively and efficiently as effect-cause. In this case, the effect is explored first and then causes are identified.

As an example, let's assume you are the supervisor of a manufacturing operation that has experienced a work slowdown. You are interviewing your workers about the situation, and you want to find out what is causing the problem. You would briefly describe the slowdown and then pursue questions related to what is causing it. After the causes have been identified, you might want to pursue the effects these causes are creating and move on to a verbal linking of the causes to the effects.

In performance appraisal interviews the ability of the interviewer to get the interviewee to link causes and effects through appropriate selection of questions is vital. The same is true for problem-solving interviews, where the ability of the interviewee to articulate for himself or herself how the effect is created often is therapeutic.

4. *Problem-Solving Pattern.* The use of the problem-solving structure is prevalent, as its name implies, in problem-solving interviews where the goal is to help the interviewee overcome a specific problem by articulating its causes and effects. It is also useful as a subunit structure for information-gathering, employment, performance appraisal, and persuasive interviews.

Like the cause-to-effect structure, problem solving is based on the idea that identification of a problem and how it is defined will lead to a better method of finding a solution. When using this structure, it is helpful to divide the body of your interview into two parts—discussion of the problem and discussion of the solution—and link the solution sequence to the problem sequence. Another approach to using a problem-solving pattern is to develop the problem, its significance, and solutions in a series of interviews.

The above four strategies suggest ways of planning for the developmental questioning sequence of the body of an interview. There are others, of course, that pertain especially to particular contexts. These will be presented when the particular contexts are discussed.

Determining the Kind of Structure Needed

At this point in our discussion of interviewing structures, we turn our attention to how much structure is appropriate for interviews. To answer this question we will explore the relative merits of nonscheduled, moderately scheduled, highly scheduled, and standardized agendas.

Nonscheduled.   A nonscheduled interview is one that has no preplanned questions. The interviewer may have a general goal for the interview, but has not taken the time, or perhaps could not take the time, to write down specific questions. In short, this interview is usually guided by a series of topics that may or may not be written. The interviewer, as a result, has the advantage of nearly complete freedom in phrasing and posing questions. The nonscheduled interview is useful when it is impossible to plan meaningfully because not much is known about the interviewee or that person's grasp of the topic.

There are several reasons that we do not recommend this structure as a general strategy. First, without prior planning, certain questions may be overlooked or missed, requiring an additional interview of a more scheduled variety to address what was missed. Thus the nonscheduled interview can be a waste of time.

Second, unless the interviewer is highly skilled, a nonscheduled interview can create an atmosphere of unprofessionalism. The interviewee arrives on time ready to do business, but the interviewer may not be able to conduct the interview with a free-flowing sensible question sequence. The result may be frustration and, again, a waste of time.

Third, the nonscheduled interview can drift with whatever topic comes to mind, thus making it easier for the participants to move away from the established topic and enter more esoteric or personal areas. The result is that the important questions never get answered because they never get asked, and so it too is a waste of time.

Finally, the nature of this interview makes it difficult to replicate. Thus, an interviewer who needs to collect the same information from several different people may not be able to do so meaningfully.

As you can see from our discussion of the disadvantages of a nonscheduled approach, the common thread uniting all the problems is a potential waste of time and a possible impression of poor preparation. It simply may not be an economical way to conduct an interview and may reflect badly on the organization.

Consider, for example, Mona's case:

I arrived for a job interview and was greeted by a woman who apologized for not having had time to read my resume. She then said my resume probably didn't give an accurate account of my background any-way, which angered me because I spent a lot of time putting it together and thought it did a very good job of just that! So she asked me to talk about myself, which I was prepared to do, but she kept interrupting me with little discussions of her philosophy on this or that. After that, we were both a little uncomfortable, so she asked me what I thought she needed to know about me and I told her I thought it was summed up nicely on my resume. She took out my resume and read it for the next couple of minutes, and then said, "You're right." That was it. I left her office with a bad taste in my mouth, and I promise you I will never work for that company. If she is representative of what it hires, it will surely go out of business.

Enough said. The nonscheduled approach often does not answer the practical or the expressive needs of the interview, and does not encourage the interviewer to exert control over the situation in a way conducive to overcoming ambiguity or feelings of apprehension.

Despite these disadvantages, we often find ourselves in a position that requires an on-the-spot interview. We must gain experience organizing our ideas and translating them into questions that will achieve our purposes. For the journalist this is an especially critical skill, as on-the-spot information-gathering interviews are a frequent occurrence.

Moderately scheduled.   A moderately scheduled interview comprises the major topics along with possible probing questions under each. It is one of the most often used interviewing formats. Journalists prefer this structured approach because it allows them first to work from a list of key questions to guide the telling of a story and then to employ the give-and-take of conversational interplay to fill in important details. Employment interviewers also use this format in all phases of the selection process. In addition, appraisal, problem-solving, and persuasive interviews can be successful with the moderately scheduled approach. The essential features of this approach include:

1. *Careful development of key questions to guide the body of the interview.* For example, assume you will be interviewing candidates for an assistant managerial position. This job requires a college degree, some management experience, and a willingness to work closely with people who have highly specialized and technical backgrounds. What key questions could you use?

Given what you know about interviewing structures, you would probably choose a topic structure with topics and questions arranged chronologically. Moving from the candidate's past to the present to the future, you would need to ask key questions concerning those areas specified in the job description: What was your college career like? What was your major? What supervisory or managerial experience have you had? What strategies would you use to deal produc-

tively with people who have highly specialized or technical backgrounds? If hired for this job, what do you expect to happen to you in
the next five years?

2. *Key questions to be answered in ways that encourage responsive
probes and follow-up queries.* Using the employment interview example, you can see how the candidate's responses to each one of the
key questions would naturally lead to probing or follow-up questions.
For example, if the candidate explained that her major was communication and her minor was business management, the interviewer could
ask for elaboration on the reasons for that choice. If she had no supervisory experience but had served in several leadership positions
while at college, the interviewer could follow up with a question
about what she learned about leadership from her campus experience
that would help her at work. And if her plans for the future called for
the acquisition of computer skills, the interviewer could probe for
whether or not she planned to pursue graduate coursework or participate in sponsored training programs.

3. *Positive relational development.* The give-and-take nature of conversational exchanges engendered by the moderately scheduled approach encourages the participants to pursue practical and expressive
needs. By allowing flexibility in responses and follow-ups, the participants are free to provide details, examples, illustrations, and other
sources of spontaneously created information that contribute to a productive relational climate.

As you can see from our discussion, the moderately scheduled approach is
widely used. We believe the reason for this is due to its flexibility. It both
builds in structure, allowing interviewers to control the direction of the interview by listing the salient issues to be discussed, and provides leeway, allowing
interviewers to develop a positive relational climate by going with the flow of
conversational exchange. It encourages interviewees to be open and to elaborate on answers given, and to provide important details and examples that can
be helpful to the interviewer. However attractive this approach may seem,
though, there are times when a less flexible schedule is needed.

Highly scheduled.   A highly scheduled interview contains all the questions,
including those to be used for probing, ordered and worded as they will be
asked. This approach is recommended for use in screening interviews when
the group or organization wants to carefully compare qualifications from
candidate to candidate. It is also appropriate under tightly controlled or
organizationally stringent conditions. For example, this approach is sometimes required of journalists interviewing government officials.

A screening interview for employment or recruitment purposes features
a list of key questions and follow-ups that are asked to every candidate,

with the purpose of screening out those less qualified. This kind of interview allows personnel maximum objectivity in making initial decisions. The screening interview is generally followed by a call-back interview that can be more flexible.

In cases where journalists are granted an interview with a government official, particularly an official whose statements may have international ramifications, the questions usually must be tightly monitored and in some cases approved before the interview, and follow-up or probing questions may also need to be specified. Asking the "wrong" questions can be hazardous. In particular, many journalists have faced imprisonment or torture because their questions led to charges that they worked for the CIA or other espionage agencies. While we sincerely hope that you will never face such charges, it is important to recognize the use and limitations of a highly scheduled interview. When it must be used, it is wise to not venture beyond its boundaries, however arbitrary they may seem. One of our acquaintances describes how sensitive such a situation can be:

> I was working in South America, free-lancing for Canadian newspapers and anyone else who would buy my stories. I got a big break through a friend to interview one of the Sandanista officials. I was told that I could only ask questions that would reflect positively on Nicaragua, and that I only had five minutes to do it in. I wrote out three questions, one of which had to do with the Contras. I got halfway through that sentence and the interview was canceled, my notes were confiscated, and I spent the next four days in jail. Some big break.

Highly scheduled, standardized.   This kind of interview provides not only questions worded as they will be stated, but options to answers as they will be offered. The highly scheduled, standardized interview is used in settings where there is a need to quantify answers or place them in specific categories. Thus this format is used in surveys and in some health care interviews.

The purpose of a survey interview is to determine how a sample of persons responds to the same series of carefully worded questions or statements. For example, suppose you were preparing a report for a marketing firm. Your task was to assess the likely impact of a new product—candy-flavored yogurt—in a particular market region. To complete this task would require developing a survey instrument capable of generating data about the likely impact of the product. You would need to use a highly scheduled, highly standardized format to be sure that what your sample responded to was the same in each case.

The highly scheduled, standardized approach is also used by health care service agencies. When you visit a dentist's or physician's office for the first time, the interviewing conditions are similar to those of a screening session. In order to assess your health or diagnose a particular problem, it is necessary to ask a series of standardized questions concerning your personal his-

Context	Appropriate Type of Format
Screening/recruitment	Highly scheduled
Employment	Moderately scheduled
Appraisal	Moderately scheduled
Survey	Highly scheduled, standardized
Problem solving	Moderately scheduled
In-depth information gathering	Moderately scheduled or highly scheduled
Computerized health care or diagnostic	Highly scheduled, standardized
Persuasive	Moderately scheduled

Figure 3.1   Summary of structural choices for interviews.

tory, any record of medication or treatments, and the often essential question, "Where does it hurt?" Many of these questions can be answered with a yes or no or with a number, date, or name.

The choice of an interviewing schedule should be based on the particular demands of the situation. Figure 3.1 summarizes the uses of the nonscheduled, moderately scheduled, highly scheduled, and highly scheduled, standardized formats just discussed.

CONCLUDING THE INTERVIEW

As with the opening and body of an interview, the conclusion of an interview also suggests the need for structure. Most of the time, the same criteria for opening an interview are useful for closing an interview.

There are five important tasks that should be accomplished in closing most interviews. *First, the interviewer needs to review the major topics and the responses given to them.* This procedure allows the interviewee to listen to how his or her answers were recorded and interpreted, and to modify or change them if necessary. This goal is especially important in in-depth information-gathering, appraisal, problem-solving, and persuasive interviews. It is less common in selection interviews, but if there are doubts about any of the points covered, it would be wise to review them.

Second, the interviewer needs to inform the interviewee of what will be done with the information and when decisions will be made. For individuals performing informative interviews this often means explaining how the notes will be written up, when the story may appear, or what other potential uses may be found for the data. For employment and appraisal interviews it is important to explain to the interviewee when a decision will be made, how she or he will be informed about the decision, and what other procedures need to be completed. For problem-solving interviews, and particularly health care interviews, the interviewee will need to be informed about how and when the process will continue (for example, see the physician, schedule the next appointment), and what, if any, preliminary conclusions can be drawn from the data given. In a persuasive interview, this might mean discussing a time frame regarding the proposal.

Third, for most interviews, the interviewer should provide an opportunity for the interviewee to add information that may have been left out. No matter how careful the planning, there may be topics that have been overlooked. Valuable information can be obtained if the interviewer sincerely solicits it from the interviewee. A simple question such as "Is there anything else we need to discuss regarding _____ that you would like to bring up at this time?" may fill in any gaps that exist.

Fourth, the interviewer needs to lay the groundwork for another interview, if necessary. When the work of the interview cannot be completed in a single session, it is important for the interviewer to set a specific time for the next meeting. Sometimes it is difficult to tell if another meeting is needed. If so, the interviewer can tell the interviewee that there may be additional questions at another time. Then if there is a call-back, the interviewee will not be surprised.

Finally, the interviewer should formally end the interview. In most instances, the interviewer should ask if there are any additional questions or concerns that need to be covered, cover them to the satisfaction of the interviewee, and then announce that the interview has concluded. Usually, some formal closure ritual will be involved—a handshake, walking the interviewee out of the office, introducing the interviewee to the next person to be consulted. In the persuasive interview, formally ending the interview means reviewing the agreement and then taking leave.

These tasks are important sources of accomplishment, but they should be accomplished within the context of situational constraints and relational sensitivities. For example, applicants interviewing for a job, or whose work is being appraised, tend to expect some personal statement toward the end of the interview that sums up where they stand. An interviewer might choose to say: "That concludes the formal part of the interview. I want to tell you that I have enjoyed this opportunity to talk with you, and feel that you have provided me with the information I need." It is important *not* to lead the interviewee on by suggesting that the interviewee has gotten the job (unless you will be offering the person the job), or that a raise and promotion are in order (unless you have the authority to make this declaration and act upon it).

In health care and counseling sessions, there is perhaps an even greater relational need to be fulfilled at the close of an interview. Because of the emotional nature of these settings, care should be taken to reassure the client and to provide positive relational feedback. An interviewer might choose to say: "I know it is difficult, but I want you to understand that correcting this problem requires time and patience. You are making progress, and that is the most important thing you can expect at this point in our work together."

In the persuasive interview, whether an agreement has been reached or not, you will want to maintain the rapport you worked so hard to build. A friendly and sincere "thank you" without promising anything you can't deliver is in order.

Closing the interview *on time* is also a sign of professionalism and courtesy. It is appropriate to announce at the end of the interview that you have another appointment (if you have one) or that you are scheduled to talk with another person. To waste time with small talk at the conclusion of an interview is to extend unnecessarily the possibilities of the relationship and should be avoided.

A note of caution regarding the closing of an interview: There will be times when the interviewer should be sensitive to the needs of the interviewee. Perhaps the interviewee wishes to make an important point as the allotted time for the interview is up. Being sensitive to this kind of a situation will allow the interviewer to show his or her concern. The interviewer might say, "I sense that there is more you want to say. This is the time we agreed to close. Do you want to continue or would you like to schedule another time?"

SUMMARY

This chapter addressed the issue of developing a basic structure for interviews. We began with an example drawn from the experience of one of our students, Patricia, who was so impressed by the structure of an interview that she changed her mind about the image of the company. We used this example because it illustrates the dramatic impact that structure can have on perceptions of interviewing effectiveness.

We went on to describe how to open an interview. In this section we pointed out that there are three interrelated goals for an opening: to make the interviewee feel welcomed and relaxed, to provide the interviewee with a sense of purpose, and to preview some of the major topics to be covered during the interview. We further discussed the importance of relational concerns during the beginning of an interview, particularly the need to balance the practical and expressive dimensions of behavior.

We then examined how to develop a basic pattern of questioning for the body of an interview. In this section we emphasized the exchange nature of questions and answers, and the importance of planning question sequences. We showed why it is necessary to correlate the purpose of a question with the pattern of organization appropriate to it and the situation. We discussed four basic patterns: topical, time, cause to effect, and problem solving.

Next we addressed the issue of the kind of structure needed to conduct interviews. In this section we detailed the differences among nonscheduled, moderately scheduled, highly scheduled, and highly scheduled, standardized formats. We pointed out the conditions under which each of these formats is best selected.

Finally, we explained the importance of concluding the interview properly. In this section we stressed the need to review the topics covered in the interview and to inform the interviewee about what will be done with the information and when decisions will be made.

NOTES

[1]Meryl R. Louis, "Surprise and Sense-Making: What Newcomers Experience on Entering Unfamiliar Organizational Settings," *Administrative Science Quarterly, 23* (1980), 225–251.

[2]H. Lloyd Goodall, Jr., and Gerald M. Phillips, *Making It in Any Organization* (Englewood Cliffs, NJ: Prentice-Hall, 1985); H. Lloyd Goodall, Jr., and Donna Bogar Goodall, "The Employment Interview: A Selective Review of the Literature with Implications for Communication Research," *Communication Quarterly, 30* (1982), 116–123.

[3]Edward W. Miles and Dale G. Leathers, "The Impact of Aesthetic and Professionally Related Objects on Credibility in the Office Setting," *Southern Speech Communication Journal, 49* (1984), 361–379.

[4]Barry Z. Posner, "Comparing Recruiter, Student, and Faculty Perceptions of Important Applicant and Job Characteristics," *Personnel Psychology, 34* (1981), 329–339.

[5]Janice M. Beyer and Harrison M. Trice, "How an Organization's Rites Reveal Its Culture," *Organizational Dynamics, 15* (1987), 4–25.

EXPERIENCES

1. Compare the effect of a nonscheduled interview with that of a scheduled interview. Conduct a ten-minute, nonscheduled interview with a friend using a tape recorder. Then plan and conduct a ten-minute, moderately scheduled interview with another friend using a tape recorder. Now compare the results. Are there any differences in the way the interviews progressed? Which interview yielded the best information? Why? What can you conclude about the effect of planning and scheduling an interview?

2. Prepare an interview on a topic that interests you, to be conducted with a person who is reasonably well informed on the topic. Construct interview schedules that follow two different methods of organizing. What circumstances might dictate using each of these patterns?

3. Gain practice in constructing a purpose statement, an opening, and a closing by using several of the situations below:

a. You are interviewing the president of your student government about his or her views of the student newspaper.
b. You are taking a survey of attitudes about substance abuse in your community.
c. Your friend has just broken a romantic relationship that she or he has had for the past year. Help is needed in coping with the situation.
d. You are the representative of a company that is hiring people for a position in your area of expertise.
e. You are a supervisor who is to conduct a semiannual performance appraisal interview.
f. Your computer has broken six times in the last two months. You decide to persuade your boss to buy you a new one.

RECOMMENDED READINGS

Benjamin, Alfred, *The Helping Interview* (Boston: Houghton-Mifflin, 1981).

Einhorn, Lois J., and Patricia Hayes Bradley, *Effective Employment Interviewing: Unlocking Human Potential* (Glenview, IL: Scott, Foresman, 1981).

Killenberg, George M., and Rob Anderson, *Before the Story: Interviewing and Communication Skills for the Journalist* (New York: St. Martin's Press, 1989).

Kreps, Gary L., and B. C. Thornton, *Health Communication: Theory and Practice* (New York: Longmans, 1983).

Manning, Gerald L., and Barry L. Reece, *Selling Today: A Personal Approach* (Boston: Allyn and Bacon, Inc., 1987).

Mishler, Elliot G., *Research Interviewing: Context and Narrative* (Cambridge, MA: Harvard University Press, 1986).

CHAPTER 4

UNDERSTANDING
QUESTIONS

OBJECTIVES

After reading this chapter, you should be able to:

Identify questions as being open or closed, primary or
    secondary, neutral or leading.
Explain when and why to use a particular question.
Specify the drawbacks of particular kinds of questions.
Utilize secondary questions to achieve your goals.
Utilize leading questions when appropriate.

Ask the right questions and you may be rewarded with the information you need. Ask the right kind of questions and you may get the kind of response you want. Consider this excerpt from an employment interview where Linda, a department manager, is interviewing Mario, her most promising candidate:

Linda: It's nice to meet you, Mario. How are you today?

Mario: I'm fine, thank you.

Linda: I'd like to begin by talking with you about your education. I see you attended the University of Wisconsin. Tell me how you happened to select Wisconsin.

Mario: I decided that the kind of school you attend can significantly affect the choices you can make later. I had heard that the journalism school at UW was difficult. That scared me a little at first, but I decided that I could handle it. I was right. It was a good decision for me because I learned a lot at Wisconsin.

Linda: And so you majored in journalism. Why did you pick journalism over some other area?

Mario: I was young and idealistic when I first made my decision. I thought that some of the journalists that write for the local news weren't very sharp—and I didn't like some of the criticism about ethics. So, I decided that since I liked to write, I would study journalism.

Linda: And now?

Mario: Since then, my reasons for the major have changed; I have matured. Now, I think there is a need for good journalists who will fulfill the responsibility of keeping the people informed.

Linda: So one of the reasons you picked journalism is because you feel a need—a social responsibility. What does it mean to you for a journalist to fulfill his or her social responsibility?

Mario: You know that is a really good question. What is social responsibility to some may be radicalism to others. It is important for you to know what I mean by social responsibility. I mean....

You can tell that this interview was going well for both Linda and Mario. Mario was unresponsive at first, but Linda considered contextual factors and knew how to encourage him so that she got the information she needed. Linda went away from the interview feeling satisfied because Mario had excellent credentials and a fine work record. He was her best hope for a replacement for a reporter she was losing. And Mario did perform well in the interview. If Linda had not understood how to use questions as well as she did, things might have gone differently. But they didn't. Linda knew how to analyze the context, and she knew about questions and the questioning process. She knew how to ask the right questions, and she discovered that, indeed, Mario was exactly the person she needed for the job.

It is possible to study the questioning process in great detail. In fact, whole books have been written about asking questions.[1] Our purpose here, though, is to provide the basic information you will need to become an effective interviewer. First, we present a system that will allow you to classify questions you are considering for use. It is essential to be able to classify questions in order to know the effect that particular kinds of questions will have. You will want to ask a particular question so that you can obtain the kind of response you desire. And you will also become familiar with a variety of questioning types so that you are able to expand your repertoire. We explore with you questions that are either open or closed, primary or secondary, and neutral or leading. We also provide guidelines that will help you determine when a particular kind of question is most useful.

OPEN QUESTIONS

An *open question* asks for information that is broad and general. A reporter might say, "Tell me about your inventions," in contrast to, "What is your latest invention?" Asking this open question generally produces a great deal of information that is focused by the interviewee's thought process. Some open questions allow considerable freedom, while others are more restrictive.

Highly Open Questions

A *highly open question* suggests a general topic area but allows almost complete freedom of response. A recruiter for South Central Bell, for example, might ask a job candidate, "What can you tell me about yourself?" If the marketing department there were asking an open question in a survey, it might be, "What has been your experience with our call-waiting service?" On the other hand, the head of engineering might ask in a performance appraisal interview, "How would you describe your performance over the past six months?" All of these are highly open questions because of the freedom of response they allow. Here are some more examples of highly open questions.

An interviewer talking to a candidate in a selection interview: What is it like to live in New York City?

A journalist conducting a street corner interview: What are your feelings about unemployment?

A scholarship selection committee member interviewing a scholarship candidate: What is the meaning of an education?

Moderately Open Questions

Sometimes the interviewer wishes to restrict the interviewee to a narrower response. A *moderately open question* is used in this situation to produce a less lengthy and more focused response. Contrast these questions with those asked by the telephone company representatives above. Instead of "What can you tell me about yourself?" the recruiter might say, "Why did you choose to go to school at the University of New Mexico?" Instead of "What has been your experience with our call-waiting service?" the marketing person might ask, "How have your callers responded to the interruption by the call-waiting signal?" Instead of "How would you describe your performance over the past six months?" the head of engineering might ask, "What have been your major accomplishments over the past six months?"

Here are some additional examples of highly open questions compared with moderately open questions.

Highly Open Question	*Moderately Open Question*
1. What is it like to live in New York City?	1. What is it like to live in Queens?
2. What are your feelings about unemployment?	2. What are your feelings about teenage unemployment?
3. What is the meaning of a university education?	3. What benefits did you get from your liberal arts education?

When Should You Use Open Questions?

Open questions are used for specific reasons in a number of different interview situations. A survey interviewer may ask such a question to supplement questions that require very restricted responses. This allows the interviewer to get some direct quotes to use to give the "flavor" of how respondents feel.

Sometimes an open question is asked to conclude a survey. A journalist might ask, "Is there anything else you want to tell me about the raised expressway?" This "clearinghouse question" allows the interviewee the freedom to bring up ideas that are important but may not have been raised by the interviewer.

A recruiter who was interviewing a candidate for a management position for Gulf Cargo Corporation said, "Now, tell me how you feel about Gulf Cargo's reputation in the community." If, instead, the recruiter were to ask an open question, he might ask, "What do you know about Gulf Cargo?" The interviewer might ask the more open question to see what the interviewee might decide to say and to see how well the person could communicate his or her viewpoint. If a Gulf Cargo manager were conducting an appraisal interview, he might say to an employee, "How do you think you have been doing these past several months?" In this case, the interviewer is asking the open question to allow freedom of choice in order to discover the interviewee's thinking.

A well-trained interviewer will use an open question when it is needed, and the interview will be stronger because of the choice. The ineffective interviewer may use open questions whenever one pops into his or her head. Here are some guidelines that will help you be most productive when making decisions about using open questions.

When to Use Open Questions

1. When you want to make the interviewee feel relaxed and the question is easy to answer and nonthreatening. (Often an interview will begin with such a question.)
2. When you want to discover what the interviewee thinks is important about the topic.
3. When you want an opportunity to evaluate the communication skills of the interviewee.
4. When you want to evaluate the information the interviewee possesses.
5. When you are interested in discovering the interviewee's values or feelings toward a topic.
6. When you wish to open a new area of questioning and intend to follow with questions prompted by the information the interviewee provides.

There are some drawbacks to open questions. It may not be possible to avoid some of these drawbacks, but being aware of them may help counter their effect. First, keep in mind that coding and tabulating responses to open questions is very difficult. Consider the possible responses to this question, asked by a group of students who were conducting a survey: "When you think of campus problems, what comes to mind?" The first respondent listed five responses: the health center, athletics, fees, scheduling classes, and graduation requirements. The variety of answers made recording, coding, and reporting the data difficult. Open questions are not often used if the purpose is to collect specific information and compare it among interviewees.

Second, remember that the interviewee has greater control when you use an open question. That person may not choose to talk about the information you want. Further, the interviewee may omit information that he or she thinks you already know. If one of these situations develops, you may have to take control. Be prepared to ask follow-up questions and even abandon the use of open questions if necessary.

Third, understand that it is difficult to record the kind of information received from an open question. Stan Friedman, an interviewer from a personnel department, was investigating employee complaints. He said, "Millie, you have been working for us for twenty years and we value your opinion. Tell me. Are there any problems in the plant of which I should be aware?" Then Millie began. Ten minutes later she stopped. Had Stan not been an experienced interviewer, he would have had difficulty sorting through Millie's long and involved response.

Responses to open questions can be rambling and lengthy when the person has poor communication skills. If you intend to ask a number of open questions, be prepared to look for key factors to record. You also might consider taping the interview if taping would not interfere with the process. If you do decide to tape the interview, you must be sure to inform the interviewee.

Finally, open questions present problems in interviews where different interviewers will be collecting information for comparison. One problem comes from the difficulty in recording the data. The different interviewers may not record enough information to make comparisons. But even if the interviewers do an adequate job of recording, they may not all select the same kind of information. Remember that interviewers are individuals and each focuses differently and considers different information important when evaluating interviews. It is best to use a standard interview schedule and agreed-upon forms of response when there are multiple interviewers.

CLOSED QUESTIONS

The *closed question* narrows the options for responding to an interviewer's question. Closed questions give the interviewer more control because they focus on the specific information wanted. For example, consider the following case of the law enforcement officer who used a series of closed questions to interview a driver he stopped in a residential area.

Officer: Good afternoon, sir. Do you know the speed limit on this street?

Driver: I believe it is 40.

Officer: The limit here is 35. Did you see the speed limit sign in the last block?

Driver: No, I didn't.

Officer: How fast do you think you were going?

Driver: Between 40 and 45.

Officer: I clocked you at 47.

Just as with open questions, there are two types of questions: moderately closed and highly closed.

Moderately Closed Questions

A *moderately closed question* asks the interviewee to supply a particular piece of information. Here are some examples of moderately closed questions so you can see what they would be like in different contexts:

A selection interviewer talking to a candidate for a job: How many years did you work for the First National Bank?

A health care professional interviewing a patient: When did you first experience the pain in your arm?

A marketing representative questioning a consumer: What other brands of toothpaste have you tried?

A journalist interviewing a voter: For which city council candidate do you intend to vote?

A sales representative talking to a prospective customer: How many computers are in operation in your department?

Highly Closed Questions

The second type of restrictive question, the *highly closed question*, supplies a short list of responses, or implies a very limited response, from which the interviewee is expected to select. This is the type of question that makes up a multiple-choice examination. The highly closed question is most appropriate for surveys, but is occasionally used in other contexts. Here are three examples from different contexts: one from a survey-taker, one from a market researcher, and one from an employment interviewer:

What is your yearly salary?

_____ Under $5,000

_____ $5000 to $10,000

_____ $10,001 to $20,000

_____ $20,001 to $30,000

_____ $30,001 to $40,000

_____ Over $40,000

Other than the brand you buy, which of these coffees would you most likely purchase?

_____ Folgers

_____ Nescafe

_____ Maxwell House

_____ Sanka

_____ Store brand

Which of these is the most important as you look at a prospective employer?

_____ Growth industry

_____ National reputation

_____ Responsibility/challenge

_____ Location of facility

Another format for a highly closed question is a *rating scale*. An interviewer for a moderate-sized paper company in Mobile, Alabama, recently asked its employees a number of questions about their job. One of these questions was a closed question using a rating scale:

On a scale of 1 to 5, with 1 being very satisfied and 5 being very dissatisfied, how satisfied are you with your job?

Satisfied   1   2   3   4   5   Dissatisfied

This type of question is often used as part of a survey, as it allows the researcher to collect data that can be quantified and compared.

A third format for a highly closed question asks the interviewee to *rank-order* a series of responses. In the paper company's survey of employees, this question, requiring a rank ordering, was asked:

Using the numbers 1 to 4, with 1 being the most important and 4 being the least, how would you rate the following with respect to your work?

_____ Challenge

_____ Job security

_____ Opportunity for advancement

_____ Opportunity to be involved

A final type of highly closed question is the *bipolar question*. Bipolar questions, by the way they are worded and the information requested, limit the respondent to one of two answers. The most frequent type of bipolar question is the yes/no type. For example, a recruiter from Commonwealth Edison might ask, "Did you say that you worked for Texas Power for two years?" A Commonwealth Edison Company nurse might ask an employee, "Do you think you can continue working if I give you some Tylenol?" The marketing department might ask customers, "Are you satisfied with your electric service?" A Commonwealth manager might ask one of his supervisors, "Do you think our plan for production in your department will be seen as fair?" All of these are bipolar questions.

This type of question assumes that the interviewee has a stand on the issue, as there is generally no provision for an "undecided" response. It also includes the assumption that there is no middle ground. For example, the question "Do you think that inflation will be higher or lower next year?" assumes this. Yet the interviewee might be thinking, "Things are going to be about the same." Thus as an interviewer you must be sure that a bipolar question really only has two options. Here are some sample bipolar questions from a reporter's interview of communication workers after a union collective bargaining vote:

Did you vote in the union election?
Do you think that the election will provide a true picture of how
   members feel?
Did you vote for or against the new contract?
Will you be willing to support the decision whatever the outcome?

When Should You Use Closed Questions?

Closed questions are an important tool for the well-trained interviewer. They have a distinct advantage when you have learned to use them effectively. They can improve the quality of information you obtain. Here are five guidelines to help you decide when to use a closed question.

When to Use Closed Questions
1. When it is important for the interviewer to have control over both the questions and answers
2. When specific information is needed and the time for interviews is short
3. When multiple interviews are being administered and ease of coding, tabulating, analyzing, and replicating is important

4. When you are not particularly interested in "why" and/or the feelings behind the interviewee's answer
5. When the interviewers you will use for multiple interviews are not particularly skilled

To know when to use closed questions, you need to understand the major difficulties associated with them. Most of the problems associated with closed questions are related to the control that this type of question exerts over the interviewee.

First, the controlled nature of the responses makes it easy for an interviewee who does not know about a topic to fake understanding. It does not necessarily take any knowledge of the topic to say "yes" or "no," or "agree" or "disagree." Because of this you must watch for puzzled looks and other cues that suggest an interviewee's uncertainty.

Second, the limited nature of the response does not allow the interviewee to reveal information about which he or she has not been asked. The interviewee may wish to volunteer valuable information but has no convenient way to do so. This disadvantage can be overcome. The police officer in the interview that we reported above, asked the driver: "Do you have anything you want to say about this situation?" This, of course, allowed the driver to volunteer his version of what was going on.

Third, there is not much opportunity to work at building rapport when closed questions constitute the major part of an interview.

The lack of opportunity for the interviewee to respond with greater freedom and flexibility can be frustrating for that person. The interviewee may feel that the interviewer is the focus of the interview and that the interviewer does not care about how the questions are answered. If the interviewee senses this, he or she may be unwilling to cooperate. A reluctant interviewee may affect the quality of the information you receive.

Finally, the shortness of the answers to closed questions does not allow the interviewer to easily assess how the interviewee is feeling. The verbal and nonverbal cues are limited. For example, a question that asks if the interviewee "approves" or "disapproves" does not allow the interviewer to know the strength of that approval or disapproval.

Here is a short segment from a performance appraisal interview that demonstrates effective use of open and closed questions. Notice how the questions asked allow the interviewer to obtain the information she wants.

Carla: Good morning, Franz. How are you today?

Franz: I'm fine. But I'm a little nervous about our interview.

Carla: Why do you say that?

Franz: John didn't do performance interviews, so this is my first one.

Carla: Then let me tell you a little about what I expect. My goal for our interview is for both of us to get a better impression of how you are doing on the job. All folks have strengths. All folks, including me, have areas where they might improve. We can be pleased about your strengths and work toward improving your performance in other areas—and I'll help you. Do you have any questions about how I see our goal?

Franz: No. I see.

Carla: Great. Now, I need to know how you see yourself on the job. What do you view yourself as doing well?

Franz: I haven't missed a day's work in six years. I haven't been tardy either. Maybe that is just good health and good luck. I'm also proud of the working relationship I have with my staff.

Carla: Yes, I'm aware of these strengths too. What goals for improvement have you set for yourself?

PRIMARY QUESTIONS

Primary question is the designation given to a question that initiates a new line of questioning within the overall interview schedule. A primary question makes sense when you take it by itself. For example, a physician said, "Tell me about the pain in your arm." This is a primary question—the meaning of the sentence is clear. When he asked, "How often does it bother you?" he did not ask a primary question. We cannot tell what "it" refers to without first knowing the primary question. A boss who was becoming acquainted with a new employee began a conversation by asking: "So you lived in Indianapolis for four years?" This is a primary question, as its meaning is clear and it began a line of questioning. But the question "What did you think of the north side?" is not a primary question. We do not know what "north side" refers to without knowing the primary question.

SECONDARY QUESTIONS

A companion classification to the primary question is the secondary question. Secondary questions derive their significance from the function they perform in the overall sequence of questions. *Secondary questions* are the follow-ups to the primary questions that give depth to the interview. They are also referred to as *probing questions,* as they "dig deeper," they illuminate, and they add to the information that was received when the primary question was asked. Effective probing requires the listening skills we discussed in Chapter 2.

When secondary questions are used effectively, they perform specific functions for the interviewer. Stewart and Cash[2] suggest that secondary questions are important when the answer to the primary question is:

- Incomplete
- Superficial
- Vague
- Suggestive
- Irrelevant
- Inaccurate
- Not answered

These situations call for follow-up in the form of one or more of five kinds of secondary questions: the elaboration probe, the clarification probe, the reflective probe, the clearinghouse probe, and the internal summary. We will look at each of these and show how they may be used to ensure an effective interview.

Elaboration Probe

Sometimes the interviewee gives an incomplete answer to your question. The *elaboration probe* is used to encourage the person to provide additional information that will amplify or extend this incomplete answer. You can see how a probe might be used when amplification is needed by examining the following examples.

In responding to the statement "I had trouble with my boss," a selection interviewer said, "Tell me more about that."

After discovering that a store owner was upset about plans for an elevated expressway, a journalist asked, "How do you feel about that?"

Upon learning during a performance appraisal interview that a coworker was distracting an employee, a supervisor asked, "What else is there to this?"

After listening to his patient complain of having headaches a physician responded by saying, "Please say more about your headaches."

If what you need is an extension of what has been said, you can use a probe like one of these:

What happened next?
And then?
Go on.
Is there more to say about this?
Please continue.
Yes?

Clarification Probe

Frequently what is called for in an interview is a clarification probe. A *clarification probe* is a follow-up question that is asked to gain further information because the interviewee gave a vague answer. The following exchange between an interviewer and a job candidate for a minister of music position illustrates how this kind of probe gains clarification.

Interviewer: Why do you want to leave your current position?

Candidate: Well, it has to do with pace. The pace is too much for me.

Interviewer: I'm not sure I understand what you mean by pace. Would you say more?

Sometimes, on the other hand, the answer is clear but you want to know the feeling or attitude associated with the answer. Another job candidate for the position of minister of music answered the question differently.

Interviewer: Why do you want to leave your current position?

Candidate: It has to do with my relationship with the senior pastor. I feel held back in what I'm trying to do.

Interviewee: Why do you say "held back"?

If the answer you receive is vague, a probe like one these interviewers used might be helpful:

In a performance appraisal interview, the interviewer responded, "You say you think your work is average. What do you mean by 'average work?' "

When an interviewee, who had obviously known of an issue for a long time, suggested he hadn't had time to consider the issue, a journalist asked, "What do you mean by 'We haven't had proper time to consider the issues'?"

A marketing researcher who was collecting data about banking said, "I'm not sure I understand. Can you say more?"

An employee's boss replied to the employee's proposal with, "I don't see how we can afford this." The employee asked, "Can you say more about what you mean by 'I don't see how we can afford this'?"

When you would like to know the feeling or attitude behind a statement, you might use a question like one of these:

A journalist asked a local merchant, "How do you feel about locating a four-lane connector along the bay?"

An interviewer looking for a new secretary asked a job candidate, "What do you mean by 'I get upset when my boss pressures me'?"

In regard to a recent argument with a coworker, a supervisor asked her employee, "Why did you react that way?"

A health care professional asked a patient, "Why do you think this happened to you?"

Reflective Probe

The *reflective probe,* sometimes called a "mirror question," feeds back what the interviewee said. It is an effective technique for gaining further clarification, but it is also used to check the accuracy of an interviewee's statement.

A salesperson used the reflective probe with a customer who was purchasing prizes for use in a safety campaign:

> Okay, George, let's review the plan. You want 300 key rings with the company logo for employees who have not had an accident during the last quarter. Then you want 100 wooden plaques with the logo and the inscription "Six Month Safety Club." Finally, you want three-dozen lightweight jackets in forest green with the logo on the front right for those who have had an accident-free year. Right?

A physician reports that she typically begins her interview of patients with the question "How are you feeling today?" You can see how her use of a reflective probe operates as a follow-up in this situation. Notice that the reflective probe leads the interviewee to elaborate on his or her original response.

Physician: How are you feeling today?

Patient: I'm not feeling very well.

Physician: You are not feeling very well?

Patient: No. I....

The reflective probe is also used to check the interviewer's understanding of the interviewee's response to a primary question. This segment from an hourly worker's performance appraisal interview illustrates this use.

Worker: I think I've been on time to work lately.

Supervisor: So you haven't been late in the past three months?

Worker: That's right.

Here are several examples of reflective probes from interviews in a variety of contexts.

> After a supervisor had worked with an employee to set performance goals, he asked, "You think that the goals we have set are doable?"

A journalist, who was probing an interviewee's response to a proposed
tax increase, asked, "You think the new city tax is too high?"

A physician, wanting to confirm his patient's statement about
medication, asked, "You believe that the medicine is working for
you?"

A department head asked a candidate for a job, "Am I correct in
assuming that you think the salary offer is OK?"

It is important to exercise some caution in using the reflective probe.
The nonverbal communication that you use can signal disbelief when you
are merely unsure. A probe of this type that is encoded with vocal and facial
cues that communicate disbelief can obviously damage the climate of the
interview and affect its outcome.

Clearinghouse Probe

The word *clearinghouse* is used metaphorically to suggest clearing the interview (the house) of what remains. The interviewer asks a question that
will allow the interviewee to tell anything that might remain unsaid about
the topic of the interview.

One journalist we know typically closes her interviews with a statement
like this one and then a clearinghouse question: "I appreciate all the information you have given me about the services you provide for the deaf. Is
there anything else you would like me to know about deafness that would be
of interest to the community?"

The clearinghouse probe can also be used during the interview. When it
is used in this way, it is asked to conclude a line of questioning. Here are
some clearinghouse probes that were asked during interviews.

A health care professional asked, "Is there more you would like to
tell me about the therapy for your back problem?"

A survey-taker, investigating recruitment practices, asked, "Have I
missed any important aspects of your new recruitment plan?"

A recruiter asked a prospective employee, "What else should I know
about your education that will help me evaluate your
qualifications?"

Internal Summary

An *internal summary* seeks to check the interviewer's perception of what
the interviewee has said. *It concludes a series of answers.* It can also be
used as a reflective probe. When it is being used as a reflective probe, the
interviewee feeds back a summary of what was said with the anticipation
that there is more to be said. In this case, a "question mark" in the interviewer's voice and a pause are expected to prompt the interviewee to say
more.

A supervisor, conducting a performance appraisal, provided this example of an internal summary:

Okay, Sam, let me review to see if I've got this straight. In looking over the past six months you see your work with the problems with the roller and drying operations as places where you have been able to make a special contribution?

This kind of secondary question is valuable in three respects. First, like the reflective probe, it allows the interviewer to check his or her understanding of the content of the responses. For example, Gene, a supervisor, used it to check his understanding of how an employee saw her accomplishments during her performance review. Gene said, "Okay, June, let me see if I can summarize what you've been saying." Then he listed what he remembered. June, then, was able to confirm her boss's understanding.

Second, a summary can serve as a stimulus for further information. June was prompted by hearing the summary to recall that she had failed to mention an important initiative. Without the summary to jog her memory, it would have gone unsaid.

Finally, a summary demonstrates to the interviewee that the interviewer has been carefully attending to the information. June knew that Gene had been listening carefully because he was able to tell her what she had said to him. Listening is difficult for most of us, and so an internal summary often suggests that the interviewer cares about the interviewee and what is being said.

NEUTRAL QUESTIONS

A *neutral question* is one that the interviewee has the freedom to answer without influence in any special direction from the interviewer. The interviewer, of course, does shape the question to get at particular information. The intent is to avoid leading the interviewee toward any specific answer or attitude. In a highly closed question, such as the bipolar yes or no, the question is considered neutral if the respondent can freely answer either yes or no. It means that the interviewer frames the question in such a way as to allow freedom of choice. It means a question that is free from interviewer bias in the sense of a right or wrong answer. Here are some biased questions taken from interviews in a variety of contexts with corresponding examples of neutral questions that we have created.

Biased Question	*Neutral Question*
1. You will stay with the firm for at least two years, won't you?	1. How long would you expect to be with the firm?
2. Would you join the union if we hired you?	2. What do you think about unions?
3. Don't you think it was immature to handle the difficulty with your boss in that way?	3. So you had this difference with your boss. How would you evaluate the way you handled the situation?

LEADING QUESTIONS

The leading question is the final kind of question used in interviews. The *leading question* is one in which the interviewer—either directly or indirectly—signals the desired answer. This expectation about a desired answer can introduce bias. For example, the interviewee may try to give the answer he or she thinks the interviewer wants in order to please the interviewer. This answer even may be contrary to what the interviewee is thinking. If so, it provides a false impression of the interviewee's view.

Leading questions vary in the degree to which they push the interviewee toward a particular answer. *Mildly leading questions* may merely make it easier for the interviewee to answer in a given direction. For example, "Would you join the union if we hired you?" is only mildly leading. A *highly leading question,* on the other hand, may compel the interviewee to give a desired answer. The question "Don't you think it was immature to handle the difficulty with your boss that way?" seems highly leading. It would take an assertive interviewee to manage this question under such pressure.

Understanding Differences

To help you understand the difference between leading and neutral questions and between mildly and highly leading questions we have collected these leading questions. We have supplied a neutral question for each leading question so that you can understand the differences. Pick out the highly leading versus the moderately leading questions as you examine them.

Leading Questions
1. You want to help with the project, don't you?
2. Do you oppose the building of the interstate connector project like other residents?
3. You will contribute to the United Fund campaign, won't you?
4. I think these are fine work goals we've set. What do you think?
5. How do you feel about these jerks that are striking our Mobile plant?
6. Have you stopped cheating on your husband?
7. Aren't you *still* overeating?

Neutral Questions
1. Do you want to help with the project?
2. How do you feel about the interstate connector project?
3. Do you think you will or won't contribute to the United Fund campaign?
4. What do you think about these work goals?
5. How do you feel about the strike at our Mobile plant?
6. Tell me about this "cheating on your husband" situation.
7. How are you doing with the diet I prescribed?

8. How would you classify yourself politically—as a conservative or a radical?	8. How would you classify yourself politically—as a reactionary, conservative, moderate, liberal, radical, or other?

Although all of these are leading questions, only the first four are mildly leading. The first three are phrased as bipolar questions. Yet the leading nature of the questions suggests that the interviewers are actually asking a unipolar question. If the interviewers were truly interested in unbiased questioning, they should ask a neutral question. The interviewee might ignore the leading nature of these moderately leading questions. But even these might become highly loaded if the nonverbal cues and other context factors were strongly favoring a particular answer.

In contrast, we believe the last four questions are highly leading. Sometimes these are referred to as *loaded questions* because they contain emotionally charged words, such as *jerk, cheating,* and *radical.* Often the interviewee feels trapped in a particular choice. Who wants to challenge a representative of the company to say that the union members are not jerks? Who wants to admit that he or she is *still* cheating on a spouse or that he or she is *still* overeating? And what are the chances that the person being interviewed is either a conservative or a radical? The journalist who asked this last question allowed no middle ground, and so the interviewee picked the less offensive conservative label. You can see that leading questions can strongly bias the information being collected.

When Should You Use Leading Questions?

Leading questions are useful if they are used in the appropriate circumstances. They are used correctly when they are used for a specific purpose in a specific interview context. We suggest the following as guidelines for the use of leading questions:

When to Use Leading Questions
   1. In an employment interview if you wish to see if the applicant is the type of person who goes along with your suggestions
   2. In a performance appraisal interview if you want to guide an employee in a particular line of analysis
   3. In a persuasive interview when you want to guide the interviewee through a particular line of reasoning
   4. In a journalistic or problem-solving interview as a confrontational strategy

Inexperienced interviewers frequently ask leading questions unintentionally because they are unaware they are doing so. Something as simple as an introductory phrase can innocently bias an otherwise neutral question. For example, the phrases ''as you know,'' ''according to leading authorities," and "according to several of your coworkers" all can lead an interviewee to give answers that do not reflect his or her opinion. People want to appear to be knowledgeable and to fit into their social group, and so they may agree with such a lead. Even the interviewer's tone of voice can affect the nature of a question. If a tone is used that reflects superiority, emphasizes a particular word too strongly, or in some way emotionally charges a question, a leading question may be created from an otherwise neutral one. Even if the interviewer is unaware of the tone of voice, he or she may have biased the result of the interview. This common problem, unintentionally leading interviewees, is one you will want to avoid.

NO RESPONSE

Sometimes an interviewer will find that a question gets no response. This is a particularly difficult situation for an inexperienced interviewer to face. The important thing to remember is that there are a variety of reasons for not responding. The question might be a difficult one and the interviewee has had to think longer than he or she might normally think. Or the question might not be understood. Perhaps the question might seem to the interviewee to be inappropriate or even embarrassing. Thus it is difficult to know the reason for not getting a response.

The first action to be taken on the part of the interviewer is to pause long enough for the interviewee to contemplate an answer. If no answer is forthcoming, then the interviewer might rephrase the question. The interviewer might say, "Let me try that question another way. If you...." Even if the interviewee still does not answer the question, he or she is likely to say something. Listen carefully to what is said before you decide what to do next. One way of responding now is to explain why the information is important and try again for an answer. On the other hand, you may decide to abandon the question altogether. In a selection interview, for instance, a decision to abandon the question might be made knowing it will be asked later in the interview.

SUMMARY

There are a number of important ways to describe questions that might be asked in an interview. Questions can be classified as open or closed. Open questions ask for information that is broad and general in nature. Their purpose is to allow an interviewee considerable freedom of choice about the information he or she presents. A highly open question allows greater free-dom than a moderately open question. Open questions are useful when the interviewer wants to give the interviewee more control. Closed questions narrow the options for the interviewee's response. A moderately closed question seeks a particular, but limited, piece of information. A highly closed question goes further by supplying acceptable responses from which the interviewee is asked to select. In the case of a bipolar question, the re-sponse is limited to two alternatives. Closed questions provide greater con-trol than open questions.

Questions are also classified as either primary or secondary. Primary questions initiate new topics; secondary questions follow the initial question about a topic. Secondary questions are sometimes called probes. Probes function to elaborate, clarify, or reflect. They can also provide an opportu-nity to "clear the house"—have the interviewee tell what remains unsaid. Sometimes they provide an internal summary.

The final category pair is neutral/leading. Neutral questions do not in-fluence the interviewee to answer in any particular direction; leading ques-tions—either directly or indirectly—signal a preferred answer. Mildly lead-ing questions present less pressure than highly leading questions. Leading questions are useful when used appropriately. When not used correctly, they can seriously bias the results.

Sometimes a question is met with no response. There are a variety of reasons for this situation—a difficult question, an inappropriate question, or a question that is not understood. After the interviewer is sure that a re-sponse is not forthcoming, the question might be rephrased or abandoned altogether.

NOTES

[1]Stanley L. Payne, *The Art of Asking Questions* (Princeton, NJ: Princeton Univer-sity Press, 1951).

[2]Charles J. Stewart and William B. Cash, Jr., *Interviewing: Principles and Prac-tices,* 5th ed. (Dubuque, IA: Wm. C. Brown, Publishers, 1988), p. 63.

AN IN-DEPTH INTERVIEW FOR ANALYSIS

Here is a portion of an in-depth information-gathering interview that illus-trates effective use of primary and secondary questions. The topic of the interview is proposed cuts in an education budget.

1. Journalist: What do you understand to be the board's latest pro-posal to balance the budget?

2. Teacher: I understand that they propose to lay off all first-year teachers and, then, to increase class size to make up for the loss of faculty.

3. Journalist: Is there anything else that you have heard about the plan?

4. Teacher: I understand that each school will have a 10 percent cut in its supply money.

5. Journalist: What do you think will be the impact of increased class size?

6. Teacher: I had to teach a class with forty students in it when I worked for another school system. It is difficult to keep track of all that is going on in your room. Then, there are more discipline problems. Things get out of hand more easily. You know, then you are not as patient as you might be.

7. Journalist: Tell me more about the problems created by increased size.

8. Teacher: The quality of instruction I can provide for the individual student suffers. Some students can learn quite well if I give them individualized instruction. Without it they cannot. With so many students there just isn't time to individualize. These students do not learn as well, and I get frustrated. I know what it takes to help these students, but just cannot do it.

9. Journalist: So, you think that adding those extra students will lead to more discipline problems, will tax your patience, and will prevent you from individualizing instruction for those who need it. These students will learn less.

10. Teacher: Yes.

11. Journalist: Tell me more about the situation. What will a 10 percent cut in your supply budget mean?

EXPERIENCES

1. Test your understanding of questions by classifying each of the following questions as open or closed, primary or secondary, neutral or leading, bipolar or not. If you believe that the question is a probe, tell whether it is an elaboration probe, clarification probe, reflective probe, clearinghouse probe, or internal summary.

   From a survey interview:
   Did you participate in the vote for the proposed increase in the tax rate for the city schools?
   Do you think we should support the schools in such a generous style?

From a journalistic interview:
> Tell me about your favorite painting.
> How can you *say* that?

From a selection interview:
> By *boss,* do you mean your immediate supervisor?
> What are the most important skills for a manager to have?

From a performance appraisal interview:
> Is there anything else you want to tell me about your view of how you are doing before we go on?
> So you think that you will check with Phil, then sit down and work on a plan, and we can meet again next week?

From a persuasive interview:
> It's important to provide good reading material from the very beginning. Don't you think so?
> How many do you want?

From a problem-solving interview:
> Movement will be painful for a couple of weeks.
> Um-hum?

2. Test your understanding of kinds of questions by completing the experiences that follow and then comparing your answers with those provided by your instructor. First, tell what kind of primary question is being used. Is it moderately or highly open or moderately or highly closed? Next, provide a suitable secondary question for each of the interview situations. Remember that secondary questions function as a probe—they do not open a new area of questioning. Be sure that you word each question carefully. Identify what type of secondary question you used. Does it ask for elaboration or clarification? Is it a reflective probe or clearinghouse probe? Is it an internal summary? Finally, classify each question as either neutral, moderately leading, or leading.

From a survey interview:
a. **Interviewer:** What do you think about the company's new incentive plan?
   Interviewee: It's OK.
   Interviewer:

b. **Interviewer:** Are there specific things about the company's new incentive plan that you like?
   Interviewee: Gee, I don't know.
   Interviewer:

From a in-depth information-gathering interview:
c. **Interviewer:** Tell me how you got started with your career as an artist?
   Interviewee: A high school art teacher noticed some of my work and liked it.
   Interviewer:

d. **Interviewer:** What do you think about the proposal for a city-owned art museum?
   Interviewee: It's not a bad idea.
   Interviewer:

From a selection interview:

e. **Interviewer:** Why would you want to leave your current position?
Interviewee: I don't find the work challenging.
Interviewer:

f. **Interviewer:** We all have strengths and weaknesses related to our work. What would you say are some of your weaknesses?
Interviewee: I'm impatient sometimes.
Interviewer:

From a performance appraisal interview:

g. **Interviewer:** I am interested in how you think you are doing. Let's begin by your telling me how you see yourself on the job.
Interviewee: It's not bad.
Interviewer:

h. **Interviewer:** We have set three goals for you to work on during the next several weeks. Do you think you will be able to accomplish all three?
Interviewee: Yes.
Interviewer:

From a persuasive interview:

i. **Interviewer:** How do you feel about the need for a new secretarial position?
Interviewee: I'm not sure we need it.
Interviewer:

j. **Interviewer:** So you agree that our current secretarial staff is overworked?
Interviewee: Yes.
Interviewer:

From a health care interview:

k. **Interviewer:** Have you had a history of diabetes in your family?
Interviewee: My mother had it.
Interviewer:

l. **Interviewer:** You seem to be anxious about something. Are you?
Interviewee: (silence)
Interviewer:

RECOMMENDED READINGS

DeVito, Joseph A., "Relative Ease in Comprehending Yes/No Questions," in Jane Blankenship and Hermann Stetzner (eds.), *Rhetoric and Communication* (Urbana, IL: University of Illinois Press, 1976).

Dillman, Don A., "Writing Questions," *Mail and Telephone Surveys: The Total Design Method* (New York: John Wiley, 1978), pp. 79–118.

Dohrenwend, Barbara S., "Some Effects of Open and Closed Questions on Respondent's Answers," *Human Organization, 24* (1965), 174–184

Dohrenwend Barbara S., and Stephen A. Richardson, "A Use of Leading Questions in Research Interviewing," *Human Organization, 23* (1964), 76–77.

Richardson, Stephen A., "The Use of Leading Questions in Nonscheduled Interviews," *Human Organization, 19* (1960), 86–89.

CHAPTER 5

USING
QUESTIONS

OBJECTIVES

After reading this chapter, you should be able to:

Construct questions that are tailored to your purpose.
Avoid wording questions in a way that will hinder the
  collection of accurate information.
Select and utilize an appropriate question sequence.

Ask the right question, a question that is the correct type for the situation and is carefully worded, and you often will be rewarded with the information you need. Ask the wrong question and you often will not be. In fact, you can enhance the whole climate of the interview if you ask carefully chosen and appropriately worded questions.

Consider how you would feel if you were this interviewer. A journalism intern decided that he would like to do a feature story for a local newspaper. He had been prompted to investigate teenage pregnancy by a short television news clip he had viewed. He secured an interview with a social worker who was quite knowledgeable about the topic. His first question was, "What effects do you think teenage pregnancies have on teenagers and their families, and what do you think can be done about them?" The social worker didn't know what to say. Instead of answering the question, she took over the interview and told the journalism intern what she wanted him to know about teenage pregnancy. The result, of course, was not the kind of story the intern had hoped to write.

The result might have been different if the student had asked a more carefully worded question. Perhaps he could have asked: "How serious a problem do you believe teenage pregnancy is in Mobile?" This might then be followed by: "What effect do you see this situation having on teenagers?" Then, he might ask: "What difficulties do you see for families in coping with teenage pregnancy?" And, finally, he might ask: "What do you think might be done to solve the problem?" You can undoubtedly envision the difference in outcome that would have been achieved by knowing how to select and word an appropriate sequence of questions.

We begin this chapter by addressing the issue of effectively phrasing questions. Then, we turn to a discussion of sequencing questions.

DEVELOPING QUESTIONS

Phrasing questions involves several important considerations. First, the interviewer must begin the process by establishing the purpose of the interview. Then, with a clear purpose in mind, the interviewer can begin wording questions aimed at achieving this goal. Wording questions requires decisions about language, knowledge level of the interviewees, complexity level, and propriety.

Establishing the Purpose

The first consideration in writing effective questions is making a clear statement of your overall purpose and goals for the interview. Failing to do so may lead to questions that are neither clear nor focused toward achieving your goal. A supervisor we know conducts performance appraisal interviews without clear goals. The outcome is often a mixture of counseling and discipline. Although both counseling and discipline might be appropriate goals for the same interview, this supervisor's inability to focus on a particular goal causes confusion and hostility. Being specific about his purpose would undoubtedly lead him to be more effective.

Some goals that this supervisor could have for a performance appraisal interview are:

1. To help the employee assess strengths and weaknesses in job performance
2. To recognize employee accomplishments
3. To agree upon areas for improvement
4. To develop practical plans for improvement
5. To discover aspirations of the employee
6. To determine training needs, if any

You can see from this list that there might be multiple goals for an interview. The goals we present here are compatible with one another and relate to an orderly progression through such an interview. An interviewer could take each goal, arranged in a sequence, and develop specific questions that would allow attainment of each one.

A similar set of goals might be developed for each of the contexts in which you might want to interview. We have presented this sequence of goals here to illustrate how an interviewer might develop such an interview. We will develop similar lists for each context as we approach the interview situations in the chapters to come.

Wording the Questions

Wording questions you expect to ask the interviewee in ways that will allow you to be successful in accomplishing your purpose is a second step in effective interview planning. This process involves four choices: language choices, knowledge-level choices, complexity-level choices, and propriety choices.

Language choices.   The wording you use in your questions must be understandable to the interviewee. Of course, an interviewer would not intentionally ask a question that she or he believes the interviewee would not understand. However, word choice is based on a person's experience, and sometimes the interviewee has a different experience from the interviewer's. The more you know about the interviewee, the more accurate you should be at selecting language that the person will understand. But you cannot always know your interviewee well enough to be able to predict the person's ability to understand language. In such a case, you will want to avoid jargon that the interviewee might not understand.

You can improve your language choice if you are able to plan your interview a day or two in advance. Word your schedule of potential questions and set them aside. Go back to the questions the next day and read them carefully. Locate and change technical words that might be too difficult for the interviewee. These will be fairly easy to locate.

Now, look for common words that may be ambiguous. Common words that suggest some kind of quantification are particularly problematic. Notice the ambiguity of the italicized words from these interview questions:

> A manager asked an employee during his performance review, "Would you describe your performance as *average?*"
> This same manager asked of a plan for improving performance, "Is this a *fair* plan for improving in that area?"
> A physician asked a patient, "Would you say you have made *a lot of* improvement?"
> A counselor asked, "Would you say you are a *heavy* drinker?"
> A marketing manager included this leading question in a telephone survey, "Would you describe the services offered by First National Bank as *excellent?*"

Average performance, fair plan, a lot of improvement, heavy drinker, and excellent services are phrases that all contain ambiguous words. Frame of reference is important in each case for determining what the quantification word means. Check to see if the inability to define the word with precision will make a difference in your being able to gather information. If so, change the wording to make it more precise.

Phrasing and labeling can cause problems. Again, it is impossible to give specific rules to guard against faulty phrasing. Yet it is easy to find examples where wording makes a difference. Two researchers who carried out surveys on performance appraisal got different results when they asked what they thought were the same question. They were interested in discovering how many of the organizations they sampled conducted performance appraisal interviews with their employees. One asked the question, "Do you conduct performance appraisal interviews with hourly employees?" The other researcher asked, "Do you conduct formal appraisal interviews with hourly employees?" The likely reason for the contradictory results is the word *formal* in the second question. Some managers consider any discussion of performance to be a performance appraisal interview, while others consider a performance appraisal interview to be the formal annual review. This word made a difference in interpretation.

Finally, pretest your questions if that is possible. The ideal pretest is to ask the questions to someone of similar background to the person you will interview. This is not always possible. You may, however, be able to ask some other person to help you look for misleading language. As you gain experience in the interviewing process, you will be better able to rely on your judgment to refine your questions.

Knowledge-level choices.   Careful analysis of the interviewee is essential to understanding how much knowledge the person has of your topic. Under-estimation of a person's knowledge can be insulting to the interviewee. For example, a tax attorney confided after the completion of an interview with a reporter: "I don't know why he wasted my time. He should have asked me something important. He could have found out what he wanted to know by calling any IRS agent." On the other hand, overestimation can produce frustration for the interviewee as he or she struggles to answer your questions. Misjudging the level of knowledge may even introduce bias into the information you collect, since most interviewees will try to answer your questions.

One way to avoid this problem is through careful selection of interviewees. Consider what your purpose dictates. Do you need an expert? Do you need a person who is well informed? Are you interested in what an average citizen can tell you? Do you want the opinion of a novice? Once you have made a decision about the type of person you want, you can begin the effort to locate such a person. If someone you know has knowledge of the interviewee, ask that person to help you verify the interviewee's level of knowledge.

You can rely on some questions—early in the interview—that will allow you to assess the person's knowledge when you are unable to assess this through some other means. Here it is important to guard against asking questions that will allow an interviewee to fake an answer. Yes and no questions will obviously not work. People like to appear knowledgeable and will sometimes claim knowledge if you allow them to do so. Asking open questions will reveal whether the person actually possesses the knowledge you desire. You might use a sequence, like the following one, which was used in a survey related to building an interstate connector.

Interviewer: Are you familiar with the plan to build an interstate connector between I-10 and I-65?

Interviewee: Yes.

Interviewer: Briefly, tell me what you understand the plan to be.

Sequences like this allow you to know if the interviewee is faking knowledge.

Complexity-level choices.   Complex questions do not usually allow you to gather the kind of information you need. We do not refer to difficult questions here, but to questions that are constructed in such a way that it is difficult for the interviewee to understand what information is being requested.

There are four primary sources of this complexity problem. First, the complex question is complicated because of its length. Here is an example of such a question.

> The mayor has recently come out in favor of the I-10 connector. She believes that, on balance, such a project will benefit the city by bringing more people into the downtown area. Businesses in the area have differing views on the benefits of such a plan. Hotels along the proposed path of the connector think it will detract from their business because it will block the view of the bay. Retail stores, on the other hand, favor the plan because they believe it will add to the ease of customers from the suburbs getting to their location. There are more retail businesses than hotels along the proposed route. Council members who represent the area are supporting the voters on their views. What do you believe is the most reasonable position on this project?

Could you sort through all of this and answer the question even if you were a reasonably well-informed citizen?

Sometimes it is the instructions for answering a question that create the complexity. Consider these instructions about rating a new educational program.

> We would like to know how you view our Baldwin County program. As you rate each of these aspects of the program, give them a number between 0 and 10. If you think that the item is not at all important, give it a 0. If you believe that the item is very important, give it a 10. If you do not know whether it is important or not, give it a 5. Decrease your rating from 10 depending on how much less important you see it. Increase your rating from 0 depending on how much more important you see it.

Imagine how confused some interviewees might be. Instead, simple instructions like the following would have been appropriate.

> We would like to know how important you think these aspects of our Baldwin County program are. Give each a rating, with 5 being very important and 1 being not important. Give the item a 0 if you do not have enough information to rate it.

A third complicating factor is the use of too many clauses and/or qualifiers in the question. Consider the following question from a first draft of an in-house survey. It was to be conducted by a medium-sized wholesaler in San Diego.

> Although the plan for reorganization of the company is not yet complete, given what we have on the drawing board, and knowing that it

doesn't include our divisions in Phoenix or Albuquerque, but that it does include our locations in Dallas and Houston, give us your overall impression of the benefits and liabilities of such a reorganization.

Before being administered, the question was revised to say:

Tell us what you see as the strengths and weaknesses of the tentative plan to reorganize our southwest territory.

The fourth source of undesirable complexity is the tendency to ask more than one question as if they were a single question. This type of question we call a *double-barreled question*. Sometimes the questions are even phrased as if they were a single question. Suppose a physician asked:

How do you feel today? Are you having more pain in your leg? And how is the heart today?

The patient is likely to answer whatever of these is the most important to him or her and ignore the others.

Valuable information may be lost if more than one question is asked at the same time. Of course, the interviewer can come back to the unanswered questions. The best plan, however, is to ask one question at a time and avoid confusion.

Propriety choices.   Some kinds of information you will want to collect may be of a sensitive or personal nature. For example, questions about personal income, political and religious beliefs, and sexual matters traditionally have been considered private.

When an interviewee is asked questions that he or she considers to be personal, the interviewee may be reluctant to respond. This circumstance requires special attention to the phrasing of questions if the interviewer is to be successful. There are three techniques that are of help here—asking indirect, rather than direct, questions; substituting a less personal word or phrase for one that seems too personal; and arranging the setting.

An *indirect question* is one that does not ask specifically for the information you would like the interviewee to provide. Here are several examples of direct questions asked in interviews with a corresponding indirect question that we have constructed.

Direct Question	*Indirect Question*
From a selection interview:	
How many workdays have you missed during the past three months?	How do you define good work attendance?

From a performance appraisal interview:

What do you see as your weaknesses on the job?	What would you like to improve in your work skills?

From an in-depth information-gathering interview:

How do you evaluate the mayor's performance?	How do you think most people see the mayor's performance?

A second technique is to soften the wording by selecting a substitute, a euphemism. Instead of saying "sexual intercourse," say "lovemaking." Instead of saying "weakness," say "area of needed improvement." Instead of saying "atheist," say "disbeliever in God." You will have to be sensitive to wording that may be too personal to others if you are to use different and less personal wording. But you may not always know what will be sensitive and personal to the interviewee. Experience will help you with this problem. A pretest of the planned questions with someone who is similar to the interviewee may also help.

A final consideration in managing this problem is the setting. First, try to interview in a place where there is some privacy. An interviewee may be less reluctant to reveal personal information if he is talking just to an interviewer than if he thinks he is talking to an interviewer *and* others. Second, pay attention to your interpersonal distance. Being physically too close or too far away can affect the feeling of the interviewee about the interviewer. Aim at 3 to 3½ feet as an appropriate interpersonal distance. Finally, take time to build some rapport with the interviewee. Pay careful attention to your opening remarks. Ask a series of other questions before you launch into those that are more personal. And make sure the interviewee understands the important purpose of your interview.

SEQUENCING QUESTIONS

Matching the purpose of an interview to appropriate sequencing of questions is another key to using questions effectively. A *sequence* is a series of interconnected questions that are organized around some overall plan. Four frequently used schemes for linking questions are the tunnel sequence, the funnel sequence, the inverted funnel sequence, and the quintamensional design sequence. We describe each of these, provide example questions, and tell when the sequence is most useful.

Tunnel Sequence

The *tunnel sequence,* a term coined by Charles Stewart, is one that uses a series of questions with a similar degree of closedness or openness. There is no narrowing or enlarging of the scope of the questioning. There also is no probing, as the interviewer is interested in the answer to a series of primary questions. Generally the sequence does not lend itself to the kind of in-depth gathering of information that other sequences provide.

Sometimes the tunnel sequence is employed to gather data through a series of bipolar questions. For example, the evaluator of a training session might use this sequence of questions:

Please help me evaluate the instruction in this session by responding to the following questions:

1. Did the instructor listen carefully?
2. Was the instructor open-minded?
3. Did the instructor encourage thinking?
4. Did the instructor know his subject?
5. Did the instructor use methods that were suited well to the class?
6. Did the instructor criticize constructively?
7. Would you recommend this instructor to teach additional courses for our organization?

The sequence is also useful for a series of open questions. The traditional journalistic questions of who, what, when, where, why, and how can be used with this sequence. In this case, all of these questions are related, but they do not necessarily need to be asked in a particular sequence.

When to Use the Tunnel Sequence
1. When you want to quantify reactions from an interviewee that can easily be quantified
2. When in-depth opinion or attitudinal information is not desired
3. When the information desired is rather simple
4. When adaptation to individual interviewees is not important

Funnel Sequence

This sequence is labeled as such because the interviewer begins with a broad, open question—the top of the funnel. The questions that follow narrow the focus of the topic, becoming more specific and closed. Closed questions may or may not be used, but if they are, they are used toward the bottom of the funnel. Here is an example of a funnel sequence that was used to collect impressions of the same training session noted above:

1. What do you think about your training experience today?
2. What did you think were the strengths of this training?
3. What did you think were the weaknesses of this training?
4. Of these strengths you mentioned, which was the most important?
5. Of the weaknesses you suggested, which was the most serious?
6. Would you recommend this training for other employees in our organization?

Knowing when to use a funnel sequence is important to your success as an interviewer. If, for example, you use it when an interviewee is unsure of her information, the initial, open question may be difficult for her to answer. Here are some guidelines that will help you know when to use the funnel sequence.

When to Use the Funnel Sequence
1. When the interviewee is familiar with the topic
2. When the interviewee is willing to talk
3. When the interviewee needs an opportunity to express feelings
4. When later questions, because of their specificity, might bias or restrict the flow of information

Inverted Funnel Sequence

An *inverted funnel sequence* is the direct opposite of the funnel sequence. It begins with a relatively closed question and moves progressively to more and more open questions. If the interviewer who was collecting data to evaluate the training program had decided to use an inverted funnel sequence, the questions from the previous interview would look like these:

1. Would you recommend this training for other employees in our organization?
2. What was the most important strength of this training session?
3. What was the most serious weakness of this training session?
4. What were other strengths of this training session?
5. What were other weaknesses of this training session?
6. What do you think about your overall training experience today?

Like the funnel sequence, the inverted funnel sequence is especially effective under some circumstances. Suppose, for example, that the interviewee has a good deal of information but hasn't organized it very well. Since most highly open questions require that a person organize information in order to answer, the interviewee may find it too difficult to answer a highly open question first and may refuse to respond. A natural reaction in such a situation seems to be: "I don't really know about that." On the other hand, the interviewee would be able to answer specific questions because he or she possesses adequate knowledge about the topic. You can see here how using the inverted funnel sequence would work. These are some guidelines for knowing when an inverted funnel sequence is appropriate.

When to Use an Inverted Funnel Sequence
1. When the interviewee may not have thought through an issue
2. When the interviewee has adequate information about the topic
3. When initial closed questions may motivate the interviewee to talk
4. When you want the interviewee to give you a final judgment about your topic that is based upon his or her answers

Quintamensional Design Sequence

The quintamensional design sequence was developed by George Gallup[1] to survey opinions and attitudes. This five-step approach begins with an *awareness step* that acts as a filter to determine how well the interviewee is informed. This step is followed by a question or questions that attempt to collect *uninfluenced attitudes*. Here the goal is to get the interviewee to talk about the issue in his or her own words. The third step is a bipolar, usually a yes or no, question that attempts to discover a *specific attitude*. The fourth step consists of a question or questions that follow up the bipolar question. This provides the interviewee an opportunity to reveal his or her *reasoning*, giving the interviewer insight into the person's motivations. The approach ends with a question that measures the *intensity of the specific attitude* revealed. Sometimes questions are not asked in all five areas. Asking for a specific attitude may, for example, prompt the interviewee to tell you why he or she feels that way. In this case, the interviewer would move directly to the intensity area.

Here is an example of questions used by a social worker employing the quintamensional design format.

AWARENESS
Tell me what you know about the city of Indianapolis's program to
   employ disadvantaged youth.

UNINFLUENCED ATTITUDE
What, if any, should the city of Indianapolis's role be in helping
   disadvantaged youth find employment?

SPECIFIC ATTITUDE
Do you approve or disapprove of the city of Indianapolis's program to
   employ disadvantaged youth?

REASONING
Why do you feel this way?

INTENSITY OF ATTITUDE
How strongly do you feel about this?

Here are guidelines for using the quintamensional design sequence.

When to Use the Quintamensional Design Sequence
   1. When you are interested in surveying attitudes or opinions
   2. When you wish to begin an interview by discovering first the
      person's knowledge and then his or her general and specific
      attitudes

SUMMARY

Phrasing questions effectively is an important skill. This can be accomplished, in part, by constructing a clear statement of purpose and keeping it in mind as you formulate your questions. Beyond this, attention must be given to language choice. The interviewer should be alert for technical language, ambiguous wording, faulty phrasing, and an interviewee's knowledge level and ability to understand the question. An interviewer should carefully analyze these factors and pretest the questions if possible. A final difficulty in phrasing is sensitive words. Questions that are too personal must be avoided.

Sequencing questions appropriately is another important factor in effective interviewing. A tunnel sequence uses a series of questions with a similar degree of closedness or openness. This ordering of questions is useful when the interviewer seeks reactions that can be easily quantified. It is not used to collect in-depth data and attitudes. A funnel sequence begins with a broad, open question and moves to progressively narrow, closed questions. This sequence is especially useful if the interviewee is familiar with the topic and is willing to talk. An inverted funnel sequence is the direct opposite of the funnel. It is particularly useful when the interviewee has not organized his or her thoughts, but has adequate information about the topic. The final sequence, the quintamensional design sequence, is used to survey opinions and attitudes. It is a five-step approach that solicits awareness, uninfluenced attitudes, specific attitudes, reasoning, and attitude intensity.

NOTE

[1]George Gallup, *A Guide to Public Opinion Polls* (Princeton, NJ: Princeton University Press, 1948), pp. 40–49.

A SELECTED INTERVIEW FOR ANALYSIS
RENÉE PAUL AND MS. HAMMOND

This simulated interview was conducted by two communication majors at the University of South Alabama. Ms. Hammond has applied for an internship in physical therapy. Renée Paul is head of the department of physical therapy.

  1. **Interviewer:** Come in.

  2. **Interviewee:** Hi, I'm Ms. Hammond.

3. Interviewer: I'm Renée Paul, and I'll be doing your interview today.

4. Interviewee: Nice to meet you.

5. Interviewer: Thank you. Nice to meet you too. I see you are applying for an internship in physical therapy in an acute care setting. This internship involves working closely with one of our staff members. Duties include planning, assisting, and evaluating physical therapy programs for patients. Are there any questions?

6. Interviewee: Not at this time.

7. Interviewer: OK. If you wish to ask any questions during the interview, please feel free to ask and I'll answer them to the best of my ability.

8. Interviewee: Thank you.

9. Interviewer: I would like to begin the interview by asking you why you chose a career in physical therapy.

10. Interviewee: Well, at first I was just interested in sports medicine, as you saw in my resume. I'm involved in the martial arts and have attended several tournaments and things of that nature. I have been involved in a lot of the extracurricular activities, and some of them involved helping people who were injured during tournaments. I became interested in sports injury and rehabilitation of sports injuries. From there, I quit my job as manager of a clothing store. I had been there for six years and decided that I needed to do something different. I was in the highest position, but I still was not happy there. It was a family business, and I would have been next in line to own the business. I decided to go back to school and take some courses. I took sports rehabilitation and physiology. I found that I had an interest in physical therapy, so I joined the physical therapy program. I started working in rehabilitation settings—acute care, hospice care, and volunteer work. I found that I had a real interest in just the physical therapy itself. My sports medicine interest is still there, but with my physical therapist degree, I feel that I have more to offer in acute care or rehabilitation.

11. Interviewer: And when did you decide to seek an internship with this hospital?

12. Interviewee: Well, I began to investigate internship options, and I found that you have a fully loaded staff in comparison with the other hospitals I checked. You have a more even patient load for the therapists that work here, and I think that's important. I like to spend a little bit of time with my patients and not have such a demanding load that I'm not able to devote the time I need to them. I also know that you have other facilities in the area, Pro-Health and Rehabilitation, and the new Re-evaluation Center down on Springhill Avenue. I thought that with those branches you were involved with more than just acute care in PT, and that there might be opportunities for me in those areas also.

13. Interviewer: OK. How has your college experience prepared you for a career in physical therapy?

14. Interviewee: Physical therapy involves spending a lot of time with patients; it involves being able to set goals for the patients and help them reach those goals. You have to be motivated and be able to motivate the patients themselves. In college, I found that time is not always kind. You have to rearrange your schedule to reach the goals you set. I had three part-time jobs and carried a full load. In school I learned how to manage my time well; I learned to set goals and discipline myself so that I was able to finish school with a good GPA and still keep my jobs. School and the experience in the field itself showed me how to manage my time. I think that I can carry that over into my management of time skills with my patients and the work load here at the hospital.

15. Interviewer: I see. Why did you choose to receive your education here at the University of South Alabama?

16. Interviewee: Mostly because of the location. I am married, and I have a family here, and I did not want to relocate. It was a convenient location, and I felt that South Alabama had an excellent physical therapy program. I checked the credentials at South and the accreditation of the Physical Therapy School itself. I found that it was highly acclaimed and felt it would be a good place for me to earn my degree.

17. Interviewer: I noticed that you are an exceptional student. Do you think your grades are a good indication of your academic achievement?

18. Interviewee: I think they show that I worked hard; and I did work hard at school. I was out for several years when I worked retail; when I went back to school, I was a better student. I was less involved in social activities and things of that nature than I was when I first went to school several years before. So, yes, I think my grades show how hard I worked.

19. Interviewer: What are some of the accomplishments that have given you the most satisfaction and why?

20. Interviewee: I'm proud of my time in school and my decision to go back. It took me a lot of time to decide to return to school, and when I did, I was pleased with my decision. And I am very pleased with my grades in school; they are very important to me. I worked hard and I reached my goal to have a high GPA. I'm also very proud of the black belt that I earned; I worked several years to get it and it taught me a lot of self-discipline. I was the second female to receive a black belt in the seventeen years that the school has been opened. I also received that school's Student of the Year award and was very proud of that.

21. Interviewer: Lastly, I would like to ask you how you would describe yourself?

22. Interviewee: I think I am very assertive and outgoing. I think this is an advantage working with patients, as I do in physical therapy. To be able to set up a good rapport with the patients and communicate well with them is a great advantage, and I feel I am able to do that. I am very motivated, and I can carry that over to motivate my patients and help them reach the goals that they have set. It's very hard asking people to do certain things in physical therapy in order to reach their goals. Therapy can be very painful, and you have to be able to empathize with the patient. I think that I am able to do that.

23. Interviewer: Do you have any questions you want to ask before we conclude the interview? If so, please feel free to ask them at this time.

24. Interviewee: No, I don't have any questions right now. I'm fairly familiar with your internship program.

25. Interviewer: Thank you for your time. We'll be getting back to you.

EXPERIENCES

1. Test your understanding of question sequences by telling how you would sequence questions for each of the following situations. Be prepared to explain your choices.
   a. As a part of the marketing department, you are taking a survey of potential users to discover the effect of a recent campaign to increase sales of a new line of cameras.
   b. You are a journalist who is conducting an attitude and opinion survey related to renovation of the downtown shopping area.
   c. You are conducting selection interviews for a management position.
   d. You are the manager of a retail grocery store who is conducting employee performance appraisal interviews.
   e. You are a police officer who has the assignment of interviewing a person whose house has just been vandalized.

RECOMMENDED READINGS

Dillman, Don A., "Constructing Mail Questionnaires," *Mail and Telephone Surveys: The Total Design Method* (New York: Wiley-Interscience, 1978), pp. 119–159.

Dillman, Don A., "Constructing Telephone Questionnaires," *Mail and Telephone Surveys: The Total Design Method* (New York: Wiley-Interscience, 1978), pp. 200–231.

Gottlieb, Marvin, "The Interview Structure," *Interview* (New York: Longmans, 1986), pp. 16–40.

Killenberg, George M., and Rob Anderson, "The Question of Questions," *Before the Story: Interviewing and Communication Skills for Journalists* (New York: St. Martin's Press, 1989), pp. 47–88.

Payne, Stanley L., *The Art of Asking Questions* (Princeton, NJ: Princeton University Press, 1951).

PART III

Organizational Contexts

CHAPTER 6

THE SELECTION
INTERVIEW:
THE INTERVIEWER'S
PERSPECTIVE

OBJECTIVES

After reading this chapter, you should be able to:

Explain the importance of job descriptions, initial questions, EEOC guidelines, and setting in preparing for a selection interview.

Distinguish between legal and illegal questions that might be asked in a selection interview.

Prepare materials for use in a selection interview.

Develop interview strategies for beginning a selection interview, motivating an interviewee to talk, avoiding bias, and concluding the selection interview.

Discuss ethical considerations.

Develop interview methods that allow careful interpretation of data collected from a selection interview.

Phil Williams, a senior at an eastern university, was heavily into the process of interviewing. He had scheduled three interviews for the day through the university placement service. This last one was the most important one for him because it represented the most promising career opportunity. The interview was with a well-established firm that was large enough to give him the opportunity to move up quickly in the organization. After Phil interviewed, he was encouraged because he believed that he had been impressive. He also had worked hard in school and knew that his credentials were very competitive. The interview reinforced his excitement about taking a job with the firm. The interviewer, the very man he would have to work under, was impressive and personable. Phil could actually imagine working for this man who acted so competently in the interview. Interviews can be exciting for the interviewee if the interviewer understands his or her role and performs it well.

You may not have thought much about the role of the interviewer in a selection interview because most of us have had our experience in this setting as the interviewee. Yet skills in conducting a selection interview are most important to acquire. If you work long enough for your organization, you might be involved in selecting and recruiting new professionals. You must understand how to create a positive experience for the interviewee. But beyond making a good impression, you must know how to make the right choices for your organization. A personnel manager for Arvin Automotive put it this way: "When I make a bad hire, it costs the company. If I make very many bad hiring decisions, it affects my reputation. I interview people very carefully." What we say here will serve as a valuable reference to help you make positive impressions and secure the information you must have to make the right hiring decision.

Selection interviewing is a term used to describe several interview situations where the purpose is to make decisions about whether or not to include a person in some activity. The purpose might be to select candidates for scholarships or graduate school. It might be to search for a person to honor for outstanding service to your organization. By far the most common, of course, is to select a candidate for employment. What we say here applies to all of these settings, but our focus will be on the use of the selection interview for employment.

This chapter focuses on the selection interview from the perspective of the interviewer. We move through the planning process: consulting the job description, preparing materials, checking Equal Employment Opportunity Commission guidelines, reviewing applications and resumes, structuring the interview, and arranging the setting. Then we turn to the interviewing process. We provide suggestions for beginning the interview, motivating the interviewee, probing, avoiding biases, and closing the interview.

THE EMPLOYER AND THE SELECTION INTERVIEW

The interviewer needs to prepare for interviewing by following a sequence of steps. This is especially important for the person who is interviewing prospective candidates for the first time or who interviews candidates infrequently. These steps should include:

1. Consulting the job description
2. Preparing materials
3. Checking Equal Employment Opportunity Commission (EEOC) guidelines
4. Reviewing resumes and applications
5. Deciding on a structure for the interview and preparing initial questions
6. Arranging the setting

Consulting the Job Description

Most tasks related to selection interviewing are not as easy as they seem— and consulting the job description is one that is not. When you consult a job description, you may find that it is outdated and does not reflect what is required in the particular job. This is because a person's duties evolve and change as the needs of the organization change. You may need to update the job description before you begin if you are to be an effective interviewer. In *How Effective Executives Interview,* Walter Mahler provides a helpful list of steps to use in updating the specifications for executive positions.[1] Most job descriptions will differ from those Mahler discusses, but with a little effort you will be able to adapt the list that follows—which is based on his list—to any job situation.

1. Do not leave the task of updating the job description to the staff. It is your responsibility.
2. Check your list of duties with other people who are familiar with the job.
3. Check to see if the position description is up to date.
4. Consider what factors contributed to successes and failures for those who hold or have held the job.
5. Consider the impact of whatever changes might occur in the job.
6. Separate the critical qualifications from those that would be nice to have.

Now that you have consulted the job description and made any necessary changes, make a chart that lists the responsibilities and qualities needed for the job. One useful type of chart is called a *two-column job analysis*. Table 6.1 presents an analysis used in the screening process for a departmental secretary in a university setting. Once you have completed this analysis, you are ready to move on to the preparation of materials to be used in the search.

Preparing Materials to Be Used in the Search

The advertisement.   An advertisement for a position usually includes the nature of the position and basic qualifications. Sometimes a salary range is included. Your organization is likely to have a policy about the kind of in-

Table 6.1   Two-Column Job Analysis

Job Responsibilities	Qualities Needed
1. Greet people and make them feel comfortable	1. Articulateness, good communication skills, personableness, self-assurance
2. Solve problems for students and faculty	2. Attentiveness to detail, good judgment, ability to be convincing but not pushy, analytical-mindedness
3. Type and reproduce handouts and tests for classroom use	3. Ability to pass typing test, follow a list of priorities, and be punctual
4. Take dictation and produce departmental correspondence	4. Ability to pass shorthand test, transcribe accurately, and spell and punctuate
5. Keep departmental records, including financial records	5. Honesty, mathematical accuracy, elementary bookkeeping skills
6. Manage interpersonal relations among departmental personnel	6. Liking for people, integrity, ability to be supportive, social sensitivity
7. Supervise student workers	7. Ability to organize, plan; tactfulness, good judgment

formation that is considered appropriate for an announcement. Also, in most larger organizations, someone in public relations, personnel, or management will be responsible for approving your advertisement before it is placed.

The rule about where to advertise a position is simple: advertise it where qualified applicants will be prone to look for job listings. Generally, for professional positions that means listing the position with the appropriate professional societies' placement services. If there is a professional trade publication, an advertisement should be placed in it, as well as in the local newspapers. Other locations where advertisements are found include school placement centers, union offices, company bulletin boards, and company publications. If your selection is for an award, you may need to do some research to find out how to contact those who would qualify.

Organizational literature.   Most organizations have professionally prepared material that can be used for any selection purpose you might encounter. If such material is not available, you should publish a one-page flier to be used for your selection purpose. Include a brief history of the company, some information about the community, and the major products or services of the organization. You might also include some of the materials used to advertise your products or services.

Secure a copy of the organization's application form. Check the form to see that it is appropriate. Often there is more than one form—one for professionals and one for hourly employees, or even a special form for selecting award recipients. Some organizations merely rely on the candidate's resume if they are recruiting for a professional position. Sometimes if the selection is for a scholarship or other award, the person might be asked for a short essay on a stated theme. Check the application form for illegal questions. You should eliminate all categories that ask for such things as pictures, age, marital status, religion, physical characteristics, arrest record, credit references, and type of military discharge. These are all illegal bases for selection.

Reviewing EEOC Guidelines

Employment decisions based on race, color, religion, sex, marital status, or national origin are forbidden under Title VII of the Civil Rights Act of 1964. Employment discrimination based on age was outlawed in 1967. Further, the Rehabilitation Act of 1973 prohibited certain discrimination against the handicapped. In 1974, the Vietnam Era Veterans Readjustment Assistance Act was passed, which mandated preferential treatment in employment and promotions for veterans of the Vietnam era.

Federal legislation has created several governmental agencies to police and enforce these laws. The aim of this legislation is to provide an opportunity for all qualified members of the work force to compete for jobs. The governmental agency with the primary charge of policing the laws is the

Equal Employment Opportunity Commission (EEOC). The commission has the authority to bring employers who do not comply with the law to court. The litigation undertaken in enforcing the law has further clarified what are illegal practices. Beyond this, some states have laws regarding equal opportunity. Check with your personnel office for information regarding state law.

As a basic rule, organizations are expected to confine questioning to *bona fide occupational qualifications* (BFOQs). We have compiled a list of *illegal* areas of questioning:

1. Change of name (may reveal national origin).
2. Maiden or former name of spouse (may reveal marital status).
3. Previous foreign address (may reveal national origin).
4. Birthplace of applicant, applicant's spouse, parents, or relatives (may reveal national origin).
5. Applicant's religion. (Unless being interviewed for a position in a religious organization.)
6. Applicant's complexion or color of skin.
7. Applicant's citizenship or national origin.
8. Applicant's foreign military service.
9. Name and address of relative to be notified (may reveal foreign-born parents). You can ask for a person to be notified.
10. Applicant's arrest record. (Law assumes a person is innocent unless proved guilty in court.)
11. Applicant's height—unless height can be demonstrated to be a bona fide occupational qualification.

A young woman in search of a position in a marketing firm reported being asked: "Do you plan to have a family? And if so, what are your plans for caring for the children while you work?"

These questions, of course, have nothing to do with whether she was qualified for a marketing position. Moreover, they are not only impertinent but illegal. The young woman handled the question well, we thought: "I want to assure you that I keep my personal life separate from my professional life. If I have children, I will be sure that they have reliable care."

The reason we think her answer was particularly good is that it took all possibilities into account. She told them that she understood the law and that she was assertive enough to deal with violations of it in this high-risk situation. She also was able to show that she was tolerant of ignorance but prepared to treat the ignorance with information. Finally, she communicated that she would answer the question because she felt it was innocent enough, however impertinent it seemed. We will say much more about answering illegal questions when we address the interviewee's role in the next chapter.

Guidelines cannot be formulated for all possible violations, but there is a commonly understood test to be applied when in doubt. You must ask the question, "Does this information pertain to the job qualification?" In other words, would the answer to the question actually reveal anything about the person's qualifications to do the particular job? Some employers are interested in personal affairs that could affect an employee's work. We know of interviewers who have asked about arrangements for child care, plans women have for childbearing, marriage plans, divorces, activities related to activist groups, and the like. Any of these could affect the person's work indirectly, but all are illegal bases for making employment decisions. They are none of the employer's business and are, therefore, grounds for complaint to the EEOC.[2] The laws that relate to equal opportunity employment are summarized in Table 6.2.

Understand that it is difficult even if you know the law to apply it. Court interpretations of the law are just as important as the law because they give more specific guidelines about what kinds of questioning might be illegal. Also, you must check the laws of your state since some state laws are more restrictive than those at the federal level. The personnel officer of your organization should have the latest information. Check with this person if you have any doubt about what is appropriate questioning.

Reviewing the Resume and Application Form

This process involves reading the applicant's letter, resume, and application form (if your organization uses one). Look for continuity in the person's work and employment experience. Do you notice any time gaps? You will want to probe these gaps to see if they are significantly related to how the candidate might perform for your organization. Be careful, though, that you do not wander into illegal questioning here.

Examine the candidate's references if they are included. Are the people given as references in a position to observe the candidate's relevant skills? Sometimes a candidate will include personal friends, clergy, and neighbors in the list of references. These people are not going to be helpful to you for obvious reasons.

Next, check the candidate's reference letters. Most reference letters are positive—after all, who would ask a person who might reveal damaging information to write a recommendation on his or her behalf. Sometimes these letters can be useful though. A middle-of-the-road letter, one that is not enthusiastic, can be a bad sign. Notice if any of the letters speak specifically about outstanding contributions and/or past performance. Make a note of this because these are areas that you may choose to pursue in the interview. For example, an interviewer for a small tool manufacturer noticed that a reference talked about a sales award. A set of questions was framed to probe this: "Tell me about how you came to win a sales contest in your company." "Who was involved in the competition?" "What do you think it takes to win such an award?"

Look to see what kinds of educational experiences the person has had. Generally, this information is limited to the names of the schools attended

Table 6.2   Federal Laws That Apply to Selection Interviews and Employment

CIVIL RIGHTS ACT (1866)

This legislation gave all persons the same contractual rights as "white citizens." It was the first federal law that prohibited discrimination.

EQUAL PAY ACT (1963, 1972)

This act made it unlawful to pay different hourly rates for the same work on the basis of sex. It amended the Fair Labor Standards Act. It exempts academic, administrative, and professional employees. The Wage-Hour Division of the Department of Labor administers this act.

CIVIL RIGHTS ACT (1964, 1972)

This comprehensive act addressed discrimination in such areas as education, federally assisted programs, and voting. Title VII of the act forbade employers, employment agencies, and unions to discriminate on the basis of race, color, religion, sex, or national origin. It established the Equal Employment Opportunity Commission. (An amendment in 1972 allowed the EEOC to bring compliance by court action.) Provisions of this act are administered by the Office of Civil Rights of the Department of Health and Human Services and by the EEOC.

AGE DISCRIMINATION IN EMPLOYMENT ACT (1967, 1978)

This act makes it unlawful to discriminate against applicants or employees who are between forty and sixty-five years old. (In 1978, this act was amended to raise the age to seventy years of age, but it exempted employees covered by collective bargaining contracts.) Some job categories are exempted if a bona fide occupational qualification is involved. The act applies to employers with twenty or more employees. The Wage-Hour Division of the Department of Labor administers the act.

EQUAL EMPLOYMENT OPPORTUNITY ACT (1972)

This amended Title VII of the Civil Rights Act of 1964 to broaden coverage to include state and governmental agencies and educational institutions and to give the EEOC authority to bring lawsuits. The EEOC has administrative authority.

AMENDMENTS TO HIGHER EDUCATION ACT OF 1965 (1972)

These amendments prohibit sexual discrimination in federally assisted educational programs and place educational institutions under the Equal Pay Act. Sexual discrimination provisions are enforced by the Department of Education.

REHABILITATION ACT (1973)

This act mandates affirmative action to employ and promote qualified handicapped people. It applies to federal contract holders employing fifty or more persons. The Departments of Labor and Health and Human Services administer this act.

VIETNAM ERA VETERANS READJUSTMENT ASSISTANCE ACT (1974)

Employers with government contracts of $10,000 or more must take affirmative action to employ and promote Vietnam era veterans. This act is enforced by the Department of Labor when complaints are received.

IMMIGRATION REFORM AND CONTROL ACT (1987)

This act prohibits discrimination on the basis of citizenship, providing an alien has a work permit and appropriate visa. The act is enforced by the Departments of Labor and Health and Human Services.

and courses of study. You can make a judgment here, though; try to assess the quality of these programs from your organization's perspective.

Finally, check the application form if there is one. Look here for completeness. Are all necessary blanks filled out? If not, there may be a reason for leaving a blank. Make a note of missing information in case you decide to interview the candidate later. Check also for the same kinds of information discussed above.

Deciding on a Structure and Planning the Initial Questions

You should usually work for a moderate degree of structure in your interviews, especially if you will be talking to a number of candidates. Research shows that structuring an interview will (1) force you to be more consistent, (2) cause you to talk less than you would otherwise, and (3) allow you to achieve higher agreement with other interviewers if you are a part of an interviewing team.[3] A good way to approach structuring is to begin with planning topics. Cal Downs found that certain topics arise in most selection interviews.[4] Although not all were initiated by the interviewer, the topics most often covered, arranged in order of the frequency with which they were discussed, are:

1. Job expectations
2. Academic background
3. Knowledge about the job and organization
4. Scholastic record
5. Work experience
6. Geographical preference
7. Goals
8. Extracurricular activities
9. Strengths and/or weaknesses
10. Salary expectations

Framing questions for each of the topics you plan to approach can be a difficult task if you are an inexperienced interviewer. We recommend that you structure your interview by content areas, taking advantage of one of the lists of questions composed by veteran interviewers. Once you have gained some experience, you will want to refine your questions based on how the questions you used served your interests. Table 6.3 displays an excellent list of questions. Keep in mind that these are only a start and must be tailored to the particular job description. Also, understand that you may want to eliminate some of the less relevant content areas, especially if you are limited by time. And, of course, you would not usually ask all the questions in a content area.

A useful technique for beginning questioning in a content area is asking a broad question. For example, an interviewer from an accounting firm might say: "What can you tell me about your accounting major?" An inter-

Table 6.3   Questions and Follow-up Questions for Selection Interviews

I. EDUCATION

1. Why did you select your major area of study?
2. Why did you select your college/university?
3. If you were starting college again, what would you do differently? Why?
4. What subjects were most interesting? What were most useful? Why?
5. What subjects were least interesting? What were least useful? Why?
6. What classes/subjects did you do well in? Why?
7. What classes/subjects were difficult for you? Why?
8. Other than the things you learned in the courses you studied, what is the most important thing you learned from your college experience?
9. What did you learn from your extracurricular activities?
10. What would be your advice to a student entering college regarding participation in extracurricular activities?
11. What elective coursework did you take? Why did you select these courses?
12. What does it mean to you to have a college degree?
13. How did you finance your college education?

II. EXPERIENCE

14. Describe each of your work experiences.
15. What do you see as your strengths as an employee?
16. You say that a strength you have is _____ . Give me some indication, perhaps an example, that illustrates this strength.
17. Describe the employee with whom you most enjoy working.
18. Describe the employee with whom you least like working.
19. What is an ideal boss like?
20. What traits in a boss do you least like?
21. What were the best aspects of your last job?
22. What were the worst aspects of your last job?
23. What were some of your achievements in your last job?
24. What were some of the disappointments in your last job?
25. Do you see yourself as a leader/manager of people? Explain your answer.
26. What kind of work situations would you like to avoid? Why?
27. What skills are needed to be successful as a _____ ?
28. What are some of the pressures you've encountered in your work experience?
29. How have you worked to manage these work-related pressures?
30. In considering potential employers, what are the most important characteristics? What is *the most important?*
31. What frustrations have you encountered in your work experience? How have you handled these frustrations?
32. What aspects of your last job were difficult for you?
33. Sometimes a work assignment requires frequent travel. How do you react to the prospect of frequent travel?
34. How would you evaluate the progress you made in your last job?
35. Do you think the progress you made in your last job is representative of your ability? Why? Why not?
36. How can a boss help an employee develop his or her capabilities?
37. What areas has your boss suggested you improve? What did you do to improve?
38. Most employees and bosses have some disagreements. What are some things about which you and your boss have disagreed?
39. What does it take to be a good leader?

III. POSITION AND COMPANY
40. Why did you select this company?
41. Why did you decide to apply for this particular position?
42. How do you see yourself being qualified for this position?
43. What about this position is especially attractive to you?
44. What do you see in the position that is not attractive to you?
45. Why should I hire you?
46. What do you know about our company?
47. Are you willing to relocate?

IV. SELF-EVALUATION
48. Tell me a little bit about yourself. Describe yourself.
49. If you could relive your life, what might you do differently?
50. What do you see as your strengths? good qualities? talents? How do you know that you possess these? Give examples of each.
51. What do you see as your weak points? areas for improvement? things you have difficulty doing? What have you done to deal with these?
52. In what areas of work do you lack confidence? Explain. What are you doing about these?
53. In what areas of work are you most confident?
54. Describe a specific work problem you had. Tell what you did to solve this problem.
55. What traits or skills are most important to being successful? Why? Evaluate yourself in relation to these traits or skills.
56. What do you consider to be your greatest work achievement? Why?
57. What does it mean to you to be a self-starter? Do you see yourself as a self-starter? Explain.
58. What factors in a work situation provide motivation for you?

V. GOALS
59. Where do you see yourself being in your profession in five years? In ten years? How did you establish these goals? What will you need to do to achieve these goals?
60. What are your salary expectations for this position? Starting salary? Salary in five years?
61. Elaborate on the career objective you presented in your resume.
62. What has influenced you most to select your particular career goal?

VI. MILITARY SERVICE
63. What kind of specific responsibilities did you have in the service?
64. What traits make a successful leader in the (name branch of service)?
65. What did you learn about work from your tour of duty?
66. What traits are needed to be a successful military person?
67. What traits detract from success as a military person?

---

viewer for a church that was hiring a minister of music might say: "What is your philosophy of church music?" A manager for a retail food store might say: "How is your work experience relevant to retailing?" A director of graduate study might say to a prospective graduate student: "Why do you want to undertake graduate study?" These questions, because they are unfocused, force the applicants to focus and organize their ideas and tell the interviewer what they, as candidates, think is important. When you ask for such information, it will also allow you to check the applicant's ability to analyze and organize—important communication skills that you will want to be able to evaluate. Keep in mind, though, that the broad nature of such a question does not allow you to easily collect the specific information needed to compare candidates.

You will also want to ask some of your easier questions in the very early part of the interview. Save the difficult questions for later, when the interviewee has relaxed and has warmed up to answering questions. If you ask a difficult question early in the interview and the candidate is not answering it well, move on to another question. It is often better to come back to the difficult question, rather than risk changing the climate of the interview too early.

Arranging the Setting

The arrangement of the setting can have a significant impact on the climate of the interview. Try to arrange for a private location. We know from reports from interviewers that it is not always possible to use a private location, but you can usually stay out of the traffic flow.

You may also wish to have some degree of formality in the setting. If you are interviewing someone who will work for you, you may select the formality of your office. Keep in mind that the choice to stay behind your desk will communicate something about you.

Some college recruiters prefer an informal setting because they believe it relaxes the interviewee. If this is what you want, you might arrange for seating that is direct and an atmosphere that is less imposing than your office. If you use your office, try moving away from your desk if this is possible. Often an informal area is arranged so that the seating arrangements convey relatively equal status, with a table on which to set coffee cups.

Don't be afraid to change locations if it seems warranted. An interviewer for a large insurance company in Indianapolis told us how her willingness to be flexible allowed her to recruit a top candidate. She had been quite impressed with a particular candidate's credentials, but the interview was not going well. The interviewee was tense and not providing the kind of information that she wanted. About ten minutes into the interview, the interviewer suggested that they move to the company cafeteria so that they could have coffee. She conducted the remainder of the interview in this setting. The interviewee relaxed and was able to show how really sharp she was. Consequently, the candidate was hired and turned out to be a very talented employee. Willingness to be flexible in arrangements can pay off.

Arranging the setting is the last step in the planning process for the selection interview. Now that we have finished studying the planning process, we can turn our attention to conducting the interview.

CONDUCTING THE SELECTION INTERVIEW

Beginning the Interview

There are a number of theories about how to begin a selection interview. One recommendation is to take a few minutes to build some rapport and make the interviewee feel relaxed by making small talk. This is a good plan as long as it takes only a few minutes. A student of ours reported that an interviewer from a local bank took this approach, carrying on social conversation for twenty minutes. This student was anxious about the interview and wanted to get on with it. She realized that interviewers make decisions early in the interview, so she thought that this behavior was some sort of a ploy. We believe this is not wise behavior. Extensive small talk can make the interviewees more nervous than they already are as they sit wondering when the "real" interview will begin.

We think it is good also to give the interviewee a brief orientation. You can orient interviewees by discussing the job specifications and providing a brief overview of how you will proceed. Candidates, in our view, are better able to respond to the organization's needs when they have some information about the job. You may choose not to be specific, but you should at least tell the candidates in general terms what is involved. This will allow the candidates to tell you why they think they are qualified—which we presume you want to know.

Motivating the Interviewee to Talk

Avoid asking difficult questions during the first part of the interview. Most interviewees usually feel nervous at the beginning of an interview, and difficult questions will only heighten the tension level. Increased tension frequently means that the candidate will say less. Also, avoid areas of sensitivity until later in the interview. If you begin a line of questioning and it turns out to be a sensitive area, bypass probing it until later in the interview. For example, during an interview for a secretary/receptionist, the candidate revealed that she had been terminated from a job. Instead of probing the topic, the interviewer said: "Many people experience difficulties with employers early in their careers. Let's talk about what you did in your next job." Later in the interview the interviewer came back to the termination and probed. In an interview for a church music program, a person revealed early in the interview that he left a church because of infighting of the membership. The interviewer merely said: "That must have been an unfortunate situation." Later he came back to the topic and probed.

Ask questions that are both open and clear. This means that you should try to avoid questions that can be answered by a yes or no. Encourage the applicant to tell you more by using elaboration and clarification probes. Ask, "And what happened next?" Be sure that these are questions rather than statements, and do not interrupt. Interruptive statements are significant predictors that the applicant will judge the interviewer not to be an empathic listener.[5] Be careful not to be concerned about short pauses in the talking. Sometimes a pause merely means that the candidate is thinking about what ought to be said next. A pause can motivate the interviewee to continue. Wait. You need not fill pauses with either chatter or a new question. But do not allow long pauses. These may have a negative effect on the applicant's perception that you are an empathic listener.[6]

Probing

Sometimes the motivational strategies you use will not cause the interviewee to say as much as you would like about a particular area or concern. Here you will want to use the techniques described in detail in Chapter 5. Probing requires careful listening because it is based upon what the candidate just said; you often cannot plan these questions. Consider this sequence of questions asked by an interviewer from a local telephone company when the candidate did not provide all the information the interviewer wanted. She began with, "What were some of your favorite courses in your major?" Then she asked, "Why was your study of small-group communication your favorite?" She concluded the line of questioning with, "How do you see these experiences you indicated as being related to the professional goals you have?" This kind of probing allowed her to gain in-depth information and analyze this candidate's communication skill.

Some answers to your questions must be probed because they do not directly answer the question you asked. An interviewer asked an applicant for a college scholarship: "What do you see the basic importance of a college education to be?" The answer the candidate gave told the applicant's plans for a major area. The interviewer did not immediately assume that the person was avoiding her. Also, she did not assume that the applicant was to blame for misinterpreting the question. She assumed that she might not have clearly communicated her question. In a tense situation such as that created by a selection interview, it might be better to say something like the interviewer did: "I guess I was not clear with that question. Let me try to rephrase it." If the candidate does not answer you directly after you rephrase a question, make a mental note of the question and come back to it later.

Avoiding Biases

It is easy for bias to inadvertently slip into an interview. One source of bias may be your own questioning. Some interviewers telegraph the preferred answer by the way they ask the question. For example, a member of an interviewing team in a church said, "That's interesting. Tell me more about it." This was a cue to the interviewee that, at least for that person, this was an important area of questioning. Another member of the team began a question with, "I think that outreach is an extremely important part of this job. What do you think about this area of the job?'' Again, the interviewee knew how to treat the information requested by the interviewer. You can tell how revealing biases may lead interviewees to respond as they think you would like, rather than from their own experience.

A second source of bias—one that the novice interviewer might never consider—is the order in which candidates are interviewed. Researchers have discovered that the quality of the preceding candidate can influence an interviewer's opinion of the candidate being interviewed.[7] Kenneth Wexley, for example, found that when an average candidate was preceded by two very good candidates, the average candidate seemed much better than the person actually was. The good feeling generated by the previous interviews apparently helped the average candidate. This effect, a halo effect, was observed only for the average candidate and not for either very good or poor candidates. The best defense against this kind of bias is being aware that it exists. If you have just interviewed some very good candidates, be extra careful to evaluate fairly the third. Also, after a series of interviews, carefully check your notes against the candidates' resumes.

Time of day is a third source of bias. Harvey Tschirgi and Jon Huegli[8] investigated decisions to hire candidates based on the time of day. They found a high percentage of negative decisions were made just before the lunch hour and just before the end of the day. Their hour-by-hour analysis, based on interviews conducted by seventeen private companies at Ohio University, is presented in Table 6.4. When interpreting these data, one has to assume that the worst candidates did not always end up with interviews

Table 6.4 Hour-by-Hour Analysis of Interviews with Recorded Decisions

Time of Day Interview Held	Number of Interviews	Number of Positive Decisions	Percentage of Positive Decisions	Number of Negative Decisions	Percentage of Negative Decisions
A.M.:					
9–10	22	12	55	10	45
10–11	22	14	64	8	36
11–12	12	4	33	8	67
P.M.:					
12–1	4	3	75	1	25
1–2	17	9	53	8	47
2–3	23	15	65	8	35
3–4	21	13	62	8	38
4–5	15	5	33	10	67
5–6	3	1	33	2	67
Totals	139	76		63	

SOURCE: Reprinted from the Winter 1979 *Journal of Career Planning & Employment* with the permission of the College Placement Council, Inc., copyright holder.

scheduled at these times. Clearly, time of day affects hiring decisions negatively.

Not weighing positive information properly is a final source of bias. Thomas Hollmann[9] was concerned that interviewers might be influenced too heavily by negative information revealed by the interviewee, particularly when it comes early in the interview. He discovered that interviewers are biased in this way. The bias came not from misinterpreting the negative information, but from paying too little attention to positive information. In other words, the presence of negative information causes the interviewer to pay less attention to equally important positive information. The outcome of such behavior is to pass over some potentially good employees. While you will not want to ignore negative information, be aware of this bias so that you can put positive and negative information in proper perspective.

Concluding the Interview

One of the goals for the closing of an interview is to conclude with the interviewee having a positive image of your organization. There is a sense that you serve as your organization's public relations officer in the interview situation. Try to conclude on a positive note. Do not end the interview with a series of difficult questions or the probing of negative information. Instead, move to an area of questioning where the candidate can experience pleasant, free-flowing conversation. An interviewer from a drug store chain, whom we recently observed, talked about the organization and why he enjoyed working for it. He was selling the organization in order to create a positive image. He continued by telling the candidate about the organization's growth and image in the community. You might do as he did. You could also say something about the key benefits. Do not overdo your pitch, but let the candidate know that your organization is a good place to work.

Give the interviewee an opportunity to ask questions. Be prepared to answer questions about duties, opportunities for development and training, opportunities for advancement, salary and benefits, and the decision process with respect to filling the position.

Tell the candidate when you plan to make a decision if he or she does not ask. Give a time frame that allows enough time to make the decision, but do not tell the person that he or she will be hired. An interviewer for a university position once said: "You are our number one candidate. We have to interview one more person, but we will get back to you within a week." A month later the candidate received a letter stating that another candidate was hired. You may think the person you interviewed is the best candidate, only to find that the next person is even better. Or, on the other hand, you might tell a candidate that she doesn't possess one of the important qualifications for the job and later discover that this person is actually the best of your applicants. You do not know whom you will hire until the decision is made and the candidate accepts. It is best not to either encourage or discourage the candidate.

	Poor	Fair	Good	Very Good	Excellent
Preparation for the interview	_____	_____	_____	_____	_____
Attitude	_____	_____	_____	_____	_____
Level of maturity	_____	_____	_____	_____	_____
Level of motivation	_____	_____	_____	_____	_____
Self-confidence	_____	_____	_____	_____	_____
Ability to get along	_____	_____	_____	_____	_____
Communication ability	_____	_____	_____	_____	_____
Appearance	_____	_____	_____	_____	_____
Knowledge of organization	_____	_____	_____	_____	_____
Academic preparation	_____	_____	_____	_____	_____
Work experiences	_____	_____	_____	_____	_____

Respond to each of these:
1. How well prepared was the applicant?
2. Describe the applicant's strengths.
3. Describe the applicant's weaknesses.
4. How does the applicant compare with other applicants?
5. How well does the applicant's qualifications fit the organization's present and future needs?
6. What is the applicant's potential for development?
7. How well does the applicant understand what is required in this position?
8. How well does the applicant understand our organization?
9. Should we hire this person? Why or why not?

Figure 6.1   Applicant evaluation form.

INTERPRETING INTERVIEW DATA

As soon as practical after the interview is complete, you should record your impressions. Your organization may have a form for this purpose. If not, you can make your own. Figure 6.1 is a typical two-part evaluation form—the first part is a rating scale and the second is a series of open questions. You can use this check sheet in conjunction with the two-column job analysis you did before the interview to analyze your data.

Data interpretation is not an easy task because it is tied to an individual's value system. We cannot tell you what makes a good employee for your particular job; that depends on what you value, the job, and situational constraints.[10] However, the task can be made easier by following these suggestions.

Keep in mind the information we have presented about biases. Research about bias indicates that (1) the time of day in which you interview may bias choices, (2) the order in which you interview may cause a contrast effect, and (3) positive information may be given much less attention in the face of negative information.

Keep in mind that you may have biased the information by the way you presented the question. Be sure not to signal the appropriate response to the interviewee by the way you asked the question. Some candidates will pick up on your cue more than others and, thus, may appear to be the better candidate when they actually are not.

Use a check sheet of qualifications with space in which to write about each candidate. Take time to fill out the sheet for each candidate after that person's interview. One difficulty in interpreting data is not focusing on the same qualities for each candidate. Use of a check sheet—such as the one described on page 129—will give you a basis for comparison among those you interview.

You will think more carefully about the candidates if you force yourself to write about each. Be careful, however, not to make marks on the resume or application form since such forms are considered by the EEOC to be official employment documents. The EEOC discovered that certain employers marked applications to signal that the applicant was a black person, a woman, a Hispanic, and so on. As a result, any marks or comments may be suspect if the EEOC examines your files because of a complaint. We advise you to keep the notes you make after the interview together in a file separate from the applicant's. Also, do not write evaluative comments during the interview. Write only factual information and not inferences. Notes taken during the interview become part of the candidate's file, and a candidate who thinks you have illegally discriminated can legally demand to see them later.

Invite promising candidates for a second interview. Often a lower-level candidate gets only a single interview. We think that this is often a mistake. The time and money required to train an employee makes hiring the wrong person costly. Many organizations have someone other than the initial contact person conduct the second interview. The two interviewers can then compare and contrast their impressions in the hope of arriving at the best applicant.

Prepare a list of specific questions for use in the second interview. The second interview is usually considered an opportunity to take a closer look at the candidate. Usually more time is allotted to such an interview, and there is more opportunity to match a job description to the candidate's skills and experience. Experience with the candidate will allow you to prepare specific questions in advance. You should take the time to do this.

INTERVIEWER'S QUESTIONS FOR EVALUATION

We think that the way to keep your interviewing skills sharp is to carefully evaluate your effort from time to time. It is easy to assume that you are doing well, and you may be. The only way you will know for sure how you are doing is to evaluate yourself. Here are some questions you can use in this evaluation process.

1. Did I update the job description and conduct a skills analysis?
2. Did I give the applicant the information he or she needed, but did not know before the interview?

Ethics and Responsibilities in Interviewing

There are several rather clearly established guidelines for the ethical behavior and responsibilities of the interviewer in the selection interview. The first of these is backed by federal legislation.

The interviewer should not ask illegal questions. Asking for the kind of information that is prohibited, even if there were no such laws, has ethical implications. The law is based upon the notion that this material has nothing to do with bona fide occupational qualifications. The principle of fairness would rule out this kind of questioning.

Likewise, *the interviewer should not use any illegal information that comes out in the interview.* Sometimes illegal information is given when the interviewee inadvertently volunteers it. The interviewer should interrupt the interviewee and explain that the particular information is not of interest as it is not a basis for selection decisions.

The principle of intentional deception applies to the third ethical guideline. *Interviewers should not intentionally misrepresent themselves or their company.* The interviewers may be tempted to exaggerate about their organization and the benefits of being associated with it. Interviewers should consider the truth of what they are saying.

Finally, *the interviewer should not intentionally deceive the interviewee with respect to the employment decision.* Sometimes interviewers will make statements that will lead an interviewee to believe that he or she will be offered a job. The principle of fairness is violated when this guideline is not observed. Rarely does the interviewer know if the person will be hired, unless the interviewer has direct responsibility for hiring and will not be interviewing more candidates. Members higher up in an organization do veto choices, and other more impressive candidates do come along.

3. Did I review EEOC guidelines?
4. How effectively did I open the interview? Did I help the candidate relax? Did I encourage the person to speak freely and openly?
5. Did I explore the candidate's attitudes, maturity, motivation, self-confidence, ability to get along, communication ability, knowledge of organization, academic preparation, and work experience?
6. Did I provide an opportunity for the candidate to ask questions?
7. Was I careful to avoid bias-creating situations?
8. How effectively did I close the interview?
9. Did I follow up on the interview by making notes and fulfilling any promises I made to the candidate?

SUMMARY

Selection interviews produce particular constraints on the communication process. For the interviewer a reputation and the well-being of the organization may be at stake. For the interviewee the possibility of meaningful employment and a career is at stake. We provided advice based on our experience and what researchers have said to help people know how to manage these communications.

The interviewer must prepare carefully by (1) consulting the job description, (2) preparing materials to be used in the search, (3) checking EEOC guidelines, (4) reviewing applications and resumes, (5) structuring the interview, and (6) arranging the setting.

Because the interviewer must be concerned with techniques for conducting the selection interview, we presented strategies for beginning the interview, as well as for motivating the interviewee. We pointed out that both beginning and ending the interview are very important since they set the tone, serving to relax the candidate, get the necessary information, and build a favorable image of the company. Obtaining full responses is important, and so we presented techniques for probing. In interpreting the data, the interviewer should keep in mind possible sources of bias. Bias can be eliminated by following carefully worked-out check sheets for listing qualifications needed for the specific job and by conducting multiple interviews.

Finally, we presented some guidelines for the interviewer's use in evaluating the effectiveness of the interview. These follow the basic structure and concerns we presented regarding the selection interview.

NOTES

[1]Walter R. Mahler, *How Effective Executives Interview* (Homewood, IL: Dow Jones/Richard D. Irwin, 1976), pp. 77–83.

[2]For further analysis of illegal questions asked in employment interviews, see Fredric M. Jablin, "Use of Discriminatory Questions in Screening Interviews," *Personnel Administrator, 27* (March 1982), 41–44.

[3]D. P. Schwab and H. G. Heneman, III, "Relationship between Interview Structure and Interviewer Reliability in an Employment Situation," *Journal of Applied Psychology, 53* (1969), 214–217.

[4]Cal W. Downs, "A Content Analysis of Twenty Selection Interviews," *Personnel Administration and Public Personnel Review* (September 1972), 25.

[5]Karen B. McComb and Fredric M. Jablin, "Verbal Correlates of Interviewer Empathic Listening and Employment Interview Outcomes," *Communication Monographs, 51* (December 1984), 367.

[6]McComb and Jablin.

[7]Kenneth N. Wexley et al., "Importance of Contrast Effects in Employment Interviews," *Journal of Applied Psychology, 56* (1972), 45–48.

[8]Harvey D. Tschirgi and John M. Huegli, "Monitoring the Employment Interview," *Journal of College Placement, 40* (Winter 1979), 39.

[9]Thomas D. Hollmann, "Employment Interviewers' Errors in Processing Positive and Negative Information," *Journal of Applied Psychology, 56* (1972), 130–134; Also see Arthur A. Witkin, "Commonly Overlooked Dimensions of Employee Selection," *Personnel Journal, 59* (1980), 573–588.

[10]Donna Bogar Goodall and H. Lloyd Goodall, Jr., "The Employment Interview: A Selective Review of the Literature with Implications for Communication Research," *Communication Quarterly, 30* (Spring 1982), 116–124.

A SELECTION INTERVIEW FOR ANALYSIS

This simulated selection interview was conducted by two communication majors at the University of South Alabama. The interviewee is Hayley Maulsby, who is applying for a position as assistant promotion director. The interviewer is Sherry Demest, manager of the marketing department.

1. Interviewer: Come in please.

2. Applicant: Hi.

3. Interviewer: Hi.

4. Applicant: How are you?

5. Interviewer: I'm fine, thank you. Please have a seat.

6. Interviewer: I'm glad you have come in today. I see from looking at your resume that you are applying for the position of assistant marketing promotion director.

7. Applicant: That's right.

8. Interviewer: I'm sure you are aware that our company works with entertainment and brings different types of entertainment into this community. I don't know if you are aware of the fact that we also bring it into the entire southeastern district, and I wanted you to be aware of that before we begin. Do you have any questions before we start?

9. Applicant: No. That sounds great.

10. Interviewer: OK, good. Well, let's start out with your college experience. What did your college education mean to you?

11. Applicant: Well, I feel like a college education helped me to learn a little bit more about myself. I went to school for a while, and then I quit and got a job. Soon, I realized that there were so many opportunities out there and that I really needed to get a better education. That's when I went back to school and explored several areas of studies. I took different classes and found that my talent was in the area of public relations, promotions, marketing, and that type of thing. That's one of the things I'm really excited about, because when I went back to school, I discovered what I was really good at doing.

12. Interviewer: Good. Well, that leads me into the next question then, about subjects in your major. Can you tell me something about what made them appealing to you—specific subjects?

13. Applicant: Some of the courses I took, especially the public relations courses, helped me understand how to develop a formal campaign—every aspect of it. You learned everything from writing a public service announcement to doing an advertising campaign. We also learned to do a brochure, lay out an ad, do a radio spot, and do a video. I really enjoyed doing those kinds of things. It was "hands-on" experience; you don't just read about it in a book; you actually do the campaigns. One of the things that helped me was the chance to do some directed studies and internships. One of them was at WABB, a radio station in Mobile. I was given the opportunity to use my own judgment to pick out the public service announcements that would be put on the air. I was also responsible for my own promotions. I had to develop them from scratch, make my own contacts, set up any promotion—for instance, in a local area, movie theater, restaurant, that type of thing. I ended up learning what public relations was all about.

14. Interviewer: That's good. I noticed that you did have a variety of experiences and that they were heavily into the field that you're going into. Now, let's talk about work itself. What type of work environment are you most comfortable in?

15. Applicant: Well, I'm sort of a go-getter. I like to have a project handed to me, and I like to do it. I work really well on my own. I'm not the type of person who will wait until the last minute. If you give me a job, I'll get it done. I would rather not be in a very structured environment, and I think that's why I'm in this field. You go and work on your own time, but actually you are still doing your job. You know, you are not just out gallivanting; you are out running here and there, but you are doing your job while you are doing that. That's the kind of situation that I work best in.

16. Interviewer: Good. Let's talk about some of the jobs that you have had. What type of things have you done particularly well in or did you have pride in when you were working in these particular jobs?

17. Applicant: I think what made me feel the most pride was when I would set out to do a certain promotion and it was a success. I knew that I was the one who promoted the event, and I was the one who got the people there and got it altogether. For example, we had a concert at the university that I attended last year, and I was in charge of the whole promotion and ad campaign. I went into all the radio stations in the southeast, and I developed the posters for the concert and handled the promotion with the school. I dealt with the record companies, and I dealt with the promotion people that the band dealt with. I kind of tied it altogether and made a really big success of the concert. That's what gives me the most pride. I just felt like I accomplished something. I did something that I felt pleased the students, which is kind of hard to do, you know.

18. Interviewer: You sound like a self-starter. Would you call yourself one?

19. Applicant: Yes. I kind of go in there and just take it...take it and go with it. This is why I chose this field, because I think this is one of the only fields that you can do that in. At a lot of places you know you can't, and you have to sit back and wait for someone to tell you what to do. But this is the kind of job where you can use your own imagination and creativity.

20. Interviewer: Well, what would you expect to be your greatest rewards from this type of work?

21. Applicant: I think the greatest rewards will be to continue to come up with new, exciting, and creative ways to promote events and to come up with new advertising and new forms of advertising. Today, advertising and promotions are a major element in every company. I think that the key, the *reward* that I could find in it, would be the ability to come up with new and different ideas.

22. Interviewer: Good. Well, of all the things you have done, which, would you say, was the hardest thing for you to do and why?

23. Applicant: The hardest thing that I probably had to do was a certain promotion I did. It involved over twenty companies in the area, and it was really difficult to make the contacts. Once I made the contacts, I had to call back every day to set up the promotion. The companies were supposed to come out to the campus and set up a display and give away a prize. It ended up being really hard. To deal with a couple of companies at a time was not too hard, but to deal with over twenty different ones was! All the people I was dealing with were salespeople in that area. They were always out, and I was trying to convince them that my promotion was good for them. They were trying to tell me what they wanted out of it. It's really difficult when you are dealing with so many different people. That was the hardest thing.

24. Interviewer: Let me ask you one more question. What qualifications do you have that make you think that you'll be successful in this business?

25. Applicant: I have a lot of motivation and ambition to work in this business. This business really excites me. You know, I get an idea and to me it's just really exciting. I just want to go and make up this great campaign. In this field, you have to be a promoter. You have got to have the personality too. These are the qualities you learn about when you are studying—the key to successful PR. And I feel I have these qualities.

26. Interviewer: Good. Do you have any questions you would like to ask me?

27. Applicant: I would like to ask how many employees you have in your company who do advertising and promotion work.

28. Interviewer: Well, at the moment, we have a working force of approximately thirty-five people.

29. Applicant: And they all are in the advertising department?

30. Interviewer: No, not all of them. In advertising we have ten.

31. Applicant: I see. And how do you split up the work? Does the assistant director give the employees assignments? Does the manager say, "you'll do the brochure; you'll do the PSA"—that type of thing? Do you all split it up like that? Or do you have...how do you all handle campaigns like that?

32. Interviewer: We do split it up. We have some people who specialize in certain things, but we also encourage people to try to get a taste of the different things so they can become well-rounded.

33. Applicant: I see. And as far as being appointed the assistant marketing promotional director, I would be directly under the director, right? What kind of duties would I be doing?

34. Interviewer: Yes, you would be working under the director, and you would have different duties, as they would come up. He would hand down assignments to you and then he would explain to you what you would need to do further.

35. Applicant: This sounds like a really good opportunity. I've worked with tour promotion companies before with the university. They've dealt with the university a lot.

36. Interviewer: Do you have any other questions?

37. Applicant: Not at this time.

38. Interviewer: I've enjoyed talking with you. I noticed that you brought some samples of your work. We'll look these over and get back to you in a couple of weeks.

39. Applicant: I appreciated the opportunity to talk with you.

EXPERIENCES

1. Plan and carry out an interview with a member of your class. Evaluate your effort using the criteria presented at the end of this chapter.

2. Assume that you are interviewing for an organization that employs people with your expertise. Develop a job description and a two-column job analysis for this position. Now develop a moderately scheduled interview for an applicant for such a position.

3. Ask an employment officer about his or her experience regarding the EEO law. What does this person's experience tell you about the law and its application to selection interviews?

4. Interview a person who regularly conducts screening interviews for people in your area of expertise. Find out what this person looks for in a person he or she would classify as a fully qualified candidate. Ask too about aspects of candidates that promote disinterest. Does anything you found out surprise you?

5. Test your knowledge of illegal questioning. First, without looking back in this chapter, list as many areas of illegal questioning as you can. Then check the chapter to discover what areas you may have omitted.

RECOMMENDED READINGS

Goodall, Donna Bogar, and H. Lloyd Goodall, Jr., "The Employment Interview: A Selective Review of the Literature with Implications for Communication Research," *Communication Quarterly, 30* (1982), 116–124.

Jablin, Fredric M., "Organizational Entry, Assimilation, and Exit," in Fredric M. Jablin et al. (eds.), *Handbook of Organizational Communication* (Beverly Hills, CA: Sage, 1987).

Jablin, Fredric M., "Use of Discriminatory Questions in Screening Interviews," *Personnel Administrator, 27* (1982), 41–44.

Jablin, Fredric M., and Craig D. Tengler, "Facing Discrimination in On-Campus Interviews," *Journal of College Placement, 42* (1982), 57–61.

Springston, Jeff K., and Joann Keyton, "The Prevalence of Potentially Illegal Questioning in Pre-employment Screening," in S. J. Bruno (ed.), *Global Implications for Business Communications: Theory, Technology, and Practice* (1988), pp. 247–263.

Witkin, Arthur A., "Commonly Overlooked Dimensions of Employee Selection," *Personnel Journal, 59* (1980), 573–588.

CHAPTER 7

THE SELECTION INTERVIEW: THE APPLICANT'S PERSPECTIVE

OBJECTIVES

After reading this chapter, you should be able to:

Do a preinterview informational interview.

Do a self-analysis of job skills and performance.

Research an organization to gather preemployment information.

Prepare for typical questions asked by employment interviewers.

Prepare a list of questions to ask an employment interviewer.

Suggest appropriate answers to difficult and illegal questions.

Identify the rules of behavior that should be observed during a selection interview.

Discuss ethical behavior in employment interviews.

Prepare a strategy for handling a group interview.

Formulate a career plan.

Consider what you did to get ready for your last selection interview. How did you secure the interview? What did you do to get ready? If it was an interview for a nonprofessional position, did your preparation consist of merely dressing appropriately? If it was for a professional position, did you prepare by writing a resume, considering some questions that might be asked, and wearing appropriate clothing?

How close are these descriptions to what you actually did to prepare? We suspect that they are quite close. But there is a great deal more you can do for a selection interview that will help you be successful.

In this chapter we look at selection interviewing from the perspective of the applicant. Because the role of interviewee is so vital to most who will study this book, we look at it in detail. We suggest that you do preinterview informational interviewing and conduct self-analyses. We discuss choices for how you present yourself in cover letters and resumes. We tell you how to research an organization and prepare for typical questions. We provide suggestions for questioning the interviewer and managing the interview. We help you know how to evaluate yourself as an interviewee. Finally, we talk about the career planning process.

DOING PREINTERVIEW INFORMATIONAL INTERVIEWING

It is worth your time and effort to interview one or two professionals in your field. This kind of interview will give you information that you otherwise would find difficult to collect. This interviewing ought to be done several months before you begin to interview for actual positions. Otherwise, your interview may seem to be a ploy merely to gain access to information to better present yourself as a candidate. You may lose an important opportunity to be considered by these firms if you do not begin the preinterview information-gathering process several months in advance of a selection interview.

The usefulness of a preinterview information-gathering interview is pointed up in the following account: Four personnel managers from industrial firms sat in a forum to answer questions from college students about the selection process. One complaint that the managers all registered was that the students they interview seem to lack the practical experience necessary to handle their new job; they do not know what work in their chosen profession is actually like. A fact-finding interview can give you more practical information about what a particular field is like. Here are some good questions to ask a professional in your field:

1. What is a typical day like?
2. What kinds of skills are most valuable?
3. What kinds of courses were most valuable?
4. What are the most difficult problems that you face?
5. How do you manage these problems successfully?
6. What are the most rewarding parts of your job? Why?
7. What are typical starting salaries? What salary can be expected after five years?
8. Which major firms or organizations in this region employ people in your profession?
9. What are some other job titles for people with your training?
10. What would be a reasonable career goal for a person in this position, say, in five years? In ten years?
11. What professional organizations would a person in your position join?
12. What are the main benefits of working for an organization like yours?

You can readily see the value in knowing the kind of information these questions can provide. Some professionals will be flattered and willing to share with you; others may not want to take the time. Don't be discouraged if the first person you call turns you down. An alternative that might be more attractive to the professional would be to invite him or her to a meeting of your student organization. Our public relations student association invites a practitioner to its meetings once each year. You could follow a question-and-answer format where these same questions would be asked.

CONDUCTING A SELF-ANALYSIS

Two types of self-analysis are helpful in preparing to interview. The first is an analysis of your personal characteristics that might be valuable to an employer. The second is an analysis of your preferences with respect to a job and organization.

All of us have strengths that would make us good employees. The problem comes in identifying these strengths so that we can take advantage of them. Table 7.1 presents an inventory of personal traits developed by Lois Einhorn for the Career Center at Indiana University. Rate yourself on each of these categories. Remember that careful evaluation will produce the most useful results for you. Once you complete the form, then take each trait you rated yourself highly on and write down a work or school example that illustrates the trait. Remember that most employers will ask you about your strengths. Use this preparation in answering this question.

Once you've rated yourself on your strengths, rate yourself on your preferences related to a job and an organization. Table 7.2 lists some characteristics of jobs and organizations that might be important to you. When you have completed the rating process, make a list of items that you consider to be very important. Use this list as you do research on organizations and examine job descriptions. Ask people who know about the organization if it is the type of organization that offers the job factors you have listed.

There are some interesting correlations between preferences in job factors and grade point averages (GPA). Tom Reardon[1] compared ten preferences with whether the persons had a high GPA or an average GPA. The results are displayed in Table 7.3. We think it is interesting to see what factors each category of student valued. Note that the factors associated with the above-average student might be good areas for asking the interviewer questions. One group of researchers speculate that the questions asked by the applicant are a source of evaluating the person's motivation.[2] This supports Reardon—if high-GPA people are highly motivated.

Generally you will be given an opportunity to ask questions. You can base some of your questions on the information in Table 7.3. One of our students asked: "What is your company's policy on continuing education?" Notice that this topic is high on the list of employer characteristics that above-average students "buy into." The interviewer reported to us that he was pleased with the question, as it was a signal to him that the student valued keeping up with the field. We will return to the issue of asking questions of the interviewer later.

Continue your analysis of your strengths and weaknesses by asking yourself about your training and experience. This will lead to preparing a resume. Begin by listing the courses that relate to your designated professional goal. In which courses did you excel? How were your grades in these courses? Were there any special projects or term projects that allowed you to gain practical experience? Might any of your college professors be helpful to you in locating jobs?

Table 7.1   Inventory of Personal Traits

	RATING				
	Poor		Average		Excellent
Trait	1	2	3	4	5
1. Dependable	( )	( )	( )	( )	( )
2. Honest	( )	( )	( )	( )	( )
3. Motivated	( )	( )	( )	( )	( )
4. Assertive	( )	( )	( )	( )	( )
5. Outgoing	( )	( )	( )	( )	( )
6. Persistent	( )	( )	( )	( )	( )
7. Conscientious	( )	( )	( )	( )	( )
8. Ambitious	( )	( )	( )	( )	( )
9. Punctual	( )	( )	( )	( )	( )
10. Creative	( )	( )	( )	( )	( )
11. Intelligent	( )	( )	( )	( )	( )
12. Mature	( )	( )	( )	( )	( )
13. Emotionally stable	( )	( )	( )	( )	( )
14. Enthusiastic	( )	( )	( )	( )	( )
15. Flexible	( )	( )	( )	( )	( )
16. Realistic	( )	( )	( )	( )	( )
17. Responsible	( )	( )	( )	( )	( )
18. Serious	( )	( )	( )	( )	( )
19. Pleasant	( )	( )	( )	( )	( )
20. Sincere	( )	( )	( )	( )	( )
21. Analytical	( )	( )	( )	( )	( )
22. Organized	( )	( )	( )	( )	( )
23. Having a good appearance	( )	( )	( )	( )	( )
24. Able to get along with coworkers	( )	( )	( )	( )	( )
25. Able to get along with supervisors	( )	( )	( )	( )	( )
26. Having oral communication skills	( )	( )	( )	( )	( )
27. Having written communication skills	( )	( )	( )	( )	( )
28. Having good references	( )	( )	( )	( )	( )

Consider your work background. If you have held a job, you are in a better position to be hired than a person who has never held a job. List all the positions you have held and the names of your supervisors. Would your supervisors describe you as a good employee? Why? What work skills did you use that might be valued by other employers? How do these skills relate to the strengths you discovered in your personal trait analysis? Have the jobs you held helped you finance part of your education? If so, this is important to emphasize.

Were you involved in any extracurricular activities? (If not, get involved now—if it is not too late.) Have you invested any time in community service or projects? (This is easy to do because service groups are generally looking for help.) Have you held any leadership positions in clubs or organizations? If so, list them, and anything else that might be an asset. Put everything you can think of on your worksheet; you will edit this later.

Table 7.1   **Inventory of Personal Traits** (*Continued*)

	RATING				
Trait	Poor 1	2	Average 3	4	Excellent 5
29. Having good school attendance	( )	( )	( )	( )	( )
30. Having good job attendance	( )	( )	( )	( )	( )
31. Willing to work long hours	( )	( )	( )	( )	( )
32. Willing to work evenings and weekends	( )	( )	( )	( )	( )
33. Willing to relocate	( )	( )	( )	( )	( )
34. Willing to travel	( )	( )	( )	( )	( )
35. Willing to commute a long distance	( )	( )	( )	( )	( )
36. Willing to start at the bottom and advance according to own merit	( )	( )	( )	( )	( )
37. Able to accept criticism	( )	( )	( )	( )	( )
38. Able to motivate others	( )	( )	( )	( )	( )
39. Able to follow through on something until it is done	( )	( )	( )	( )	( )
40. Able to make good use of time	( )	( )	( )	( )	( )
41. Goal- (or achievement-) oriented	( )	( )	( )	( )	( )
42. Healthy	( )	( )	( )	( )	( )
43. Able to take initiative	( )	( )	( )	( )	( )
44. Able to follow directions	( )	( )	( )	( )	( )
45. Detail-oriented	( )	( )	( )	( )	( )
46. Able to learn quickly	( )	( )	( )	( )	( )
47. Willing to work hard	( )	( )	( )	( )	( )
48. Having moral standards	( )	( )	( )	( )	( )
49. Poised	( )	( )	( )	( )	( )
50. Having growth potential	( )	( )	( )	( )	( )
51. Others	( )	( )	( )	( )	( )

SOURCE: Adapted from Lois Einhorn, *Interviewing...A Job in Itself*, pp. 4–5. Used by permission of the Career Center at Indiana University.

PREPARING A COVER LETTER AND RESUME

The primary goal of a cover letter and resume is to persuade the employer to grant you an interview. The cover letter gives you the opportunity to arouse the interest of the prospective employer, to demonstrate that you can write well, and to show that you can adapt your presentation of self to a specific job and organization. The resume serves to highlight your background, education, and achievements. Its primary purpose is to cause the reader to want a personal interview with you.

The Cover Letter

There are some rather specific expectations with respect to cover letters, and it is important that you know them. Here are some of the most important dos and don'ts:

Table 7.2   **Preferences in Job Factors**

	Importance		
Factors	Not Important	Average Importance	Very Important
1. Challenge	( )	( )	( )
2. Responsibility	( )	( )	( )
3. Stability of organization	( )	( )	( )
4. Security of job within organization	( )	( )	( )
5. Size of organization	( )	( )	( )
6. Training program	( )	( )	( )
7. Initial job duties	( )	( )	( )
8. Advancement opportunities	( )	( )	( )
9. Amount of contact with co-workers	( )	( )	( )
10. Amount of contact with the public	( )	( )	( )
11. Starting salary	( )	( )	( )
12. Financial rewards "down the road"	( )	( )	( )
13. Degree of independence	( )	( )	( )
14. Opportunity to show initiative	( )	( )	( )
15. Degree of employee involvement in decision making	( )	( )	( )
16. Opportunity to be creative	( )	( )	( )
17. Type of industry	( )	( )	( )
18. Company's reputation in the industry	( )	( )	( )
19. Prestige of job within the organization	( )	( )	( )
20. Degree of results seen from job	( )	( )	( )
21. Variety of duties	( )	( )	( )
22. What the boss is like	( )	( )	( )
23. What the co-workers are like	( )	( )	( )
24. Suburban or metropolitan community	( )	( )	( )
25. Hours	( )	( )	( )
26. Benefits	( )	( )	( )
27. Commuting distance involved	( )	( )	( )
28. Amount of overnight travel involved	( )	( )	( )
29. Number of moves from one city to another involved	( )	( )	( )
30. Facilities of office or plant	( )	( )	( )
31. Spouse's desires	( )	( )	( )
32. Others (list)	( )	( )	( )

SOURCE: From Lois Einhorn, *Interviewing...A Job in Itself,* p. 3. Used by permission of the Career Center at Indiana University.

1. Always send an original copy of the letter. Do not send a photocopy or a carbon copy. If you cannot type, hire a professional typist.

2. Address the cover letter to a real person. Do not send it to "Dear Sir or Madam." It is worth the expense to call the firm and ask the

Table 7.3   The Top Ten Employer Characteristics Students "Buy Into"

Above-Average Students (3.2 to 4.0 GPA; $N = 325$)	Average Students (2.0 to 3.2 GPA; $N = 443$)
*1. Employer in a growth industry	1. National or local reputation
2. Potential for advancement	2. Location of employer
*3. Past history of growth/success	3. Potential for advancement
*4. Opportunity for continued education	4. Salary
5. Salary	5. Responsibility/challenge/freedom
†6. National or local reputation	6. Fringe benefits
†7. Location of employer	7. Prestige of working for employer
8. Fringe benefits	8. Employee is in a growth industry
†9. Responsibility/challenge/freedom	9. Past history of growth/success
10. Prestige of working for employer	10. Opportunity for continued education

*Significant at .01 level
†Significant at .05 level

Source: Reprinted from the Winter 1980 *Journal of Career Planning & Employment* with the permission of the College Placement Council, Inc., copyright holder.

receptionist for the name of the person who hires people for the position of interest. Say "I would like to address a letter to the person who hires people for _____ . Could you tell me this person's name, spell it please, and give the person's title?"

3. Do not allow any misspelled words or excessive erasures or white-outs. Do not misspell the word *personnel.*
4. Follow one of the typical business letter formats. (The one we use in Figure 7.1 is always appropriate.)
5. Use high-quality, cotton-content paper, white or off-white. Do not use flashy colors or erasable bond paper.
6. Space the letter attractively on the page. Leave a little more margin at the top than at the sides; allow approximately one-inch margins on the sides. Confine the letter to one page and do not run it too close to the bottom.

Structure the letter to include at least three paragraphs. The first paragraph generally should state the purpose of the letter, the particular position for which you are applying, and how you came to know about the position.

At either the end of the first paragraph or the beginning of the second, you might explain why you are interested in the particular position, the organization, and its products or services. You should highlight your academic background and explain how it qualifies you to be a candidate for the position. If you have had work or other special experience, briefly tell about this and relate how it gives you unique qualifications for the position. Refer the prospective employer to an enclosed resume that summarizes your qualifications, training, and experiences.

The third paragraph should ask for an interview and may suggest times when you are available. Repeat your telephone number in the letter and of-

"Exact form I should use"

1000 Hillcrest Road
Mobile, Alabama 36695
January 10, 19--

Mr. G. L. Lee
Personnel Manager
XYZ Corporation
3000 Executive Park
Mobile, Alabama 36604

Dear Mr. Lee:

    Please consider my application for a position in train-
ing and development with XYZ Corporation. I am especially
interested in your company because of its successful history
and record of continuous growth and stability. I will be
graduated in May from the University of South Alabama with a
bachelor of arts degree in communication with an emphasis in
organizational communication.

    The enclosed resume will give you the pertinent facts
about my education and past record of employment, which I
believe qualify me for a position with your company. My
particular interests lie in the areas of personnel development
and training, especially human relations. The confidence I
have in handling personnel contacts has been gained from both
my work experience and classes I have taken in communication
and psychology. The variety of my work experience has given
me the ability to adapt and relate to people easily and
quickly. I am free to travel if the position warrants it.

    I would appreciate the opportunity to discuss employment
possibilities with you personally in an interview. I believe
that would enable us to discuss more fully my training and
experience. I would be available sometime next week if that
would be convenient. I may be reached at the above address
or by phone at 205-661-1000. Thank you for the consideration
of my application.

                        Sincerely,

                        John Q. Student

Figure 7.1 Sample cover letter.

fer to provide any additional information that your prospective employer
might find helpful in evaluating your credentials. Finally, close your letter
with thanks and some statement about anticipating their future contact.
Say, in some way, "I look forward to hearing from you."

    Figure 7.1 displays a sample cover letter. Remember that each cover
letter *must be tailored to the particular job* and should be freshly typed or
word-processed.

The Resume

Imagine your resume somewhere in the middle of a stack of 200 others. If you can imagine this situation, then you know what your task in resume preparation must be. You must discover what you can do to make your resume stand out as deserving of special attention. There are some things you can do. You can print your resume on off-white paper. You can also give it some "graphic appeal" by using quality paper, allowing adequate margins, underlining various important parts, and the like. Beyond these suggestions there are no guarantees. The average resume in a pile of 200 will receive less than a minute of attention. However, if you violate certain expectations, it will be rejected immediately.

We think that the best way to call attention to your resume is to anticipate the needs of the reader. Consider that resumes serve at least three purposes: to open the door to an interview, to provide an outline for an interview, and to act as a reminder of the interview. Therefore, the following concerns are important, both for the purpose of attracting attention and for substantive reasons as well.

1. Neatness and attention to expectations of employers
2. Information retrieval
3. Completeness of information, but in a condensed form

Some important research is helpful in understanding what employers expect. Edward Rogers,[3] vice president and director of personnel for a major advertising agency, surveyed 170 major American corporations concerning these expectations. Fifty-eight percent responded to his inquiries. He asked about factors that cause disinterest in candidates. Nearly 90 percent of these personnel people cited poor grammar or spelling errors in the interview or written materials. Further, about 70 percent agreed that poor organization of ideas or overpromise in representing one's self created disinterest. Rogers asked these same representatives of American corporations questions about issues of form and style of resumes. Over 80 percent agreed that a resume should be printed on 8½ × 11-inch paper and should be a maximum of two pages long. And nearly 40 percent said they would be unlikely to pursue a candidate whose resume was longer than two pages. Sixty-six percent preferred a one-page resume.

Beverly Culwell went beyond issues of form and style to ask employers to react to categories of information that might be included in a resume. Table 7.4 displays their advice from most-important to least-important items.

You can see that there is considerable agreement about the causes of disinterest in candidates and about many of the items to be included in the resume. There is also good agreement about the appropriate form the resume should take.

The resume is an information sheet. It should be designed in such a way that it gives the expected information in an easy-to-read form. It should contain:

Table 7.4   **Employer Reaction to Resume Data**

Resume Item	Yes, Should Appear	No	No Opinion
Career objective	66%	8%	27%
Extracurricular activities	76%	15%	9%
College(s) attended	76%	3%	20%
College grade-point average	57%	14%	29%
Specific courses taken	57%	23%	20%
Interests and hobbies	53%	11%	37%
Honors/awards	56%	9%	35%
List of references	8%	47%	45%

SOURCE: Beverly Culwell, "Employer Preferences Regarding Resumes and Application Letters," unpublished paper, School of Business, Missouri Southern State College.

1. Name, addresses, and telephone numbers.
2. Career objectives or goals. This is usually the kind of job you are seeking.
3. Educational background. Degree(s), major, minor, special training, and other significant educational experiences are listed with their dates. Grade-point average can be given here also. If yours is not particularly impressive, omit it.
4. Experience. List the jobs you have had, beginning with the most recent and working backward. Include job title, name of employer, specific duties, and scope of responsibilities. List any special accomplishments.
5. Honors. List any special awards, recognitions, and scholarships.
6. Activities. Here you should list service clubs, professional societies, other clubs, and interests. Be sure to list any offices held or other leadership you provided.
7. References. These may be given, but we recommend just saying "References furnished upon request."

Should you put personal information on your resume? There is no correct answer to this question. Research shows that about 26 percent of employers expect to see it, but this is not a good enough reason to include it. It does add a personal touch that allows the employer to get a better picture of you. At the same time, such a section often includes irrelevant material that can be used for illegal discrimination. You will need to make a personal decision about including this information, but we recommend that you don't include it.

We think some good model resumes will help you plan your own resume. Figure 7.2 displays a sample resume that reflects our suggestions. It is a one-page resume of a person who has had considerable experience. Note how John arranges his strengths so that they stand out. Figures 7.3 and 7.4 show alternative ways of arranging information. Figure 7.3 is a res-

```
                          JOHN DOE
                      1111 ZALE AVENUE
                   MOBILE, ALABAMA 36691
                      (205) 000-0000
```

*Neat &
easy
2 read*

```
           JOB OBJECTIVE:  Entry-level management track position
                          personnel staffing.
```

EDUCATION

```
1986-1990      University of South Alabama, Mobile, Alabama
               B.S.: Psychology, minor in economics. GPA: 3.4
               (A = 4). June 1990.
```

SKILLS

ADMINISTRATIVE AND MANAGEMENT SKILLS

— Supervised staff, budgets, and facilities in business and nonprofit organizations.
— Directed programs for University Placement Office, planned workshops, coordinated public relations, and evaluated effectiveness.
— Attended to detail. Challenged by making systems work. Gathered sophisticated information as research assistant, processed orders for meat company, and routed truck logistics (increasing efficiency by 20 percent).

HUMAN RELATIONS AND COMMUNICATION SKILLS

— Able to communicate in speaking and writing--clearly, concisely, and effectively.
— Attentive listener, able to help people "think out loud," reflect on experiences, identify problems, and develop solutions.
— Seasoned interviewer, skills developed as stringer for newspaper.
— Able to develop rapport quickly and easily.

EXPERIENCE

```
                    Ponder Meat Company
                      Mobile, Alabama
```

```
1987-1990      Assistant Manager for Inventories. Enjoyed industrial
               side of management by assisting in maintenance of inven-
               tories, processing orders, and directing transportation
               strategies.
```

```
                      Counselors, Inc.
                      Mobile, Alabama
```

```
1985-1987      Supervisor of Training. Recruited, trained, and super-
               vised staff for program to educate high-risk students
               about self-management skills.
```

```
                  University of South Alabama
                      Mobile, Alabama
```

```
1984-1985      Placement Assistant. Worked part-time for several years
               to present "Career Orientation" workshops to students.
```

```
                    Mobile Press-Register
                      Mobile, Alabama
```

```
1983-1984      Journalist. Worked part-time "stringer," conducting
               interviews, gathering facts, writing news and features.
               Published 50 articles.
```

```
               Other Part-Time and Summer Experiences. Student intern
               in psychology department; tutor in english, math, and
               other subjects, waiter, and busboy.
```

INTERESTS AND ACTIVITIES

```
               Vice-President, senior class, in college.
               Salutatorian in high school.
               Active in Student Council and debate and swim teams
               at the University of Alabama.
```

CREDENTIALS AVAILABLE UPON REQUEST

Figure 7.2 Sample resume.

```
Jane Rodriguez
300 S. Western Street
Mobile, Alabama 36608              Telephone: (205) 000-0000
            JOB OBJECTIVE    Career as a certified public accountant
                             with a well established firm.
```

```
1986-1990    EDUCATION
             University of South Alabama, Mobile, Alabama
             Candidate for B.S. in accounting, June 5, 1990
             GPA 3.78 on a 4.0 scale
             Honors and Awards: Dean's List              4 quarters
                                President's List         3 quarters
                                Scholarship              2 years
                                Nominated for Who's Who Among
                                American Colleges and Universities
                                Selected for service on the Dean's
                                Student Council, College of Business
                                President, Alpha Lambda Delta,
                                1987-1988
                                Member, Beta Alpha Psi, Accounting
                                Honorary
                                Member, Beta Gamma Sigma, Business
                                Honorary
                                Member, Omicron Delta Kappa, Academic
                                Honorary
```

```
             SKILLS

             TECHNICAL

             — Able to analyze and solve accounting problems and
               apply knowledge of accounting practices to a particular
               situation.
             — Can compile, interpret, and present data in an orga-
               nized manner.
             — Able to systemize and catalog information in a logical
               order.
             — Skilled in making mathematical computations without
               the aid of a mechanical device.
```

```
             HUMAN RELATIONS AND COMMUNICATIONS

             — Able to communicate in speaking and writing--clearly,
               concisely, and effectively.
             — Able to manage and direct others.
             — Attentive listener, able to identify problems and
               develop solutions.
```

```
             EXPERIENCE
                             Auburn Water Systems, Inc.
                                  Crestview, Florida
1989         BOOKKEEPER AND OFFICE ASSISTANT--Completed books for
             review by auditors at end of fiscal; prepared books
             for new fiscal; prepared bills; posted payments.
1986-1990    GENERAL WORK EXPERIENCE--Have worked many part-time and
             full-time jobs, learning how to handle various situations
             and communicate effectively with fellow workers.

             INTERESTS AND ACTIVITIES

             Member, Phi Chi Theta; traveling; swimming; sewing;
             cooking; sailing; canoeing.

             PERSONAL DATA

             Single, 21 years old, excellent health.

             REFERENCES AVAILABLE UPON REQUEST
```

Figure 7.3   Sample resume.

Cheryl Robinson

ADDRESSES:

HOME
000 Hillcrest Road
Mobile, Alabama 36609
205-000-0000

COLLEGE
Smith Residence Center
University of South Alabama
205-000-0000

OBJECTIVES: My immediate objective is to obtain a position in business in the field of public relations. My long-range goal is public relations management.

EDUCATION: B.A., University of South Alabama, expected May 1990. Major area: Organizational communication and public relations. Minor area: Marketing.

GPA: Overall: 3.2; Major area: 3.5; Minor area: 3.3 (4.0 scale)

EXPERIENCE:

1988-89 Information clerk, Smith Residence Center. Responsible for answering phone and giving information.

1987-89 Editorial Staff, Vanguard, student weekly newspaper. Researched and wrote news stories and editorials, assisted in layout and design.

Summer 1986 Part-time assistant, public relations, Illinois Bell Telephone Company, Dekalb. Helped to design brochures; wrote a speech for use in the high school; edited in-house newspaper.

1985-86 Part-time salesperson, Hall's Shoe Store, Mobile. Sold men's and women's shoes, took departmental inventory.

Summer 1985 Lifeguard, municipal swimming pool, Mobile. Taught swimming and enforced water safety programs.

HONORS: Dean's list for junior and senior years. Outstanding student in Communicatin Arts, 1988-89.

ACTIVITIES: Member, Public Relations Council of Alabama, Student Chapter, 1986-90, and vice-president 1989-90.

REFERENCES: Furnished upon request.

Figure 7.4 Sample resume.

ume that is structured to call attention to honors and awards. There is a secondary, but clear, focus on Jane's skills as well. Finally, Figure 7.4 shows an emphasis on the applicant's administrative and human relations skills. This applicant is looking for a management position. As you can see from these examples, there are a number of ways to structure a resume and to focus the reader's attention in a specific way.

CONDUCTING THE JOB SEARCH

At some place in the search for employment, you are going to come to the question: "Where should I begin looking for prospective employers?" This might be one of your first considerations, or it might happen later—after you have prepared credentials. There are a wide range of places for you to

Table 7.5   Searching for Job Opportunities

THE SEARCH FOR JOB OPPORTUNITIES AND SUCCESS RATES
 1. Go to professional placement agencies, 1%
 2. Go to state placement offices, 2%
 3. Go to university placement offices, 10%
 4. Go to professional association placement services (AMA, SCA, ASTD), 40%
 5. Check with relatives, 25%
 6. Check with professional associates, former colleagues, and/or friends, 75%
 7. Check with former teachers, 30%
 8. Consult newspaper and magazine advertisements, 25%
 9. Use mass mailing to job lists, 5%
10. Use mass mailing to the Fortune 500 lists, 5%
11. Check with people holding a similar job, 50%
12. Ask for leads from former employers, 5%
13. Check with social acquaintances (from clubs, PTA, scouts, etc.), 10%
14. Attend workshops or seminars, 60% long-term, 15% short-term
15. Take your classes on field trips, 50% long-term, 1% short-term
16. Create your own, 1%
17. Write corporate officers, 5%
18. Ask for leads from fellow students, fraternity brothers, or sorority sisters, 60%
19. Check with voluntary organizations (United Fund, Community Center, etc.),
    15%
20. Work for the local chamber of commerce, 15%
21. Advertise your qualifications in particular journals, magazines, and other
    publications, 2%

SOURCE: Charles J. Stewart and William B. Cash, Jr., *Interviewing: Principles and Practices,*
4th ed. Copyright © 1985 by Wm. C. Brown Publishers, Dubuque, Iowa. All rights reserved.
Reprinted by permission.

consider. Most of us will be overwhelmed—especially if we are in school or
are employed—by the time it takes to conduct a vigorous search. You can
save considerable time by understanding where the most promising places
to look for job opportunities actually are.

The most promising source of jobs depends upon the kind of job for
which you are looking. When you are determined to stay in your local area,
local sources are best. Table 7.5 suggests what local sources seem to be the
most promising. If you are willing to move and are conducting a national
search for a position, you will want to pursue a different set of contact
points.

RESEARCHING THE ORGANIZATION

You will be more impressive than most candidates for a job if you research
the organization carefully. Just as you are impressed when an interviewer
takes the time to study your resume thoroughly, employers are gratified
when you take time to study their organization. Your willingness to put in
the effort means you are interested.

Organizations have been known to ask specific questions about an applicant's knowledge of their firm. One interviewer we know routinely asks:

"Tell me what our company's stock was selling for at yesterday's close." One of our students reported being asked by a paper company representative: "How much paper is produced in our mill across the street?" He knew the answer because he had taken the time to read the trade journal for the paper industry. He got the job too.

There are two types of information you want to know: that which is public and that which only the employees of the organization know. Sources of public information are numerous. Consult your school's placement center; the chamber of commerce; the organization's annual report; *Thomas' Register of American Manufacturers; Moody's Industrial Manual; Standard and Poor's Industrial Index and Register;* Dun and Bradstreet's *Middle Market Directory, Million Dollar Directory, Reference Book; Fortune's Plant and Product Directory; US Industrial Outlook;* and *Business Index*. Also, check to see if the organization's business is the focus of a trade journal.

Here are some questions to answer from these sources:

1. Where are the company's plants, offices, and branches located?
2. How old is the organization and what is its history?
3. What services does the organization offer or what products does it produce? What are its yearly sales?
4. What is the company's growth and potential and its rank within the industry?
5. Who are its competitors in the industry?
6. Answer questions that are specific to a particular field. For example, for a social service agency: What are the agency's objectives, program, and funding sources? For a newspaper: What is the newspaper's circulation, affiliations with other media, competition, and growth history?

Securing private information can be difficult. You may be able to get answers to some of these questions if you do informational interviewing. Check with alumni, friends, stockbrokers, and anyone else who might have experience with the organization. Sometimes a direct telephone call to the personnel department of the organization can get you the information you desire.

These are some questions that will help you secure information:

1. In your opinion, what kind of public image does the organization have?
2. Is there high turnover? If so, why?
3. What educational and training programs does the organization provide?
4. Will the organization help employees return to college for advanced study?

5. What is a realistic starting salary for an entry-level position in your profession?
6. What kind of benefits does the organization offer?
7. What is the organization's policy on transferring people to other locations?
8. What is the general work climate like?
9. Do subordinates participate in decisions?
10. What are the most serious problems faced by people in the part of the organization in which you will be employed?
11. What is the company's stock selling for at yesterday's close?

You can tell by the nature of some of these questions that you might not want to ask them of an interviewer. Yet, often, they are important for your future. We think doing your homework is impressive to interviewers because many candidates don't bother!

PREPARING FOR TYPICAL QUESTIONS

You will be asked questions that you never imagined an interviewer would ask. One of your authors, in an interview with a dean, reported that a graduate school friend was studying communication problems related to talking to the aged. The next question was a surprise, "Why would anyone want to talk to old people anyway? They just want to be left alone." Then the dean paused for a response. What would your response be to such a question?

A partner from a law firm asked a law student another unusual question: "Suppose you were in a building and the top floor was a library with every book ever published in it. The building caught fire and you have the opportunity to save yourself and five books. You must throw the books out the window in order to get out yourself. What five books would you save and why? And some, because they are heavier, will hit first. In what order will these five books hit?" Could you answer this one?

You cannot prepare for every question, but some very good lists are available to help you know what are typical questions. In the previous chapter we presented a list (in Table 6.3) that will be helpful. In addition, we think the list in Table 7.6 will help you be prepared for unexpected questions. We recommend that you practice answering questions from the lists we have provided.

Videotape yourself answering if you can. Perhaps your college or university placement service provides taping service. If you cannot, at least audiotape the answers so that you can analyze both the verbal and nonverbal content of your answers. (Ask a friend to play the role of interviewer.) You may be surprised by what you hear.

For example, taping might reveal a choppy delivery—one that is punctuated by excessive pauses. One of our students found this to be his problem. The interviewer decided that the excessive pauses meant that he was

Table 7.6   Typical Interview Questions

1. What are your long-range and short-range goals and objectives? When and why did you establish these goals? How are you preparing yourself to achieve them?
2. What specific goals, other than those related to your occupation, have you established for yourself for the next ten years?
3. What do you see yourself doing five years from now?
4. What do you really want to do in life?
5. What are your long-range career objectives?
6. How do you plan to achieve your career goals?
7. What are the most important rewards you expect in your business career?
8. What do you expect to be earning in five years?
9. Why did you choose the career for which you are preparing?
10. Which is more important to you, the money or the type of job?
11. What do you consider to be your greatest strengths and weaknesses?
12. How would you describe yourself?
13. How do you think a friend or professor who knows you well would describe you?
14. What motivates you to put forth your greatest effort?
15. How has your college experience prepared you for a business career?
16. Why should I hire you?
17. What qualifications do you have that make you think you will be successful in business?
18. How do you determine or evaluate success?
19. What do you think it takes to be successful in an organization like ours?
20. In what ways do you think you can make a contribution to our organization?
21. What qualities should a successful manager possess?
22. Describe the relationship that should exist between a supervisor and those reporting to him or her.
23. What two or three accomplishments have given you the most satisfaction? Why?
24. Describe your most rewarding college experience.
25. If you were hiring a graduate for this position, what qualities would you look for?
26. Why did you select your college or university?
27. What led you to choose your field or major study?
28. What college subjects did you like best? Why?
29. What college subjects did you like least? Why?
30. If you could do so, how would you plan your academic study differently? Why?
31. What changes would you make in your college or university? Why?
32. Do you have plans for continued study? An advanced degree?
33. Do you think that your grades are a good indication of your academic achievement?
34. What have you learned from participation in extracurricular activities?
35. In what kind of a work environment are you most comfortable?
36. How do you work under pressure?
37. In what part-time or summer jobs have you been most interested?
38. How would you describe the ideal job for you following graduation?
39. Why did you decide to seek a position with this organization?
40. What do you know about our organization?
41. What two or three things are most important to you in your job?
42. Are you seeking employment in an organization of a certain size? Why?

(Continued)

Table 7.6   Typical Interview Questions (*Continued*)

43. What criteria are you using to evaluate the organization for which you hope to work?
44. Do you have a geographical preference? Why?
45. Will you relocate? Does relocation bother you?
46. Are you willing to travel?
47. Are you willing to spend at least six months as a trainee?
48. Why do you think you might like to live in a community in which our organization is located?
49. What major problem have you encountered and how did you deal with it?
50. What have you learned from your mistakes?

We think it would be helpful to be able to answer these additional questions:
51. Did you do the best job you could in school? If not, why not?
52. What kind of boss do you prefer? Why?
53. Describe a typical day at the company for which you worked.
54. What are some important lessons you have learned from jobs you have held?
55. What type of books do you read? What was the last one you read?
56. What kinds of things cause you to lose your temper?
57. Are you a leader? Give an example.
58. Are you a creative person? Give an example.
59. Are you analytical? Give an example.
60. What are the most important books in your field?

SOURCE: Questions 1–50 from *The Northwestern Lindquist-Endicott Report 1988,* by Victor R. Lindquist, The Placement Center, Northwestern University, Evanston, IL.

unsure of himself and his answers. This was merely a speaking pattern, but the interviewer had no way of knowing this. If this were your problem, a little effort would allow you to change the pattern.

Next, analyze your answers, keeping in mind that the organization wants to know that:

1. You have selected it for a good reason.
2. You are reasonably ambitious, but not unrealistic.
3. You are a hard worker.
4. You know your strengths and weaknesses.
5. You can be relied upon to follow through on the job.
6. You have some goals, and they are reasonable.
7. You are trustworthy.
8. You like people and are likable.
9. You get along with people and will "fit" with other employees.
10. You will have the interest of the organization in mind when you act.

Do you provide answers that give evidence of some of these items? For example, telling the interviewer that you have been active in clubs and organizations will say that you probably like people. The fact that you have taken difficult courses and have been successful and that you have carried out special projects in school will show that you are ambitious and probably a hard worker. Judgments that interviewers make are based on speculation. Decisions they make are based on what they think is true—although they may actually be wrong.

An interviewer for a northwestern telephone company actually provided this kind of analysis. After completing a demonstration interview for a class, he said of the interviewee: "I have a feeling that you don't like people and that you are not ambitious and do not like hard work. Let me tell you why I say this. You do not belong, and have not belonged, to any groups or organizations. You have said that you dislike certain courses—all of which are the more difficult courses. And you have quit jobs because too much was required of you for the pay." True or not—the interviewer believed his judgment.

QUESTIONING THE INTERVIEWER

A personnel manager for a small tool manufacturing company said: "One problem with many of the college graduates I interview today is that they have a bad attitude. They come to an interview wanting to know what the company will do for them, rather than telling me what they can do for my company. I'm not interested in hiring that type of person." A manager from a food company agreed. He added: "Yes. They want to know about our retirement benefits. That is so silly as they are unlikely to be with us at retirement anyway."

If you ask about salary, retirement, and other benefits at your initial interview, the interviewer may decide you are a person who is too concerned about what the organization can do for the employee. Many interviewers see this as an inappropriate priority for a candidate. If you ask questions about the organization that could be answered by research, you may also be viewed negatively.

Ask questions that will point to your strengths, show that you have researched the organization, and help you know when you might hear from the interviewer. Ask questions like, "Will I be involved in decisions in my department?" Or ask, "What kind of training and professional development opportunities might I expect as I progress in the organization?" Keep in mind, though, that a personnel manager might not be able to answer specific questions about your area. Also, do not ask so many questions that you appear to be quizzing the interviewer. Here are some questions from which you might select.

1. What are some of the things you have enjoyed most about working for your organization?
2. Will there be a training program or period? If so, what can I expect?

3. If I do well in my initial position, what would be my next step?
4. Is there anything else you would find useful to have in evaluating my qualifications?
5. When might I expect to hear from you about your decision?

The question about time frame can be an important one. It opens the door to a continuing relationship with the interviewer. A call to the interviewer toward the end of the time frame may allow you to find out if the position has already gone to another candidate. Employers operate in different ways. Some may not be planning to fill a position for a month or more; others will make a decision in a couple of weeks. You will want to know when you can quit worrying about a particular position. The time-frame question can provide another advantage. You may prefer a position in one organization but be offered a job in another. The time-frame question provides an opportunity to contact the preferred organization without seeming too anxious.

MANAGING THE INTERVIEW

You might feel a little overwhelmed at this point because there is so much to do to merely be prepared for the interview. Selection interviewing is complex, but you will discover you have gained a good deal of expertise from the study and practice you experience in this course. One of our students recently reported that an interviewer ended the interview by asking: "Where did you learn to interview like this?" The student replied: "I have studied interviewing as a communication major." The interviewer responded: "You are to be congratulated. You handled the interview very well."

In the next several pages, we will help you discover how to manage the interview. We begin by discussing frequent complaints of interviewers. Next, we address the issue of answering illegal questions. Then, we discuss interviewee behavior during the interview. Finally, we offer suggestions for managing the group interview.

Frequent Complaints of Interviewers

Table 7.7 lists the most frequent complaints employers make about interviewees, as reported by the Placement Center at Northwestern University. These complaints can be avoided. The preparation we recommended will allow you to have the information to show that you are prepared and do have appropriate interests and expectations. If you practice interviewing, you will sharpen your communication skills. As you interview, keep these complaints in mind and avoid them.

Table 7.7   Most Frequent Interviewer Complaints about Interviewees

Rank	Complaint
1	Poor personality, manners, lack of poise, confidence, arrogant, egotistical, conceited
2	Poor appearance, lack of neatness, careless dress
3	Lack of enthusiasm, shows little interest, no evidence of initiative, lack of drive
4	Lack of goals and objectives, lack of ambition, poorly motivated, does not know interests, uncertain, indecisive, poor planning
5	Inability to express self well, poor oral expression, poor habits of speech
6	Unrealistic salary demands, overemphasis on money, more interested in salary than opportunity, unrealistic concerning promotion to top jobs
7	Lack of maturity, no leadership potential
8	Lack of extracurricular activities, inadequate reasons for not participating in activities
9	Failure to get information about our company, lack of preparation for the interview, inability to ask intelligent questions
10	Lack of interest in security and benefits, "what can you do for me" attitude
11	Objects to travel, unwilling to relocate

SOURCE: *The Northwestern Lindquist-Endicott Report 1988,* by Victor R. Lindquist, The Placement Center, Northwestern University, Evanston, IL.

Answering Illegal Questions

You are likely to be asked illegal questions.[4] Our students always want to know how to answer them, but there aren't any perfect answers to illegal questions. There is always a risk. You may choose to answer the questions and forget about the fact that they are illegal. If you answer them directly, the employer may actually discriminate against you. On the other hand, you may politely refuse to answer. However, if you avoid answering them, the employer may not hire you because she thinks you are evasive. You will want to do a quick analysis of the interviewer's motives, as best you can, to make a decision about how you want to answer.

Research shows that when most interviewees are presented with an illegal question, they answer it straightforwardly.[5] We also know that typical interviewees experience illegal questions as inappropriate even if they do not understand that the question asked is illegal.[6] These two statements taken together are a bit disturbing and lead to a question. Why do people who are uncomfortable with an illegal question answer it? It seems reasonable to suppose that they believe they have no other option if they are interested in securing employment in the particular organization. While we do not deny that the interviewee is at a disadvantage when asked an illegal question, we do think that there are options other than answering the question directly.

There are actually a range of options to be used as the interviewee sees fit. These options convey messages that range from answering the question

Table 7.8 Questions and Exemplary Responses

1. Terminating the interview
   Example: "It's interesting that your company uses such questions as a basis for hiring. I expect to file a complaint with the Equal Employment Opportunity Commission because you discriminate on an illegal basis.

2. Giving a direct refusal
   Example: "I'm sorry. This is not a question that I am willing to answer."

3. Giving a direct refusal with reason
   Example: "I'm sorry. This is not a question that I am willing to answer because this information is personal."

4. Asking how information relates to job qualifications
   Example: "I am not sure how this question pertains to my qualifications for this job. I'd be happy to answer it if I can understand how it pertains to my qualifications."

5. Telling that information is personal
   Example: "This information is personal. I don't mix my personal life with my professional life. I'd be happy to talk about my job qualifications."

6. Acknowledging concern/asking for information
   Example: "I'm not sure what you want to know by asking this question. Could you tell me what it is you want to know?"

7. Answering perceived concern
   Example: "I take it that your question about my plans for child care is a concern about the likelihood that I may be absent from work when my children are ill. I want to assure you that I see myself as a professional person and will behave in a professionally responsible manner when they are ill."

8. Answering the question and the perceived concern
   Example: "I am married. If you are concerned about how my marital status might affect my staying with the school system, I can assure you that I am a professional and intend to continue working regardless of the events in my personal life.

and the perceived concern to terminating the interview. The strategies we will present here are based on the work of Joann Keyton and Jeff Springston.[7] The assumption for each strategy, except the terminating strategy, is that it is used with the goal of doing the least damage to the interviewee's candidacy.

Three criteria are offered for making a decision about which strategy will work best for you. These are (1) the perceived use of the information, (2) the importance of revealing information to the interviewee, and (3) the desire to secure the position.

Let's examine how these might be used. First, what seems to be the intent of the interviewer? The primary interest here is whether the interviewer seems to want the information in order to discriminate illegally. Sometimes the tone of the interview will allow this judgment to be made. Second, how important is revealing the information? Perhaps, the interviewee may judge that giving the information is not particularly important or objectionable. Third, how important is securing the position? The position may be so important to the interviewee that he or she is willing to risk providing the information.

Table 7.8 presents eight response strategies with exemplary responses. These are meant to serve as a model for you to use in practicing response strategies.

Below are some answers that students have reported using that illustrate these strategies. The first two questions were asked of a woman who was interviewing for a job with an Oregon school system. The last question was asked by the owner of a grocery store in Alabama.

Q: Are you married or single?

A: That's a personal question. I'd be happy to answer any questions about my qualifications.

An alternative answer:

A: If you're concerned about how my marital status might affect my staying with the school system, you should know that I am a professional and intend to continue working regardless of events in my personal life. I am single [or married].

Q: How old are your children? Who will be baby-sitting with them?

A: I don't see how that information would be helpful in evaluating me as an employee, but I have children and have made arrangements for their care.

Alternative answers:

A: I'm not sure what information you want by asking these questions. Could you tell me what it is you want to know?

A: I'm not sure how these questions pertain to my qualifications. I'm, of course, willing to answer any question you'd like to ask about my training or experience.

Q: Do you participate actively in a church?

A: My religious activities are personal. I do not mix my professional life with my personal life. I'd prefer to talk about my job qualifications.

Alternative answers:

A: I'm not sure how this question relates to my qualifications. [Then you might say] I prefer to pass on that one; [or] I'd prefer to tell you more directly what you want to know. [You could stop here.] I'd be happy to answer questions about my training and experience.

A: [If you are sure you do not want the job and would like to put a stop to this kind of questioning, you might say] This is a highly illegal question. It is interesting that your company uses such questions as a basis for hiring. I expect to file a complaint with the Equal Employment Opportunity Commission because you discriminate on an illegal basis.

Sometimes an interviewer may ask an illegal question with the intent of getting at job-related information. An interviewer for an insurance company once asked about family ties. She was trying to determine what social bases the interviewee had for finding clients and for selling insurance. If the interviewee understands the basis for what is being asked, an answer that will provide the information without giving out illegal information can be given.

There are many other illegal questions that might be asked. Remember that the answers to illegal questions asked by inexperienced interviewers may not serve as information used in making hiring decisions.[8] Sometimes, the interviewer is just trying to be friendly and does not understand the law. You have to decide what the situation is and then formulate an answer. These examples are meant to serve as guidelines—you need to decide how to answer based on what your goals are and what you feel comfortable in doing.

Abiding by the Rules

Candidates are often turned down because they do not observe the rules of behavior rather than because they do not have appropriate qualifications. We provide a discussion of rules that you will want to follow as you engage in the interview.

Be at the interview ahead of the appointed time.   Plan to arrive at least fifteen minutes ahead of the time set for the interview.[9] You may want to take care of personal needs, have difficulty finding the personnel office, or even get stuck in traffic. Fifteen minutes is not much time, but enough to handle most last-minute details. If you are late for the interview, that is one strike against you. Most interviewers consider promptness very important.

Dress appropriately.   You need to dress in a manner that would be appropriate for the work situation in which you would find yourself. If you are uncertain, it is reasonable to err on the conservative side.[10] What we mean by this is that it is better to slightly overdress—dress up more than you need to—than to underdress. Remember also that proper hair length, appropriate use of colognes and perfumes, and other grooming are important concerns. Incidentally, we think that it's good advice to remove any outside clothes—heavy coats, hats, and the like—before you enter the office for an interview.

Be friendly and responsive.   Smile. Try to show that you are enjoying the conversation. Use gestures in your conversation that are appropriately smooth and emphatic. Observe someone in a lively conversation and you will understand what we mean. Make sure that you get the interviewer's name right, and use it once or twice—*Mr. Smith* and not *John*.

Do not take over the interview. Most interviewers expect to control the interview; let them. Also, don't interrupt the interviewer—that's very rude. Do not be surprised, however, if a few interviewers expect you to carry the interview. We've found that such people are in the minority. Look for cues that might signal this. Broad, general questions are often a sign of this situation.

Give more than one- or two-word answers to questions. Most interviewers will want you to talk. Very short answers show a lack of thoroughness. This may be interpreted as a lack of preparation. The interviewer may think that you have difficulty carrying on a conversation. So, give the interviewer something with which to work. On the other hand, do not drone on forever with meaningless chatter.

Avoid the negative. Do not criticize your present or past employers. Think, instead, of positive reasons for leaving your job. You might say, "I left because the job did not allow me the opportunity to grow professionally." If the situation was bad, you can mention it, but don't dwell on it or explain it in detail unless the interviewer insists.

Suppose the situation at one of your jobs was such that you were terminated. Sometimes interviewees believe that if the interviewer knew of the termination, it might damage their chances of being hired. Often they want to hide the fact. Our advice is that such an effort is fruitless at best—and probably counterproductive. Many people get terminated, and that fact suggests, or should suggest, that there is no disgrace involved. Moreover, every personnel director, and almost every interviewer, knows how to find out about a candidate's successes or failures on the job.

We advise you not to hide your firing or dismissal. You can and should make a positive statement if possible. You might say, as one of our graduates did: "I was terminated because I disagreed with my boss and didn't have enough sense to present my case and quit arguing. I've learned a lot from the incident, and I think I've become a better employee because of it." The student got the job. The risk you expose yourself to in not telling is great. Suppose you hide the firing and the interviewer discovers it later. That discovery is likely to yield an attitude that you cannot be trusted.

Be prepared to sell yourself. The interviewer usually will ask what training you have had to prepare you to do your job. Do not brag. Say that you have had some good educational and work experiences and that you have been successful. Give some examples of your success. Mention that you believe you can do the job because of these successful experiences that relate to the job.

One of our students used her part-time job at a fast-food restaurant to sell herself. While interviewing for a marketing position, she was asked:

"Are you a leader?" She replied: "I think I am. While I worked for McDonald's, they were short of team leaders because someone was on vacation. I was asked to fill in until the person returned. She did return, but left two months later. I was asked to take the job because of my good performance as a temporary replacement. I think this speaks to my ability to lead people well."

Show an interest in the company.   Do careful research about the company. If there is an opportunity to display that knowledge, use it. You may be asked why you selected to interview with the organization. You may even be asked to tell the interviewer something about the company. These are opportunities to show your interest. Plan and be ready for them. Also, tell the employer that you want to work for the organization (if you do) and why. Do not beg for a job, however.

Common sense and simple courtesy suggest these additional rules:

Do not use profanity or slang—even if the interviewer does.
Do not continue talking while the interviewer is studying your resume.
Do not try to interpret items on the resume unless asked to do so.
Do not lie.
Do not look at your watch to keep track of the time.
Do not talk about salary in the first interview until and unless the interviewer raises the issue.
Do not appear to be too interested in telephone conversations that might take place during the interview.
Do not fiddle with hair or clothing.
Do not read papers on the interviewer's desk or pick up things on the desk.
Do not smoke.
Do not drink alcoholic beverages if the interview takes place in a restaurant.

Take a few notes if you want.   There may be some information you will want later. Be sure it is accurate; write it down. But do so courteously. You might ask, "Do you mind if I take a note or two?" You can also write some of the questions you will ask on the same pad. When you ask when the interviewer might get in touch with you, you may want to write the information down so you will remember it.

Handling the Group Interview

A different kind of interview that is used by some organizations is the group interview. The personnel department arranges for several candidates to be present at the same time. Then these people are interviewed as a group. This has several advantages for the organization, though it can be unnerving for the interviewees. The purpose of such an interview seems to be very much like the technique referred to as the "stress interview." The organization wants to discover how the interviewees will handle themselves in a very stressful situation, what personality characteristics will emerge (who will take charge, or who is willing to be thoughtful and cautious but assertive under pressure), or how the several interviewees vie for control of the situation.

While this type of interview allows for comparisons and contrasts, it is not useful, in our opinion, because it produces a kind of tension in candidates not likely to be encountered in normal working situations. If you can avoid a group interview, we recommend that you do so. If you cannot—and there are situations in which you will not be able to—then here are some techniques you can use to manage the situation.

1. Ask the interviewer—or some representative—before the interview why the organization uses this technique. Most of the time the organization knows why it is using the technique; and if you can discover the reason, you will be that much ahead. You might say something like: "Mr. Jones, would you mind telling me what you are attempting to discover by using this method of interviewing? It would help me greatly to know how to respond to the situation." Such a statement is a take-charge statement. It shows that you are reflective, that you like to plan ahead, and that you are concerned about your image and like to live up to expectations. Even if the organization's representative declines to answer the question, you are still likely to earn some respect from such an insightful cross-examination.
2. Prepare as you would normally prepare to answer the typical questions as suggested in the first part of this chapter.
3. Be doubly sure to do organizational research. The other candidates may not do the research, and this will set you apart from them.
4. Listen carefully to the questions. Under these circumstances you do not want to be the person who asks that the interviewer repeat the question.
5. Pay close attention to what other candidates say. You may be asked to react to what they have said. If you have not been listening, then you will not be able to respond. Be sure you have paper so that you can take notes.
6. Be careful about the questions you ask. If you can think of an especially good question or two, be sure to word them carefully before the session. Write them down so that you have them ready and look for opportune moments to bring them up during the interview.

By using these suggestions, you may be able to turn a difficult situation into an advantageous one.

Ethics and Responsibilities in Interviewing

Three ethical guidelines should be observed by interviewees in the selection interview. First, *interviewees should not intentionally misrepresent themselves or their credentials*. Unethical behavior in this area might range from exaggerating about some skill or ability to lying about credentials and employment history. Claim all that you have done and present it in as positive light as possible.

The ethical decision often arises when there is damaging information in the interviewee's educational or employment record. Perhaps the person received low marks in school or was terminated from a position. Ethical behavior dictates that the interviewee tell the truth. Interviewees who have experienced such unfortunate circumstances should plan how they will answer questions regarding this part of their life, rather than intentionally deceive.

Second, *the interviewee has a responsibility to prepare for the interview so as not to waste the interviewer's time and resources*. The interviewee may be an ideal candidate but may be ill prepared for an interview. Lack of preparation, if noticed, will undoubtedly lead to rejection of the candidate. Thus, the interviewee has wasted time and resources of the organization. We believe this violates the ethical principle of justice.

Finally, *interviewees should not schedule interviews for positions that they do not intend to take*. This guideline is especially important if the interview is scheduled in a placement center, but it is important for on-site interviews too. Generally, the number of interviews an organization can schedule is limited. Scheduling an interview for a job that is not of interest can violate the principle of justice. Others may be deprived of an interview because no time slots are available to them.

APPLICANT'S QUESTIONS FOR EVALUATION

An applicant can learn much about interviewing through careful analysis of how he or she did with each interview. This must be done within the context of the specific interviewer, because some interviewers are not very well trained themselves. You might be doing the best job possible, and still be frustrated if the interviewer is inexperienced. With this caution in mind, ask these questions to help you evaluate your interview experience.

1. Were my materials—cover letter, resume, application form— adequately prepared?
2. Did I adequately research the organization? Did I make use of this knowledge in the interview?
3. Did I check out my dress with someone who could help me judge its appropriateness?

4. What situations during the interview made me uncomfortable?
5. Were there any surprise questions? How did I handle these?
6. What questions did I not handle well? How can I improve my answers?
7. Where were there opportunities to sell myself? Did I make use of these?
8. Did I give examples of my abilities where appropriate?
9. Did I help the employer understand what I could do for the organization?
10. Did I ask questions of the interviewer that allowed me to show appropriate interest (and abilities if appropriate)?
11. Did I obtain enough information about the position and organization to allow me to make a decision?

FORMULATING A CAREER PLAN

A Career Plan

Career planning is a concept that makes good sense to most of us. Yet we think that some young people do not do very much career planning because they do not know how. Our purpose in this book is not to explore every issue but to give you the basics so you will be knowledgeable about how to best undertake the process.

Manuel London and Stephen A. Stumpf[11] present an excellent set of suggestions for guiding you in a career plan. We describe what they suggest are the important elements in such a program. These are establishing a career path, seeking feedback, having realistic expectations, and managing information.

Establish a career path. The first step in a career plan is to define work activities that you are capable of doing. You may determine these by examining what your educational training is or what you do on your job. Look for logical extensions of what you are now capable of doing. For example, if you find that people respond well to your suggestions, you might project that you have potential leadership skills.

Next, identify job families that relate to your capabilities. A career counselor can help you with this task. A career family includes jobs that follow a logical progression so that they develop your potential by giving you an opportunity to develop the necessary skill for the next level. If you are employed, your organization will probably have someone in the personnel department who can help. Your first job is an important one because it gives you access to a career family. Research suggests further that it is important that this job be the one that provides challenge, opportunity for growth, and independence.[12]

Finally, decide what it will take to get you through each step of your plan. Determine for each level in the plan what kinds of education, training, and skills will be necessary to achieve your aim. You may be able to develop a two-column job analysis as suggested for the recruitment process earlier in Chapter 6. If you are in an organization that has positions similar to the ones you expect to take, look for role models that you can observe as you look toward advancement.

Solicit feedback on your performance.   Performance appraisal literature suggests that feedback on your performance is important to your success.[13] Feedback helps you understand what it will take to enhance your performance—the kind of behavior that is likely to be rewarded. Feedback will help you have a sense of accomplishment and, thus, motivate you to strive. Moreover, feedback will help you know if your plan is moving you in the right direction. You may want to reevaluate your plan if feedback tells you that you have been unable to develop certain necessary skills.

Adopt realistic expectations.   Goal theory suggests that the most realistic plan will be one that is achievable, but moderately difficult.[14] A plan that embraces easily attainable goals will not be as effective in providing motivation as one that is moderately difficult. On the other hand, a plan that is too ambitious very quickly becomes a source of discouragement. Many factors can interrupt a career plan—for example, suppose someone ahead of you was not promoted as you expected—and lead to frustration.

A more realistic plan is likely to be generated if you can involve either a mentor or your supervisor in the process. A person who is close enough to you to observe your work is likely to be able to help you more realistically evaluate your performance and help you monitor your progress. Your supervisor can help you understand what standards it will take and what job family is most realistic for you.

Manage information.   Your ability to problem-solve about your career is closely tied to the kind and quality of information you have for making decisions. You must gather relevant information carefully and use it in the process of problem solving. Here are some records you should keep to help you:

> Assessment of your skills
> Past and current performance evaluations
> Career interest test results
> Description of the next assignment you anticipate
> Statements of policies and procedures for filling new positions
> Available training programs
> Information on career paths

Implementing a Career Plan

The important elements in implementing a career plan are pictured in Figure 7.5. They are joint planning sessions with your supervisor or mentor if pos-

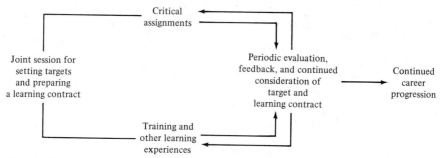

Figure 7.5   A model of career development. [*Manuel London and Stephen A. Stumpf,* Managing Careers *(Reading, MA: Addison-Wesley, 1982), p. 164.*]

sible, critical job assignments, training and learning experiences, regular evaluation and feedback, systematic rewards, and thorough and timely career progression.

A career development counselor or your supervisor can help you learn to implement this model by helping you engage in certain activities that will move you along the path. If you follow this model, you see that it involves setting targets (understanding the skills required, having job descriptions, preparing learning contracts to specify training plans, setting goals), obtaining developmental activities (training, role models, education), experiencing critical job assignments (challenging, but doable, with clear expectations), receiving clear feedback and evaluation (periodic review of goals and progress), and obtaining reassignment. The model works best for you when your organization has a clear commitment to career planning and development. Otherwise, you can use the model, without the aid of your supervisor, to guide your own efforts toward career development.

SUMMARY

In this chapter we examined selection interviewing from the applicant's perspective. We pointed out the importance for the interviewee of (1) gathering information about the job and problems related to it through informational interviewing and library research, (2) doing a self-analysis to gain understanding of his or her strengths and weaknesses, (3) preparing a cover letter and resume that conform to the expectation of interviewers, (4) researching the organization by conducting interviews and library research, (5) preparing to answer typical questions by rehearsing answers and by looking critically at his or her taped responses to these questions, and (6) preparing a list of questions to ask an employer.

Next we addressed issues related to managing the actual interview. Interviewees ought to understand what interviewers find to be inadequate in interviewees. They should handle illegal questions tactfully but firmly. They should also follow the guidelines we provide for appropriate interview behavior. Finally, they should use the techniques suggested for managing possibly stressful group interviews to turn them into an advantage. We also provided questions that an interviewee can use to evaluate his or her performance.

Finally, we addressed career planning. Steps in career planning include establishing a career path, soliciting feedback on performance, adopting realistic expectations, and managing information.

NOTES

[1]Thomas Reardon, "Preselection: How Students Prescreen Employers," *Journal of College Placement, 40* (Winter 1979), 53–55.

[2]Robert Gifford, Cheuk Fan Ng, and Margaret Wilkinson, "Non-verbal Cues in the Employment Interview: Links between Applicant Qualities and Interviewer Judgment," *Journal of Applied Psychology, 70* (1985), 735.

[3]Edward Rogers, "Elements of Efficient Job Hunting," *Journal of College Placement, 40* (Fall 1979), 55–58.

[4]Jeff K. Springston and Joann Keyton, "The Prevalence of Potentially Illegal Questioning in Pre-Employment Screening," in S. J. Bruno (ed.), *Global Implications for Business Communications: Theory, Technology and Practice,* Proceedings of the Annual Meeting of the Association for Business Communication (1988), pp. 247–263.

[5]W. D. Siegfried and K. Wood, "Reducing College Student's Compliance with Inappropriate Interview Requests: An Educational Approach," *Journal of College Student Personnel, 14* (1983), 66–71.

[6]Siegfried and Wood.

[7]Joann Keyton and Jeff K. Springston, "I Don't Want to Answer That! A Response Strategy Model for Potentially Discriminatory Questions," paper presented at the annual meeting of the Speech Communication Association, San Francisco, November 1989.

[8]If you wish further counsel on answering illegal questions, see Fredric M. Jablin and Craig D. Tengler, "Facing Discrimination in On-Campus Interviews," *Journal of College Placement, 42* (1982), 57–61.

[9]Gifford, Ng, and Wilkinson.

[10]A research report provides data that women might consider in selecting clothing for the interview. Sandra Forsythe and her associates discovered a positive correlation between a particular costume that they called "masculine." This costume consisted of a beige, tailored suit with a blazer jacket and a rust blouse with a narrow bow at the top. See Sandra Forsythe, Mary Frances Drake, and Charles E. Cox, "Influence of Applicant's Dress on Interviewer's Selection Decisions," *Journal of Applied Psychology, 70* (1985), 374–378.

[11]Manuel London and Stephen A. Stumpf, *Managing Careers* (Reading, MA: Addison Wesley, 1982), pp. 137–147.

[12]Joseph A. Raelin, "First-Job Effects on Career Development," *Personnel Administrator, 28* (August 1983), 71–92.

[13]D. R. Ilgen, C. D. Fisher, and M. S. Taylor, "Consequences of Individual Feedback on Behavior in Organizations," *Journal of Applied Psychology, 64* (1979), 349–371.

[14]R. B. Zajonc and J. J. Taylor, "The Effects of Two Methods of Varying Group Task Difficulty on Individual Performance," *Human Relations, 16* (1963), 359–368.

A SELECTION INTERVIEW FOR ANALYSIS

This simulated selection interview was conducted by two communication majors at the University of South Alabama. Joey Wilkinson has applied for the position of district manager. Cheryl South is the store manager.

1. Interviewer: Joey Wilkinson?

2. Interviewee: Yes.

3. Interviewer: Hi, I'm Cheryl South. Nice to meet you.

4. Interviewee: Nice to meet you.

5. Interviewer: I see here you are applying for our assistant manager position.

6. Interviewee: That's correct.

7. Interviewer: I would like to start this interview off with a little about yourself, just to kind of relax the atmosphere and get things going.

8. Interviewee: Okay. So you want me to tell you a little about myself?

9. Interviewer: Yes, why don't we go ahead and start with that.

10. Interviewee: I'm currently twenty-two years old. I'm enrolled at the University of South Alabama. I'm majoring in history and minoring in communications, and I have got a 3.2 overall average. When I'm not doing schoolwork, I've got a part-time job in a local restaurant here in Mobile...where I am a waiter. I consider myself a very hardworking individual and very efficient. I am well organized, and overall I consider myself to be a very good worker, giving the best I can give. As far as hobbies and things, I like photography, bicycling, and just about any kind of sport. I really like baseball.

11. Interviewer: I see you are majoring in communications. I majored in communications.

12. Interviewee: I'm minoring in it.

13. Interviewer: Oh, minoring, excuse me. Okay. I see. You are majoring in history.

14. Interviewee: That's correct.

15. Interviewer: It's not clear to me, with your major in history, why you are applying for this job.

16. Interviewee: The reason why I am applying for this job is because, number one, I see it as a good opportunity, and, number two, I have good experience in retail already. I worked about 3½ years at a couple of retail stores, and I gained a great deal of knowledge of what is required in retail jobs. I also gained a great deal of experience with the job itself and working in that field. Basically, I consider this a good opportunity for me to get employment in a good corporation and develop some skills that come pretty naturally to me.

17. Interviewer: What are some of your long-range plans?

18. Interviewee: My goal right now is to pursue a retail-type job, because I do have some experience in it from the past, and if I don't use that experience, it will be wasted. As far as long-range goals, I would like to continue my education. Possibly go to graduate school and pursue a degree in history with emphasis later on maybe doing some teaching in college.

19. Interviewer: Okay. I was running over your resume and one of the things that sparked my interest was the partnership you formed in the summer of '86. Could you tell me a little bit about that?

20. Interviewee: Sure. What I did was form a partnership with a friend of mine to do lawn work. For a period I was unemployed, while the store I was working in was being remodeled. So my friend and I formed a partnership and passed out brochures all though the city and conducted our own research on the type of yards we wanted to take, whether residential or business. We received responses from the brochures we passed out. We developed a clientele and basically did yard work after that and supported ourselves through the summer. It was hard work, but it was a valuable experience.

21. Interviewer: That's great. It shows a lot of enthusiasm. I noticed on your resume that you didn't mention anything about inventory, unloading, or pricing. Did you ever take a formal inventory?

22. Interviewee: Yes. One of the jobs that I didn't list on my resume was a three-day job in a clothing store, where you were called in specifically to do an inventory, so I do have some experience in inventory on that level. I can see it is very difficult work, but I thought I did a very good job. It is a very important type of job. Also, one of the retail stores I worked in, we had inventory each year. The first year I was there we actually did the inventory ourselves. We counted each item, and we listed inventory. As far as the pricing you asked about, that is something we did daily. We had merchandise come in every day; and if it wasn't priced, we priced it. We had to work up the price using whatever procedure was necessary.

23. Interviewer: Well, we would train you to do the inventory here. I do realize that different shops use different inventory methods. But it is good that you have some past experience. That way you wouldn't be without any information.

24. Interviewee: No. It won't be a mystery to me.

25. Interviewer: It will be a lot quicker training.

26. Interviewee: Yes.

27. Interviewer: I noticed on your resume, and you had mentioned at the beginning of the interview, that you are working at Quincy's Restaurant.

28. Interviewee: That's right.

29. Interviewer: Tell me a little bit about your job there. You specified that you work with customer services a good bit. I would like to get an idea of how you handle customer service.

30. Interviewee: Well, our main duty revolves around helping customers. When they come into the restaurant, we are responsible for seating them, bringing their food, making sure their drinks are filled, and taking care of anything else they may need. So the job itself centers on what we can do for the customers when they come into the restaurant. It's not filled with little tasks where you clean this or move that or you set up. It's more of what you can do for someone who is eating. We are not there to talk to the customer very much, though we do stress a certain amount of public relations. We are mainly concerned with keeping the customer happy at all cost.

31. Interviewer: What type of approach do you feel works for you when there may be a problem with a customer or when someone just gives you a smart-aleck answer.

32. Interviewee: Well, it depends upon the situation. Most of the time we have been instructed that if we have problems with a customer, the best thing to do is not try to handle it ourselves. I'm not in a management position; therefore, if I take the responsibility and I deal with the situation badly, then it's going to reflect badly upon me. What I try to do is find an assistant manager on the floor, who is trained to deal with a customer and has the authority to say if the meal was bad and give a free meal. Whatever the situation may be, I try to go and get higher help. I'm not saying that I can't handle it, but there are proper channels to go through.

33. Interviewer: Right. I also see that you have worked with registers. It's very, very rarely that assistant managers have to work with registers, but sometimes when it gets to be busy or somebody gets sick and doesn't come in that day, we do have to put assistant managers on registers. What type of register do you have experience with? What's the latest type of register you have used?

34. Interviewee: The most modern I've been trained on is computer-operated. A lot of the assistant managers where I've worked didn't have to know how to work the register per se. They did, however, have to understand how the register operated, because they would have to override if there was a problem. Cashiers don't have the authority to correct a mistake that involves a large amount of money.

35. Interviewer: Well, our policy is that the assistant manager and manager are the only people that can correct a cashier's mistakes, and they need to know how to do it.

36. Interviewee: Okay.

37. Interviewer: This is a basic question that I ask everybody. What were the reasons for leaving your past jobs? It's interesting to us. I would like to know if, perhaps, there were any problems—if you have been fired from any of the jobs or if you just left most of them on your own.

38. Interviewee: I have never been fired from a job.

39. Interviewer: Good.

40. Interviewee: Most of the time I quit my jobs to gain more work experience. In my resume, you will notice I did work at a couple of jobs for several years. I worked at Zayers Corporation for about three years. It was a good job for me, and it worked in with my schedule. The people were good to work for, and it gave me good experience. Toward the end, though, it didn't work in well—with my schedule or my goals. I had to work long hours, and I also wanted to gain more experience. That's why I pursued other interests.

41. Interviewer: Well, I have to tell you, your resume looks impressive. You have a lot of experience; you aren't new. You really would need very little training. However, we have some stores in some other states, and since you are still in school, it might be a problem to travel. But if we did need you to travel during holidays or maybe a trip on the weekend to help out the other stores, could you do this?

42. Interviewee: That would not be a problem as long as you would be able to work around my schedule. And I'll be graduating within the next year, so it would not be a problem for long.

43. Interviewer: The last question I would like to ask is, what are your feelings about salary?

44. Interviewee: As far as salary, it depends upon the corporation. A lot of times corporations have a set range for each job category. I feel certain South Alabama has a system like that, so you already have a set salary range for assistant managers. I feel with my experience I'm worth a little bit more than the bottom of the range, but I would consider negotiating. I feel that $1500 to $2000 above the base of the range would be fair because of the past experience I have.

45. Interviewer: That's definitely reasonable. And we could review your work after a certain period of time to see how you are doing.

46. Interviewee: That's what I had intended. I would definitely like a review in about six months or a year, whatever is considered appropriate.

47. Interviewer: Good. One thing I would like to explain to you concerns moving from the position of assistant manager to the position of manager. We would hire you for the position of assistant manager. However, we will be moving a number of people around since we are opening new stores. We will have to send some of our managers from the stores we already have to new stores. You might find that you would be thrown into the manager position sooner than you were hoping for. I think you could handle the position. What would you think of being trained for assistant manager and having to become manager?

48. Interviewee: Well, first I believe it wouldn't take me very long to become accustomed to doing a manager's job, and I believe I could handle the job. The key to it, I believe, would be the training. I wouldn't want to be thrown into a situation where I was expected to know things and not have the training for it. A manager is expected to do a large variety of things. If he goes in unprepared, in the end he is going to be the one who suffers, and I don't want that to happen to me.

49. Interviewer: The company agrees with you. You would definitely be trained; it would be our loss if you weren't. Well, that is all I have to ask you. Is there anything you have to ask me?

50. Interviewee: I have about three questions I would like to ask. Would it be OK for me to continue my education along with pursuing the assistant manager's job?

51. Interviewer: Absolutely, absolutely. We also have seminars and meetings we like to send our managers and assistant managers to. We think that the more they can learn, the more we can gain. So, definitely your education is very important.

52. Interviewee: Well, that definitely helps out. One more thing: Is there any material or past records from my previous jobs that I could send you that could help you evaluate me better?

53. Interviewer: Well, if there is anything that you may not have put in your resume such as previous jobs or maybe special accomplishments, we would like to know about these. Give us as much information as you can. Is there anything else?

54. Interviewee: Just one more thing—when can I expect to hear from you?

55. Interviewer: I have several applications to go over, so I would say in about two weeks.

56. Interviewee: That sounds good to me.

57. Interviewer: Thank you for coming.

58. Interviewee: I would like to thank you for giving me the time.

59. Interviewer: No problem.

EXPERIENCES

1. Develop a resume that you might use to apply for a position. If you have not had extensive working experience, do not worry about it. Just include what you can to represent yourself as you are now. Bring copies of the resume to class to share with other members, and examine their resumes. Then discuss the following questions:
   a. What features of the resumes were attractive to you?
   b. What features seemed to control eye movement and attention?
   c. Do you think that some resumes would be easier than others for an interviewer to use? What are the differences?

2. Suppose you were going to interview the person whose resume you found most attractive. Make a list of questions you would ask this person. Now tell how the resume contributed to the questions you selected.

3. Two or three pairs of students should role-play an interview while the remainder of the class observes. Then discuss as a class the following questions:
   a. How effective were the questions asked by the interviewer and interviewee? Why do you think these were effective?
   b. How successfully did the interviewer guide the exchange? Did the interviewee have any influence on guiding the exchange?
   c. What suggestions would you make to the interviewee to improve the performance?

4. Review the lists of questions found in Chapters 6 and 7. Pick out the five most difficult questions to ask a classmate. In class, select dyads and ask the questions. Consider the effectiveness of the answers as well as ways of improving them.

5. Identify the two illegal questions that you believe would be most difficult to answer. Share with the class how you might go about answering these questions.

RECOMMENDED READINGS

Babbitt, Laurie, and Fredric M. Jablin, "Characteristics of Applicants' Questions and Employment Screening Outcomes," *Human Communication Research, 11* (1985), 507–535.

Bolles, Richard N., *What Color Is Your Parachute? A Practical Manual for Job Hunters and Career-Changes* (Berkeley, CA: Ten Speed Press, 1990).

Einhorn, Lois J., Patricia Hays Bradley, and John E. Baird, Jr., *Effective Employment Interviewing* (Glenview, IL: Scott, Foresman, 1982).

Sears, Rosalie, "Nonverbal Communication in the Employment Interview: A Review of the Literature," *Indiana Speech Journal, 18* (1986), 20–31.

Stanat, Kirbey W., *Job Hunting Secrets & Tactics* (Milwaukee, WI: Westwind Press, 1977).

CHAPTER 8

THE PERFORMANCE
APPRAISAL
INTERVIEW

OBJECTIVES

After reading this chapter, you should be able to:

Cite specific purposes of a performance appraisal interview.

Describe these approaches to performance appraisal interviews—tell and sell, tell and listen, and problem solving—and explain when they might be adequate.

Identify several strategies likely to produce a positive climate for the performance appraisal interview.

Explain the techniques critical to employee-centered problem solving.

Create and implement a plan to conduct an employee-centered strategy in appraisal interviewing.

Develop and implement a plan for participating, as an employee, in an appraisal interview.

Pose ethical considerations for the performance appraisal interview.

The performance appraisal interview provides an opportunity to motivate an employee to achieve his or her potential. It presents a chance for the supervisor and employee to work together to celebrate the employee's performance strengths. It also gives an opportunity to discover ways to redirect non-productive energy into rewarding achievements. One of the most difficult types of interview for both parties involved is the performance appraisal. And herein lies one reason that the promises of celebration and renewal are not fully realized as often as they might be. The participants need to better understand the performance appraisal interview process and be able to implement behaviors that will increase the likelihood of productive outcomes.

This chapter has as its aim helping participants know how to make performance appraisal interviews more productive. We begin by addressing the role of the interviewer. In this section we discuss the processes of planning and managing the interview. Next, we turn to the role of the interviewee. Here we present information to help the interviewee prepare for and communicate in the interview. Then, we discuss a special case of performance appraisal—the disciplinary interview. Finally, we look at ethics and responsibilities in performance appraisals.

THE INTERVIEWER'S PLANNING

For the interviewer, planning for the interview begins with establishing and selecting an orientation to the interview. Then, legal requirements must be reviewed and met. Next, performance is measured and performance goals set when appropriate. Finally, the interview structure is planned.

Setting the Purpose

A decision about the general purpose of a performance appraisal interview is an easy one to make. Most people agree that the performance appraisal interview has as its aim communicating an evaluation of the employee's performance. Yet when specific purposes are posed, there is far less agreement. Our research has identified these fourteen specific purposes.[1]

1. To help the employee do the job better
2. To give the employee a clear picture of how well he or she is doing
3. To build a stronger, closer relationship with the employee
4. To develop practical plans for improvement
5. To recognize employee accomplishments
6. To communicate the need for improvement
7. To counsel the employee and provide help
8. To discover what the employee is thinking
9. To let the employee know what is expected
10. To set objectives for future performance
11. To warn or threaten the employee
12. To reveal the employee's ideas, feelings, and/or problems
13. To discover the aspirations of the employee
14. To determine training needs

Begin the activity of setting goals by examining this list. Which of these are important goals for your interview? Then consider what additional goals are relevant because of the particular circumstances. Once you have completed this assessment, organize your thinking about these goals by classifying them as employee self-development goals and organizational goals. A *self-development goal* is one that seeks to increase the ability of the employee to cope successfully with work-related problems. For example, the interviewer may wish to help the interviewee learn how to be a better problem solver. An *organizational goal* is one that relates to setting performance standards. For example, the interviewer may wish to set a production goal. This classification of goals makes it easier to visualize them.

Choosing an Orientation to the Appraisal Interview

There are a number of orientations to the appraisal interview, each of which centers on a view of how employees are motivated and what is an appropriate supervisor-employee relationship. Some of these views seem to be more productive than others. We base our criteria for judgment of productivity on whether the orientation is likely to meet the two overall goals we suggested above, self-development goals and organizational goals.

Norman Maier suggests three orientations to performance appraisal interviews from which he has formulated three approaches.[2]

1. *Tell and sell.* The supervisor communicates the evaluation and then persuades the employee to improve performance. This plan assumes that the employee is willing and able to improve weaknesses if they are pointed out; the employee believes that the supervisor is qualified to do the evaluation; and the employee appreciates being given advice. Maier claims that the tell-and-sell approach is most useful for the new employee who does not know how to improve.

2. *Tell and listen.* The supervisor communicates the evaluation and then encourages the employee to release defensive feelings. No particular attempt is made to discuss a plan of action, however. The assumption is that the employee will improve if the feelings of defensiveness and resistance are relieved. Maier suggests that change is brought about because the employee feels accepted by the supervisor.

3. *Problem solving.* This approach requires the supervisor to listen and reflect feelings and ideas, explore by asking questions, and summarize. The supervisor stimulates and encourages the employee to grow and develop. Problem solving as conceived by Maier "has *no provision for communicating the appraisal* [our emphasis here], and indeed it may be unessential for this purpose. If the appraisal is required for other purposes, it may be desirable to delay making it until *after* the interview."[3] This philosophy is based on the assumptions that the supervisor can help the employee grow without talking about performance shortcomings and that mutual discussion of job-related problems leads to improved performance.

These three proposals do not meet the criteria we set for orientations to performance appraisal interviews. Specifically, none of these meet both employee self-development and organizational needs. The tell-and-sell approach does not consider employee development to be important, and the tell-and-listen approach does not make any attempt to meet organizational needs. On the other hand, Maier's problem-solving approach comes closest to meeting both these needs, but—because it makes no provision for conveying the appraisal—it does not satisfy organizational needs.[4]

An approach that shows promise is the General Electric Work Planning and Performance Review Program. This program grew out of the research of John R. P. French, Jr., Emanuel Kay, and Herbert H. Meyer.[5] The essential ingredient of the approach is periodic meetings between manager and employee. In these meetings, the two talk about daily work activities, focusing on planning work, reviewing progress toward goals, and engaging in mutual problem solving with respect to any difficulties they discover. This process does not involve formal ratings, but does require the supervisor to keep notes about the meetings for the employee's record. Discussion about salary increases is kept separate from discussion of performance issues. A separate formal interview is designated for salary discussion.

We believe that the basic idea adopted by French and his associates has merit for planning performance appraisal interviews. This kind of participative mutual problem solving and planning has promise for meeting both employee self-development and organizational goals.

Reviewing Performance Appraisal and the Law

Performance appraisal interviews, like selection interviews, require that the interviewer be familiar with laws that have impact on the participants. Begin by carefully reviewing your organization's procedures and regulations regarding employee evaluation. These are a source of valuable information as they are generally written by your organization's personnel specialist.

Consider also the provisions of the law. Secure copies of Title VII of the 1964 Civil Rights Act (as amended) and the Equal Employment Opportunity Commission's guidelines and interpretations.[6] Do not overlook the fact that this aspect of personnel practice is regulated by the Equal Opportunity Commission and subject to the same civil rights legislation and Equal Opportunity Commission guidelines as the selection process. These laws do not require that the organization carry out performance appraisals. But when the organization does, the laws require that the appraisals be carried out in a standardized fashion, that they measure actual work performance, and that they be applied equally to all levels of employees. What this means is that employees with similar levels of experience and seniority in jobs that require essentially the same skill level be evaluated similarly and receive equal compensation for their work.

Appraising Performance

Basic research for conducting a performance appraisal interview involves collecting data about the interviewee's performance and evaluating those data. It is important to ensure that the evaluations are valid, productive, and acceptable to employees. These goals can be achieved more readily if the evaluation process follows accepted practices for assessing performance. We present a set of guidelines that will allow achievement of these aims. Then we discuss different types of formats used for evaluation and give an example of an effective evaluation system that one organization is using for its evaluation process.

Guidelines for evaluating performance.   Systematic collection of data for each employee is important. Here are suggestions that will guide you in the process.

1. *Keep a file for each employee which covers the period of the evaluation.* This file should contain periodic evaluations of the employee's performance as well as critical incidents that describe in specific terms effective and ineffective performance. Include also in this file letters, reports, and any other pertinent information. The file should fully cover the period, rather than contain materials gathered in anticipation of the upcoming review. After each evaluation period, move materials into a backfile so too much weight is not placed on performance that is no longer relevant.

2. *Base the evaluation on job-related factors.* Careful job analysis and setting of criteria for evaluation will help to ensure that the appraisal is based on job-related factors. What are the factors that contribute to performance of the particular job? How important is each factor in the overall picture? What can be measured and what cannot be measured? Answers to these questions are important "up-front" work necessary to the collection of performance data. If the factor can be measured, decide how you will accomplish this. Some measurement standards for performance are quantity, quality, time, and cost. Measurement of other factors may not be possible. For those, you will want to collect examples of the effective or ineffective behavior.

3. *Focus the evaluation on no more than six to eight major performance objectives.* The word *focus* means just that. It is possible to measure large numbers of objectives, but it is difficult to focus on large numbers of objectives. The failure to focus makes it difficult to present the information in a way that can be comprehended meaningfully by the employee.

4. *Strike a balance between objectives that are too complicated to be measured and those that are too simple to be useful.* There is an important balance you need to achieve. A simple objective is easy to understand and easy to measure. Yet in the overall performance picture it may not be particularly meaningful. On the other hand, a complicated objective may be both difficult to comprehend and difficult to measure. Strike a balance between the two extremes.

5. *Recognize that there is a difference between actual performance and potential for performance.* Try to view performance in terms of that which adequately does the job. It is easy to fall into the trap of evaluating a person on the basis of potential, either low or high, rather than what is necessary to do the job. An employee who is doing an adequate job but has greater potential might be rated lower than a coworker, even though both employee's performance is the same.

6. *Be sure to collect data about both favorable and unfavorable performance.* Another difficulty in evaluation of performance is bias in the direction of either favorable or unfavorable data. Try to achieve completeness in the data collection if balance actually exists. You will want to be able to affirm the positive aspects of the employee's performance *and* improve the weak areas.

Formats for performance evaluation.   The actual evaluation can take one of several formats. You will want to select one or a combination of these to create a framework within which to measure the objectives you have drawn.

An *essay* appraisal uses the narrative form to discuss the strengths and weaknesses of an employee. Normally, four or five general objective areas will be designated for comments. A form is created that lists these areas, with a space after each for comments. Essays of this type tend to be highly subjective and dependent on the writing skill of the evaluator. They can, however, provide a richness of detail that might not be achieved by other methods. Essays are usually used in conjunction with other standardized rating formats.

A *critical incident* appraisal is a more focused version of the essay. Here the assessor is asked to write a specific example of good and poor employee performance. Usually, the objectives drawn for the particular position are listed, with a space for the description of a critical incident under each. This kind of evaluation is more job-focused and therefore gives the interviewer and interviewee more specific information to discuss during the interview. One drawback to this method of reporting the appraisal is that it, like essays, is dependent to some extent on the evaluator's writing skill and is time consuming.

A *conventional rating form* generally consists of a series of items—either employee characteristics or job behavior—with some type of a high-to-low rating scale. For example, the category may be "knowledge of work," with a 5-point scale, 1 being low and 5 being high. These forms differ in the categories chosen to be rated and the number of points used on the scale. You will find Figure 8.1 helpful in constructing such a scale since it displays some of the frequently used categories. The major difficulty with a conventional rating form is that such categories, without definitions, may be vague. This makes the meaning associated with the term highly dependent on the unstated, and perhaps highly personal, definition in the mind of the rater.

A *behaviorally anchored rating scale* (BARS) has been developed to overcome some of the difficulties associated with the conventional rating scale. The BARS scale is constructed through job analysis and, thus, is unique to a particular job. The instrument is developed in a five-step process: (1) collecting critical incidents from managers and employees for a particular job; (2) identifying general categories of performance from an analysis of these incidents; (3) clarifying and rewording the incidents so that they are clear to all concerned; (4) asking knowledgeable people, including employees, to assign these incidents to the categories, keeping only those with the highest agreement on the first and second ratings; and (5) scaling

Figure 8.1　Frequently used rating characteristics [*From R. I. Lazer and W. S. Wilkstrom,* Appraising Managerial Performance (*New York: The Conference Board, p. 21*)].

1. Knowledge of work	16. Motivation, commitment, industry, effort
2. Leadership, influence	
3. Initiative	17. Organization
4. Quality of work, accuracy	18. Interpersonal relations, tact, courtesy
5. Quantity of work	
6. Cooperation	19. Planning
7. Judgment	20. Follow-up
8. Creativity, innovation, resourcefulness	21. Decisiveness
	22. Control
9. Dependability	23. Grooming
10. Evaluation/development of personnel	24. Responsibility
	25. Attendance
11. Planning and organization	26. Objectivity, openness to criticism
12. Communications	27. Stability
13. Alertness, intelligence, adaptability	28. Self-control
14. Analytical ability, problem solving	29. Self-expression
15. Delegation	

the incidents on a performance-category continuum. Figure 8.2 provides an example of the end product of a BARS scaling process.

Employers who use the BARS format do so because they believe that including specific job behaviors produces more reliable results. They also believe that those involved in the appraisal process will be more satisfied with the system because they had a hand in developing the scale. Employees do in fact report a high level of satisfaction, feel that they have greater impact on the process than with other rating systems, and perceive their supervisors as supportive.[7]

A *forced-choice* rating requires the assessor to select a description of a category from choices supplied. For example, if the category is *initiative,* the supervisor would be required to select one of these responses:

Initiative
1. Does not show initiative
2. Frequently does not show initiative
3. Often shows initiative
4. Usually shows initiative
5. Almost always displays initiative

A *ranking* system forces the rater to compare employees within a particular work unit of the organization. Usually there is no provision for ranking employees in a tie, and so decisions must be made about whose performance is better. This system has an advantage in making salary decisions, but has little advantage in bringing about actual performance improvement since no indication is given of why a worker was rated as he or she was.

Figure 8.2 Sample behaviorally anchored rating scale [*From William C. Donaghy,* The Interview: Skills and Applications, *reissued by Shefield Publishing Company, 1990, p. 324. (Copyright © 1984). Used with permission of this publisher.]*

POSITION: Custodial Zone Supervisor   Date: _____

NAME: _____ Unit: _____

On each of the following pages:

1. Read the description of each task/objective and the examples of job behavior.
2. Then, as you review and discuss the employee's performance in relation to each task/objective, circle the number on the rating scale that indicates your evaluation of the employee. Always circle the number. Do not place an *X* or a checkmark.
3. If you wish to rate an employee on an important task/objective of his/her job that is not included on this form, please develop the blank rating scales provided. If possible, assign mutually agreed upon examples of behavior to points on the rating scale and then rate the employee's performance in relation to these examples.

Task/Objective #1:

> Receive oral and written reports from subordinates, employees, and occupants of buildings regarding damaged facilities, fixtures, and equipment, and process work orders through proper channels.

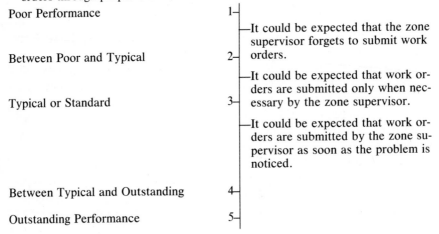

(*Note:* This BARS form would go on with similar scales until all important task/objectives are completed, with blank scales at the end for any the rater wishes to add.)

This system can also create morale problems because the lowest-ranked employee may actually be fully competent.

The final rating technique, *management by objectives* (MBO), is widely used.[8] The process of developing the standards for performance takes place in an interview where the manager and subordinate work together to set goals (objectives) rather than to stipulate activities to be performed. The performance is later assessed using these preset and agreed-upon standards.

Several advantages result from the fact that MBO is a joint process. Research suggests that MBO (1) accounts for more complexity than behaviorally based ratings, (2) relates more to what the employee actually does, (3) is less ambiguous and subjective than other measures, and (4) facilitates feedback by encouraging meaningful supervisor-employee discussion of employee strengths and weaknesses.[9]

MBO is not without its problems, however. One difficulty is that the agreed-upon goals may not coincide with organizational goals. For example, it is possible that goals set by people in production are not sufficient to meet goals set by people in sales. This difficulty can be overcome to some extent by a technique called *layering*. Layering is a goal-setting process that flows from the top of an organization down. Thus, the setting of objectives in a university environment would work like this: the university sets goals first, next the college sets goals based on its role in the university goals, then the departments set goals in relation to college objectives, and, finally, the individual sets goals as they relate to the department's goals.

Another problem associated with MBO is a tendency to be overly optimistic. This results from the difficulty of predicting the future. Thus, once goals are set, they must be reviewed periodically to make sure that they are still realistic.

Example of an effective rating system.   We promised an example of a currently used successful rating system. Figure 8.3, found on pages 188–189, is just such a system. It is the evaluation procedure used by the McCormack & Dodge Corporation, a fast-growing computer software firm headquartered in Natick, Massachusetts.

MANAGING THE INTERVIEW

Skillful management of the interview requires that the interview be carefully planned and executed, that attention be given to achieving a productive climate, and that appropriate techniques and practices be applied.

Planning and Carrying Out the Interview

The plan we present next and the sample stimulus questions embody the employee-centered problem-solving approach we've suggested. The plan begins by immediately involving the employee in the process.

Ask the interviewee to prepare for the interview.   The employee might consider these four questions in preparation:

1. What are the important duties and responsibilities of my job?
2. What are the major problems I encounter on the job?
3. How does my job performance meet the goals and duties of my job?

Figure 8.3   Evaluation procedure used by McCormack & Dodge. [*Used by permission of Dun & Bradstreet Software Services, Inc., Framingham, MA.*]

The employee information and signature section across the top of the inside pages of the evaluation form will be completed as follows:

Please print: Signatures: Date:

Employee name_____   Employee_____
Reviewing manager_____   Manager_____
Department cost center_____   Next level manager_____
Date of hire_____   Personnel_____

Managers evaluate each performance factor on two scales. The first scale is a determination of how heavily each item should be weighted, or how important it is in relation to all other factors. The second scale is a determination of how well the employee performs in relation to the manager's expectations.

These performance factors are *weighted* as:

Critical: the performance factor is absolutely vital to job performance. *Each* factor weighted as critical is unquestionably necessary to fulfilling the function of that job. The evaluation of the employee's performance would alter significantly if the employee did not meet the manager's expectations in those critical areas.

Important: the performance factor is very significant to job performance. Each is important, but *no one single* factor is critical to job performance. Rather, the successful performance of an individual is determined by the *overall* accomplishment of *all* important components.

Desirable: the performance factor is included in the evaluation, not as a necessary component to the job, but as a complementary component. It would be positive if the individual performed at or above the manager's expectations for these factors, but the overall impression of performance would not alter significantly if the individual did not perform well for these factors.

The performance factors are then *rated* as:

1. **Exceeds expectations:** the employee *consistently* and *significantly* exceeds the expectations of performance for this factor—*unusually high level of excellence.*
2. **Meets expectations:** the employee demonstrates good performance for this factor. The manager's standards are essentially met.
   A rating of "(2) Meets expectations" does not mean average or mediocre performance. Expectation standards for performance are high and should be communicated as such.
3. **Does not meet expectations:** the employee does not meet expectations of performance for this factor. Improvement is required.
   The Plus (+) or Minus (−) signs allow for further indication of how well each factor was performed.

The performance appraisal includes three categories of *performance factors:*

   I.   *General performance factors:* job components that apply to all positions, such as quality of work, organizing skills, initiative.

Figure 8.3 *(cont.)*

(1) *Job knowledge:* depth of understanding of the content and procedures of the job and of the field of specialization.
(2) *Quality of work:* thoroughness, accuracy, and completeness exhibited in routine assignments and special projects.
(3) *Responsiveness to supervision:* timeliness of pursuing and completing tasks and objectives; acceptance of responsibility.
(4) *Organizing skills:* planning, scheduling, coordinating tasks and assignments effectively.
(5) *Judgment:* analyzing and evaluating situations; success in reaching correct and optimum decisions.
(6) *Attitude:* ability and desire to cooperate with others toward the best interest of all concerned.
(7) *Initiative:* ability to organize and develop constructive ideas; to perform new or assigned tasks in a self-directed manner.
(8) *Self-development:* desire to improve performance and to strengthen both personal and job skills.
(9) *Communication skills:* ability to communicate with superiors, peers, and subordinates.
(10) *Supervisory skills* (if applicable): *Human Factors:* ability to select, motivate, and develop subordinates.
(11) *Supervisory skills* (if applicable): *Managerial Factors:* skill in planning, organizing, controlling, and coordinating departmental activities; cost control effectiveness.

II. *Performance to job standards:* the standard functions of the employee's job. Any individual in a particular job should be rated on the standards of the job which are taken from the job description.

III. *Performance to goals and objectives:* the goals that the manager and the employee have *previously* determined. These should be relevant to the particular employee's performance, as opposed to being generic to the job description.

Comments
The manager's comments are *required* for all factors weighted as critical and any factors that exceed or did not meet expectations. Any additional comments related to performance of an individual in each performance category are welcomed.

The purpose of the comments section is to document for the employee *why* the manager chose to put an X in the box for that factor. What was going through the manager's mind when he or she decided to put an X in:

Exceeds expectations—What did the employee do above and beyond the expectations for the factor?
Did not meet expectations—What was not accomplished? How could the employee improve performance?

An X in the box simply indicates the result of the manager's decision—not the reasons why that decision was made. Neither praise (exceeds expectations) nor criticism (did not meet expectations) really alters performance. It simply makes the employee feel good or bad for a short period of time. By providing information as to *why* performance was rated as it was, an employee can understand what actions need to be continued or improved. These comments make the "performance to goals and objectives" section much easier to complete and to relate the goals and objectives to actual performance.

4. How does my performance compare with the performance of others doing similar work?

Establish or reestablish goals related to the specific job.   Ask the employee:

1. What kind of things does a person in a job like yours need to do to be successful?
2. What do you think are the most difficult parts of your job?
3. What are the less difficult parts of your job?

Ask the interviewee to analyze his or her performance.   A study by Ronald J. Burke and his associates found that subordinates who were encouraged to talk about their ideas were more likely than those who weren't to see their supervisors as helpful, constructive, and willing to assist them in resolving job problems.[10]
Ask the employee:

1. Which of the activities you listed do you think you were most successful with? Least successful with?
2. Would you take each of the difficult and less difficult parts of your job that you have listed and talk with me about how you see yourself handling each?

If the interviewee has missed a key issue, an appropriate response might be: "I have been thinking about what is important in a job like yours and have been wondering if [you name it] might also be important. What do you think?" (Employee talks.) Then, "How do you see yourself doing with respect to this?"

Summarize any difficulties with performance that came out.   Examine your findings. Summarize the difficulties you've identified. Then explore alternatives for managing them with the employee through brainstorming. You might say, "You listed these difficulties. [List them.] I'm wondering what you think you might do to overcome [name the difficulty]. Can you suggest several ideas?"
You should have some suggestions to contribute if the interviewee is unable to make any. You might say, "I have thought about the difficulties you suggest. I can think of an alternative or two that might be helpful. I wonder what you think of each of these."

Assist the interviewee in selecting a solution.   Review the ways the employee has suggested the problem might be resolved. Then ask, "Which of these ideas do you think are best? Which are most reasonable?"

Ask the interviewee to consider the outcome of the selected solution.   The employee needs to go through the process of understanding what it will take to do what he or she has agreed to do. This is an important transition to the next step, goal setting. If the employee discovers a defect in the original idea, it might lead the person to discard the proposal in favor of another. Ask, "What are the likely results if you do [describe the solution]?"

Establish new goals and obtain the interviewee's commitment to them.   Goal setting is most important for attaining success with the plan. Chances of success are greatly lessened if the goals set are not clear and manageable. Remember also that the goals must be accepted by the employee if the employee is expected to strive for them. A goal also is more likely to be accomplished when a person perceives it to be set through his or her choice.[11]

The interviewer can manage goal setting by asking these questions: (1) "What have you decided to do?" (2) "When will you do it?" And if the interviewee has not improved from previous appraisal and goal setting, (3) "What shall I do if you don't do what you say you will do?"

Plan for training if it appears to be the solution to a performance problem. Keep training in mind as you conduct performance appraisal interviews. Sometimes a problem is a function of the employee not knowing how to do something or not having developed a particular skill, rather that the employee not being willing or able to perform.

Plan for evaluation and follow-up.   Determine jointly how you will know when the goals are met. Decide also what would be an appropriate schedule for checking on goal accomplishment. The employee should help. Ask, "How will you know when you have achieved these goals?" "When shall we get back together to see how you are doing?"

If you are the supervisor, let the interviewee know that you will help.   Most employees are likely to feel supported if you offer help. In a recent study, Gary Blau found that an offer of this kind is especially important when the task is complex or ambiguous.[12] You have greater expertise, power, and control than the employee, and it may be comforting to the employee to know that you are available if needed. You might say, "Be sure to let me know if I can help you in achieving these goals."

Keep in mind that an important rationale for the employee-centered performance appraisal interview is employee self-development. Each time employees move through this sequence, they should be learning to solve work problems.

Climate

A significant body of research concludes that, in general, the more employees participate in the appraisal process, the more satisfied they are with the appraisal interview and the supervisor.[13] An interview in which the employee does most of the talking, in contrast to an interview in which the boss does most of the talking, is employee-centered. Such an interview also appears to increase the employee's commitment to carrying out the goals discussed, but measures of "air time" might be misleading.[14] If during much of the time the employee is displaying defensive reactions, these objectives might not be met.[15]

An employee's defensiveness can be reduced or perhaps avoided by activities that promote supportiveness. Jack Gibb, in his classic essay "Defensive Communication," suggests that defensive behavior is "that behavior which occurs when an individual perceives or anticipates threat."[16] Gibb believes, as we do, that defensive-producing behaviors involve an attempt to win, dominate, impress, or escape punishment. Further, Gibb says that defensive behavior causes an "ensuing circular response [that] becomes increasingly destructive."[17] What Gibb means by this is that our defensive behavior promotes defensive behavior in the other person. Then, in turn, the other's defensive behavior causes our defensive behavior to become more intense. Thus, a defensive spiral is created.

What, then, is the solution to the problem of choosing defensiveness-producing communication? Gibb suggests six pairs of behaviors that foster a supportive climate. Each is contrasted with its opposite, defensiveness-producing behavior. Table 8.1 presents these and a description of each.

Since performance appraisal by definition is an evaluative activity and evaluation tends to produce defensiveness, the interviewer needs to understand and be able to implement the supportive alternatives. Instead of evaluating, the interviewer might describe a problem behavior: "I've noticed that you have been fifteen minutes late for work once a week over the past six weeks." Rather than displaying neutrality and certainty, the interviewer might continue with empathy and provisionalism: "I understand that circumstances sometimes get in the way of intentions—at least they do for me. I'm not sure what is going on here. Would you tell me about this situation?" Instead of controlling, the interviewer might follow with a problem orientation: "I see that circumstances are making it difficult for you to be on time for work sometimes. What are some things you might try that would help you around these?"

A positive climate is also facilitated if the interviewer adopts other behavior. Two researchers have reasoned that because employees are generally apprehensive about being appraised, reduction of the number of negative criticisms and removal of the discussion of salary from the appraisal process reduce defensiveness.[18] Beyond these, W. F. Nemeroff and Kenneth Wexley found that taking the attitude of helper, treating the employee as an equal, and showing respect for the employee as a person yields more satisfaction with the session and supervisor.[19] In addition, Gary Latham and Lise Saari discovered that supportive behavior can result in higher goals being set.[20]

Table 8.1 Supportive and Defensive Climates

Defensive	Supportive
Evaluation: To make a judgment about the other; to make an assessment of the other; to raise questions about the other's viewpoint, motives.	*Description:* To be nonjudgmental; to ask straightforward questions; to request factual information; to present "feelings, events, perceptions, or processes that do not ask or imply that the receiver change behavior or attitude."
Control: To try to manipulate the other; to attempt to impose an attitude or viewpoint on another; to try to keep the other from doing something; "implicit in all attempts to alter another person is the assumption of the change agent that the person to be altered is inadequate."	*Problem orientation:* The antithesis of imposing one's view; to communicate "a desire to collaborate in defining a mutual problem and seeking its solution"; to suggest by your words and actions that you have no preplanned solution, viewpoint, or behavior to impose on the other; to give the opportunity for "the receiver to set his own goals, make his own decisions, and evaluate his own progress—or to share with the sender in doing so."
Strategy: To preplan what you want and trick the other into thinking he or she is making the decision; to cause the other to feel that you have an interest in her or him when you do not.	*Spontaneity:* To express straightforward, "above the table" behavior; to avoid deceiving; to have unhidden, uncomplicated viewpoints and motives; to be honest.
Neutrality: To show little or no concern for the other or his or her problems and viewpoint; to treat the other as an object rather than a person.	*Empathy:* To identify with the other person's problems and feelings; to show respect for the other's value system; to affirm the other's worth as a person.
Superiority: To communicate that you are "superior in position, power, wealth, intellectual ability, physical characteristics, or other ways" to the other; to suggest that the other person is inadequate in comparison to you; to convey the attitude that the speaker "is not willing to enter into a shared problem-solving relationship, that he probably does not desire feedback, that he will be likely to try to reduce the power, the status, or the worth of the receiver."	*Equality:* To avoid "pulling rank"; to show the other respect; to minimize differences in ability, status, power, and intellectual ability.
Certainty: To be rigid in your viewpoint; "to seem to know the answers, to require no additional data"; to adopt the attitude of teacher in the sense that you try to correct the other; to take on a win-lose position.	*Provisionalism:* To be willing to be tentative with respect to your behavior, attitudes, and views, to convey the attitude that more data might change your mind; to problem-solve with the other rather than impose your view; to share data and work jointly on a task in a give-and-take fashion.

SOURCE: Adapted from Jack R. Gibb, "Defensive Communication," *Journal of Communication* (September 1961), 142–145. Reproduced by permission of the International Communication Association and the author.

Techniques and Practices

Certain techniques and practices tend to contribute to the success of a performance appraisal interview. Be aware of each of these and implement them when appropriate.

Give the employee a worksheet in advance of the interview.   A worksheet allows the employee to prepare for and be more active in the interview. It also focuses the employee's attention on issues related to the job and performance. Ronald Burke and his associates found that giving the employee a worksheet was associated with a positive outcome.[21] Such a worksheet might include these questions:

1. What are your duties and responsibilities?
2. What are the problems you encounter on the job?
3. What is the quality of your performance with respect to the duties you listed above?
4. How do you see your work in comparison with that of others in similar positions?

Encourage rather than praise.   Common wisdom suggests that people ought to be pleased with and motivated by praise. Limited praise can have a positive effect in the appraisal interview. Some, though, have argued that too much praise can produce several negative outcomes and cause defensiveness.[22] Praise may be viewed as threatening—a statement of superiority. It might also increase the distance between the supervisor and employee and also decrease contact between the two. Meyer and his associates concluded in their essay in the *Harvard Business Review* that praise was not useful "because it was regarded as the sandwich which surrounds the raw meat [of criticism]."[23] Undoubtedly, the important factors are the sincerity and amount of praise—if praise is sincere and limited, it may have the desired positive effect.

We believe encouragement is a desirable alternative to direct praise. If as an interviewer you ask the interviewee to evaluate his or her areas of accomplishment, you can then affirm what was said and acknowledge the person's feelings about the success. This affirmation and acknowledgement is encouraging to the employee in that you are jointly celebrating the success. This kind of "praise" seems more genuine and less manipulative because you are reinforcing the interviewee's assessment of accomplishment that he or she sees as praiseworthy. You might say, for example, "You seem pleased with the way you handled that." Or when the employee mentions an accomplishment, you can say, "I appreciate what you did."

Listen actively and feed back the employee's important ideas.   Active listening is a skill we addressed in Chapter 2. Recall that the listener paraphrases what is heard and feeds it back to the speaker. Paraphrasing is casting what you have heard into your own words; it is not parroting. The employee is encouraged by paraphrase because it makes clear that the supervisor is listening carefully enough to understand. This kind of listening also provides the employee an opportunity to correct any faulty impressions the supervisor may have formed.

Keep an employee-centered perspective in the interview. The interview should focus on the employee's reasoning, analysis, and solutions, when possible. Suppose you say to an employee, "I noticed that you've been late to work several days. I want you to get up earlier in the morning so you can get here on time!" This response would not be focused on the employee's reasoning or analysis or solutions to the problem. An employee-centered response might be "I noticed that you've been late to work several days. I'm wondering what the problem is and if there is something either you or I can do to solve it." This response allows the employee to present his or her viewpoint and is therefore likely to cause less resentment. This kind of approach has been shown to yield better performance.[24]

Don't criticize too much. Too much criticism destroys the climate for productive problem solving. Limiting criticism produces less defensiveness and a greater chance of the employee achieving the desired improvements.[25] Research reveals that those areas of a job that were most criticized were the ones in which the least improvement was actually made. When similar areas received less criticism, more improvement was achieved. In addition to these two findings, the overall number of criticisms was positively correlated with the number of defensive reactions by the employee.[26]

Discuss salary increases in an interview separate from the performance appraisal interview. Some researchers believe that discussion of salary has a negative effect on discussion of improvements.[27] They argue that the employee who believes what he or she says may influence the overall dollar increase in salary may promise whatever is necessary to get it. In other situations, the employee may turn the interview into a session where he or she seeks to justify a greater increase. Or the employee might enter into a debate over the smaller increase planned. Whatever the employee's reaction, discussion of salary can have the effect of increasing the tension associated with the interview.

Establish specific performance goals. Setting specific goals is very important for improvement.[28] Meyer, Kay, and French discovered that setting specific performance improvement goals produced twice as much improvement as did talk about general goals or criticism without goal setting.[29] Be specific about the target and the time frame for achieving it. Say, for example, "We agree, then, that you will try to increase your production to 150 units per day by the end of next month." Don't say, "We agree, then, that you will increase your production."

Establish checkpoints to review progress toward goals.   Periodic checking is necessary if the employee is to make regular progress. Kindall and Gatza suggest that there are often points in the completion of a project, or other company-imposed reporting dates, that are logical checkpoints.[30] Work with the interviewee to mutually agree on reasonable checkpoints. Ask, "When should I get back with you to see how things are going?"

Conduct interviews at least semiannually.   Most employees will be better motivated by more frequent performance reviews.[31] The anticipation of an upcoming interview can move the employee to consider how he or she is progressing with the current goals and attempt to meet the targets. Waiting a whole year to talk formally about performance also allows goals to become no longer appropriate and to be forgotten.

Be consistent in your style of approaching employee problems.   If you do not practice a problem-solving, coaching orientation in managing employee problems, this style will seem insincere in the interview. The supervisor who acts as judge in day-to-day interactions and as coach/helper in the performance appraisal interview will be seen as a phony.

THE INTERVIEWEE'S PREPARATION AND PARTICIPATION

The appraisal interview represents an opportunity for the interviewee if he or she engages in preparation and is aware of what constitutes effective participation.

Preparation

Preparation for the interviewee involves conducting a self-assessment. Guide your assessment by answering the following questions in writing and then thinking about the implications of your answers:

1. What are my principle duties? What are the performance objectives I have agreed to meet?
2. How well have I carried out each of these?
3. How does my performance compare with that of my coworkers who are in similar positions?
4. What problems have I encountered on the job?
5. What are several approaches I might take in dealing with these problems?
6. Would I promote myself if I were the boss? Why? Why not?

These questions cover most of the major concerns of supervisors and will help you anticipate questions you might be asked. Be sure to go beyond these questions if you can think of issues that have been of recent concern to your boss.

Managing the Interview

You will undoubtedly want to draw upon the knowledge and expertise of your supervisor in the discussion of your performance. This can be done most productively by phrasing questions that do not challenge, but that will provide you with the information you desire. In asking questions, keep these guidelines in mind:

1. Try to get the interviewer to give you as much information as possible about your performance. If the interviewer is not using an employee-centered approach, you may hear evaluative comments about your performance.
2. Try to get the interviewer to give specific examples to illustrate what is meant, if possible.
3. Ask if the interviewer has additional suggestions about what you can do to improve.
4. Be prepared to discuss your performance difficulties. An interviewer following an employee-centered style will want you to be able to solve any problems you are experiencing.
5. Summarize and check out whatever conclusions are reached so that you make sure you understand what is expected.
6. Ask for information and suggestions from the interviewer if the interview seems to be stalled. Avoid questions or statements that challenge. Examples of informational, as opposed to challenging, statements are given in Table 8.2.

Table 8.2   Examples of Informational and Challenging Statements

Informational	Challenging
I'm wondering what I have been doing that leads you to that conclusion?	I don't see how you can say that! How do you know?
Would you describe some specific difficulties you have observed so I can know how to improve?	What do you want me to do?
Looking at my performance, can you suggest particular things you'd like me to do that I'm not now doing?	I'll do anything you say. You're the boss!
Sometimes people do things that irritate or frustrate others. Am I doing anything you'd like me not to do?	And I'll refrain from doing what you tell me not to do. You're the boss.

SOURCE: Michael S. Hanna and Gerald L. Wilson, *Communicating in Business and Professional Settings,* 2d ed. (New York: Random House, 1988), p. 249.

Table 8.3   Examples of Supportive Statements

Category	Example
Description	From my perspective, this is what I thought I was doing.
Provisionalism	There are several ways of attacking this problem. I thought that what I did had a good chance of working even though other methods might also work. What other methods would you suggest?
Equality and problem orientation	I recognize your point of view on this issue and wonder if there is some way we can work together on this problem.
Empathy	I believe we both want to get the best product from our effort, and I am beginning to understand how difficult it is to coordinate our effort. If we can find a specific solution to this problem, it will help us achieve this optimum effort.

SOURCE: Michael S. Hanna and Gerald L. Wilson, *Communicating in Business and Professional Settings,* 2d ed. (New York: Random House, 1988), p. 250.

You may wish to avoid challenging the interviewer, because it is difficult to challenge a person without creating defensiveness on the part of him or her. We do not believe, though, that you should avoid challenging altogether. However, it is smarter to challenge ideas than to challenge the person. If it is necessary to challenge an idea presented by the interviewer, keep in mind the defensive behavior categories in Table 8.2 and Jack Gibb's essay on defensiveness and behaviors that foster a supportive climate. Table 8.3 gives examples of how you might use supportive behavior in a conversation about your performance.

Finally, you will want to employ principles of language use that will promote clarity. Here are some basic ideas you should consider:

1. Personalize your statements by the use of the word *I*. For example, "I believe that...."
2. Realize when you are making a statement of inference, and choose your words to reflect this.
3. Clarify the fact that you are hearing an inference when that is what is being presented.
4. Say explicitly what you want rather than what you don't want.
5. State your wants in terms of actions you can control.

THE DISCIPLINARY INTERVIEW

The focus of a disciplinary interview is different from that of the usual performance appraisal interview. Some situation has developed that is serious enough that immediate action must be taken. Perhaps lives are endangered or conduct is such that productivity is clearly in jeopardy.

Planning for the Disciplinary Interview

The first step in planning for this interview is to be sure that you have the facts straight. Carefully review what you know about the situation. Describe the situation in writing. Did you observe the circumstances directly? How reliable are others who may be witnesses? Will they stand behind you if need be? What kind of harm is being created by this situation? How extensive is the harm?

Now consider possible causes of the behavior. Was the behavior deliberate? Was the behavior avoidable? Was the behavior caused by lack of training? Is there any pattern of this kind of behavior from the employee? Might the behavior be caused by some outside factor such as drug abuse, marital problems, or emotional problems? Is this behavior likely to continue if you do nothing?

Ask yourself what kind of action is needed in this case. Will you merely need to talk with the employee? Will you need to take some punitive action? What will the punishment be? Do you have the authority to administer the kind of punishment you are considering? What is the organization's policy with respect to this kind of punishment? Will your boss stand behind you?

Schedule the interview at a time when you will have plenty of time to spend with the person involved. You will not want to be pressured into hasty action. Also, schedule the interview for as soon after discovery of the situation as possible. Of course, you will want to allow enough time to properly prepare. Since the interview may be upsetting to the person involved, you may also wish to schedule it at a late enough time in the day that it will not disrupt the work schedule of the employee involved.

Managing the Disciplinary Interview

Hold the interview in a private location. Generally, you will find that discipline administered in public intensifies the hard feelings created by calling someone's behavior into question.

Consider having another manager or union representative present if the situation is a serious one. Keep in mind that such a witness may be asked to testify about what was said. You might wish to ask the person to take notes. Make detailed notes for yourself too.

Be direct about the purpose of the interview. Stick to the facts in describing behavior and infractions. State specifically what your organization's and/or union's policy is with regard to the situation. Allow the employee to tell his or her side of the incident. Ask questions that will draw out the person's feelings and explanation for the behavior. Do not name-call or make conclusions that you are not qualified to make. For example, avoid words like *lying, thief,* or *drunk.* Do not try to make any medical or psychological diagnosis.

If discipline is clearly appropriate, give it. Do not debate, argue, or negotiate the penalty. But be sure that whatever you do is in line with the infraction. If you are not sure what you want to do or if your company has a rule about waiting to administer punishment, you may delay for some reasonable time. You might say, "Report [or call] to me tomorrow at nine o'clock for my decision." Or if you wish medical data to be collected, you might say, "I've arranged for you to go to the company physician for a test. Bring me a slip from the doctor when you return." Your organization may also have prescribed discipline for certain infractions. Theft is generally grounds for dismissal. Employees who have drug problems are sometimes counseled and may be offered the opportunity to enroll in a drug treatment program rather than be removed from the position. Whatever the punishment, be sure that you administer it equally to all employees.

SUMMARY

Performance appraisal interviews provide an opportunity to motivate an employee. The interviewer plans with this general purpose and others that meet the specific situation. An orientation is selected based upon a view of how employees are motivated and what is an appropriate supervisor-subordinate relationship. Several approaches are available: "tell and sell," "tell and listen," problem solving, and employee-centered problem solving. The orientation that meets both self-development needs and organizational needs is the employee-centered problem-solving approach.

The interviewer must appraise the employee's performance. This involves being familiar with the law and developing and administering an appropriate rating scheme.

The interviewer must also manage the interview by fostering a productive climate, applying appropriate techniques and practices, and carefully executing a plan. A productive climate will generally be one where the interviewee participates, the interviewer utilizes supportive communication, and the number of negative criticisms is limited. Appropriate techniques include giving the employee a worksheet, providing encouragement, using active listening, maintaining an employee-centered perspective, separating salary discussion from performance discussion, establishing appropriate goals and checkpoints, and conducting semiannual interviews in a style consistent with the supervisor's day-to-day style. Carrying out the interview involves asking questions that will help the employee analyze his or her performance, considering solutions for performance difficulties, and

Ethics and Responsibilities in Interviewing

Interviewers who are conducting performance appraisal interviews should consider a broad guideline which has its basis in the principle of fairness. *Treat the interviewee and his or her ideas with respect.* In practice, this guideline can be observed by engaging in certain behaviors. These have already been presented, and so they are merely listed here.

1. Base your appraisals, as much as possible, on objective standards of observation and data collection.
2. Give the interviewee an opportunity to prepare for the interview.
3. Give the interviewee an opportunity to provide input into his or her evaluation.
4. Solicit the interviewee's suggestions for solving performance problems.
5. Ensure that any solutions to performance problems fit the particulars of the situation.
6. Follow through on any agreements made.

Two additional guidelines are important. First, *ensure that information revealed in the interview is available only to those who have a legitimate claim to know*. There is a natural tendency to want to talk about work, and, especially, the triumphs in solving problems. Discussing information revealed during a performance appraisal interview will violate the ethical principle of justice and, perhaps, deception. Employees may believe they have been deceived by the smoke screen of presumed confidentiality surrounding these interviews.

Second, *do not deliberately misrepresent your view about the interviewee's performance or company policies*. Sometimes interviewers are tempted to encourage an employee by saying things about his or her performance that are not true. This unethical behavior may backfire if the employee is at all realistic in assessing his or her own performance. This kind of behavior, of course, violates the principle of intentional deception.

Interviewees assume several ethical responsibilities. First, *interviewees should take on the responsibility to prepare for the interview*. Preparation means reviewing the strengths and weaknesses of the employee's performance. It also means considering possible solutions to any performance problems.

This view stems from the assumption that a responsible member of an organization attempts to show respect for other organizational members as well as the organization's resources. Failure to prepare may waste valuable time of the interviewers as well as deprive the organization of resources the interviewees might provide through improved performance.

(Continued)

Second, *interviewees have a responsibility not to misrepresent themselves, the facts, or their motives.* This means making an honest attempt to evaluate their performance. This means also not to promise to do what they intend not to do or believe they cannot do. Not following this guideline violates the principle of intentional deception.

Finally, *interviewees have the responsibility to ask for help in solving performance problems if needed.* Interviewers will not always know when interviewees will need help in meeting the agreed-upon goals. Failure to reach goals because help was needed and not asked for wastes resources. Wasting resources can be seen as violating the principle of intentional harm.

setting goals. Training is a solution that should be considered for some performance problems.

The interviewee should also prepare for the interview. This involves carrying out a self-assessment. Preparation also includes understanding what is wanted from the interviewer and using interviewing techniques that will help to make the interview more productive. The interviewee will want to get as much information as possible about how the employer views his or her performance, utilizing behavior that will be viewed as supportive.

The disciplinary interview is a type of performance appraisal that focuses on a behavior that is serious enough to warrant taking immediate action. Planning involves a thorough understanding of the situation and organizational rules regarding the type of behavior. Schedule the interview to allow for sufficient time, and hold the interview in a private location. Be direct about the purpose of the interview, and stick to the facts. Know also what kind of discipline is appropriate, and administer it equally to all employees.

NOTES

[1] Gerald L. Wilson and H. Lloyd Goodall, Jr., "The Performance Appraisal Interview: A Review of the Literature with Implications for Communication Research," *Southern Speech Association Meeting*, Winston-Salem, NC, April 1985. Also see Hermine Zagat Levine, "Consensus on Performance Appraisals at Work," *Personnel* (1986), 63–71.

[2] Norman R. F. Maier, *The Appraisal Interview: Three Basic Approaches* (San Diego, CA: University Associates, Inc., 1976).

[3] Maier, p. 12.

[4] Human resource development professionals agree with us that these are essential ingredients of an effective performance appraisal. See Donald L. Kirpatrick,

"Performance Appraisal: Your Questions Answered," *Training and Development Journal, 40* (1986), 68–71.

[5] This research is reported in E. F. Huse and Emanuel Kay, "Increasing Management Effectiveness through Work Planning," in *The Personnel Job: A Changing World* (New York: American Management Association, 1964).

[6] Steven D. Norton, "Performance Appraisal Advice for a New Supervisor," *Supervising Management 27* (1982), 30–34. Robert Layer, "The Discrimination Danger in Performance Appraisal," *Conference Board Record* (March 1976), 60–64.

[7] Stanley Silverman and Kenneth N. Wexley, "Reaction of Employees to Performance Appraisal Interviews as a Function of Their Participation in Rating Scale Development," *Personnel Psychology, 37* (1984), 703–710.

[8] Surveys indicate that this technique is now used by approximately 50 percent of organizations, and that almost three-fourths of the managers using it find it effective. See William C. Donaghy, *The Interview: Skills and Applications* (Glenview, IL: Scott, Foresman and Company, 1984), p. 329.

[9] Kenneth N. Wexley and Richard Klimoski, "Performance Appraisal: An Update," *Research in Personnel and Human Resources Management, 2* (1984), 40; G. P. Latham and Kenneth N. Wexley, *Increasing Productivity through Performance Appraisal* (Reading, MA: Addison-Wesley, 1981); Daniel Ilgen, Richard Peterson, Beth Ann Martin, and Daniel Boeschen, "Supervisor and Subordinate Reactions to Performance Appraisal Sessions," *Organizational Behavior & Human Development, 12* (1981), 311–330.

[10] Ronald J. Burke, William F. Weitzel, and Tamara Weir, "Characteristics of Effective Employee Performance Review and Development Interviews: One More Time," *Psychological Reports, 47* (1980), 683–695.

[11] Mirian Erez and Frederick H. Kanfer, "Role of Goal Acceptance in Goal Setting and Task Performance," *Academy of Management Review, 8* (1983), 455.

[12] Gary Blau, "The Effect of Source Competence on Worker Attitudes," *Journal of Applied Communication Research, 14* (1986), 33.

[13] See Maier, *The Appraisal Interview;* A. R. Solem, "Some Supervisory Problems in Appraisal Interviewing," *Personnel Administration, 23* (1960), 27–40; M. M. Greller, "Subordinate Participation and Reactions to the Appraisal Interview," *Journal of Applied Psychology, 60* (1975), 544–549; W. F. Nemeroff and K. N. Wexley, "Relationships between Performance Appraisal Interview Characteristics and Interview Outcomes as Perceived by Supervisors and Subordinates," paper presented at the 1977 Academy of Management Meeting, cited in R. J. Burke et al., "Characteristics of Effective Employee Performance Review and Development Interviews: Replication and Extension," *Personnel Psychology, 31* (1978), 903–905; and K. N. Wexley, J. P. Singh, and G. A. Yukl, "Subordinate Personality as a Moderator of the Effects of Participation in Three Types of Appraisal Interviews," *Journal of Applied Psychology, 58* (1973), 54–59.

[14] Maier, *The Appraisal Interview,* pp. 1–20; Solem, "Some Supervisory Problems"; Greller, "Subordinate Participation."

[15] Greller, "Subordinate Participation."

[16]Jack R. Gibb, "Defensive Communication," *Journal of Communication, 2* (1961), 141.

[17]Gibb.

[18]Huse and Kay, "Increasing Management Effectiveness."

[19]Nemeroff and Wexley, "Relationships between Performance Appraisal Interview Characteristics and Interview Outcomes."

[20]Gary P. Latham and Lise M. Saari, "Importance of Supportive Relationships in Goal Setting," *Journal of Applied Psychology, 64* (1979), 151–156.

[21]Burke et al., "Characteristics of Effective Employee Performance Review," 903–919.

[22]Herbert H. Meyer, Emanuel Kay, and John R. P. French, Jr., "Split Roles in Performance Appraisal," *Harvard Business Review* (January–February 1965), 123–129. Richard E. Farson, "Praise Reappraised," *Harvard Business Review* (September–October 1963), 61–66.

[23]Meyer, Kay, and French, "Split Roles," p. 127.

[24]Latham and Saari, "Importance of Supportive Relationships."

[25]Emanuel Kay, Herbert H. Meyer, and John R. P. French, Jr., "Effects of Threat in a Performance Appraisal Interview," *Journal of Applied Psychology, 49* (October 1965), 311–317.

[26]Huse and Kay, "Increasing Management Effectiveness."

[27]Meyer, Kay, and French, "Split Roles," pp. 124–127.

[28]Feedback and goal setting have been found to be significantly related to subordinates' perception of equity and to the accuracy and clarity of information exchanged. See John M. Ivancevich, "Subordinates' Reaction to Performance Appraisal Interviews: A Test of Feedback and Goal Setting Techniques," *Journal of Applied Psychology, 67* (1982), 581–587.

[29]Meyer, Kay, and French, "Split Roles," pp. 124–127.

[30]Alva F. Kindall and James Gatza, "Positive Program for Performance Appraisal," *Harvard Business Review* (November–December 1963), 158.

[31]Wilson and Goodall, "The Performance Appraisal Interview."

AN APPRAISAL INTERVIEW FOR ANALYSIS

The interviewer, John Graham, is the sales department manager. He is forty-three years old, and he is married. It is the time of the year to distribute bonuses to his sales representatives. John has been an excellent sales representative himself, being promoted on that basis five years ago with the charge to modernize the department and upgrade the skills of the salespeople. He has been rewarding outstanding contributors with merit pay increases and opportunities to attend professional development conferences. In spite of his effort, Linda Anderson's performance has slipped to a minimally satisfactory level. Linda does enough to keep her from being fired, but not much more. She is nearing retirement and seems to have given up. Linda also gossips about John's management and generally tries to undermine his effectiveness. He is determined to stop this behavior, but has resigned himself to the fact that he will not be able to improve Linda's performance.

Linda Anderson is fifty-eight years old. She has worked for the company for thirty years. She admits privately that she is tired of "busting her behind" for a few dollars in merit raise money. She believes she is giving the company enough effort—especially after all those long years of "hard work and very little recognition." She believes she is underpaid and not appreciated. She thinks her performance is better than average.

1. Mr. Graham: Come in. Hi, Linda, how are you doing today?

2. Ms. Anderson: Fine. Just fine, John.

3. Mr. Graham: Have a seat. First of all, glad to have you here today. I know you've been through the performance appraisal interview a million times.

4. Ms. Anderson: Yes, all too often sometimes.

5. Mr. Graham: Yes, but you know it's important. It's good for both of us to discuss some things that we've had problems with or haven't had problems with, good things and bad things. Not necessarily bad things, I should say, but just things that come up and goals we want to work on—things we want to talk about. First of all I want to talk to you a little bit about the questions I asked you to prepare before you came into the interview. I know you've done this before, but I think it's important for you to reevaluate your goals and look at them again and see how they compare with your performance at this time. I want you to tell me a little bit about what you feel your responsibilities are in your job as a sales representative that are important for you to do your job effectively.

6. Ms. Anderson: Well, I guess I have two basic responsibilities. One is to take care of our current customers—to call on them frequently enough that they have access to our new product lines and to make sure that they remember we're around when they are doing their ordering. Another job, which is sort of secondary but important too, is to call on potential customers and establish new accounts, as time permits, because one of the things we are supposed to do is to try to expand sales in our particular territory.

7. Mr. Graham: You used the phrase *supposed to do.* Do you feel these things are things you have to do or things you want to do because...

8. Ms. Anderson: Well, you have to do them to some extent. Otherwise, you get fired and the company goes broke. They have to be done to some extent, you know, deal with people. Some do more or less, depending on who they are.

9. Mr. Graham: Is that your main objective, not to get fired? Is that what you feel is most important?

10. Ms. Anderson: I don't want to get fired. That's pretty important to me. I am going to retire in a few years, and I don't want to be left without a pension.

11. Mr. Graham: Well, we see that you've been with us for a long time and that you have performed well through the years. As you near retirement, do you notice any differences in the way you feel toward your customers or the people that you call on or make regular stops to see?

12. Ms. Anderson: No, I enjoy them. I've had some long-lasting relationships. I don't really feel any differently about my customers. I take care of them. It's probably a little harder to establish new accounts. I'm not as young as I used to be, and getting around as much as I used to do is difficult. I'm not like those twenty-six-year-old youngsters who can put in twelve-hour days and that kind of thing. At the crack of dawn they are off and on the road somewhere.

13. Mr. Graham: So, you see this as a problem with calling on new accounts, not being able to get out or to get around?

14. Ms. Anderson: Well, it's just harder when you get a little older to move as fast as some of the younger people. Frankly, sometimes you just don't feel like it. You've made your career, and you're respected. You know you're doing a good job. Why kill yourself? Those other people are doing it because they have to make their name. I've already made mine.

15. Mr. Graham: You think you've already made your name?

16. Ms. Anderson: Yes, yes I do. My customers respect me.

17. Mr. Graham: What about the younger employees? As they get older, will they get a philosophy like yours?

18. Ms. Anderson: I don't know. That frequently happens. You have to establish yourself when you're a younger person. Once you've established yourself and you have a reputation, then there's no need to keep doing those same kinds of things all the time.

19. Mr. Graham: Do you think there is any way that we could prevent this from happening to some of our younger sales representatives?

20. Ms. Anderson: Well, you know sometimes we think we are working for a pittance here. We need to build up a better incentive program. You get out there every day and work yourself to a frazzle and what do you get from it? My paycheck isn't very much smaller than it was when I was out there busting my behind.

21. Mr. Graham: So, you feel that things other than just pay....

22. Ms. Anderson: It seems like just a few dollars, maybe more incentive. People at one of our competitors gave their top salesperson a Mercedes, one of those spiffy little Mercedes convertibles, for having the top sales for the year.

23. Mr. Graham: So, you think we ought to offer more incentives?

24. Ms. Anderson: I think it would help people keep moving. It seems to me that an increased incentive might help people achieve certain goals.

25. Mr. Graham: Well, I think this is a matter that we probably need further discussion on, maybe at another time, as far as salaries and other incentives go. Our main goal here is for us to discuss any problems you think you're having in performing your job. We've talked about how you think you can't get about as much as the younger crew does, but yet you seem to be making your quota. Is it important to you to set new goals, to strive a little bit above your past accomplishments?

26. Ms. Anderson: If I'm rewarded for it. People don't like to work if they are not being appreciated. I like to be appreciated just like anybody else. I don't mind striving for it, if there is something to be had out of it. If there is nothing to be had, then why bother?

27. Mr. Graham: Sometimes we work a little bit harder for people that we respect a little bit more. I've noticed some attitude differences among the employees in our organization concerning my management. Are there some things that you think that we should talk about to improve upon my relations with some of the sales representatives?

28. Ms. Anderson: Well, I don't know. It is kind of hard to work for a younger person. I think that's a disadvantage that you might have. When an organization promotes younger people ahead of the older folks, that probably creates some problems for people. They might not like to take instruction from a person that is younger than they are. You know, the person has less experience than they do.

29. Mr. Graham: Has this been a problem for you?

30. Ms. Anderson: Sometimes. I think that I know more than people that have a lot less experience than I do. I've been here for quite a few many years.

31. Mr. Graham: You think that you should have been promoted before some of the younger people in the company?

32. Ms. Anderson: Frankly, yes. I think that's a mistake to promote younger people ahead of folks who are tried and true and have proved themselves and have the knowledge.

33. Mr. Graham: Do you feel this makes a younger person any more ineffective in his or her administration, because of the age?

34. Ms. Anderson: Yes. Younger people don't have all of the knowledge and experience that they might have, and that affects some of the decisions that they make.

35. Mr. Graham: So, maybe if you were part of these decisions with the older or younger administration, you would feel more a part of the organization? You would be lending some of your knowledge and experience to the organization. Would this help you feel more a part or more in compliance with the administration?

36. Ms. Anderson: Yes, I just didn't know anybody really cared about that.

37. Mr. Graham: Oh, Linda, we care a lot about you. We've noticed your work, and I see through the years you have been on the receiving end of some of our incentive programs for people who have made outstanding contributions to the organization. Maybe if we discuss the things that you've done a little bit more and give a little more recognition for the things that you've done, this would help us to make your job a little more effective. Can we agree on that?

638. Ms. Anderson: I would be happy to help if I can.

39. Mr. Graham: The only other thing I can think of that we need to discuss is maintaining communication between the two of us. I would feel better about things if you would come and talk to me when you think that I'm making the wrong decision. We could get it out in the open and talk about it like we have today. I appreciate your explaining to me how you feel about a younger person and how it affects your performance. And I really think you could offer some suggestions that would be helpful. I think we need to get together a little bit later and discuss this, maybe in a few weeks, and see where things are going. Is that agreeable with you, Linda?

40. Ms. Anderson: Sure.

ROLE-PLAYING CASES FOR THE APPRAISAL AND DISCIPLINARY INTERVIEW

Sue Angelino, Office Manager

The interviewer, Jerry Harper, is the manager of the regional sales office of a large publishing house. He has recently been promoted from a position as sales representative, a job he had held for ten years. He had some contact with Sue Peterson, the office manager, through his previous position. He is conducting his set of performance appraisal interviews with those who work in the regional sales office.

Sue Angelino has held her position as office manager for five years. She is very intelligent, efficient, and capable of handling the details of her work. There is one difficulty that makes her less than an excellent employee. Now and then she will approach one of her subordinates in a way that results in bad feelings. She knows after the fact that her behavior is not appropriate for a manager.

Sue's behavior is such that the employees feel "put down"; they think that Sue feels she is better than those who work for her. One employee said of this behavior, "Sure, Sue is the boss. But she doesn't have to have such a superior attitude. She's no better than the rest of us." An example of her behaving inappropriately was the time she just walked up to Peter Alexandrovich's desk, tossed some work on it, and walked away without comment. Sue also berates people who make errors, and she does so in front of their coworkers.

Sue does not do these things all the time. They happen occasionally and not always to the same people.

Max Moskowitz, Development Officer

The interviewer, Hannah Williams, is the director of public relations and former development officer for Central University. Several months ago the areas of public relations and development were merged and both operations placed under the direction of the head of public relations. Hannah was appointed to head the department. At that time a recent college graduate, Max Moskowitz, was hired to do development work. Hannah is in her late thirties and has her degree in public relations. Her first job was with Central University as the development officer. Her success as a development officer is clear. When she left the post, the university was receiving in excess of $3 million per year in contributions from alumni and various local businesses and industries. In the six months that Max has been heading development, donations have been off slightly. But the dip in giving doesn't seem to be the only problem. Hannah has received four or five angry notes from alumni over the "hard sell" approach Max is using. During this first performance review, Hannah is determined to help Max resolve this problem.

The interviewee, Max Moskowitz, is an enthusiastic graduate with a degree in communication arts and marketing. He enjoys his work and is concerned about the slight drop in giving. Being the type of person who believes in action, he has stepped up his campaign to increase alumni giving. He believes strongly that alumni have an obligation to support their alma mater. He is determined to get this point across. Max believes that he is doing the right thing and that his work is considerably above average.

Joe Harper, Hourly Worker

The interviewer, Phil Irwin, is the supervisor on the stamping line of Southern Industries. He is responsible for fifteen stamping machine operators and six sheet metal handlers. A morale problem has been developing on his line during the past six months. A little more than six months ago, the company needed to replace an operator. Rather than fill an operator's slot with an inexperienced worker, Joe Harper was transferred from the Lake Forest plant to do the job. Joe's record shows that he is one of the line's hardest workers. His production is above average, with a very low level of waste. He always arrives for work fifteen minutes early and is never absent due to illness. His one problem is that his only topic of conversation with coworkers is complaints about work. It has gotten to the point that his coworkers avoid him and have come to Phil Irwin with the issue. Sue Marcos, the operator on the machine next to Joe's, has asked to be moved to a different position on the line.

Joe is thirty-five years old and has been a laborer since being graduated from high school. He has held a number of jobs, but has not generally been in any one for more than five or six years. He is a hard worker and knows it. He resents others around him who don't work as hard as he. He likes Southern very much and hopes to stay with them. He believes in speaking his mind, and he does so frequently. Most of the time he has a good point in his complaints, but his coworkers get tired of hearing him and have tried to get him to stop.

Michael Turner, Assistant Training Director

The interviewer, Marie Longman, is director of training for a large paper manufacturing firm in the south. She is fifty-two and very good at her job. She believes that training is serious business and that a no-nonsense approach is the only way to proceed. She has recently hired a graduate from Normal University to structure and teach an ongoing program in communication skills for the plant's technical personnel. Mike Turner has been conducting a training series for engineers. An older engineer and long-time friend of Marie, George, is attending the series of classes. George complained to Marie, "Mike has been quitting class early and inviting people to go have a drink with him. Then he sits in the bar and flirts with the women engineers. He even spends more time talking to them in class."

Mike Turner is twenty-six years old. He has been in this job for six months, but has worked in training for three years for a competitor. He views himself as a good trainer. He is fun-loving and enjoys people—particularly members of the opposite sex. He knows that it is important to develop a sense of cohesiveness in a group—especially when they are going to be together for ten weekly classes. Twice he has stopped fifteen minutes early and urged the group to socialize a little at the corner pub. Everyone had a good time, and he believed that it increased the camaraderie of the group.

June Chung, Assistant Product Marketing Manager

The interviewer, Richard Merrill, is a forty-five-year-old director of marketing for a local bank. He has been in this position for twelve years and prides himself on his well-run department. He believes in his people and rewards them for superior performance. June has received above-average raises over the two years she has been in the department. She is one of his best young professionals, with an impressive record of not only high-quality imaginative approaches to marketing, but also adherence to her commitments. Lately something seems to have happened to June's drive. Her work isn't exactly poor—it can only be described as average. Her last program report was a week late.

June is an amiable, single person who is twenty-four years old. She is personable but slightly on the shy side. She had been engaged, but broke off the engagement six months ago. That was when Paul, a married man who has a desk next to hers, began to take an interest in her. She has no interest in him, but he talks to her during working hours—taking valuable time from the projects she is working on. He has called her at home and even stopped by twice in the evening. Each time she has told him that she is definitely not interested. June knows that if she tells Richard, Paul may be terminated. Richard doesn't believe in allowing this sort of harassment by either sex.

EXPERIENCES

1. Interview a person who conducts performance appraisal interviews. Discover as fully as possible what goals the person has for appraisal interviews and what approaches are used in the process. Write a short essay which compares and contrasts these practices with those presented in this chapter.
2. Investigate disciplinary policies for two organizations. What seem to be the important features of a disciplinary policy? For what kinds of problems are employ-

ees likely to be terminated? What kinds of employee assistance programs are in place for employees who are experiencing difficulties? Are these assistance programs optional? Why or why not?

3. This chapter discusses the BARS approach and the MBO approach to evaluating performance. Locate an organization that uses each approach. Collect information on members' reactions to each method. What are the strengths and weaknesses of each method?

4. Consider the various methods of performance appraisal interviewing discussed in this chapter. Write a short paper that describes each method. Tell also what seems to be the most appropriate circumstances for employing each method, including your rationale for deciding appropriateness.

5. The employee-centered problem-solving performance appraisal plan has been described as a developmental approach. Discuss in small groups what it means to take a developmental approach. Tell what aspects of this approach can be characterized as developmental.

RECOMMENDED READINGS

Beer, M., "Performance Appraisal," in J. W. Lorsch (ed.), *Handbook of Organizational Behavior* (Englewood Cliffs, NJ: Prentice-Hall, 1987), pp. 286–300.

Cusella, Louis P., "Feedback, Motivation, and Performance," in F. M. Jablin, L. L. Putnam, K. H. Roberts, and L. W. Porter (eds.), *Handbook of Organizational Communication: An Inter-disciplinary Perspective* (Beverly Hills: Sage, 1987), pp. 624–678.

Goodall, H. Lloyd, Jr., Gerald L. Wilson, and Christopher L. Waagen, "The Performance Appraisal Interview: An Interpretive Reassessment," *Quarterly Journal of Speech, 72* (1986), 74–87.

Patton, T. H., Jr., *A Manager's Guide to Performance Appraisal* (New York: Free Press, 1982).

Pearce, J. L., and L. W. Porter, "Employee Responses to Formal Performance Appraisal Feedback," *Journal of Applied Psychology, 71* (1986), 211–218.

PART IV

Professional Contexts

CHAPTER 9

THE IN-DEPTH
INFORMATION-
GATHERING
INTERVIEW

OBJECTIVES

After reading this chapter, you should be able to:

Explain the purpose of an in-depth information-gathering interview.

Discuss at least three uses of an in-depth information-gathering interview.

Describe how to complete an oral or written assignment using an in-depth information-gathering interview.

Develop a strategy and plan for collecting information that makes productive use of a variety of primary and secondary questions.

Utilize various strategies for managing difficult interviewees.

Discuss the ethics of an in-depth information-gathering interview.

Mark and Sandra Sanford are entrepreneurs. In addition to holding down full-time jobs, they maintain a side business devoted to publishing a business directory for the rapidly expanding community where they make their home. However, when you ask them, as we did, what they do for a living, you do not hear about their full-time jobs nor their own small business. Instead they both respond, in unison and with confidence, that they are in the "informational interviewing business."

They explain that informational interviewing is one of the most important occupations in America's service-related economy. They point out that every business is only as profitable as the information within it—information used as the factual and interpretive bases for decision making, problem solving, and strategic planning—and that persons who are skilled in locating and eliciting information are therefore highly valued.

Mark's full-time job is as a computer programmer. In his work he is responsible for developing and certifying software designs, a business goal that cannot be accomplished unless various interviewing processes are effectively employed. For example, he must discover what customers want a computer program to do before he can write a program to do it. To find out what customers want means interviewing them for information about how they plan to use the software, what design features they prefer, and what problems they have had using existing programs.

Similarly, Sandra works in her full-time job as a technical documentation specialist. She writes technical manuals for computer software developed by people like her husband. She explains that in order to carry out her assigned duties she is constantly interviewing for information. She must discuss the features of a software package with its programmers and designers as well as personnel in the training department who will be using the documentation to teach new users. She must interview customers to discover if there are any "holes" in the documentation, or explanations that aren't written clearly. For Sandra, the ability to interview for information is essential to the performance of her job, even though her job is, strictly speaking, writing documentation.

But it is in their own small business that their informational interviewing skills have had the most dramatic payoff. To research and publish a business directory requires directing their interviewing energies toward customers who want to communicate a personalized message about their business to potential users of the directory, but who often do not possess the marketing and technical documentation know-how to do so. Mark and Sandra work with them by asking questions about the unique features of their business, service, or product; discuss with them how that information can be used in the directory; and help them make decisions about their entries based on these interviews.

As you can see, Mark and Sandra's definition of their jobs as informational interviewers is accurate. And it is smart. Rather than defining their jobs by the businesses that employ them or by the products they produce, they define them by the one skill that is necessary to accomplish all of their tasks.

This chapter is about informational interviewing. It speaks to the use of interviews to acquire, analyze, interpret, and communicate information. Our purpose is to reveal how one-on-one interviewing for information is important to organizations and to prepare you for assignments that require the strategic development and use of these interviews.

To accomplish our purpose we will begin with an explanation of the uses of informational interviews. We will then examine research strategies that are useful in the gathering and evaluating of information, including techniques for preparing for the interview, for developing question sequences that help you to open up and probe important areas, for handling difficult interviewees, and for checking out or validating the information received. Next, we point out the usefulness of recording the interview. Finally, we address ethical issues and responsibilities.

USES OF IN-DEPTH INFORMATIONAL INTERVIEWS

We begin this chapter by focusing on the relationship between informational interviewing and its outcomes: *informational interviews must be understood in terms of what will be done with the information.* Improving your skill as an informational interviewer means understanding the *uses* to which your information can be put. In the following subsections we will discuss the four principal uses for information acquired through interviews.

To Learn More about a Person, Subject, Event, or Experience

Mark and Sandra Sanford started to become interested in publishing a directory when they began to talk to people for the purpose of learning more about what was needed in their community that they could provide. They were interviewing for information, although in most cases they simply appeared to be having a conversation about community needs.

The outcome of these early interviews was a list of possible small business enterprises. They learned more about the community, expanded their business contacts, and acquired what at first appeared to be seemingly unrelated details that they would later piece together for a larger purpose. Viewed this way, these initial informational interviews had as their goal personal growth and an enhanced understanding of persons, subjects, events, and experiences.

For our purposes, personal growth and enhanced understanding represent the most fundamental type of informational interviewing. Examples include exchanging small talk at a business lunch or function, discussing a current event with an expert, attending a lecture or class on a subject of importance to you and then discussing relevant issues with the lecturer, or conducting a person-on-the-street interview to gauge public reactions to a current event.

When you go into an informational interview with the goal of enhancing your personal experience, you have the least rigid agenda for asking questions and the most flexibility in the direction and scope of the conversation. This sort of interview doesn't feel like an interview at all; it feels like conversation. Therefore, it should be conducted as you would conduct a conversation. Consider this example, drawn from one of Sandra's early interviews about starting a small business directory:

Sandra: What do you think gives a growing community a unique identity?

Ellen: Certainly it is in part its ability to say something about itself that distinguishes it from its neighbors.

Sandra: You mean...?

Ellen: I mean perhaps its architecture is different; or its business district has a particular look or style.

Sandra: But how do you bring people here? I mean Madison has a unique downtown area, and yet we know people still go to Huntsville, Birmingham, Nashville, and so forth to do their shopping.

Ellen: I think that is because if you are new to an area, as many of our residents are, you tend to rely on either the newspaper or the Yellow Pages for information about where to find things. And you will travel the extra hour or so to bigger cities like Birmingham or Nashville just because you expect more shopping opportunities.

Sandra: I see. And I agree. But are you saying that if we had a Madison Yellow Pages, we might be able to attract more business?

Ellen: Yes, I think so.

As you can see from this excerpt, Sandra wanted to gain information from Ellen (who is, by the way, the owner of a fashion store in Madison) about how to establish the uniqueness of a community. From Ellen's initial responses, Sandra narrowed the topic to sources of advertising, which led to the topic of a local business directory. It was an informational interview, but it looked and felt like a conversation. While it had a general goal orientation (community uniqueness, how to attract customers), Sandra was less interested in gathering specific information than she was in enhancing what she knew about the business needs of the community.

Now let's examine a more structured, goal-oriented form of informational interviewing.

To Gather Information to Complete a Brief Oral or Written Assignment for a Class or a Company

Mark Sanford was given the responsibility of developing a written report for his employer on the feasibility of implementing a new programming review cycle. His task was to collect information about the current review cycle procedures—their advantages and disadvantages—and to solicit new ideas to improve or replace the procedures. Mark's assignment was a written report, but the report could not be written without first doing a series of informational interviews.

The outcome of an informational interview with this goal will be a presentation and/or document that will reveal the context, content, and character of the fact-finding mission that will be acceptable for the intended audience. In addition to Mark's assignment, other examples include interviewing a rocket scientist over the telephone about current research for a column in your campus newspaper, talking with a soldier about his or her feelings about an upcoming battle for a "news report" segment of a local news broadcast, and discussing literary criticism with an English professor to help you prepare a term paper.

This type of informational interview should be characterized both by attention to the questions you need to ask to fulfill your purpose and by a moderately loose style of conducting the actual interview. Here again, the interview will feel like a conversation; however, it will have more structure than a chance meeting with a stranger because you will have planned out specific questions and you will have a more specific goal in mind for the purposeful exchange of talk. Consider the following excerpt from one of Mark's discussions about the review cycle:

Mark: As you know, I am here to talk about the review cycle. What I need to find out is how well the current system is working, and if there are any problems, what suggestions you have about overcoming them.

Catherine: Fine. I'm glad to see we are looking into these procedures.

Mark: Really? You sound concerned.

Catherine: Yes, I am. The current review cycle takes too long, and doesn't allow for dialogue between the programmer and anyone else in the cycle who registers a complaint.

Mark: I see. Do you have an example?

Catherine: Sure. Last month my project was held up for four days because somebody over in sales thought that there weren't enough bells and whistles to make the program attractive to his customers.

Mark: And...?

Catherine: And so I lost four days of work, and this company lost a competitive advantage—our competitor in the meantime introduced a clone of my design. When I finally found out about the sales objection, I wrote a two-line memo that resolved the problem. It said—here, I have a copy of it if you'd like to see it—it said: The bells and whistles are to be customer-dictated. The beauty of this program is that it is infinitely flexible.

Mark: So you are saying that all it took was a two-line response and we could have gained a market advantage.

Catherine: Exactly. And now our product—my program—looks like a clone of the competition's instead of the other way around.

As you can see from this excerpt, Mark's strategy was to begin by discussing the general nature of his assignment and then to allow the interviewee to provide the information. His goal was to complete his assignment, but to do that would mean gaining information from others. Notice that he does not try to evaluate that information, or to question it. His job is to acquire it.

To Develop an In-Depth Piece of Writing or Broadcast Journalism

The outcome of this third type of informational interviewing will be a feature story, book, or documentary capturing the essence of the subject and designed for a target audience. Examples include CBS's *60 Minutes;* ABC's *20-20;* MTV's *Star Attraction;* Tracy Kidder's "The Soul of the New Machine"; Frances Fitzgerald's "Cities on a Hill," a story about a handicapped person for *Parade Magazine;* a story about a celebrity for *People* magazine; and a story for the *Atlantic Monthly* (or the *New Yorker* or *Harper's*).

When preparing for interviews with these goals in mind, you will need to do preparatory research before interviewing the experts or authorities; you will need to very carefully plan out your questions and question sequences; and you will need to validate the information you receive before using it in your work. These outcomes require relatively long periods of time to complete, and the interviewer aiming for these goals should keep careful and detailed records of everything. The interviews tend not to be singular experiences, but multiple ones, and so it becomes very important to build rapport with the interviewees over time and to be flexible in your approach to their material.

Beth, a local television news journalist, found out about Mark and Sandra's business directory. She decided it might be worth a story and contacted them for an interview. She was interested in how two hardworking, fully employed people found time to develop a small business, but she knew that they would also be interested in plugging their product. Her interviewing strategy had to balance her goals with those of the interviewees while not appearing to give her station's endorsement for their product. Consider the following excerpt for evidence of how Beth accomplished her task:

Beth: So you decided to devote your Saturdays to gathering basic information for the directory?

Sandra: Yes. We divided the labor, and each took about four or five potential customers in the morning and four or five more in the afternoon. We stressed to them the advantages of a local directory, explained to them how we planned to provide it free of charge to all area residents, and then went into the comparative cost of our directory versus the Yellow Pages.

Beth: You realize, of course, I'll have to edit out those last comments. We can't appear to be endorsing your product. I'm mostly interested in how you managed to find time to do all of these things while maintaining your job.

Mark: The answer is simple. We wanted it very badly. If you want something badly enough, you will sacrifice to do it.

Beth: Is that also how you felt, Sandra?

Sandra: Yes. Certainly. But there is the satisfaction that comes from owning your own business, making it profitable, providing a needed service to the community.

Beth: How long did it take to develop your database?

Mark: About two months.

Beth: So you didn't do any shopping, go to any movies, for two months?

Sandra: More like four months, actually. There was a lot of planning that went into it before we actually started collecting the information. And then we had to use our desktop publishing system to design the pages. And make an agreement with a printer.

Beth: Sounds like a lot of time and effort.

Mark: That's right. But it was worth it.

As you can see from this excerpt, Beth had to balance her concerns for a story with the interviewees' desire for some free publicity. By addressing that issue in a straightforward manner when it occurred naturally in the interview, she avoided later problems and was able to follow her plan for the interview. Notice how she kept redirecting her questions back to the theme of her story. To complete an interviewing assignment such as this one requires maintaining the focus of the interview.

To Begin, Develop, or Complete a Research Project to Satisfy a Predetermined Organizational Goal

The outcome of this fourth type of informational interviewing goal will be a research report, article, or statement capable of demonstrating the satisfactory accomplishment of the initial purpose. Examples include a presentation by the marketing division of Procter & Gamble on the feasibility survey of a new toothpaste flavor, an advertising campaign by Nike Corporation using a series of "people-on-the-street" interviews, an article for the *Journal of the American Medical Association* on the toxic interactants in a baked potato skin, a briefing for a professional meeting of the Decision Sciences Institute on artificial intelligence applications of expert systems that will be published in their proceedings, and preparations for hosting a news conference for the media.

Here again there will be a preparatory research requirement to complete the assignment and interviews in terms of working out questions and sequences in advance. In many cases there will be a need for more than one interview with each interviewee in order to complete the assignment, and there will be an ethical demand that you check out or validate the information you report as factual before using it in your work.

Sandra and Mark's business directory became a success. News of their product and its success reached other neighboring communities, and soon there were calls for information by local residents about how they did it. Sandra decided that she should write an article about their experiences. The article would, of course, advertise their success, but also it would serve as a guide to beginning and running this sort of project for others.

Sandra did not feel that the article should be limited to their own experiences. To be complete, she would need to interview other publishers of business directories. Perhaps she would find that there was a pattern to successful business enterprises. Perhaps she would also learn some ways of improving their business efficiency and operation. Below is an excerpt from one of her interviews with a publisher in the midwest. Notice how she uses a moderately structured approach to gain information:

Sandra: You have been publishing this directory for three years. Could you tell me how your initial vision for the business has changed during that time?

Bill: Sure. In the beginning I thought I would make a little money on the side by putting out this directory. I didn't think of it as a full-time job, nor did I think it would need to come out every four months.

Sandra: Every four months? Really?

Bill: Oh yes! Our community is growing, and new businesses open every week. To be accurate I need to update the directory every four months.

Sandra: I can see how that would eat up a lot of your time.

Bill: So much so that last year I quit my other job. I just couldn't do everything that needed to be done.

Sandra: What prompted that decision? I mean, was there a specific incident that encouraged you to make the decision?

Bill: Let me think. Yes, Yes, there was. It was the day the local Boy Scout troop told me they wouldn't be able to help me with the deliveries.

Sandra: Did I hear you correctly? The local Boy Scout troop did your deliveries?

Bill: That's right. They are a service organization. I made a donation to them. They hand-delivered each and every directory in all of our neighborhoods. It saved me a lot of postage and trouble.

Sandra: Why couldn't they help you that one time?

Bill: It was my fault. They had a Jamboree planned for that weekend, and I had just forgotten all about it. So when my boss told me I had to work that weekend and I knew I would have to make the deliveries myself with only the help of my two boys, I quit.

Sandra: You quit? On the spot?

Bill: Right there on the shop floor. I was polite about it, but when I told him I couldn't work that weekend because of my delivery schedule, he told me I had to choose between my business and his business. So I did.

Sandra: I see. I think I would have made the same choice, given the circumstances. Now let's discuss how you decided on a printer.

As you can see from the above excerpt, Sandra controlled the interview by her skill in asking questions. Her moderately scheduled format allowed her to probe when she heard potentially useful information for her article, and at the same time allowed her to accomplish her interviewing objectives.

In each one of these situations the interview is linked to a specific outcome—enhanced understanding of a general situation, a business presentation, a segment on television, a professional article. Having a specific outcome in mind is important to informational interviewing because it defines the uses to which the information will be put, which in turn helps you figure out how to create a research strategy for the interview.

In the following section we will examine research strategies. We will move beyond Sandra and Mark's experiences and look at ways in which you can design and carry out an informational interview.

CREATING A RESEARCH STRATEGY FOR THE INTERVIEW

To create a research strategy requires determining (1) where you can go to acquire information to prepare you for interviewing, (2) what questions to ask, (3) how to probe into answers you receive, (4) how to handle problematic interviewees, and (5) how much checking out or validating of the information you will need to do to satisfy the requirements of the job. Let's examine each of these steps in order, and in more detail.

Preparing for Interviewing

The information you receive from an interviewee is dependent upon the quality of questions you ask, which in turn is largely dependent on the level of knowledge, skill, or understanding you bring to the interviewing situation. This means you need to prepare for the interview by determining who can be interviewed and by investigating alternative sources of information.

Determining who can be a subject for an interview can be accomplished by answering these basic questions:

1. Who is available?
2. Does the person (or persons) have the information?
3. Will the person (or persons) willingly provide the information?
4. Can the person be persuaded to be interviewed?

Answering these questions should lead you to investigate alternative sources of information that can help you (1) to locate the individuals who are knowledgeable on the subject and (2) to develop a strategy for evaluating and checking out the information they provide.

As you probably know, there are three fundamental sources of information: experts, libraries or other sources of written or computer-accessible data, and opinion polls or surveys. To prepare for an interview may mean you need to consult one or more of those sources. In most cases you will find you need to consult all three.

For example, assume you are preparing a short documentary film on the subject of local housing problems. You want to feature in your film the plight of a homeless family who was made homeless because the father was laid off from a factory job and has no other marketable skills; and the mother, in addition to rearing three small children, suffers from chronic arthritis which makes her unable to use her secretarial skills. Your interviews of these individuals will be the focus of your documentary, but to do justice to their story you need to acquire additional information.

First, you consult the local housing authority. You conduct a brief, exploratory interview about local housing problems, and in addition to this information you are given a few pamphlets that illustrate current statistical data. In the course of your interview you ask the housing authority what other sources of information you should consult, and are given the names of three articles in professional housing journals to read.

Second, you visit the library. Here you locate the three articles and also, through the cooperation of a librarian, find a book on the new urban poor that illustrates the extent of the problem.

Third, you schedule an interview with a local professor of community planning. In this interview you explore possible solutions for the problems of housing, and learn of two additional library sources that may be of use to you when you plan your film.

Fourth, you decide to conduct a random sample opinion poll with residents of the city about their awareness of the shortage of housing. (To aid you in this task, you might consult Chapter 10 on survey interviewing. This explains sampling techniques, question formats, and reliability of results to you.)

Fifth, you return to the library and find only one of the two sources the professor recommended. The helpful librarian orders the other book using interlibrary loan. While you are there, you browse through the popular magazine section and find a really good story about the same things you want to feature in your film. You ask the librarian to help you use a computer search to see if any other popular articles have been written.

Sixth, you return to your documentary family for the actual on-film interview. You have used the available information, have read the books and articles, have talked with experts, and can design your questions for maximum utility. You can fill in the story of this family with information you received from all of those sources. With luck, and the proper lighting, you can finish your project!

As you can see, preparing for the interview involves a variety of steps and a variety of sources. The essential feature of preparing for an interview is to keep in mind that you are spending time (and in some cases money) to educate yourself about a topic worth pursuing. It's your education, and its your time, so be sure that what you get out of it is worthwhile.

Asking Questions

As you learned in Chapters 4 and 5, the art of interviewing is largely an art of asking intelligent, skilled questions designed to induce the interviewee to respond appropriately. When you conduct an informational interview, you need to be concerned with three key issues about the questions you ask:

1. *What are the most important sources of information for me to consult in order to complete my assignment?* How you answer this will determine who you need to interview and what major questions you need to ask.
2. *What information do I want to receive from the interviewee?* How you answer this will determine your major topics and sequences of questions.
3. *What specific use can I envision for answers I receive to each set of questions?* How you answer this will determine how the interview can be made more economical and still accomplish your objectives.

To see how these issues can work to your advantage, consider the following statement made by a technical writer for a computer software firm:

I was assigned to write the technical documentation for a new product. This meant interviewing members of the programming staff, a quality assurance representative, and two people in our training department. Each interview was important to the documentation because it would allow me to better understand how the system worked and what potential problems an end user would face, and it would also establish a format that would be used by the training department when the system was sold.

Each interview was different. I had to spend time researching the product, developing questions for the interview, and on two occasions scheduling a second interview with someone when I wrote up my notes and saw that I was still lacking some important information.

In this example the interviewer was keenly aware of what she needed to do with the information she received, and those objectives guided her research strategy. Notice that she defined each of the interviewees as a source of a particular kind of knowledge—the programmers know the system, the quality assurance representative knows the potential user problems, and the trainers know what formats are appropriate for instruction. By defining the types of knowledge to be gained from each interview, the technical writer was able to design questions capable of speaking to each interviewee's level of expertise. Her job, then, was to combine the three sources of information into a technical document that would be friendly to the user, technically correct, and capable of being used for corporate training tasks.

Planning Your Probes

How can you receive sufficient details from the interviewee? How you answer this will determine the words and phrases you use to probe or follow up primary questions, and will help you understand what sort of examples, illustrations, and other data you should seek.

As you learned earlier in this book, planning for probes is one of the most difficult aspects of interviewing. This is the case because probes tend to suggest themselves to experienced interviewers during the flow of conversation, and often the most effective probes or follow-ups are less planned than they are spontaneous. However, it wouldn't be fair for us to suggest that inexperienced interviewers will simply "get better at probes with experience." In fact, there are useful strategies that you can employ to gain access to details, and details are the major reason why you use follow-up and probing questions in an informational interview.

For example, assume you are interested in doing a news story on Star Wars researchers. You realize that this is a highly controversial subject, as well as a highly technical one. Assume further that you have done the necessary homework to prepare for a series of interviews with people engaged in Star Wars research, including reading a few popular books and articles on the subject, researching news accounts of federal debates on the subject, and interviewing two physics professors with opposing views on whether the research effort on Star Wars projects can actually produce workable results. Now you need to interview the principals: a research director at an army installation, a computer programmer who works on simulations of Star Wars defense strategies, and a defense contractor who is responsible for developing one of the essential fiber optic links in the system.

You know that each one of these interviewees may be somewhat guarded on the subject. After all, each one of them may feel the need to protect his or her job as well as some military secrets. Furthermore, you know from your research efforts that claims are made by both sides that are difficult to prove given the current state of technology and the fact that no one ever predicts the future very accurately. How do you ferret out the necessary details to complete your work?

Of course, you are unlikely to get these people to reveal classified information. But you can make use of two of the techniques of probing to obtain examples, illustrations, and other data from these interviewees: *elaboration* and *clarification*. In this case it would be advisable to plan only your opening questions (and plan those based on what your research has told you), and then use a question such as "Can you elaborate on that, please?" or "Would you mind clarifying that statement for me?" or "Could you give me an example of how that would work?" to gain the level of detail you are seeking.

These two techniques can also help you acquire additional information from an interviewee. They elicit examples, illustrations, and other data such as imaginary scenarios, technical specifications, statistics, or nonpublished test results. However, informational interviewing requires more than simply getting answers to questions; it also involves checking out or validating information you have been given by your sources. And in some cases, as we will see later, it requires you to validate information using your own experience.

Dealing with Problematic Interviewees

The nature of in-depth interviewing can produce special circumstances that are difficult for the interviewer. Part of what you are trying to achieve is to bring out into the open the interviewee's attitudes, values, and beliefs, as well as reasoning that underlies decisions. Journalists, in particular, may find themselves interviewing people who have the experience of some of life's most trying moments fresh in their minds. You need to be prepared to manage several problems if they surface.

Reluctant interviewees.   The *reluctant interviewee* is a person who has agreed to be interviewed, but does not seem to want to fully participate in the interview. It may be difficult to tell if the person is unwilling or unable to talk.

There are a variety of reasons for this kind of behavior. The reason might be something having to do with the topic, situation, other people, or even you. It also could be none of these, but, instead, a trait of the interviewee which has been acquired in the process of growing up in a particular home environment. If the interviewee verbalizes his or her uneasiness, you should take time to talk through the problem if possible. Sometimes you can encourage an interviewee to participate more if you talk less. Are you using pauses effectively? Perhaps a change in interviewing environment will ease the situation. You might move to a lounge or cafeteria to relax the interviewee.

Think, too, about the style of communicating you are using and the type of questions you are asking. If you are being informal, you might switch to a more formal style. If you are asking primarily open questions, you might try a series that are more closed. Consider, too, the level of difficulty of your questions. Can you pursue for a while an easier line of questioning?

Finally, make sure you are showing interest. You might try active listening.

Hostile interviewees.   A *hostile interviewee* is a person who displays defensive communication behavior. Recall that we discussed defensive and supportive communication in Chapter 8. You will want to have the ideas discussed there firmly in mind if you are working with a hostile interviewee.

Be sure that what you are observing is hostile behavior. Sometimes a person is cool and aloof because this is that person's general temperament. Once you are satisfied that the interviewee is showing hostility, you might decide to deal directly with it. There are so many possibilities for the source of hostility that you will probably want to come out and ask the interviewee about it. You might try a nondirective statement or question like one of these:

"I've noticed that you appear to be angry. Could we talk about it?"
"You appear to be very upset."
"You seem to be very critical. Is something wrong?"

What follows your probe might very well be a venting of anger. Be prepared and supportive in your behavior.

Emotional interviewees.   The *emotional interview* is the person who is displaying intense feelings. These might range from anger to sorrow. We dealt with the topic of anger above, so we will turn here to sorrow.

The in-depth interview may very well take place regarding some disaster, crime, death, or scandal. The person who is displaying the strong emotion, therefore, is probably psychologically involved in the incident. Our first thought is to say something like, "Don't feel sad. Everything is going to be all right." A statement like this is usually a mistake. It is saying in effect, "You shouldn't feel the way you feel. Everything will turn out fine." This denies the person's right to feel sad and makes a statement that might not be true. It might be reassuring to say something like, "It's OK to cry. I know you are sad about...." A sincere expression of condolences is almost always appropriate. And don't be afraid to refer to people involved by name.[1] If you are personally close to the person, it can be appropriate to make a gesture of support, such as holding the person's hand.

If the situation is such that you do not seem to be making any progress with the interview, you may want to pause for a moment or set another time. Simply say something like, "We're not in a hurry. Take as long as you need." Or you might say, "Perhaps we should talk some other time. Would you like to set another time to talk?"

Validating Information

One of the most important skills you will learn from your study of interviewing for information is how to check out or validate that information *before* you use it. Not only will this step in the research process help you avoid legal problems such as slander, libel, or fraud; it will also provide you with a healthy dose of skepticism about believing what others tell you.

Remember that one of the most common problems affecting communication between people is the false assumption of shared understandings about situations, meanings for words, or goals for talk. Given this background it should not be surprising to you to discover that what you "innocently" wrote down as a fact during an informational interview may not have been intended to be recorded as a fact, but merely as speculation by the interviewee. Conversely, what you may put together based on inferences made from your notes may not, in fact, turn out to be valid.

To guard against such problems you need to develop procedures (and sources) for checking out or validating your work before completing your task. We recommend that you use the following heuristics (rules of thumb) to guide you:

1. An expert is a person with information and a point of view; because every issue contains more than one point of view, it is wise to seek out contrasting opinions from other experts before reporting as fact what one expert tells you.

For example, consider the following excerpt from an interview one of our students, Jennifer, conducted with a city planning expert:

Jennifer: So you believe that our traffic flow problems can be solved by gaining access to the army arsenal's land?

Mr. Franklin: Absolutely. Of course, they don't want to give us access because they claim it will ruin their security.

Jennifer: Are there other proposals for reducing traffic flow problems?

Mr. Franklin: Oh yeah, sure. But none of them have the advantages of this plan. They either cost too much or will take too long to complete.

Jennifer: What about Councilwoman Silverstein's recommendation for tapping into state highway moneys?

Mr. Franklin: You'd have to discuss that plan with her. But I still think that even if you got the state money, access to the arsenal land is essential.

As you can see, this expert came equipped with a definite point of view. Jennifer learned about his plan, but she also discovered she needed to schedule an interview with Councilwoman Silverstein.

2. Information, even specific technical details such as numbers or statistics or findings, is necessarily ambiguous. This means that it is capable of being interpreted differently by different people. If you can only think of one way to interpret information, it usually means you need to talk to more, and to different, people.

Consider the following excerpt from an interview between a news reporter and a consultant on the city's business growth:

News Reporter: You have been quoted as saying that we can expect a

15–20 percent increase in new businesses over the next five years. What does this mean for our city planners?

Consultant: That was a conservative estimate. I think our planners need to get busy with improvements to our roads, to our schools, and to our commitment to business investment.

News Reporter: So you have confidence in your figures?

Consultant: Yes. Of course, every good statistic can be overturned by poor city planning. What we need is planning.

If you were the news reporter in the above scenario, what would you do? How would you try to verify this information?

3. Information about historical events can be checked out easily. Information about the evolution of a fact (such as who actually invented a product, who originally came up with a new idea, or where someone was on the night of the murder) is usually more difficult to verify. You can report history as verifiable fact, but beyond that you can seldom rely on verifiable facts.

Consider the following excerpt from an interview conducted by a marketing manager with a customer:

Marketing Manager: So you are telling me that you would buy this product if it had a more useful index?

Customer: I'm saying I would be more inclined to do that, yes. But without an accurate index I don't think I'd even consider it.

Marketing Manager: Could you give me an example of how the index could be improved?

Customer: That's not my specialty. I just know I don't particularly like this one.

Marketing Manager: What is it that annoys you?

Customer: The whole thing. I don't know. You'd have to do some work on keying the major functions, maybe using more color.

Marketing Manager: So if we key the major functions with a color code, that would satisfy you?

Customer: That would be a start.

In this excerpt the interviewer has trouble getting specific information from the customer. So how reliable do you think the information that is finally given about color coding actually is? What would you advise the marketing manager to do to check on the reliability of this information?

4. College professors are good sources of a wide variety of information. They are also members of disciplines at war with other disciplines, they are believers in research methods that often discount the importance of other research methods, and they are prone to speak generally of things they may only have specific data about. When you interview a college professor, learn to ask for research citations you can use to check out the information you are given. And remember, there are always opposing points of view in any profession.

Consider the following brief excerpt from an interview conducted by a graduate student in speech with a professor of anthropology:

Student: I was interested in finding out why so many communication scholars are turning to the work of anthropologists, particularly in organizational studies.

Professor: Probably because of the recent, faddish interest members of your discipline seem to have in the idea of culture.

Student: Faddish?

Professor: To be sure. Your discipline amazes me. One year it is a social science; the next it is a humanities. One year it is concerned about philosophy of language; the next it is all awash in the concert of culture. Who knows what will be next?

As you can see, this particular professor's view of the communication discipline (whether right or wrong) runs through his answers to the interviewer's questions. Separating the fact from the opinion would be difficult. What do you think you would do if you were conducting this interview?

These simple rules will help you validate information you receive from interviewees. However, there is another way to validate information you receive, and it is a way that is increasingly more popular among "new journalists." It is based on personal involvement: in order to know about an experience, one must become personally immersed in that experience.

Consider this example. A friend of ours is an investigative reporter who free-lances for popular magazines. Recently he has been writing about regional social organizations and what makes them attractive to their members. On one assignment he wrote about a local fox hunting club that happened to be one of the two privately owned fox hunting clubs in the country. It also happens to be located in a region renowned for its high-technology focus. For him the contrast between high technology and the heritage of fox hunting was appealing. Here is what he did to write the story—notice how he inserted himself into the situation with the interviewees in order to validate what he had been told:

First I scheduled an interview with the founder of the club, a man in his seventies who really knew how to be a millionaire. From him I learned about the formal history of the organization, his interest in starting it, and how it had developed. I asked him who else I should interview, and he explained to me something I otherwise wouldn't have known: a fox hunt is run by a "master of the hounds," the person who buys and trains the foxhounds and who really is the "hunter."

When I talked to the master of the hounds, he explained to me technical details about selecting and training the dogs, and how a hunt is organized and run, but he also told me that people who ride in the hunt are asked to join on the basis of the quality of their horses. I asked him to give me the names of some horse owners—a range of quality—for me to talk to. He did.

When I spoke with the horse owners, they revealed the importance of breeding and bloodlines, but the common thread in their stories had to do with a veterinarian who had introduced most of them to each other. So then I knew I had to talk to the vet. In this way I was able to interview a wide variety of people involved with the hunt, and each one of them led me to someone else who in turn led me to someone else. My questions were basic, broad, and open—"How did you get involved with fox hunting?" would take some of them half an hour to answer. They liked to talk.

However, to write a story about fox hunting meant doing far more research than simply talking to members of the club. It also meant reading some important books on the subject so that when I talked with these people I had some language in common with them. It also meant actually riding in a hunt. Now there's the part they don't tell you about in journalism school. Here I am, a middle-aged man who has never ridden a horse, and yet I knew that to capture the experience of a hunt for my readers would require me to learn how to ride.

Believe it or not, that was the core of my research experience for the article. Not only did taking riding lessons with a member of the hunt teach me how to ride; it also provided me with personal experience with an animal that I had before only observed from the sides of roads. Then I knew why people fox-hunt: there is love of the sport based on the love of the animals in it that is the point of it. Whether or not they corner a fox—which is, by the way, a bloody and awful thing to witness— doesn't matter nearly as much as the continuing of an old and noble heritage that bonds men and women to their animals. If I hadn't done what it took to actually research this article, what I would have written would have been about as useless as a travel guide written by someone whose only experience of the place was library books and other people's descriptions of their experiences.

In this example you get the feeling that a research strategy for an informational interview, or series of interviews, entails far more than simply planning questions and question sequences. For this investigative reporter it means immersing himself in the experience of what will be written about, and of actually learning how to perform the skills involved in it. Again, the outcome you seek determines the research process you will use.

Recording the Interview

You will want to take written notes of your interview. This requires some skill and practice, but it is important since you may not always be able to tape-record an interview. And even if you are using a tape recorder, you will want to take notes because there is always the chance of the machine not operating properly.

If you decide to use a tape recorder, you will want to reduce the effect it might have on the interview. Use a small recorder with a condenser microphone. Place the recorder so that it will be located in an inconspicuous spot. Also, explain to the person being interviewed that you are using the tape recorder to ensure accuracy.

SUMMARY

This chapter examined the interview as a method of acquiring and interpreting information. We began by defining the uses to which informational interviewing can be put, and by demonstrating that the skills of this type of interviewing are pervasive in our service-oriented economy.

We then discussed the importance of planning a research strategy. In this section we showed the relationship between understanding the uses to which information will be put and the types of questions and question formats appropriate to obtaining that goal. We also suggested ways to deal with difficult interviewees. In addition, we stressed the importance of checking out information, of validating facts, and of seeking out more than one source of expertise before forming an opinion. As an example of a way to validate information, we reported how a journalist immersed himself in the experience that later would be written about, quite a different approach from our earlier examples of Mark and Sandra Sanford as interviewers. Finally, we talked briefly about recording the interview.

NOTE

[1]George M. Killenberg and Rob Anderson, *Before the Story: Interviewing and Communication Skills for Journalists* (New York: St. Martin's Press, 1989), p. 150.

AN IN-DEPTH INFORMATIONAL INTERVIEW FOR ANALYSIS

In preparation for a series of newspaper stories, David McDowell is interviewing Rhonda Stewart. He has planned to center one story on a significant event in her early life. That is the topic of this interview.

Ethics and Responsibilities in Interviewing

The in-depth information-gathering interview situation suggests a number of guidelines and responsibilities. First, *interviewers have the responsibility to clearly identify themselves and their sponsoring organization.* Of course, there are circumstances in which the interviewer is well known and there is no sponsoring organization or group. But some professional interviewers, such as journalists, will usually not be known by an interviewee. The principle of fairness suggests that interviewers have a responsibility to clearly identify themselves and their organizations.

Second, *interviewers should not schedule interviews under false pretenses.* Interviewers generally reveal the purpose of an interview when it is scheduled. It is unethical to intentionally deceive, to suggest one purpose to the interviewee and then pursue another during the actual interview.

Third, *the principle of fairness dictates that interviewers do their homework.* Uninformed interviewers can waste valuable time of interviewees. But, beyond this, uninformed interviewers may misinterpret information and, thus, generate misleading conclusions in any report or action that results from the interview. Interviewers have a responsibility to be well informed.

Fourth, *interviewers have a responsibility to respect the dignity of the interviewee.* This suggests that the interviewer should not delve into personal information that is not relevant to the purpose of the interview.

Fifth, the integrity of the product of the interview dictates another responsibility. *Interviewers should be sure that any conclusions they state in the product of the interview are supported by the information they have collected.*

Sixth, *interviewers have the responsibility to use the information gathered only for the stated purpose and outlet.* So, it would be unethical to tell interviewees that material is being collected for a feature essay in the newspaper and then publish that information in a book. This behavior is intentional deception.

Finally, *interviewers should keep their promises.* If they have agreed that some information secured during the interview is "off the record," they must respect that promise no matter how important it seems to include that information. To use the information would violate the principle of fairness and might also be viewed as intentional deception.

Interviewees, too, should be careful to follow certain three ethical guidelines: First, *interviewees should be careful not to misrepresent themselves or their credentials.* To claim to have an expertise that they do not have, for example, is intentional deception and, perhaps, intentional harm.

(Continued)

Second, *interviewees should not agree to an interview and then back out.* Some professional interviewers, journalists for example, work under strict deadlines. Withdrawal from a promised interview might create harm, intentional or not.

Finally, *interviewees should prepare for the interview, if necessary.* Further, *interviewees have the responsibility to participate fully and openly as long as what is asked is within the bounds of what they have agreed to do.* The principle of fairness is violated when interviewers prepare extensively for an interview and interviewees do not prepare or participate fully.

1. **McDowell:** Ms. Stewart, I've appreciated your willingness to grant me the opportunity to do this series of interviews with you. In this first interview, we will be talking some about the early years of your life. It is important to me that you feel comfortable. Would you like a cup of coffee or a soft drink?

2. **Stewart:** No, David, I don't think so.

3. **McDowell:** Let me know, too, if you need to take a break.

4. **Stewart:** OK.

5. **McDowell:** I will be tape-recording the interview. I will just start the tape recorder and put it over here out of our way.

6. **McDowell:** From your childhood, what major event created a lasting impression?

7. **Stewart:** That would be my parents' divorce.

8. **McDowell:** Let me ask you a few questions about it. Do you mind talking about it?

9. **Stewart:** I agreed to these interviews. I don't mind talking about this.

10. **McDowell:** When did this occur?

11. **Stewart:** When I was 4½.

12. **McDowell:** Where were you when this occurred?

13. **Stewart:** Huntsville, Alabama.

14. **McDowell:** Is that your hometown?

15. **Stewart:** Yes.

16. **McDowell:** Can you tell me a little bit about the circumstances immediately preceding or leading up to the realization of the divorce? I

guess what I want to talk about is the particular point of discovery in this case when you found out they were getting a divorce.

17. Stewart: I was so young that I don't really remember that. I guess the full realization came a few years later when I realized that my family was not quite the same as other children's families. Probably when I was first entering grade school, perhaps first grade or kindergarten.

18. McDowell: So, we could say really, it began to make an impression on you when you were about six years old?

19. Stewart: Right.

20. McDowell: Who besides yourself and your parents were involved that added to making this a lasting impression?

21. Stewart: My mother's family, the other party involved that caused the divorce, and my peers with the normal mother-father-child family.

22. McDowell: How did your peers react when they found out your family was different?

23. Stewart: Well, at open-house nights and at performances, when their parents would come to those and just my mother would show up, there was a little difficulty. It was just that other kids would look at me funny, and ask, "Where's your dad?" or "Why isn't your dad here?" or "Why did they get divorced?"—that kind of thing. And of course you really can't go into all of that when you're that young. You don't fully understand. And you feel cheated because the other kids talk about what they do with their family, their fathers—where they go and what they do.

24. McDowell: What about your mother's family?

25. Stewart: What do you mean?

26. McDowell: Well, what were the reactions from them?

27. Stewart: Let's see. My mother was the only person in the whole family who ever had a divorce, and divorce has not been accepted until recent years. She never quite fit back into the family. Of course, I was too young to really know how her family generally felt. But I often heard her say things when she was on the phone with friends. I would hear her saying things like, "They don't accept me for the way I am now. I'm alone. They think I've disgraced the family." And of course that rubs off on a child. After hearing things like that, you think that maybe your family unit is not quite as good as another family unit or you're not quite as good as the other kids.

28. McDowell: You seem to be saying that a lot of your mother's trauma is what caused it to be such a traumatic or lasting experience for you. Is that right?

29. Stewart: Yes.

30. McDowell: (pause)

31. Stewart: One thing I would like to add—I guess the reason for that would be I was so young that I don't really remember family life before they had gotten a divorce.

32. McDowell: What do you remember about your family life immediately preceding the divorce?

33. Stewart: I don't remember anything before the divorce.

34. McDowell: How about afterward?

35. Stewart: I don't remember anything really until kindergarten and first grade when we had moved to Mobile.

36. McDowell: What kind of changes occurred in your life?

37. Stewart: Well, of course, I hardly ever saw my father. I didn't get to see his family—my grandmother and everybody on that side of the family.

38. McDowell: I'm looking for the kinds of changes in your life that caused this event to be impressionable.

39. Stewart: Well, as I was saying, not getting to see my father as much as I would have liked to. In fact, when I saw him, I saw him for about one weekend a year. And, of course, I didn't get to see his family, so I feel a loss there. I guess it was all one-sided. I only got one person's impression—my mother's—of what a divorce was like, and what the effects were from that. Do you understand?

40. McDowell: I understand. Is there any one specific event or action that stands out as being the most memorable or most impressionable experience of the entire ordeal.

41. Stewart: Well, I do remember one thing that occurred during the divorce. That was when my uncle had come to pick us up in Huntsville with the moving van. I remember getting to ride to Mobile in the van. I was excited about that until, I remember, he said you're never going to see your father again. That's the only thing I remember at the divorce time. That was very traumatic.

42. McDowell: At that time, what was your relationship with your uncle?

43. Stewart: I didn't know him very well. I had only seen him—well I don't know how many times I'd seen him, but I don't remember him before that. I don't remember any of my mother's family before that.

44. McDowell: What time of year did this all happen?

45. Stewart: I don't remember. I think it was during the summertime. It seems like that because I know I wasn't well, come to think of it, I was too young to be in school. Probably summer or early fall, it seems like.

46. McDowell: Can you think of anything that I have not asked you that would be pertinent to the primary question of why this created a lasting impression?

47. Stewart: Do you mean what effects it has now? For one thing, because I have not been around my father, I don't know him very well. And I'm not as close to that side of my family as I could be. I'm also not very close to my mother's side of the family because of the things that they said about each other.

48. McDowell: So, you are saying not only did the divorce create obviously a very long-lasting impression, but it had very definite effects throughout your life, even to the present.

49. Stewart: Definitely.

50. McDowell: I thank you. I think this is what I need to know at this point.

EXPERIENCES

1. As a class, view a group interview from a program such as *Face the Nation* or *Meet the Press*. Compare and contrast the interviewing styles utilized by the different interviewers. Which styles are more effective than others? Why? Now evaluate the questions asked. Which questions seemed to be more effective in gaining the information sought? Why were these questions more effective? Finally, consider the use of probing. Were there missed opportunities for probing? Were attempts to probe for additional information effective? Why or why not?

2. Plan and carry out two interviews, one with a newspaper journalist and the other with a police or insurance investigator, to compare and contrast their experiences and techniques used to conduct interviews. How does the general goal of the in-depth interview shape the techniques used? What constraints does each situation bring to the interview? What characterizes an effective interview and interviewer?

3. Attend a press conference to observe a group interview where one person is taking questions from several interviewers. How does this situation differ from those where there is a single interviewer? How do the skills needed by the interviewer differ from those needed in the one-on-one interview?

4. Contrast a planned versus unplanned in-depth information-gathering interview. Conduct two 10-minute interviews regarding a person's hobby, the first being unplanned. Do not plan the second interview until after you have completed the

first. Now conduct a planned interview with another interviewee. Tape-record both interviews. Analyze the tapes to discover the effect of planning. How does the information obtained differ regarding depth and breadth? Does the information from one of these interviews seem more complete? Are there any differences in the climate of the interviews?

RECOMMENDED READINGS

Anderson, David, and Peter Benjaminson, *Investigative Reporting* (Bloomington, IN: Indiana University Press, 1976).

Benson, Thomas W., "Another Shootout in Cowtown," *The Quarterly Journal of Speech, 67* (1981), 347–406.

Biagi, Shirley, *Interviews That Work* (Belmont, CA: Wadsworth, 1986).

Birkhead, Douglas, "An Ethics of Vision for Journalism," *Critical Studies in Mass Communication, 6* (1989), 283–294.

Goodall, H. Lloyd, Jr., *Mystery is the Detective's Metaphor: Reading Context, Self, and Other(s) as Clues* (Carbondale, IL: Southern Illinois University Press, 1990).

Killenberg, George M., and Rob Anderson, *Before the Story: Interviewing and Communication Skills for Journalists* (New York: St. Martin's Press, 1989).

Metzler, Ken, *Creative Interviewing: The Writer's Guide to Gathering Information by Asking Questions* (Englewood Cliffs, NJ: Prentice-Hall, 1976).

Michler, Elliot G., *Research Interviewing* (Cambridge, MA: Harvard University Press, 1986).

Van Maanen, John, *Tales of the Field: On Writing Ethnography* (Chicago: University of Chicago Press, 1988).

CHAPTER 10

THE SURVEY INTERVIEW

OBJECTIVES

After reading this chapter, you should be able to:

Formulate a statement of purpose for a survey interview.

Conduct background research on a particular issue.

Develop a basic structure for a survey interview.

Prepare an effective opening and closing for a survey interview.

Prepare a schedule of appropriate questions for securing the desired information and purposes.

Draw an appropriate sample using the four procedures described.

Specify considerations in selecting and training interviewers.

Pretest and refine a survey interview.

Conduct a survey interview.

Analyze the results from data collected for a survey interview.

Respond appropriately as an interviewee when called upon to participate in a survey interview.

Discuss the ethics of survey interviewing.

Rarely does an adult in our society *not* participate in a survey interview. The survey is an important means for data collection when the task is to know what the members of some identifiable group think. Advertisers use surveys to assess the results of their campaigns. Manufacturing firms use surveys to monitor how their products are being received. Organizations conduct surveys to learn various things about their external publics as well as their employees. Politicians base decisions about their campaigns on data collected through surveys of their voting constituency. Colleges survey their graduates to determine program effectiveness. Journalists use a survey technique called precision journalism[1] to gather facts on which to base news reports and analysis. Thus, it is quite likely that most adults in our society at some time have been asked to participate in a survey.

As a professional, you will undoubtedly find opportunities to use survey interviewing to collect data. Some professionals, especially those in a communication-related position, use surveys more than others. Surveys provide the solid base of information on which decisions can be made. And so whenever the collective wisdom of some identifiable group is needed to make a decision, you will need to use surveying techniques to gather it.

This chapter begins with a discussion of the step-by-step process of planning the interview. Then, we address concerns related to managing the interview. Next, we present information that will be useful in data analysis. And, then, we briefly describe responsible interviewee behavior. Finally, we address ethical considerations.

PREPARATION FOR THE SURVEY INTERVIEW

Stating the Purpose

A specific statement of purpose focuses the interviewer's attention on what needs to be accomplished and guides in the effort to achieve this end. The general purpose of a survey interview is to collect data to learn how members of some group respond to a person, topic, or event. This response might tell us what they know about the subject of interest, what their attitudes are toward it, or how they behave (or think they might behave) toward it. Let's describe each of these specific purposes in greater detail.

First, survey research might be conducted to describe what people know about a topic and where they learned about it. There are many reasons for wanting this kind of information. A company may want to find out what consumers know about its products and where they learned about it. An organization may want to discover what its employees know about its new insurance benefit. A school system may want to know what the public thinks about the schools or issues related to them. The list of reasons for such a survey is nearly endless, as this is a very common type of data collection.

Second, survey research might be conducted to collect data about some group's attitudes. This type of survey is called an *opinion poll* and often is used to measure the public's attitudes about political candidates or public issues and policies. Note that here the word *public* means something other than just the general public. A *public* is "a group of people who have a common interest and are capable of engaging in discussion of an issue in order to do something about it."[2] So organizations have all kinds of publics, both internal—their employees—and external—their consumers, clients, and others—whose attitudes might be measured through a survey.

Third, survey research might be conducted to discover how some group responds to something. One particular kind of survey that has this purpose is the market research survey. The researcher may want to know, for example, what brands of a particular item a public buys and what it is that it likes about them. People in the broadcast industry may be interested in what television or radio programs are watched and/or listened to. Political candidates and others may wish to know on a weekly basis how voters plan to vote.

In addition, researchers have created a survey that studies the relationship between information from one of these three types of surveys and some characteristic or characteristics of the people surveyed. These characteristics are referred to as *demographic variables*. They include such variables as sex, religion, age, race, education, economic status, occupation, and place of residence.

Although you can have a general purpose in mind, you cannot formulate a specific purpose without deciding which group or groups can provide the information that will allow you to achieve that purpose. Identify in specific terms the group or groups you will want to interview. Think about the specific characteristics of each group you are considering. Are there characteristics of some groups that might make them more desirable as a source of information? Take into account factors such as general knowledge of the desired information, availability of interviewees, and willingness of interviewees to participate. Consider also the amount of time you will have to gather data and to conduct each interview. There are often trade-offs related to time and available resources. You may have to set a less ambitious goal for your survey because of lack of resources.

Conducting Background Research

The beginning point for conducting background research is taking stock of what you know about the person, topic, or event of interest. Once you have determined what you already know, you will find that you will generally need to know more. Background research must answer such questions as: What is the history and current status of this particular concern? What ideas or solutions have been investigated? What ideas or solutions are currently being discussed and proposed? What questions have been answered? What questions remain unanswered? What attitudes might your particular public have toward the topic, the interview, and you?

Sources of information are numerous. Interview those who are knowledgeable about the topic—in your organization and elsewhere. Check for files and archives of organizations—yours and others. Check libraries for government documents, professional journals, and books that discuss the topic. Has the issue or person been in the news? If so, be sure to check newspapers and newsmagazines. Remember also to check references cited in those resources in order to obtain additional sources of information.

Developing the Basic Interview Structure

The next step in developing the survey interview requires planning the body, opening, and closing. One method of planning the *body* of a survey interview is to develop an *interview guide* that includes the major topics and subtopics. The guide will focus your ideas and, when examined in the perspective of your purpose, allow you to see whether you are covering the whole of the purpose. A careful examination of the interviewing guide can also help you discover areas where more research is needed.

Sometimes, you may wish to use an alternative method for developing an interview guide. Journalists have used the words *who, what, when, where, how,* and *why* as a quick reference to ensure coverage of a story. Use of these key words may give you the kind of structure you want if you are doing a simple survey.

Figure 10.1 presents part of an interview guide developed in preparation for a nationwide survey of performance appraisal practices.

The *opening* of the survey interview is not tailored to the specific interviewee, as is generally the case in other interviews. This is so because if you were to individualize the opening, you might create a more favorable climate for some interviewees than for others, and this would bias the data. Instead each interviewee is treated alike. Because of the necessity to standardize the opening, we suggest you write it out so you can memorize it and recite it verbatim.

Here is an example of an opening that was used in the nationwide performance appraisal interviews:

Hello, my name is _____ , from the Institute for Communication Research at the University of South Alabama. We

Figure 10.1 A sample interview guide.

I. Goals
    A. Organizational
        1. Affirmative action
        2. Labor contract
        3. Promotion
        4. Increased efficiency
        5. Other
    B. Employee
        1. Salary
        2. Training
        3. Feedback
        4. Improvement
        5. Other
II. Practices
    A. Before appraisal interview
        1. Written job description
        2. Worksheet
        3. Written appraisal
        4. Self-appraisal
        5. Peer appraisal
    B. During appraisal interview
        1. Limit criticism
        2. Employee self-evaluation
        3. Joint problem solving
        4. Establish checkpoints
        5. Plan for training if needed
    C. After appraisal interview
        1. Record progress
        2. Schedule periodic follow-ups
        3. Offer help
        4. Offer training

---

are studying the performance appraisal interviewing process to determine what differences in practices might exist. You have been selected to participate in this national survey because you are a personnel professional. Answers to questions of this kind will help us make performance appraisal interviews more comfortable for you and your employees. Your responses will be kept confidential. We will be pleased to send you a copy of our results as an expression of our gratitude for your participation. May I have a few minutes of your time to ask you some questions about your performance appraisal interviewing practices? (Go to first question.)

Let's look briefly at the construction of this opening. First, the interviewer and the organization represented were identified. A name can add a prestige factor that will enhance the willingness of the interviewee to participate. (*Note:* If revealing the name of the organization might bias the results—perhaps, for example, the Democratic Party is paying for a political poll—the organization's name may be omitted. Instead, the name of the group conducting the poll might be used.)

Next, the purpose of the survey was revealed. This was followed by an inducement to participate. In this case the interviewer said, "Answers to questions of this kind will help us make performance appraisal interviews more comfortable for you and your employees....We will be pleased to send you a copy of our results as an expression of our gratitude for your participation."

The person was assured that the information he or she would provide would be kept confidential. Finally, the person was invited to participate in the interview. Whether you ask the person to participate or not is a decision you will have to make. This decision is based on the particular situation. In this case, the interviewers were working with professionals who undoubtedly saw themselves as busy people. The assumption was made that they would be more likely to participate if they had the opportunity to make the decision. Sometimes, and often in surveys that are polling political opinions, the interviewee is not given an opportunity to say that he or she will participate. Instead, the interviewer moves directly into the first question.

The *closing* of a survey interview is generally brief. It is based on who the interviewees are and the purpose of the interview. When there is no need to contact the interviewee in the future, the interview may close with a simple expression of appreciation. The interviewer might say:

These are all the questions I have. Thank you for your willingness to help.

Sometimes the organization seeking the interview wants to reward the interviewee for participating. One way of doing this is to provide the interviewee with a copy of the results. This was done in the case of the appraisal interview survey discussed above. This interview was closed with the statement:

> Your contribution to this research effort is very greatly appreciated. If you would like a summary of the results, please give me your address. I'll be sure you receive a copy.

Sometimes the organization sponsoring the research wants to be able to verify that valid interviews actually took place. This can be accomplished by calling some of the people who were interviewed. A closing like this might be used if additional contact is anticipated:

> These are all the questions I have. May I have your telephone number so my employer can check to see that this interview was conducted as planned? (Interviewee provides telephone number.) Thank you for your willingness to help.

You may find that you are through with the interview, but the interviewee wishes to continue to talk. You may talk with the interviewee if you wish *and* if you have time. Ending on a friendly note will undoubtedly leave the interviewee favorably disposed to participation in another survey effort.

Preparing the Questions

Next, turn your attention to the schedule of questions to be asked. Careful attention must be given to constructing and refining questions because you will not be able to make changes after you have begun the interviewing process. Each interviewee must be asked precisely the same question to ensure that all interviewees are treated exactly the same so that no bias is introduced.

Important concerns in developing questions for a survey interview are reliability and validity. *Reliability* refers to the consistency of a question. A consistent question is one which will be interpreted similarly by various interviewees or by different interviewers who are asking the same question. *Validity* refers to the accuracy of the information elicited from a question. Here the concern is how accurately the information given in response to a question reflects the interviewee's attitudes, beliefs, or behaviors. To achieve reliability and validity, all the questions must be carefully prepared and pretested.

Begin the development of questions by considering the kinds of questions that are specifically suited to survey research. Generally, these will be highly standardized closed questions. These are asked so that the interviewee's response to a question can be tallied and compared with the other interviewee answers. Four general types of questions are used: nominal scale questions, interval scale questions, ordinal scale questions, and Bogardus Social Distance Scale questions.

Nominal scale questions.   Sometimes the kind of information you will want to collect will be nominal. A *nominal scale* uses categories (variables) that are considered to be mutually exclusive. *Mutually exclusive* suggests that the categories do not overlap, nor do they line up in some kind of continuum. For example, a nominal scale might be used to collect demographic information such as that displayed below. This kind of information is called *self-report* because it asks for information about the respondent.

Of which political party are you a member?

Republican 1

Democratic 2

Independent 3

Libertarian 4

Socialist 5

None 6

Interval scale questions.   An *interval scale* indicates choices that can form a continuum and provide distances between measures. There are different kinds of interval scales.

A *numerical interval scale* is often used to collect information about age, income, educational level, rank in an organization, and the like. A numerical interval scale like the one below might be used to collect information about annual income.

What is your yearly income?

Under $10,000 1

$10,000–$19,999 2

$20,000–$29,999 3

$30,000–$39,999 4

$40,000–$49,000 5

Over $50,000 6

A *frequency interval scale* is used to report how often the respondent does something or uses something. For example, an interviewer for a church was polling its members to evaluate use of its programs. One question asked was:

In a month that has four Wednesdays, how frequently do you attend our Wednesday night programming?

4 times a month 4

3 times a month 3

2 times a month 2

1 time a month 1

Don't attend 0

An *evaluative interval scale* may be used to seek an evaluation. A power company asked a question of this type in a survey of its customers:

How would you rate the service of the power company?

Excellent 5

Good 4

Average 3

Below average 2

Poor 1

A typical evaluative interval scale that asks the interviewee to make a judgment is an *agreement/disagreement scale* (often called a Likert scale). A question using this kind of scale allows the respondent to make a choice along a 5-point scale. The middle point on such a scale is considered the neutral point. This kind of question is frequently used to assess attitudes. Here are two questions of this type from the power company survey:

Please respond to these questions by indicating your choice. The choices you can use are *strongly agree, agree, neither agree nor disagree, disagree,* or *strongly disagree.*

The power company provides adequate service. Do you?

Strongly agree 1

Agree 2

Neither agree nor disagree 3

Disagree 4

Strongly disagree 5

The employees of the power company are friendly. Do you?

Strongly agree 1

Agree 2

Neither agree nor disagree 3

Disagree 4

Strongly disagree 5

Semantic differential questions use a scale between sets of bipolar adjectives (adjectives with opposite meaning) to indicate a response. Between each set of adjectives are five to nine points (most questions use only five points), which are used to suggest different positions the respondent might select. This type of question is often used to measure attitudes and opinions. Here are several questions of the semantic differential type:

On a scale of 1 to 5, with 1 being very satisfied and 5 being very dissatisfied, how satisfied are you with the power company's service?

Satisfied   __   __   __   __   __   Dissatisfied
        1   2   3   4   5

Now, on a scale of 1 to 5, with 1 being very important and 5 being very unimportant, how important do you think these services of the power company are?

Energy audits:
   Important   __   __   __   __   __   Unimportant
           1   2   3   4   5

Ordinal scale questions.   An *ordinal scale* asks the respondent to rate or rank variables in relationship to one another. For example, if the power company wanted to know which services its consumers thought were most important, it could use this format:

On this card there are several services that are provided by the power company. Rank them in the order of importance to you.

____ Energy audits

____ Appliance sales

____ Appliance repair

____ Energy conservation information

Bogardus social distance scale questions.   You may want to include questions that utilize the Bogardus Social Distance Scale when you find yourself engaged in a survey that has the purpose of investigating relationships. The scale generally includes responses that move from more distant relationships to closer relationships. The purpose is to discover changes in attitudes about a relationship as it moves closer in proximity to the respondent.

Suppose an organization was measuring attitudes about including female soldiers as part of the army's combat forces. It might ask the following question of infantrymen:

The army is considering the possibility of including women as part of its combat forces.

1. Would you be in favor of allowing women to take combat roles in the army?
2. Would you be in favor of allowing women to take combat roles in your battalion?
3. Would you be in favor of allowing women to take combat roles in your company?
4. Would you be in favor of allowing women to take combat roles in your platoon?
5. Would you be in favor of allowing women to take combat roles in your squad?

Reviewing your questions. Once you have finished writing your questions—no matter what format(s) you have used—it is important to go over them. Chapters 4 and 5 dealt in depth with questions and their uses. Here is a summary of the pertinent ideas presented there. Review each of the questions you have constructed using the following questions as a checklist:

1. Is the wording clear?
2. Is the question relevant to the survey's purpose?
3. Is the question appropriate to the respondent's knowledge level?
4. Is the question either too simple or too complex?
5. Will the respondent be willing to answer the question?

Bias in scales. Studies suggest that respondents may answer questions in various ways that bias the results. One way a respondent does this is by selecting answers that will allow him or her to appear to be socially desirable. A socially desirable answer is whatever the respondent thinks would be a "normal" or "desirable" answer. In terms of the scales we have discussed, that might be the safe, moderate, or middle option of an interval scale.

Another way respondents introduce bias is to try to appear knowledgeable. They may be reluctant to admit that they do not know. Thus they may pick some option that stands out or seems "safe."

Finally, respondents who may be asked to rate activities that make most people uneasy are less likely to admit that they ever engaged in such an activity. They may respond by changing the subject if they can.[3] You may be able to detect the likelihood of some of these problems if you carefully test your survey before you use it to actually collect data. The pretest might lead you to revise some of the questions in order to avoid any bias you discovered.

Determining interviewee knowledge level, consistency, and honesty.   Sometimes you will want to assess the interviewee's knowledge level, consistency of response, and honesty. You can construct questions that will allow you to assess these items.

The interviewee's *knowledge level* can be determined by using a sequence of two questions, known as the *filter approach*.[4] The sequence follows the format of this one that was asked about a proposed bypass connector:

Reporter: Are you familiar with the I-210 proposal that would connect two interstate highways?

Citizen: Yes, I am.

Reporter: What is the basic plan for the I-210 connector?

The *consistency* of an interviewee's answer may be checked by asking a *repeat question*. Generally the question is repeated several questions after it was first asked—perhaps three or four minutes later. The aim is to compare the responses for variation. Usually the wording of the questions is changed so that it seems to be a somewhat different question. Here are two examples of questions asked in a survey of church members regarding a proposed building program.

Interviewer: Are you in favor of the plan to build additional educational space?

Interviewer: Do you personally think that the plan to build additional educational space should be approved?

Interviewer: We are trying to assess what kind of financial support we might expect for this new building program. Your answer will be confidential and in no way obligates you. What amount do you think you might be able to give on an annual basis to support the program?

Interviewer: We are wondering what kind of support for this building program we can expect. I'm going to read a series of annual pledges. Stop me when I get to the range that you believe you may contribute. Your answer is entirely confidential and in no way obligates you.

Under $100	1
$100–499	2
$500–$999	3
$1000–$1999	4
$2000–$2999	5
$3000–$3999	6
$4000–$5000	7
Other	8

You may discover in the process of pretesting a question that the order in which responses are listed is biasing the results. Perhaps the list of responses is long and the last choices are receiving less attention than the earlier ones. Or perhaps the bias is a result of the tendency to select the last response presented.[5] When this is the case, you can use a *shuffle question* to counter these tendencies: merely rotate the order of responses from interview to interview. Be sure, however, that the interviewers and coders are well trained or their confusion may introduce error in the data collection or recording process.

Accommodating contingencies. Sometimes the next question asked depends on what response the interviewee gives to the previous question. The two questions are linked through *contingency* instructions. Notice how this question from an interview inquiring about programs offered at a new branch campus of a university was written.

1a. During the past six months, have you received any information about Northern Illinois University's new program in Rockford?

(20)
Yes [ ] 1—Ask q. 1b.
No [ ] 2—Skip to q. 2a.

1b. What program or programs did you hear about? (Do not read this list.)

(21)

Arts	1
Continuing Education	2
Education	3
General Business	4
Personalized Study	5
Sciences	6
Other (specify)	7

1c. (Ask only if Personalized Study Program is not mentioned in q. 1b.; otherwise skip to q. 1d.)

Did you ever receive any information about the Personalized Study Program?

(22)
Yes [ ] 1—Ask q. 1d.
No [ ] 2—Skip to q. 2a.

1d. Did you think that the Personalized Study Program might be of interest to you?

(23)
Yes [ ] 1—Skip to q. 2a.
No [ ] 2—Ask q. 1e.

1e. Why didn't you think the Personalized Study Program was something you would be interested in?

_____ (24)

_____ (25)

Accommodating indecision. A *leaning question* is one that asks the interviewee to tell what direction his or her opinion might favor regarding some idea, issue, or candidate. It is useful when respondents may be in the process of making decisions. Such might be the case when assessing voter sentiment about political candidates. The interviewer begins with a question that asks respondents where they stand if they were to vote today. If a respondent indicates that he or she is undecided, the interviewer follows up with a leaning question. Here is how the question was asked in a recent election in a northwestern community:

1a. If the County Commission election were held today, who would you vote for in Place 3? (If undecided, ask q. 1b.)

Oliveth Archer   1–1
Bill Montana   1–2
Undecided   1–3
Will not vote   1–4

1b. Well, do you lean more toward Archer or Montana at this time?

Archer   1–5
Montana   1–6
Undecided   1–7

Sometimes a question like "If you had to vote today, would you vote for Archer or Montana?" is used as an alternative to using a question with the word *lean.*

Selecting a Question Sequence

Review the question sequences presented in Chapter 5 when you are prepared to place the questions in some order. The most common sequence for surveys is the tunnel or string-of-beads type when there is no particular reason to order the questions otherwise.

You may want to choose the quintamensional design sequence if your purpose is to investigate intensity of attitudes and opinions. Recall that this sequence is a five-step approach that moves from awareness of a particular issue, to uninfluenced attitude, to specific attitude, to reasons, and then to intensity of feeling about the attitude.

Some sequences tend to include open-ended questions and therefore may not be suited to surveys unless modified in this respect. In particular, the funnel and inverted funnel sequences fall into this category. The general format of the funnel sequence does seem to be a useful model for surveys though. Research on the effects of question order indicates that general questions ought to come first and then the more specific questions.[6]

Choosing Interviewees

Most surveys are conducted to learn something about a group of people. The term *population* is used to refer to this group. A population can vary in size depending on the purpose of the survey and target group. A population might be all the workers employed by General Motors, or all the workers employed by GM's Pontiac Division, or all the workers employed by its Packard Electric Plant. And even within a plant, the population might be its union workers, or its nonunion workers, or its salaried workers. The researcher draws the boundary of a population based upon what group he or she would like to make statements about. A population may also be a public if the group is capable of discussing an issue and doing something about it.

Often the whole population about whom statements will be made is not available to the researcher. Members of the population may be physically spread out or so great in number that funds and time are factors that make them "not available." This does not mean that the research cannot be done, nor does it mean that statements cannot be made that reflect the population. The researcher chooses a group that is representative of the whole group and designates that group as a *sample* of the whole. If this sample is selected scientifically, its responses are assumed to be representative of the entire group.

Selecting a sample.   Samples are selected using four procedures and principles. First, you must clearly describe the population and its boundaries. Second, you must ensure that the sample is selected in such a way that it is representative of the total population. Third, you must be sure that each member of the population has the potential for being selected as part of the sample. Fourth, you must know the likelihood (probability) that each person might be selected to determine the acceptable margin of error. We will describe shortly techniques that will allow the requirements to be met. But first we describe some important considerations regarding sampling.

Sampling error results "when what we measure in the sample does not match what exists in the target population."[7] The error exists because by chance or by faulty selection procedures the proportionate mix of people in the sample is different from that in the population. Generally, a sample is selected that will allow a confidence level of 95 percent. This means that there is a mathematical probability that 95 times out of 100, interviewees would give results that resemble your data, within 5 percentage points either way (the margin of error). The *margin of error* suggests by how many percentage points a number reported as a result could be off from what it actually is. Two factors influence your attainment of this confidence level: sample size and sampling techniques.

Sample size. The size of the sample is determined by the size of the population and whatever is the acceptable margin of error. Rarely would a survey require a sample greater than 500 people. Gallup produces accurate results in its national surveys with as few as 1500 respondents.

Philip Meyer presented the following table as a guide for sample size for those who wish to achieve a 95 percent confidence level.[8] Notice that as the size of the population increases, the overall percentage of the population needed to meet this requirement decreases.

Population Size	Sample Size
Infinity	384
500,000	384
100,000	383
50,000	381
10,000	370
5,000	357
3,000	341
2,000	322
1,000	278

Sampling techniques. Many sampling techniques have as their basis the idea of random selection. *Random* means that every possible member of a sample has an equal probability of being selected. Sometimes we have a reason to bias the selection by deliberately selecting more members from particular groups. For example, a newspaper may know that certain sections of the city subscribe more heavily than others. Surveyers may want to select greater numbers of respondents from these areas. However, even if this is done, the selection *within* groups is made on a random basis.

One method you might employ is drawing a *simple random sample*. If you know the names of all the members of your target group, then you can use the listing to draw a sample. You might place the names on separate slips of paper, mix them up, and draw the number of names you need. A more scientific way of achieving similar results is to use a *table of random numbers*. Number the names on the list you are using. Then, as a source, use a good statistics book or research methods book that has a table of random numbers.[9]

The procedure for reading a table of random numbers is to pinpoint a starting place by pointing, *without looking,* to some spot in the table. The number you have located is the starting point for selecting numbers. The numbers in the table will have several digits, but you can use just the last few to match the same number of digits as in your largest number from the list of numbered population members. The person on your list that corresponds to the number in the book becomes the first person in the sample. Move to the next number and repeat the matching process until you have finished selecting your sample.

Sometimes the telephone book provides the population you wish to sample. There are several methods of obtaining a random sample from a telephone book. You might begin by using a table of random numbers to select pages, and then use a table of random numbers to select names from the designated pages. Or you might use a *skip interval* approach. You would pick every tenth name, or twentieth name—or some specific number—in the book. (The same technique can also be applied to other lists of names.)

A marketing researcher used this skip interval technique to gather data about customers of a food store in the Chicago area. The researcher interviewed every fifth customer who entered the store. Of course, the researcher had to decide to carry out these interviews at various times during the day and week to ensure a representative sample was being taken.

Often you will know about certain characteristics in the population that will lead you to want to include certain numbers of members who have these characteristics. This can be accomplished by selecting a stratified random sample. A *stratified random sample* is one that includes a minimum number of respondents from each of several groups or a percentage of the entire sample that represents that group's percentage in the actual population. Suppose you were working for the church we've spoken about that was surveying its members. You might want to ensure that a certain number of members in various age groups were surveyed. The church's rolls could be divided into young people, young adults, middle-age adults, and older adults. Once this has been accomplished, you could use a table of random numbers to select the number of members needed from each group.

A final sampling technique is used for door-to-door surveys. The *sample-point* technique, sometimes called *start-point,* selects city blocks by using a table of random numbers. These are used as points for starting the interviewing process. Often age and/or sex quotas are assigned for each group of blocks to be interviewed. For example, the interviewer may be instructed to interview someone in every other house, until two males and two females have been interviewed. Corner houses are sometimes skipped in this kind of survey because they are often larger and represent a different economic makeup. This technique allows selection of a sample, with visual inspection to ensure that the interviewee meets certain observable criteria, but without use of lists or telephone numbers.

Certain other considerations are necessary to avoid bias. Obviously time of day and week can affect who will be available in our sample. For example, surveying students at a college or university will usually require interviews at several locations, at various times of the day and evening, and even on the weekend. Another factor that must be taken into account if you use the telephone book is that approximately 15 percent of those people who have telephones do not have their numbers listed. If you suspect that this will make a difference, you might want to select phone numbers using a *random digit dialing* scheme.[10] Although a computer selection is often used, numbers can be generated by using the digits of the exchanges of interest and a table of random numbers to generate the last four digits.

In addition to the unlisted number problem, no doubt some folks are too poor to have a telephone or may be in a situation where they currently don't have one. There are no particularly good ways to cope with this sort of problem, except to do door-to-door interviewing if leaving these groups out will bias the data being collected.

Finally, the list you use may introduce bias. How current is the list? What are the criteria for getting a name on the list? Are certain members of the population not included for some reason? For example, a local church we know was growing so fast that, in addition to the main list of members, they had as many as two additional lists containing the names of new members.

MANAGING THE INTERVIEW

Selecting Interviewers

Selecting the appropriate interviewers will facilitate success with your survey. We suggest three considerations for making decisions. First, determine how many interviewers you require. If you have some small number of interviewees to survey, then only one or two interviewers will be needed. If, however, your sample is larger, you will need to consider your resources and how important time will be for the project. In some situations you will have to pay interviewers because you do not have paid staff available to help. You must determine what wage you will pay and how much money you have for this purpose. Also, you must take into account the time element. Sometimes whatever you are measuring may change over time. For example, the progress of a political or marketing campaign might be measured over time. In these situations you will need to complete the survey within some reasonable period of time—say, two to four weeks. As well, you need to note whether the survey is lengthy or the respondents are scattered over a large area. Either one of these circumstances may require additional interviewers to complete the project within a reasonable time frame.

Second, consider any special qualifications needed. Basic qualifications for any interviewer include a pleasing personality, good interpersonal communication skills, and the ability to follow directions carefully and consistently. These are about all that are needed if you have constructed a survey that consists of highly scheduled standardized questions and complete openings and closings.

On the other hand, if you expect the interviewers to exercise judgment about responses and ask appropriate follow-up questions, then interviewers who are knowledgeable in the subject area and skilled in phrasing questions and probing are needed. Of course, you can train interviewers in these skills, but there are no guarantees that the people you select will be able to satisfactorily master them.

Finally, select people who have personal characteristics that will enhance the interview process. Generally, those who have a positive up-beat outlook and are older will project more confidence to the interviewee. Research suggests that age yields credibility, and self-confidence and an optimistic outlook induce cooperation.[11] Apparently, similarity in ethnic heritage, sex, and, in some cases, age (German to German, black to black, woman to woman, senior citizen to senior citizen) can be an advantage to the interviewer. If the majority of your population shares one of these similarities, you might select interviewers to match.

Training Interviewers

Training the interviewer is a necessary part of all but the simplest surveys. Do not assume that those already skilled in interviewing techniques will know what to do. All interviewers should attend training to ensure that they all are following the same instructions.

During the training session an interviewer handbook should be distributed. It should contain a purpose statement, the questionnaire, maps, time sheets, nonresponse logs, an explanation of the sampling procedure, a set of instructions about the interviewing process, instructions about probing, and the deadline for completion.

An important part of training is rehearsal of the interview. Each interviewer should have the opportunity to administer the interview several times while being observed. Be sure that the instructions are followed, that the questions are asked exactly as written, that the responses are recorded accurately, and that probing is accomplished as expected. Upon completion of the training, provide each interviewer with an official identification card.

Pretesting the Interview

Pretesting the interview is a step that absolutely cannot be skipped. It allows you to discover and correct problems with questions and procedures. A critical problem that is not caught at this time can create incredible problems later.

Pretests are conducted with selected members of the target population, if possible. If this is not possible, then they should be conducted with a group that is essentially similar to the target population. The interviewer must go through the whole interview process from opening to closing. The researcher must be prepared to analyze each interview for problems. Here is a list of questions that may be used as a guide to analyzing the interviews:

1. Did the interviewee understand what was wanted? If not, why not?
2. What questions brought puzzled looks or required explanation?
3. What questions caused interviewees to hesitate?
4. What questions brought negative reactions? (Note that we are not talking about a "no" answer to a bipolar question or a "strongly disagree" on a Likert scale when we say negative reaction.)
5. Were there questions where the response categories seemed inadequate?
6. Are there any problems with data tabulation?
7. Was bias of any kind detected?

You are ready to conduct the survey once you have analyzed the results of the pretest and adjusted the survey instrument and/or procedures as necessary.

Conducting the Survey Interview

Each interviewer should be aware of how he or she is expected to conduct the interview. Well-executed interviews based on careful preparation will undoubtedly pay off with usable results. We begin with suggestions for conducting face-to-face interviews. Then we address the special case of the telephone interview.

Make the interview a pleasant communication experience for the interviewee. Interviewers can enhance the experience by asking the questions in a conversational style. By this we mean that the talk should sound like conversation rather than reading. Practicing with a tape recorder will allow you to strive also for enthusiastic delivery, without sounding like the stereotype of the door-to-door salesperson. Aim at a friendly, businesslike, and sincere image. Also, maintain eye contact and speak clearly and loudly enough to be easily understood. Attention to these factors will aid in creating a comfortable communication experience for the interviewee.

Be sure that recording answers does not get in the way of the communication process. The answers must be recorded quickly and accurately, but without undo attention to the fact that they are being recorded. A carefully constructed questionnaire, with each response having a number code that can be easily circled, will help in the recording process. Practice in the pretesting process will also help make the recording process go more smoothly.

Be sure that you are wearing appropriate clothing. A professional, well-groomed look is the aim. This does not necessarily mean formal business attire. It does mean at least the type of clothing that might be worn in a casual office setting. Also, avoid wearing any buttons or insignia that may identify you with a particular group or position. These may bias the survey results by encouraging interviewees to respond in particular ways. The symbol being worn may have nothing to do with the survey, but it may trigger some kind of an emotional reaction that affects the way the interviewee responds.

Do not allow yourself to rush through the interview. Give the respondent enough time to think. Sometimes waiting is difficult because of the tendency to want to fill silence with something. You must resist commenting, fidgeting, or looking at your watch.

Encourage people to participate, but do not pressure. Perhaps some people will say that they do not have time to participate in the survey. Try a statement like, "This will only take a few minutes" or "I can ask you questions while you are working." This kind of plea can add to the possibility of being granted the interview.

Record answers as instructed in training and prescribed on the schedule. If there are open questions, interviewers must write or print answers accurately and clearly. The analysis process is easier when uniform recording is carried out.

When interviewers have obtained the answer to the last question, they should thank the respondent for cooperating and excuse themselves. This is usually accomplished by reciting the memorized closing that is part of the questionnaire.

Telephone surveying has become widely used because of its advantages over face-to-face interviewing for certain kinds of research. There are two particular advantages to be gained by using the telephone to conduct research. First, if the respondents are located over a large geographic area, transportation costs can be cut substantially and thus the research cost cut. Second, the researcher can exercise more control over the interviewers because they are all centrally located. Interviewers can be observed and problems detected that could not be detected if they were carrying out interviews in the field. Beyond these advantages, studies show that telephone and face-to-face interviews produce similar results, with less "socially desirable" answers being given in telephone interviews.[12]

The telephone interview may produce some negative effects. A study by Lawrence Jordan and his associates[13] suggests that interviewees do not like telephone interviews, and that their attitude may affect their responses. Other studies have revealed that fewer interviewees prefer the telephone, especially older ones; that interviewees are less cooperative; and that they feel uneasy about discussing sensitive issues over the telephone.[14]

The opening in a telephone interview is particularly critical, perhaps because it is easier to hang up than to disengage in a face-to-face interview. In the case of telephone interviews, the great majority of refusals occur before the first question. One study concluded, "Respondents react to cues communicated by the interviewer's voice and may grant or refuse an interview on that basis."[15] Therefore, special attention should be given to the voice during the training of interviewers. The voice should have a conversational quality, with appropriate volume, that enhances trust in the interviewer.

Finally, pauses are inevitable and should be explained. If a particularly long answer is to be recorded, the interviewer might say, "Just a moment, please, while I record your answer."

ANALYZING THE RESULTS

Coding and Tabulating the Responses

When all the interviews are completed, you may need to work with several questions before you begin tabulation. Any open-ended questions used will need analysis so that a category and coding scheme can be developed for them.

Suppose, for example, that you had asked this question that was asked as part of a telephone survey in New Orleans, "What are the five major unsolved problems in the City of New Orleans?" One response might be, "I think walking downtown at night is dangerous in certain sections." Another response might be, "The roads where I live have potholes." Still another response might be, "We need to build more schools so that we can relieve overcrowding." You might build a category system to reflect these concerns. If this question were coded 25, you would code each of the categories with 25 and a number—1, 2, 3, and so forth.

25-1. Crime.	"I think walking downtown at night is dangerous in certain sections."
25-2. Public works.	"The roads where I live have potholes."
25-3. Schools.	"We need to build more schools so that we can relieve overcrowding."

Of course, these may not be the specific categories you would use if you were actually conducting this survey. Categories will depend on your analysis of the data and purposes. They may be developed through a content analysis procedure that we will explain shortly.

Sometimes the open questions will create problems in the coding process. If too many responses fall into the "other" category, these responses need to be analyzed to discover if there is actually another category of data that has not been used. If there is no obvious category, the data may have to be discarded because no meaningful conclusion can be drawn.

A second problem in coding open-ended questions is related to the language used by respondents. Sometimes the response may seem to belong in more than one category. For example, a response from the survey of problems in New Orleans was, "Our children need more programs that provide enrichment." It was difficult to know whether to code this as "schools" or "city recreation." Beyond this, perhaps the language used is not clear. What category does the response "Our streets are unsafe" belong under? Is the respondent talking about street repair or crime?

Sometimes careful pretesting will reveal these difficulties with open-ended questions. This will allow refining of the question and/or some follow-up questions that can lead to clarification. Otherwise, questions that were hoped to provide some meaningful data may only provide somewhat useful, but not quantifiable, anecdotal information.

Interpreting the Data

Statistical interpretation of data is not within the scope of this book. We refer you to a basic statistics book for information regarding this aspect of carrying out a survey.[16] There are two general methods of analyzing survey data: frequency count and content analysis. We will address these next.

The term *frequency count* is used to refer to how many respondents selected each of the particular answers to a question. Thus, in a poll of choices for candidates, a frequency count would refer to how many people indicated they will vote for Archer, how many indicated they will vote for Montana, and how many are uncommitted.

Sometimes you may wish to know whether two or more frequency counts are actually statistically different. Suppose the frequency count for Archer is 442, the one for Montana is 389, and the one for uncommitted is 162. The numbers for Archer and Montana are actually different numbers, but are they different from a statistical standpoint? What this last question is asking is, "How likely is it that these two numbers are actually different by chance?" Another way of saying this is, "How likely is it that we would get a similar difference if we were to conduct this survey again?" The only way to know the answer to this question, especially if the numbers are close, is to apply a statistical test. By consulting a good statistics book, you can find a formula that would allow you to determine if the numbers are actually statistically different.

You might wish to analyze open-ended questions using a technique called *content analysis*. Since open-ended questions do not provide any categories for response, the data must be analyzed to see if certain ideas, themes, or trends are present. So a content analysis does exactly what the term suggests. It analyzes particular data to see if they contain certain ideas, themes, or trends by counting the number of times the data of interest are present. One way of doing a content analysis is to have several people read through the responses and develop some ad hoc (after the fact) categories that the responses seem to fit. If you wish, then, you can go further and determine the frequency count for each category.

You will want to check on the reliability of the coders' work if you are using content analysis. After you have developed categories, ask each coder to determine how many times the responses fall into each category. Then compare their results to see if they usually agree with each other about how they categorized the responses. If there is close agreement, then the results are reliable. If there is not close agreement, then there might be something wrong with the category system or perhaps the care the raters are taking in making their determinations. You can determine the intercoder reliability by consulting a statistics book for help in how to calculate this.

RESPONDING TO A SURVEY INTERVIEWER

The data collected in survey interviews undoubtedly have an important impact on the way individuals and organizations in our society plan for the future. The part you play as an individual interviewee may seem insignificant. Yet if you are a person who has conducted survey research, you know how important each respondent is to the successful completion of the project. Of course, you may choose or not choose to participate. Whether you do or do not can be a more responsible decision if you follow some basic guidelines.

Listen carefully to who the people conducting the survey are and what their purpose is. If the purpose is not clear, ask why they are collecting the data and how the data will be used. If you do not want to participate, don't. Never agree to participate and then provide unreliable information to the interviewer.

Listen carefully to each question if you make a decision to participate. Try to hear the whole question before you decide how you will answer. Don't worry about how your answer will be taken by the interviewer. Straightforward, honest answers are really what the interviewer is looking for from interviewees. If you don't hear or understand a question, ask for it to be repeated or clarified.

Finally, if you do wish not to answer a question—perhaps it asks for personal information—you have a right to tell the interviewer that you wish to pass on the question. Your wish should be respected. If it is not, you have the right to terminate the interview.

SUMMARY

We noted that preparation for a survey must begin by stating the purpose. Another essential element is to identify the group from which data are to be collected. We suggested that a sample should be drawn following specific principles and practices that allow inferences about the entire group of interest.

Ethics and Responsibilities in Interviewing

Within a survey interview, ethical guidelines and responsibilities should be followed when performing various activities, namely, collecting data and drawing conclusions. *A researcher should adhere to certain standard procedures in order to guarantee that the reader of the results can have confidence in them.* Not devoting the time and energy to follow these might be viewed as intentionally deceiving or intentionally inflicting harm. The principles of fairness and justice also seem to apply here. The following responsibilities have been discussed throughout the chapter, so they will merely be listed here without comment:

1 *Use appropriate sampling techniques in selecting participants.*
2 *Qualify your respondents so that you are sure they are within the population you claim to represent in the data.*
3 *Thoroughly screen and train those who will carry out the interviews.* This will allow you to be reasonably sure that these people will maintain the highest professional standards in representing you and the organization sponsoring you.
4 *Use appropriate statistical techniques in analyzing your data.* This will enable you to be reasonably sure that the basis for your conclusions is sound.

Three additional ethical guidelines are important. First, *an interviewer should not misrepresent his or her credentials or organization.* An interviewer has the responsibility to clearly identify the organization that is sponsiring the research. But, beyond this, the researcher has the responsibility to ensure that the sponsoring organization is reputable and will utilize the information collected responsibly.

Second, *the interviewer has the responsibility to use the data only for a purpose consistent with that revealed to the interviewees.*

Finally, *the interviewer has the responsibility to follow through on any promises made.* Often interviewees are promised a reward as an incentive to participate in the interview. If a promise is made to provide results of the survey to participants, for example, then the researcher must be sure to do so.

The interviewee takes on ethical responsibility, too. An interviewee should participate fully and truthfully in the interview, assuming the questions are within the bounds of propriety and the announced scope of the interview.

Next, we turned our attention to planning the basic interview structure—by developing an interview guide, opening, and closing. We recommended formulating specific questions from the guide based on the kind of data to be collected and the purpose of the survey. They will generally follow one of these formats: nominal scale, interval scale, ordinal scale, or

Bogardus Social Distance scale. The questions should be sequenced using one of the recommended schemes.

We suggested that interviewees should be selected to meet the criteria of a certain sample size and a scientific sampling technique. The sampling techniques listed included the simple random sample, skip interval, stratified random sample, sample point, and random digit dialing.

Next, we focused on selecting and training interviewers. This requires attention to the number of interviewers needed, their personal characteristics, and special qualifications. Interviewers should be given a handbook with specific information and should be trained by observation and critique of actual performance.

We emphasized that before the interviews are begun, the interview instrument and procedures must be pretested. This requires that actual interviews be conducted with members of the population being studied or with a group that matches their makeup.

Next, specific behaviors regarding face-to-face and telephone interviews were discussed. Then information was given on interpreting the data collected, with special emphasis on coding and analyzing. We concluded the chapter by discussing the interviewee's conduct.

NOTES

[1]Philip Meyer, *Precision Journalism* (Bloomington, IN: Indiana University Press, 1979).

[2]Gerald L. Wilson, H. Lloyd Goodall, Jr., and Christopher L. Waagen, *Organizational Communication* (New York: Harper & Row, 1986), p. 172. This definition is based on the work of Herbert Blumer and John Dewey. See Herbert Blumer, "The Mass, the Public, and Public Opinion," in Bernard Barelson and Morris Janowitz (eds.), *Reader in Public Opinion and Communication,* 2d ed. (New York: Free Press, 1966), pp. 43–50; John Dewey, *The Public and Its Problems* (Chicago: Swallow, 1927).

[3]Norman M. Bradburn, Seymour Sudman, Ed Blair, and Carol Stocking, "Question Threat and Response Bias," *Public Opinion Quarterly, 42* (1978), 221–234.

[4]Sam G. McFarland, "Effects of Question Order on Survey Responses," *Public Opinion Quarterly, 45* (1981), 208–215.

[5]Stanley L. Payne, *The Art of Asking Questions* (Princeton, NJ: Princeton University Press, 1951), p. 21.

[6]Laure M. Sharp and Joanne Frankel, "Response Burden: A Test of Some Common Assumptions," *Public Opinion Quarterly, 47* (1983), 36–53.

[7]James A. Anderson, *Communication Research: Issues and Methods* (New York: McGraw-Hill Book Company, 1987), p. 154.

[8]Meyer, p. 123.

[9]See Fred N. Kerlinger, *Foundations of Behavioral Research,* 3d ed. (New York: Holt, Rinehart and Winston, 1986), pp. 637–644.

[10]For a discussion of random digit dialing, see Paul J. Lavrakas, *Telephone Survey Methods: Sampling, Selection, and Supervision* (Newbury Park, CA: Sage, 1987), pp. 33–44.

[11]Eleanor Singer, Martin R. Frankel, and Marc B. Glassman, "The Effect of Interviewer Characteristics and Expectations on Response," *Public Opinion Quarterly, 47* (1983), 68–83.

[12]Theresa F. Rogers, "Interviews by Telephone and in Person: Quality of Responses and Field Performance," *Public Opinion Quarterly, 39* (1976), 51–65.

[13]Lawrence A. Jordan, Alfred C. Marcus, and Leo G. Reeder, "Response Style in Telephone and Household Interviewing," *Public Opinion Quarterly, 44* (1980), 210–222.

[14]Robert M. Groves, "Actors and Questions in Telephone and Personal Survey Interviews," *Public Opinion Quarterly, 43* (1979), 190–205; Peter V. Miller and Charles F. Cannell, "A Survey of Experimental Techniques in Telephone Interviewing," *Public Opinion Quarterly, 46* (1982), 250–269.

[15]Lois Okenberg, Lerita Coleman, and Charles F. Cannell, "Interviewer's Voices and Refusal Rates in Telephone Surveys," *Public Opinion Quarterly, 50* (1986), 97–111; A. Regula Herzog, Willard L. Rodgers, and Richard A. Kulka, "Interviewing Older Adults: A Comparison of Telephone and Face-to-Face Modalities," *Public Opinion Quarterly, 47* (1983), 405–418.

[16]See William Hayes, *Statistics,* 3d ed. (New York: Holt, Rinehart and Winston, 1981).

A SURVEY INTERVIEW
FOR ANALYSIS

Context: The following dialogue recreates a survey interview conducted in supermarkets in the Rocky Mountain region. The product's identification has been changed, and the identities of the interviewer and interviewee are not revealed.

1. Interviewer: Excuse me, would you like to try our new party cracker?

2. Interviewee: Sure.

3. Interviewer: Great! While you are sampling the product, let me ask you a few questions about your preferences in party snacks. OK?

4. Interviewee: (eating a cracker) Uh-huh.

5. Interviewer: Good. First, how many times a year would you say you entertain guests or friends in your home?

6. Interviewee: Uh, I don't know, exactly. (Selects another cracker.)

7. Interviewer: Our research suggests that most people's entertaining habits can be explained by the use of these four categories: Only major occasions (Super Bowl, Christmas, Thanksgiving); major occasions plus business-related entertaining; major occasions, business entertaining, and family rituals (such as birthdays and anniversaries); or major occasions, business entertaining, family rituals, and general weekend partying. Of these four choices, which one best fits your own entertaining behaviors?

8. Interviewee: That second one, I guess.

9. Interviewer: Major occasions and business-related entertaining?

10. Interviewee: Yeah, that's the one.

11. Interviewer: About how many persons do you usually entertain at one time?

12. Interviewee: Gee, I guess it depends. I mean, for major occasions, maybe ten or so; for business-related occasions, usually only four or five.

13. Interviewer: Thanks. That leads to my next two questions. This is really going well.

14. Interviewee: Glad to help. Can I try one of those crab items?

15. Interviewer: Sure. Here's one for you.

16. Interviewee: Thanks. These are really good, by the way.

17. Interviewer: That was my next question. So you like the product?

18. Interviewee: Yeah, it's kind of somewhere between one of those wheat crackers and one of those cheese crackers.

19. Interviewer: Uh-huh. What is your usual choice of party food?

20. Interviewee: Depends on who's coming. But I always have some sort of cheese and cracker thing, you know, and some dips and vegetables.

21. Interviewer: And what are your usual choices of crackers?

22. Interviewee: Well, I always have Ritz and Stoned Wheat Thins, and lately I've been buying one of those assorted boxes that has flavored crackers in it.

23. Interviewer: Flavored crackers? Could you elaborate, please?

24. Interviewee: Yeah, you know, those with sesame seeds, and cheese flavors, and I think there is even one with peanut butter flavor.

25. Interviewer: I see. Given that range of choices, how would you rate our new product?

26. Interviewee: I like it. I guess I'd buy it. Try it out, you know; see how much is left over when the party ends.

27. Interviewer: Is that how you generally make your party food decisions?

28. Interviewee: Yeah, that and what I like. I'm the one with the leftovers. (giggle)

29. Interviewer: Of the five varieties of spreads used on our new product here today, which one did you enjoy the most?

30. Interviewee: The crab. I like crabmeat on anything.

31. Interviewer: And your second choice?

32. Interviewee: I think the cheese and peppers.

33. Interviewer: A third choice?

34. Interviewee: The rest are all about the same to me. Good variety, though.

35. Interviewer: I'm glad you enjoyed the product. Just two more questions...

36. Interviewee: Go ahead. I'll just have one more crab cracker.

37. Interviewer: Fine. If I could direct your attention to our new product's box for a minute. (Displays box.) Does anything about the packaging of the product stand out to you?

38. Interviewee: It's about like Triscuits, I'd say.

39. Interviewer: I see. And if you had to decide between our new product and a Triscuit, just based on the packaging, which one would you choose?

40. Interviewee: Triscuit.

41. Interviewer: Why?

42. Interviewee: Everybody likes Triscuits. I forgot to mention that before. I always buy a box of them.

43. Interviewer: I see. What makes the packaging of that product superior to our new product?

44. Interviewee: I guess the name of the product, because I know it, and it's a brighter-yellow box.

45. Interviewer: What is more important, the color of the box or its name value?

46. Interviewee: Name value. Color is only important when I'm trying to locate something on the shelf.

47. Interviewer: Well, that's all I need to know for our survey. I want to thank you for your cooperation. Why don't you have another one of those crab crackers before you go?

48. Interviewee: I think I will. And say, I think I'll try a box of these too. Who knows? It's worth a try.

EXPERIENCES

1. Select a topic of interest, perhaps something related to an issue at your college or university. Formulate a purpose statement and a questionnaire that fulfills the purpose. Select a population to survey and a sample that is a size which fits your time and resources. Collect and analyze data.
2. Select a product for which you might conduct market research. Develop a market survey that will allow you to collect data about that product and its competition. If time and resources permit, collect the data and analyze them.
3. Arrange an interview with a member of an organization who conducts research interviews. Organizations that collect this kind of information are your college's institutional research department, the local chamber of commerce, radio and television stations, newspapers, certain businesses, and your local and state government. Ask the person questions that will allow you to discover how he or she prepares, conducts, and analyzes the research interview. See if the person has a recent interview guide that you may have. What kind of sequencing was used for the questions? Does it cover the purpose of the interview satisfactorily? Analyze the guide for its strengths and weaknesses.
4. After you have conducted a survey interview, analyze your effort as an interviewer. Were your instructions adequate? How might they be improved? What problems did you have securing interviewees? What problems did you encounter during the interviews? How effective was your attempt to handle these problems? What did you learn from your experience as an interviewer?

RECOMMENDED READINGS

Anderson, James A., *Communication Research: Issues and Methods* (New York: McGraw-Hill Book Company, 1987).

Babbie, Earl R., *The Practice of Social Research,* 5th ed. (Belmont, CA: Wadsworth, 1989).

Cochrane, W. G., *Sampling Techniques,* 3d ed. (New York: John Wiley, 1977).

Dillman, Don A., *Mail and Telephone Surveys: The Total Design Method* (New York: Wiley-Interscience, 1978).

Lavrakas, Paul J., *Telephone Survey Methods: Sampling, Selection, and Supervision* (Newbury Park, CA: Sage, 1987).

Marsh, Catherine, *The Survey Method* (London: Allen & Unwin, 1982).

Meyer, Philip, *Precision Journalism* (Bloomington, IN: Indiana University Press, 1979).

CHAPTER 11

THE PROBLEM-
SOLVING
INTERVIEW

OBJECTIVES

After reading this chapter, you should be able to:

Explain the purpose and goals of a problem-solving interview.

Discuss how the context can be productively defined, and how the interviewer can structure the questions to create a nonthreatening problem-solving interview.

Describe strategies for dealing with difficult situations and people in a problem-solving interview.

Develop criteria to evaluate the success of a problem-solving interview.

Plan and carry out a problem-solving interview.

Discuss ethics of problem-solving interviews.

Consider for a moment how problems are solved. It doesn't matter if the problem is large or small; involves money, monotony, or love; or requires the resources of a nation, computer, community, counselor, or couple. A problem isn't a problem until it is identified, and a solution can't be a solution until it is articulated. This means that all problems—and for that matter all solutions—are created, understood, and overcome through exchanges of words between or among people.

It should come as no surprise, then, that we have chosen to study the problem-solving interview. Interviews are, after all, exchanges of words between or among people, and very often interviews are places for problems to be worked out. For example:

A friend, Catherine, is having a problem with her fiancé. She comes to you to talk about it.

A relative, Jose, has just lost his job. He has a child to raise, he has a mortgage payment to meet, and he is considering returning to school to change careers. He calls you on the phone and asks to speak with you about his situation.

A colleague, Sarah, has been missing meetings lately. You are concerned about her, puzzled about how to proceed. If this situation continues, you are certain that she will lose her job.

An employee, Jonathan, is having difficulty sustaining the level of work required to meet his group's objectives. You are his group's manager, and he has requested a meeting with you to discuss the problem.

In this chapter we will develop a more complete understanding of how problem-solving interviews can address situations such as those listed above. Before we begin, however, we need to state this important consideration: *Although the advice that we offer in this chapter is the basis for most professional counseling and therapy-intervention interviews, merely reading this chapter and learning these techniques will not provide you with the level of professional training required to handle difficult emotional and personal problems.* What we offer here is aimed at improving your understanding and skill in everyday problem-solving situations, *not* those that require the services of a physician, religious counselor, psychiatrist, lawyer, accountant, or teacher.

To accomplish our task, first we describe how to plan for the problem-solving interview. Second, we discuss techniques for managing the interview. Third, we explain how to evaluate the interview. Next, we discuss ethical considerations. Finally, we look at the role of the interviewee in the problem-solving interview.

PLANNING FOR THE PROBLEM-SOLVING INTERVIEW

There is an old saying that goes like this: "Prior planning prevents poor performance." Nothing could be truer for the problem-solving interview. There are few exchanges of talk in life that have the equal potential for help and damage as those that involve identifying an individual's problem and searching for ways to overcome it. For this reason, careful planning is essential. Without it, what could have been a mutually rewarding experience can become a devastating emotional crisis that deepens—rather than overcomes—the problem.

In this section we will describe the six steps for planning for and conducting the problem-solving interview. The steps are (1) understanding the context, (2) establishing a goal for the interview, (3) developing a productive process for identifying and articulating possible solutions to the problem, (4) asking and answering questions during the interview, (5) knowing when you've accomplished the goal of the interview, and (6) planning the close and exit. Let's examine each of these steps in greater detail.

Understanding the Context

Planning for a problem-solving interview—regardless of its context—should begin with a statement of the problem. But what is a *problem?* We usually define a problem by articulating the most visible (and often the most painful) elements of it: trouble with a fiancé, the loss of a job and possible career change, missed meetings due to drinking on the job, an employee unable to keep up with the volume of work needed to meet deadlines. However, these statements are often only the tip of the iceberg when it comes to understanding the context for a problem-solving interview. They are statements of the obvious in situations that are generally far more complex.

For this reason we believe it is productive to consider a second sense of meaning for the term *problem*. We are required to look at a problem as part of its context. As the noted family therapist Jay Haley expresses it: "A problem is defined as the type of behavior that is part of a sequence of acts between several people."[1] This is a very insightful, and strategically important, statement, and we ask you, please, to read it again. Viewed from this perspective, then, a "problem" is more than the simple statements required to point out what is wrong; a "problem" is also an appreciation of the context—the sequence of acts between several people—that have created the situation labeled as the "problem."

We think Haley's approach is useful because it focuses on relational goals and processes that come together to produce problem behavior. For example, Catherine's "problem" with her fiancé may be understood as a pattern of recurring behavior between them rather than "his attitude" or "her desire for a commitment." Similarly, Jose, the relative who has lost his job and wants a career change, may be repeating a pattern of behavior that worked well for him before he had a child to raise and a mortgage to meet. Sarah, the colleague who is missing meetings, may have unmet psychological needs. And Jonathan, the employee who is having trouble keeping up with the volume of work, may be impaired by other's treatment of him, the unavailability of necessary tools or expertise, or a lack of training that he has been afraid to admit.

In all of these cases appreciation of the "context" includes an appreciation of the forces at work behind the scenes of the problem statement. Perhaps, after reading our argument, you are saying to yourself, "I agree. It is important to understand more than simply what the problem is. But how do I accomplish that? And how do I plan for it?"

Here are a list of questions you can use to probe your own—as well as your interviewee's—understanding of the context for the problem:

1. What do I think I know about this situation?
2. What have I been told about this situation by others?
3. What have I been told about this situation by the person I will be speaking with?
4. What questions can I ask to get the person to speak freely about the situation?
5. How can I verify what I have been told so I know fact from conjecture and/or fiction?

These questions should be answered to the best of your ability before conducting the interview. In many cases our students have found it helpful to write out the answers for future reference. Although all the questions are important, they are important for different reasons. The first question attempts to get you involved in the situation by spelling out your level of knowledge about the problem, as well as what your biases may be. The second question attempts to fill in more details about your knowledge of the problem with gossip, rumor, innuendo, and reports by persons who have some access to the problem. It is important to categorize these sources of material according to their source (a close friend of the injured party) and the source's source (a rumor passed on by a person who overheard it in the cafeteria). The third question tries to get at the background given to you previously by the person with whom you will be speaking. Have there been hints about the problem? Can you recall specific details of conversation in which the problem was mentioned? Were examples used? If so, what were they?

Collectively, these three questions will help fill in information and opinion that surround the definition of the problem, and may in fact *contribute* to the solution of the problem. They help you separate fact from suspicion, and may shed light on who else is involved in the problem other than the "interviewee."

The fourth question has a different purpose. It is designed to get *you* started articulating the method you will use to explore the problem. What questions need to be addressed (Is the person aware of the problem? How does he or she account for it? What does she or he think ought to be done to overcome it?)? What information is vital to the problem (How long has this been going on? What is the level of commitment to overcoming it? Are there others involved who can help? How will the financial, logistical, or work-related issues be handled during the recovery?)? What information should not be shared initially (your concern about the effects of the problem on future growth, how others are responding to the problem)? What should not be shared at all (potentially damaging information contained in rumors or gossip)?

The fifth question, "How can I verify what I have been told?," is asked to help you remember to consider that other persons might have information that will allow you to sort fact from possible conjecture and/or fiction. Consider who has been mentioned as being involved with the problem. Of these people, to whom can you speak ethically in order to verify what you have been told? You might also decide how you can ask about information in more than one way. If different questions elicit the same response, that may add to your confidence in the information's reliability.

As we pointed out at the beginning of this section, it is absolutely essential to plan for the problem-solving interview. These questions help you select from an available array of possible statements and questions only those that can help you reach your goal. Now review what you have learned and then write a statement of the problem.

Establishing a Goal

Once you are sure that you understand the context, you need to think about establishing a goal. Consideration of the context allows you to understand what is possible before you attempt to determine what goal is preferable. This requires exploring your own understanding of the situation and its potential effects before deciding what course of action should be pursued.

Our tendency is to hope for too much. This means that we expect, perhaps during one problem-solving session, to be able to get the interviewee to agree not only on what the nature of the problem is, but also on how it must be solved. Unless you are very skilled, or the problem is very easy to understand and solve, this is asking for too much. For this reason it is advisable to take one step at a time, and to make sure that each step has been taken equally by the interviewer and interviewee before proceeding to the next one. For example, if you are a manager and an employee has come to you to discuss his inability to perform to standards, you may wish to set aside one meeting to discuss the reasons for the existence of the problem and another for possible solutions to it. If you are helping a relative think about a career change and the attendant financial and logistical stress it will incur, several sessions may be required.

The important thing to keep in mind is that problems must be understood before they can be solved.[2] In part this is because the language used to articulate the problem must fully embrace all of its components, and in part because whatever agreement is reached about how the problem is defined will ultimately determine the choice of solution. For example, if your friend Catherine is having trouble with her fiancé, and you agree that the problem is his "wandering eye," then chances are pretty good that the solution will be directed toward changing his behavior. This may work only if you have fully explored the problem and decided that it is his behavior (rather than something Catherine is doing or not doing) that is causing the problem. In this case if Catherine then confronts him with what she believes is a solution and he rejects it because "she doesn't really understand what's going on between us," then you have not solved a problem, and have probably created another one through her accusations.

So, then, what goals are preferable in a problem-solving interview? Clearly this will depend on your relationship with the interviewee, how much information is available on the problem, and how open, resistant, angry, pitiful, or stubborn the interviewee is likely to be during your conversation. Figure 11.1 displays appropriate and inappropriate goal statements for problem-solving interviews. Notice how the preferred goal statements reflect careful, precise, behaviorally specific language that focuses on observable outcomes rather than more abstract feelings, attitudes, or beliefs.

Each one of the statements in Figure 11.1 is important for examination of language usage. In the first example, the more appropriate statement focuses on what Catherine should do as a result of the session—tell her fiancé what is bothering her about their relationship—rather than on the more ambiguous goal of "expressing herself." The second example focuses on completing a financial plan before launching into a career change instead of the more abstract goal of seeing "how much is involved." The third example is useful because the poor statement is one that often reflects the feelings of a helper—"I want to help"—but does little to focus on the nature of the problem. The fourth example is important because it reflects a difference in approach to the problem—the more appropriate statement focusing on getting Jonathan to explain why he is unable to do his job, the inappropriate state-

Figure 11.1 Appropriate and inappropriate goal statements.

Appropriate Goal Statements	Inappropriate Goal Statements
As a result of our session, I want Catherine to be able to tell her fiancé precisely what is troubling her in clear words.	As a result of our session, I want Catherine to be able to express herself more openly.
I want my brother-in-law to be able to see the importance of completing a detailed financial plan before making a career change.	I want my brother-in-law to be able to see how much is involved in his career change.
I want to help my colleague to realize that his supervisor has noticed that he has been missing meetings and to understand what the probable outcomes of this behavior might be.	I want to help my colleague.
I want to explore the reasons why Jonathan is having difficulty on the job.	I want to explore the reasons for Jonathan's poor performance on the job.

ment assuming that Jonathan already knows those reasons, and furthermore that it is probably his own fault!

From this discussion of possible ways of expressing goals for a problem-solving interview, it should be clear that an appropriate goal statement includes the following characteristics:

- Clear, nonabstract language
- A focus on observable outcomes rather than internal feelings, attitudes, or beliefs
- A nonjudgmental approach to the problem

With these objectives in mind you should be able to formulate productive goals for each session. Now let's consider the third step in planning for the problem-solving interview—developing a productive interviewing process.

Developing a Productive Process for Identifying and Articulating Possible Solutions

Part of the planning for a productive problem-solving interview involves charting a path through the territory you want to cover. This means that the exchange of talk should proceed step by step from beginning to end, and that control over the movement from step to step is in the hands of the person conducting the interview.

There are four identifiable steps for a productive problem-solving interview process.[3] These steps are:

A social step.   During this step the interviewer and interviewee meet and greet each other, exchange pleasantries, and generally attempt to relax and feel comfortable. The interviewer should monitor this step by attending to the level of eye contact, the various facial expressions, and signs of nervousness or anxiety present in the interviewee. It is important not to try to rush through this step to get to the heart of the issue. Trying to talk about a problem to someone who is obviously distraught is unlikely to be productive. Try to get the interviewee to relax, to look at you, to show behavior indicative of openness instead of anxiety before moving on.

The problem step.   During this step the interviewer should inquire into the nature of the problem from the interviewee's perspective. Remember, it is important to remain nonjudgmental, particularly if potentially shocking information is presented. The idea is to get the interviewee to talk openly about her or his perceptions of the problem, why it exists, what causes it, and whether or not there is real evidence to support it. During this phase of the discussion the interviewer should try to accomplish two communicative tasks: (a) reduce the level of abstraction in descriptions of the problem (*Interviewee:* "I just know something is *wrong*! *Interviewer:* "Oh, how so?"); and (b) contain the discussion to a descriptive analysis of the problem rather than focus on possible solutions (*Interviewee:* "The problem is I need to get out of this relationship!" *Interviewer:* "That's one option. Before we explore other options, let's be clear on exactly what leads you to want to do that."). The objective of this step is to gain agreement between the interviewer and interviewee on the problem, what causes it, who is involved in it, and what are the signs of the problem.

The interaction step.   If the problem that is identified involves more than one person, it is usually advisable to set up a separate session in which the other players are brought in, and talk can be exchanged between or among them. For example, if you are Jonathan's manager, it may be helpful to bring in some of his coworkers to discuss their perceptions of the situation and then jointly work out agreements for managing a solution. However advisable this may be, it is not always practical. As a friend advising Catherine, you should not participate in a discussion with her fiancé.

During the interaction step the objective should be to discuss the problem that has been agreed upon, and to vent any emotions that may block successful attempts to manage a solution. This step is important because it may provide the interviewer with additional information or examples of the problem that can lead to a modification of your concept of what the real problem is. It is also important because it allows the interviewee to release pent-up feelings of frustration, anger, resentment, or other emotions that may later get in the way of implementing a solution.

The goal-setting step.   The final steps in a productive problem-solving interview process are to get the interviewee to articulate possible ways of solving the problem and then to decide on—and commit to—a practical course of action. This requires the interviewer to change the focus of the discussion from the problem to solutions, and is most easily and efficiently accomplished with the statement: "Now that we have a clear understanding of the problem, let's begin to explore ways of overcoming it. What do you think some possibilities might be?"

During this step in the discussion the interviewer must be alert to regression—to the tendency of the interviewee to want to go back to the safer domain of the problem rather than to the riskier domain of possible solutions. Gently prompt the interviewee with statements such as "I think we've already decided that, haven't we?" or "Let's not go into that again. We've made progress understanding what has led to this situation. Let's concentrate on what we can do to overcome it."

This step ends when the interviewer extracts a realistic statement of goal from the interviewee, or when it becomes clear that another session will be required before such a statement can be made. If the statement is articulated, it is often helpful to ask the interviewee to write it down. This will reinforce the need for action, and will reveal any hesitation. If there is some hesitation, the interviewer might then decide that more discussion is needed before anything else can be accomplished.

Asking Questions

Once you have a clear understanding of the territory you plan to cover, the next step is to plan precisely how to move through it. Hence, the fourth step in your planning process should include appropriate consideration of the questions you will use to guide the interview.

For a productive problem-solving interview you should plan questions for each of the four steps just outlined. Figure 11.2 details some examples of questions you may want to consider.

Figure 11.2 provides some open questions the interviewer can use to guide the discussion. However, follow-ups and probes are also essential to the success of a problem-solving interview because they let the interviewee know that the interviewer is actively involved in listening. Remember, people do not open up to others who do not seem interested in what they are saying. To be an effective problem-solving interviewer requires a caring, reflective, and involved attitude toward the interaction.

Knowing When You Are Finished

One of the most difficult things for a problem-solving interviewer to learn is when to end the interview. Planning for the close is an essential skill that can be acquired by paying attention to three important cues: the accomplishment of the purpose (or the realization that the purpose cannot be accomplished), the decline or dwindling of the conversation, and leave-taking

Figure 11.2   Sample questions for each step in the problem-solving interview.

SOCIAL STEP

Goal:
To relax the interviewee, to relieve anxiety, to get the interviewee to open up
  and begin talking about neutral issues.

Questions:
How are you doing today?
How is your (spouse, child, friend, etc.) doing these days?
How has your (tennis, golf, softball, etc.) game been lately?
What do you think of this weather?
Did you hear about (some nonthreatening newsworthy item)?

PROBLEM STEP

Goal:
To explore the nature and causes of the problem—to determine who is involved and what specific factors can be found that contribute to it.

Questions:
What do you think the problem is?
How do you think the problem developed?
Who else knows about this situation?
Who else is involved?
What do you think causes you to want to do that?
Do you think ignoring it will make the problem go away?
What do you think makes you feel that way?
Are there specific instances you recall that can help me understand why you
  believe this to be true?
Can you give me one (some) examples?
How do you think (he, she, they) sees the problem?
If you were (she, he, they), what would you do?
Are you sure about this? How do you know this to be the case?
Has anyone else seen this happen? Who are they?
How many times has this occurred? Do you have a record of it?
Is this all you can tell me about it?

INTERACTION STEP

Goals:
To get the interviewee to talk openly about the problem that has been agreed
  upon and to release potentially damaging emotions. In some cases, to bring
  in other parties to engage in the discussion.

Questions:
How did that affect you?
What did you think about when that happened?
Did that make you angry (sad, happy, envious, etc.)?
If you can, tell me how you felt when you found out.
Do you think (he, she, they) will understand the problem the same way you
  do? Why or why not?
Now that we've agreed upon what this problem is, how do you feel about it?
Is there anything else that you feel needs to be expressed before we go on?
Do you think you can handle this problem alone?

Figure 11.2 *(cont.)*

GOAL-SETTING STEP

Goals:

To get the interviewee to explore alternative ways of solving the problem, to help the interviewee evaluate alternatives, and then to agree on a plan of action. To commit to carrying out that plan.

Questions:

What do you think needs to be done to overcome this problem?

What do you believe the alternatives are?

Have you considered all the options? Can you tell me what they are?

Is there another way out of this dilemma?

Are you certain you want to pursue that?

What do you think needs to be done to accomplish that?

Can you see this as a solution that requires you to act in a particular way?

What is your role in implementing this solution?

How committed to this plan are you going to be?

What happens if (he, she, they) don't buy it?

If this doesn't work out exactly as we have planned, what will you do?

Are you going to be open to other possibilities?

I know this will be hard for you. Do you think you can do it alone?

Is there someone who can help you do this?

Do you understand that this is going to solve your problem but that it requires you to make a commitment to (not spend money recklessly, ask for help when you need it, work more cooperatively with others, etc.)?

Is there anything else we need to talk about before you act?

---

nonverbal mannerisms. Let's examine each one of these cues in more detail.

Obviously, the single most important cue for both parties is the accomplishment of the purpose. If the goal was to describe the problem, and it has been described to the satisfaction of both the interviewer and interviewee, then it is time to close. If the purpose was to chart a practical course of action to overcome the problem and such a course has been charted, it is time to close. When the purpose is accomplished, the end of the interview is signaled and can be done quickly and efficiently by simply saying: "Unless there is something else you can think of, I think we're finished."

However, not all purposes—even those that have been carefully planned for—actually are accomplished. For example, discussions of chronic absenteeism from a task group may reveal additional problems, perhaps a child care situation, that call for additional time. Similarly, discussions of ways to overcome a problem may get bogged down. It is essential for the interviewer to recognize when the goal is not being accomplished and to adjust to this development without showing signs of frustration or annoyance. To get out of a nonaccomplishing situation the interviewer may use any of the following strategies:

RUNNING OUT OF TIME

"We are running later than I imagined we would. I need to be someplace else in a few minutes, but I want to spend as much

time with you on this problem as you feel we need to. Can we
schedule another time?''

INFORMATION OVERLOAD

''I see that there is more going on here than we had originally
anticipated. Perhaps we should stop here for now, and come back
later with a fresh perspective.''

INFORMATION UNDERLOAD

''I see that we need more information about what can be done before
we go much further. I suggest we end this today, and plan to
meet again tomorrow morning. How does that sound?''

EMOTIONAL RESCUE

''I can see this upsets you. Perhaps we should stop for now and take
some time to think things over. Do you think that is best?'' Or
perhaps this alternative: ''I can see this upsets you. Do you want
to go on?''

PRESENCE OF POTENTIAL CONFLICT BETWEEN INTERVIEWER AND INTERVIEWEE

''I can see we disagree on this. How about if we make a date to
discuss this later, when we've both had time away from here to
think it through?''

The second cue for an interviewer to watch for is the decline or dwindling of conversation. It may be that the interview has exhausted all the
topics or that the interviewee is withholding information. In either event,
it is unlikely that anything more will be accomplished until time has passed
to reflect on what has occurred. When this is the case, the interviewer
should acknowledge the absence of things to talk about and ask for an end
to the session: ''I see that we both have run out of things to say. What do
you say we take a break? Can we get together at this same time on Wednesday?''

The third important cue is nonverbal. Lowering one's eyes and voice,
or looking repeatedly at a watch, can signal the need to exit. The interviewer should be alert to these symptoms and respond to them appropriately. Continuing the session when the interviewee does not wish to be
there is unlikely to accomplish anything other than to create a mutually embarrassing situation.

Planning the Close

In most problem-solving interviews it is necessary to plan for a close that
includes two elements: (1) a review of what has been covered or decided
and (2) a final leave-taking. Unless the interviewee is emotionally unable to

continue the interview, both of these steps should be carried out before ending the session.

To review what has been covered requires the interviewer to highlight the major ideas of the discussion and to list any specific agreements that have been made. This should be accomplished in an unhurried, positive, summary fashion, such as:

> I think we've got a good understanding of the problem and what needs to be done about it, Catherine. You admit that your fiancé never felt entirely comfortable with the idea of getting married, and perhaps did so just to please your parents. Now he appears to be interested in other women. You have agreed to talk with him about it, and to be willing to end the engagement if your perceptions match his. And you've agreed to speak with him about it tomorrow. That's a big step, and I think a very important one.

> So where are we at this point? You've agreed that making a career change is a major event in your life, and that it takes some careful planning. You've agreed to work on a financial plan to see either if you can swing it or if you need to back off for a while and pay off some debts before jumping into something new. I've agreed to check into some day care options and to see if your courses will transfer for credit to our local college. I think these are positive steps, Jose, don't you?

> I'm so glad we've had this chance to talk things out, Sarah. I didn't know that you were missing meetings to do errands for your neighbor. As we've discussed, I thought perhaps you were missing them because of your drinking. In fact, what we've discovered is that you've already decided to join Alcoholics Anonymous and that you are planning to attend their meeting on Friday. I think that is great! And I want you to know I will do anything I can to help you through this, including meeting with our boss to explain the situation before you go in on Monday.

> I think we've covered a lot of important ground today. We've seen that the problem has two basic areas—your feelings about the work you are doing and the inability of others to help out when you are under pressure. I think before we go any further, Jonathan, we need to investigate some training and development options. Let's plan to talk again tomorrow afternoon. What does your schedule look like?

Each of these closings focuses on the major topics covered and agreements made during the interview, and ends on a positive note with a future-directed action. After these statements have been made, the interview is essentially completed. All that remains is saying farewell, shaking hands or hugging, and, if needed, checking schedules for another meeting.

MANAGING THE PROBLEM-SOLVING INTERVIEW

You will want to keep a key factor in mind as you conduct the interview. Each interviewee will have some degree of intellectual maturity when it comes to thinking about and solving problems. Your role in the interview will clearly vary depending on this factor. With mature interviewees, who have thought through or are capable of thinking through the problem and posing reasonable solutions, you will be able to guide them through thinking about the problem and solutions. You will be able to focus on their reasoning to solve the problem.

On the other hand, with less mature interviewees, what is generally called for is a collaborative effort to discover mutually acceptable solutions. This means that you will share in the problem-solving process by offering your input and ideas. Consequently, your planning will be more critical because you will need to input more of your reasoning and ideas. Thus, you will need to ask questions that will lead to an analysis of the situation and solutions that the interviewee may have omitted.

EVALUATING THE PROBLEM-SOLVING INTERVIEW

Assuming the interview is conducted according to plan, the next task is to evaluate the session. Doing this helps you to analyze what was discussed during the interview, and contributes to your understanding of the problem and the likely success of the solution.

There are three major considerations for evaluating a problem-solving interview: (1) How well did I follow the plan? And if I didn't, why not? (2) What can I do to better understand the meaning of the communication exchanged during the session? And (3) what is the likelihood that what was accomplished during the session will help the interviewee improve his or her understanding of the situation and want to act to overcome the problem? Let's examine each of these considerations in greater detail.

How Well Did I Follow the Plan?

To accomplish this interviewing analysis goal, it is helpful to write down responses—not necessarily every word, but the gist of what was said—as they occurred to questions that were raised. As we have pointed out in a previous chapter, note-taking during an interview can be intrusive, and particularly in a counseling session it may be wiser to wait until the interview is concluded before jotting down your ideas. This task is made easier, of course, if, before the interview, you wrote down the questions you planned to ask and if you actually asked those questions. The important idea to remember is that the effectiveness of your analysis will depend largely on your capacity for accurate recall of what occurred during the interview. Again, listening is the essential skill.

To aid you in analyzing the interview, the following questions may be used:

- Was I fully prepared to conduct the interview?
- Did I make an effort to analyze the situation, and my perceptions of the problem, before the interview? If so, how did the information I received support, reinforce, modify, or conflict with my initial perceptions?
- Did I state my goals for the interview clearly?
- Did I listen carefully and reflectively throughout the session?
- Did I foster a situation in which insight could be gained, or did I merely serve to reinforce existing prejudices, opinions, and innuendo?
- Did I try to handle a problem larger than my level of expertise? If so, what can I do now to encourage the interviewee to seek professional help?
- Did I follow the four steps of the problem-solving process? Did I make clear transitions from step to step?
- Was I able to create a situation in which a full and complete understanding of the problem was realized?
- Did we fully explore alternative solutions?
- Was the solution arrived at in an informed, rational way, or was it forced and/or overly emotional? If it was forced and/or overly emotional, what steps can be taken to improve the situation?
- Did I take time to review our accomplishments and agreements before the closing?
- Did I end the interview properly?

These questions should help you analyze the interviewing process. It should also help you write down your recollection of what transpired during the interview. You are now ready to move on to the second stage of the problem-solving interview analysis.

What Can I Do to Better Understand the Meaning of the Communication Exchanged?

Analysis of communication exchanges in problem-solving interviews should proceed by asking questions about (1) the information that was obtained and its reliability, (2) the relationship you established with the interviewee, and (3) the potential for multiple interpretations of meanings.

The informational content of the interview is important because it establishes the facts of the case. Like a detective investigating a mystery, your job as the interviewer is to ferret out clues from seemingly innocent data. To get to the clues requires first collecting the data. The following questions should guide your analysis of the information gathered in the interview:

- What was said about the problem?
- What evidence, examples, or other proof was offered to support claims made about the problem?
- Can you find out whether any of this information is reliable and accurate?

It must be pointed out here that even if you discover that information was unreliable and inaccurate, it is possible that the interviewee nevertheless *believes* it to be entirely reliable and fully accurate. The decision you must make is whether or not to confront the interviewee with the truth. Unless you are a skilled professional, chances are good that confrontation will produce few, if any, positive results. If you are a friend or relative, your strategy may look very much like betrayal, thereby decreasing the potential you have to give help. The important thing is to know, for yourself as a helper, how reliable and accurate the information is, and to use that assessment as a gauge of how clearly or unclearly the interviewee understands the true nature of the situation.

The second consideration deals directly with the relationship you established during the interview. For many people trying to fulfill a helping role, this issue can be easily misread or misunderstood. For example, we may assume that because we know we are acting out of friendship or genuine concern for the welfare of the interviewee, she or he will know that too. Instead, it is possible that attempts to help may be read as interfering in the personal business of another, or meddling, or worse. This is why it is important to make your relationship a part of your analysis of the interview. What you were told may be as much a function of how the interviewee feels about your offer of help, and you personally, as it does with the reality of the issues involved.

To guide your analysis of the relational aspects of the interview, the following questions may be useful:

- How does the interviewee see me—as a friend, colleague, coworker, boss, relative, intruder, etc.?
- What did I do or say during the interview to make my role clear?
- What did I say or do to generate a hostile perception of my role?
- Did I offer to protect the privacy of the interviewee, or not to divulge any information to others?
- Did I respond calmly to shocking information?
- Did I reflect an attitude of caring and responsibility?
- From the interviewee's perspective, was I in a position to provide help?
- From the interviewee's perspective, am I trustworthy?
- From the interviewee's perspective, did I act during the interview in an intelligent, sensitive, and caring way?

These are often difficult questions to answer. They are difficult because they require you to try to "see yourself as others see you," in this case a person who is in trouble looking at a person who isn't. Nevertheless, if you are to find clues in the available information, it is important to look at what you have contributed to that information pool.

The third source of analysis deals with the possibility of multiple meanings for the same information content.[4] We know that in any communication situation individuals bring their unique backgrounds and interpretations to bear on exchanges of talk. We know also that these differing interpretations can and do contribute to misunderstandings and conflict over intentions and the meanings of outcomes. It is important to keep this in mind in evaluating what was said.

For example, let's assume that during our session with Jose, he made the statement: "I know it's important to try again. And again, and again. But I also know when to quit trying. When to start over by doing something completely different. And I think this is the time." Viewed merely as a statement made in the context of a question about returning to his present job with a renewed sense of purpose, this message could mean simply that he is unwilling to do that. However, viewed as a metaphor for the way in which he has responded to a variety of prior settings—his marriage, his relationships with friends, his view of his career—the statement may acquire more interpretive power. He may believe he is simply speaking about his job, but from your viewpoint he is in fact speaking about his whole life.

Who is right?

As you can easily see, the potential for the same information to acquire quite different interpretations is a real part of the problem-solving session. And there are no easy answers to the question Who is right? In truth, in many instances the fact is that both interpretations are right, because both are grounded in evidence capable of supporting them. The issue, then, becomes how to proceed.

The following questions should help you decide what to do:

- If conflicting interpretations exist, how can this be tactfully clarified—brought out for discussion?
- What is your role as a helper in this relationship—to induce understanding, to impose understanding, or to suggest possible ways of understanding the problem?
- Do you have a vested interest in the interviewee's acceptance or rejection of a possible interpretation?
- If the roles were reversed, how would you want the situation handled?

These questions should encourage you to think about conflicting interpretations as causes for openness and continued discussion. They should also encourage you to be sensitive to who owns the experiences being talked about—after all, the person experiencing the problem is also the person who must deal with the consequences of accepting one or more interpretations of what is "really" happening. When the interview is over, your life also goes on, but not in the same way as the life of the person in the midst of a crisis.

What Is the Likelihood That What Was Accomplished during the Session Will Help the Interviewee?

The final stage in postinterview analysis consists of fitting together the means and ends of the session. This stage requires careful, thoughtful consideration of the likely impact of the exchange of talk on actual outcomes.

A word of caution is in order here. There is a tendency to *overestimate* the potential for success when agreements have been reached, despite the fact that those agreements generally involve others who weren't in on the decision. For this reason it is wise to take a cautiously optimistic view of any problem-solving outcome—to encourage the level of commitment necessary to accomplish the goal while privately adopting a "wait and see" attitude. After all, what will happen if the agreed-upon solution doesn't solve the problem? Or creates another one? You need a position to fall back to that respects the understandings that have been reached but that leaves open the possibility of change.

To help you perform this part of the analysis, the following questions may be used:

- How did the interviewee respond to the preferred solution?
- Did he or she take an active role in constructing it?
- If the solution requires the commitment of outside parties, what can be done to ensure their cooperation?
- Did the interviewee understand that as reasonable as the chosen solution now seems, it may not work out? If so, did the interviewee leave mental room for alteration and change?
- What is your personal assessment of the likelihood of the solution to accomplish its goals?
- What do you honestly believe the interviewee feels about the likelihood of the solution to accomplish its goals?

Answering these questions can help you analyze the interview. Of course, the quality of that analysis will depend on the thoughtfulness and sensitivity you bring to the data.

THE INTERVIEWEE'S ROLE

The fact that you are involved in a problem-solving interview means that either you or someone who has a relationship with you sees a problem. Your approach to the interview is likely to be somewhat different in each case.

If the circumstance is that you have sought help in solving a problem, then your first step is to prepare for the interview. Begin by trying to assess the problem as objectively as you can. What harmful things are happening? Why are they happening? Next, consider your goals. What are your overall goals? Are some more important than others? How realistic are these goals? Finally, consider realistic solutions. What are some ways that you might go about reducing the effect of the circumstances that are causing the problem?

On the other hand, if you find yourself in the situation where you have been asked to discuss a problem regarding yourself, you may not have much opportunity to prepare an analysis of the problem and its solutions. Your tasks here are to try not to become defensive and to find out as much as you can about the other person's view of the problem. If possible, allow some time for analysis between the initial contact about the problem and the time to discuss it. If you have time, prepare your analysis of the problem as we suggested above.

During the interview you will want to listen as carefully as you can. If the other person initiated the request for the interview, make sure you understand what he or she sees as the problem. Ask questions to clarify the issues if necessary. If you have a different view or reservations about the issue, state this. Try to work through an understanding of the problem before you attempt to discover solutions.

Finally, ask for the interviewer's help if that seems reasonable and you need it. Support of another person can be vital in the successful management of a problem.

SUMMARY

This chapter dealt with problem-solving interviews. Our assumption was that while some problems are best handled by trained professionals, there are a wide variety of everyday situations in which problem-solving interviewing skills are necessary.

We began by exploring how to plan the interview. We detailed a six-step plan capable of moving the interview from understanding the context and defining the problem through planning the close.

We then turned our attention to how to evaluate a problem-solving interview. In this section we divided our analysis into three interrelated components: (1) analysis of the accomplishment of the original plan, (2) analysis of the meanings attributed to the exchanges of talk, and (3) analysis of the likelihood of the solution meeting the goals of the interview.

Finally, we addressed the role of the interviewee in a problem-solving interview. The interviewee should prepare by working through an analysis of the problem and its solutions if possible. Beyond this, the interviewee should attempt to understand the interviewer's view of the problem, especially if that person called the interview. Avoiding defensiveness, listening carefully, and asking for clarification are key skills during the interview.

Ethics and Responsibilities in Interviewing

Participants in a problem-solving interview should adhere to several ethical guidelines and responsibilities.

First, *interviewers should be aware of their credentials and what that implies*. This means that interviewers might find themselves in situations where they should redirect the interviewee to someone credentialed to help. Some problems are too difficult for the layperson to handle. Allowing an interviewee to assume that you have the competence to help when you don't constitutes deception.

Second, *interviewers should do not promise anything that they cannot or do not intend to deliver*. Promises might range from "call me if you need me" to financial support. Deception occurs when interviewers promise what they don't deliver.

Third, *interviewers should show respect for each interviewee and his or her ideas*. This means hearing the person out and helping the person think through ideas. It means involving the person as much as possible in the problem-solving process. The problem belongs to the interviewee, and thus, the principle of fairness is violated when he or she is not allowed to be involved in the process as much as possible.

Fourth, *interviewers should allow the other person to make free choices, and not inhibit his or her ability to do so*. This is accomplished by taking the interviewee into account and participating only as much as necessary in order to allow the interviewee to participate as much as possible in the analysis of and solution to the problem. Taking on this responsibility follows the ethical principle of fairness.

Finally, *interviewers should not reveal information gleaned from an interview with those who have no legitimate reason to know it*. Most interviewees will assume the interviewer's confidentiality. Violating this assumption might be interpreted as an act of deception.

Interviewees take on several ethical responsibilities in the problem-solving interview. First, *interviewees, as much as possible, should think through the situation so that they can make best use of the time with the interviewer*. The principle of fairness suggests that interviewees should do their part in preparing.

Second, *interviewees should not misrepresent the facts or their position on the issues*. Not telling the truth might cause harm as well as cost of the interviewer valuable time. The interviewer, if the misrepresentation is detected, will undoubtedly see this behavior as an act of intentional deception.

Third, *interviewees should not suggest that they will do things that they do not intend to do*. Promises made and not kept are seen as acts of deception that violate principles of fairness.

Finally, *interviewees should not make demands of the interviewer that go beyond what one might reasonably expect*. Of course, what constitutes appropriate demands will vary from situation to situation. Whatever the situation, though, interviewees who ask more than they ought will be seen as violating the ethical principle of fairness.

NOTES

[1] Jay Haley, *Problem-Solving Therapy* (New York: Harper & Row, 1976), p. 2.

[2] Gerald M. Phillips and Julia T. Wood, *Communicating in Relationships* (New York: Macmillan, 1983).

[3] Haley, p. 15.

[4] H. Lloyd Goodall, Jr., "The Nature of Analogic Discourse," *The Quarterly Journal of Speech* (1983), 171–179.

SAMPLE PROBLEM-SOLVING INTERVIEW FOR ANALYSIS

The following case is true. The names have been changed to guard the identities of those involved. The background on the case is as follows:

Mike, twenty-one, a graduating senior from a regional university, is seeking guidance from his advisor, Dr. V. The issue is his future employment opportunities, a situation which (as you will see) causes him a great deal of genuine concern. The situation is further encumbered by the fact that Mike has been a good student, was captain of the tennis team, and served as a leading member of his student government association for three years. His major is political science; his minor is communication.

Dr. V. is a faculty member in the department of political science at the regional university. She is also Mike's advisor, and is genuinely concerned about his welfare, although she has made it clear that she does not see her role as an employment counselor, but as an educator. She has helped Mike complete his paperwork for the university's career center, and encouraged him to complete an interviewing class during the first semester of his senior year. Privately, she has hoped he would choose to attend law school.

1. Mike: Hi, Dr. V. Are you busy?

2. Dr. V.: I'm always busy, Mike. But come in.

3. Mike: You probably get tired of seeing me ask the same old questions, but I am really concerned about getting a job—or in my case *not* getting a job—and you're the only person I know to talk to about it that doesn't tell me not to worry.

4. Dr. V.: So you come to me because I give you a hard time? (She laughs.)

5. Mike: (laughing) I guess so. You know what I mean.

6. Dr. V.: No, I'm not sure that I do. What do you mean?

7. Mike: (He shrugs.) I don't know. I think I'm having a hard time because I've worked hard to do everything right but nothing is turning out the way I planned, and...

8. Dr. V.: (interrupting) Wait a minute, Mike. How can that be true? Here you are, graduating from college on time despite your many activities. You've built quite an impressive record. What's your grade point average?

9. Mike: (sighs) Oh, about 3.2 I think. But it will probably go down this term because all I do is sit around worrying about getting a job.

10. Dr. V.: I see. Well, let's talk about that, shall we?

11. Mike: OK.

12. Dr. V.: I mean *really* talk about it.

13. Mike: (seems puzzled) What do you mean?

14. Dr. V.: I mean that we should discuss this as a problem that requires a solution. No more kidding around, no more jokes. If you're letting this problem get in the way of your studies, then it is time to give it serious attention.

15. Mike: And what does that mean? Do you have an answer?

16. Dr. V.: I said no more joking around.

17. Mike: All right. But where do we begin?

18. Dr. V.: Why don't you tell me what you think the problem is.

19. Mike: The problem is I don't have a job.

20. Dr. V.: What else?

21. Mike: I'm graduating next month.

22. Dr. V.: And...(leading him on)

23. Mike: (smiles) And I'm planning to get married the month after that.

24. Dr. V.: OK so far. You don't have a job, you're graduating, and you're planning to get married. Is this one problem or three different problems?

25. Mike: One big problem with three different parts. (smiles)

26. Dr. V.: Can we analyze them independently?

27. Mike: I guess so.

28. Dr. V.: Where do you want to start?

29. Mike: Let's start with...(he thinks about it) school.

30. Dr. V.: Why there?

31. Mike: Because I've been thinking a lot about it lately. I mean, here I am, a guy who follows the rules, who went to college so that I could get a better job, and now I'm graduating with a decent GPA and I can't find one. Makes me wonder if I haven't been missing the point— is school really worth it if I end up like this?

32. Dr. V.: That's a pretty tough indictment.

33. Mike: I'm in that sort of mood.

34. Dr. V.: Well, then. Let's begin with your perceptions of what college is good for. You said you went here so you could get a better job. Is that right?

35. Mike: Yeah. That's right.

36. Dr. V.: Who ever told you that?

37. Mike: What? Well, lots of people. You know. My mom and dad, for example. My guidance counselor in high school. My friends.

38. Dr. V.: Did any of those people tell you anything else about going to college?

39. Mike: Well, sure. They told me to study hard and to make good grades.

40. Dr. V.: What else?

41. Mike: (thinking...)

42. Dr. V.: Didn't they tell you that you should study hard because an education is a worthwhile goal? That knowledge is important?

43. Mike: Well, yeah. They did tell me that, but it was always in the context of getting a better job, making more money, and so on.

44. Dr. V.: All at once? Or eventually?

45. Mike: What do you mean?

46. Dr. V.: I mean do you expect to get a better job and make more money all at once or eventually?

47. Mike: (thinks about it) I see what you mean. But does that mean I shouldn't get some job, any job, right now?

48. Dr. V.: You can always do that. You've always been able to do that. I don't think that's a problem.

49. Mike: I don't understand.

50. Dr. V.: What did you do to help finance your education during the past four years?

51. Mike: I waited tables. I worked at the country club. I sold spa memberships.

52. Dr. V.: I rest my case. You have proved conclusively that you can walk right out of this office today and get a job.

53. Mike: Yeah, but...

54. Dr. V.: But what? Not good enough for you, huh?

55. Mike: That's it, exactly. I thought a college education meant I could do something else.

56. Dr. V.: Like what?

57. Mike: I don't know. Work in an office. Do something important.

58. Dr. V.: Don't you think that takes time? I mean, you don't really expect to do something important immediately, do you?

59. Mike: I guess I did. Maybe I'm just impatient.

60. Dr. V.: Good. Very good. I think that is part of your problem. But you said there were other parts?

61. Mike: Exactly. I'm getting married in two months and I don't have a job—excuse me, I don't have the kind of job I thought I should have when I graduated from college.

62. Dr. V.: Mind a personal question?

63. Mike: It depends. (He grins.)

64. Dr. V.: Do you have to get married in two months? You don't have to answer that if you don't want to.

65. Mike: No, I don't have to get married. But it is what we planned.

66. Dr. V.: Did you make these plans assuming you would have the kind of job you can't yet articulate?

67. Mike: Yeah, I guess so.

68. Dr. V.: Don't you think plans can change, particularly when things are not quite as you planned?

69. Mike: Yeah, but Susan is counting on it.

70. Dr. V.: Is she? Have you asked her, talked to her about it?

71. Mike: Well, sort of. (He shrugs.) No, not really.

72. Dr. V.: Do you think maybe you should?

73. Mike: She is going to be disappointed. Her parents are going to be disappointed. My parents are going to be disappointed.

74. Dr. V.: Do you know that for sure, or are you just guessing?

75. Mike: Well, what else could they be? It makes me seem like I'm backing out or something.

76. Dr. V.: Let's examine that last statement. First, they might be relieved—would you want your daughter marrying a guy who hasn't got a job yet? Would you want your son marrying a girl who would marry a guy who didn't have a job? In fact, everyone might be relieved. You're young. You've got plenty of time. I don't know about your religion, but in mine it takes only minutes to say your vows. Twelve minutes, to be exact. And churches are open every day of the week every week of the year.

77. Mike: That's easy for you to say. You're not the one who has to break the news.

78. Dr. V.: That's true. But if you are old enough to graduate college, get a job, and get married, you ought to be old enough—mature enough—to say these things.

79. Mike: You are right. (He thinks, looks away.)

80. Dr. V.: It seems that something else is troubling you.

81. Mike: Yeah. I see now how I can handle these issues. I mean, I can talk to Susan tonight, and frankly I don't think she or her parents—or my parents either—will mind a little postponement.

82. Dr. V.: Good, that's a very good start.

83. Mike: And what you said about a college education make sense. I know I'm impatient and there are jobs I can get...

84. Dr. V.: Yes, that's right. So what's the problem?

85. Mike: (looks troubled) Maybe the problem is that I'm really not ready for all this responsibility yet.

86. Dr. V.: Go on.

87. Mike: To tell you the truth, I'm a little scared. I grew up in a family that always supported me, no matter what. But they also expected me to do the right thing. And mostly, I did. But now I think maybe I need some time for myself, you know, to figure some things out.

88. Dr. V.: I can certainly sympathize with that. I spent one summer doing nothing—according to my parents—but really I was doing one of the most important things in my life. I was figuring out who I was and what I really wanted.

89. Mike: That's it. That's what I mean. You know, lately, I've been giving some real thought to going on to law school. But I can't tell anybody because I've made all these other plans.

90. Dr. V.: Haven't we just agreed that plans can be changed? By the way, I think that's a great idea about going to law school. I've hoped you would consider doing that. But have you prepared to take the LSAT?

91. Mike: (smiles) Believe it or not I've already taken it. In fact, Dr. V., I've already been admitted to law school for the fall.

92. Dr. V.: That's great, Mike! Congratulations!

93. Mike: Yeah, but…

94. Dr. V.: But what?

95. Mike: But I didn't tell anybody. Not even Susan. (He looks down.)

96. Dr. V.: Why not?

97. Mike: Because I was afraid I wasn't smart enough to get in. I thought if I kept it to myself and things didn't work out, then it wouldn't matter because nobody would know. I just hate to let people down. I can handle it, but I can't handle their disappointment.

98. Dr. V.: Who is going to be disappointed that you got into law school? I think the bigger issue is that you have some serious talking to do with Susan and some other people.

99. Mike: I know. I just don't know how.

100. Dr. V.: Nobody knows how. That's part of it. There is no one right way. It looks like you've got some important choices to make.

101. Mike: Choices?

102. Dr. V.: Yes, choices. Whether or not to get married right away. Whether or not to go to law school. Whether or not to get a job. But there is one choice that you have already made that can go a long way to helping you make all the others.

103. Mike: What's that?

104. Dr. V.: What are you going to do tonight?

105. Mike: I'm going to talk to Susan.

106. Dr. V.: What are you going to talk about?

107. Mike: (sighs) Well, I need to talk to her about law school. And we need to talk about getting married.

108. Dr. V.: Right. Absolutely. (smiles) And I thought we were going to have to talk about getting you a job.

109. Mike: (smiles) I did too. But I'm glad it didn't turn out that way.

110. Dr. V.: You see, plans can change. And for the better.

111. Mike: Thanks, Dr. V. I needed this. Do you think I could come back tomorrow and talk some more?

112. Dr. V.: Let's check with my secretary. I'm sure I can make some time.

ROLE-PLAYING CASES

The Problem Examination

The interviewee, Kazujiko Suzuki, is a new professor at Normal College. He has just given his midterm examination. The exam included sixty objective questions and six short-answer essay questions for a fifty-minute exam period. At the end of the exam period, he collected the papers and discovered that ten of the thirty students had not finished the exam. The course for which the exam was given was an upper-level course that is required for graduation. The exam grade was to be half of the final course grade. Several of these students may not pass the course if they fail this examination.

The interviewer, Joann Williams, is a colleague who has been teaching at the college for fifteen years. Kazujiko and Joann enjoy and respect each other. So, Joann has taken on the task of mentoring Kazujiko. Their relationship is friendly and satisfying to both.

An Employer-Employee Relationship

Paul Holbrook is the business manager for Midwest Chemical Company. He has worked in his present position for fifteen years and over this time has developed a number of habits that are annoying to his employees. About a year ago he started eating lunch alone in his office with the door closed. In fact, he keeps his door closed most of the time. When members of his department have a question, they often get a brief and unsatisfactory answer. For example, Kay asked for the morning off to go to a 9 A.M. dentist appointment. Paul answered, "Two hours," without even looking up from his work. George put a note in Paul's mailbox asking how to submit a report. Two days later, he got a one-word reply, "Typewritten." Upon hearing of the one-word reply, Stan, another employee, told George how lucky he was. Several months ago Stan asked Paul a question as he passed through the office. Paul acted as if Stan hadn't said a word. Recently Paul has become concerned that the atmosphere in the office has changed. He asked Mary Wright, a senior bookkeeper in his department, to talk with him.

Mary Wright has been with Midwest for twenty years. She is a careful observer of people and circumstances and is well aware of what has been happening in the office. Paul has turned to her on several occasions to help him solve problems.

A Dating Problem

The interviewee is June Stewart, a twenty-year-old college sophomore. She has been dating Sean for a little over a year. They have talked off and on about their future together and even the possibility of marriage. June is a member of St. Peter's Baptist Church; Sean is a member of Holy Family Catholic Church. They have talked at length about how they might manage this difference. June decides to talk to her pastor about the situation.

The interviewer, Pastor Smith, has known June all her life. He is not aware of the topic of the interview. He only knows that she made an appointment to talk about a problem.

A Parent Problem

Dawn Cope, the interviewee, is a sophomore at Northern University. She is a very responsible twenty-year-old woman who is majoring in communication. Her grades suggest that she is a serious student, with a grade point average of 3.2. She has elected to live at home because of economic necessity, although she has some income from a part-time sales job at a local department store. Her parents pay her college tuition, and she pays for books, clothes, and entertainment.

Dawn is particularly frustrated by the way her parents have ignored the fact that she is an adult. They continue to treat her as if she were still a high school girl. Thus they demand that she tell them where she is going and when she will return at all times. They also quiz her about the people she dates and her friends. Dawn resents this treatment and has decided to talk to a trusted professor about the problem.

Mike Szabo, the interviewer, is an associate professor of communication at Northern. He is forty-six years old, is married, and has two children. He has been a professor for ten years.

The Class Project

The interviewee, Alex Carpenter, is the leader of a group that is working on a class project. One member of the group, Jason, has missed several meetings and is often late with his part of the work. The project is due next Monday. Alex has talked to Jason about some late materials. Jason commented, "I got them to you didn't I? You're lucky I had time to do it at all." Alex is concerned that Jason's work will not be ready for the Monday deadline and decides to talk to him about the problem.

The interviewee, Jason, is an overcommitted senior student. He needs the credit for the course, but he is not particularly concerned about the grade. He is spending most of his time lining up job interviews and participating in them.

EXPERIENCES

1. Identify a recent experience in which you played the role of interviewer in a problem-solving interview. How did you help the interviewee work through the problem? What did you do to manage the climate of the interview? What things would you do differently if you were able to "replay" the interview?
2. Select one of the role-playing cases presented above. Plan an interview. Tell how you would begin. Indicate what questions you would plan to ask. Suggest what solution or solutions you see as viable. Tell how you would close the interview.
3. Interview a person who volunteers to work in a crisis center. Discover what procedures the person generally follows. Find out also what training the person received for carrying out these interviews. Ask what techniques he or she has learned that are especially valuable in this kind of interviewing.

RECOMMENDED READINGS

Benjamin, Alfred, *The Helping Interview,* 2d ed. (Boston: Houghton-Mifflin, 1984).

Combs, Arthur W., *Helping Relationships: Basic Concepts for the Helping Professions* (Boston: Allyn and Bacon, 1985).

Long, Lynette, Louis V. Paradise, and Thomas J. Long, *Questioning: Skills for the Helping Process* (Monterey, CA: Brooks/Cole, 1983).

Makau, Josina M., *Reasoning and Communication: Thinking Critically about Arguments* (Belmont, CA: Wadsworth, 1990).

Monroe, Craig, Mark G. Borzi, and Vincent S. DiSalvo, "Conflict Behaviors of Difficult Subordinates," *Southern Communication Journal, 54* (1989), 311–329.

Morris, G. H, and Marta Coursey, "Negotiating the Meaning of Employees' Conduct: How Managers Evaluate Employee Accounts," *Southern Communication Journal, 54* (1989), 185–205.

Rubenstein, Moshe Y., *Patterns of Problem Solving* (Englewood Cliffs, NJ: Prentice-Hall, 1975).

Wolfe, Christopher Sterling, and Michael J. Cody, "Perspectives on Legal Interviewing and Counseling," *Southern Speech Communication Journal, 53* (1988), 360–384.

CHAPTER 12

PERSUASIVE
INTERVIEWING

OBJECTIVES

After reading this chapter, you should be able to:

Define the purpose and goals of persuasive interviewing.

Discuss strategies for preparing for a persuasive interview.

Plan and carry out a persuasive interview.

Describe strategies for dealing with problem interviewees
and special circumstances.

Develop criteria for evaluating of a persuasive interview.

Pose ethical standards for a persuasive interview.

The persuasive interview provides a setting in which the interviewer consciously seeks to exert influence over the interviewee. Persuasion has as its aim communication designed to influence others by modifying their beliefs, values, or attitudes.[1] The interviewer asks questions and creates messages in an attempt to lead the interviewee to think, feel, and/or act in a particular way. Frequently, the interviewer has a goal in mind that involves the interviewee taking some action.

There are many uses for a one-on-one persuasive effort of this type. A sales interview is one of the most common. Eric Skopec reports that more than 6.5 million people in the United States make their living in some sales occupation.[2] Of course, not all of these millions work in situations where they are conducting one-to-one interviews, but many do.

Beyond selling of some product is the "selling" of an idea to another person. Nearly all professionals engage in interviews of this kind. First-level managers persuade mid-level managers to accept their proposals and programs. Managers and teachers convince their employees and students that they ought to do a task in a particular way. Employees and students persuade their supervisors and teachers to accept their ideas and suggestions. Architects and designers sell their their ideas to clients. The opportunity to participate in this type of interview is extensive.

Some of the interviews we discussed earlier in this book include persuasion among their goals. For example, supervisors undoubtedly hope to persuade their employees to improve performance. Recruiters would like to persuade job candidates that their organizations are good places to work. Health care professionals want to persuade their patients or clients to follow prescribed advice. Refer to the chapters that discuss these kinds of interviews for information about them.

This chapter focuses on the interview situation where persuasion is the primary aim. We begin by presenting the step-by-step process for preparing the persuasive interview. Next, we provide information on managing the interview. Finally, we suggest ways to make the role of interviewee more productive.

PREPARING FOR THE PERSUASIVE INTERVIEW

Preparing for the persuasive interview requires that you move through five steps. You begin the process by stating the purpose. The next two steps require you to analyze the interviewee and the interviewee's position. Once you have completed these tasks, you are ready to consider the setting and, finally, plan the interview.

Stating the Purpose

The statement of purpose of the interview provides the guidance needed to carry out the remaining steps of preparation. There are several things to remember in planning the purpose. For one thing, be specific, because you are focusing your effort on a particular individual. For another, keep in mind that it is unlikely that a single interview will produce a dramatic change. Ask yourself what you ultimately want this person to think, feel, or do that can be reasonably expected. Write a statement that reflects this aim. Do not expect a dramatic change after just a single interview.

Here are some statements of purpose generated by interviewers for persuasive interviews:

To persuade Helen that we should buy a Pontiac Firebird.
To persuade Bob to apply for a community block grant to upgrade
O'Neil Park.
To persuade Don to buy a Zenith Eazy PC computer for my office.
To persuade Joan that we should adopt a telephone preregistration
system.
To persuade Mike to increase my salary by $2000.

Analyzing the Interviewee

Begin your analysis of the interviewee by listing what you already know about this person. Study the list to discover what additional information you will need.

What are some of the kinds of information you will want to consider? Check to see if you have information about the interviewee's personal characteristics, socioeconomic background, orientation toward the topic, and psychological characteristics. We will say more specifically what is meant by each of these momentarily.

Sources of information about a person may be interviews with people who know the person, personnel files if the interviewee is somebody in your organization and you have access to these, and reports or documents that the person may have written that relate to the topic. Sometimes there will still be things you want to know. You may plan the first part of the interview to collect some of these data and then make use of them later in the interview.

Personal characteristics.   Personal characteristics include both physical and mental features of the individual. Consider age, sex, race, appearance, and build. Age may give you some information about the person's likely experience with the topic of interest. Does the age of the person suggest the experience level that this person may have with the topic? Does age mean that the person has a particular rank or status? Will the person's sex make a difference in outlook for this topic? Will race make a difference? Sex and race will not make a difference for most issues, but you may be considering a topic for which they do. What about appearance and build? It sometimes is helpful to be able to visualize the person you intend to persuade.

Considerations about intellectual capacity and preparation are especially important. How deeply will the person have thought about your topic and proposal? How adept is the person at analyzing an issue? To what extent has this person developed a vocabulary that will allow you to present your ideas in a sophisticated way? The person's intellectual capabilities must be assessed so that you know at what level to present your case.

Socioeconomic background.   Consideration of a person's socioeconomic background may give insights into the kinds of group associations a person has. Ask yourself what group behavior is implied by the person's status, both socially and economically. Research suggests that strong group identification will have significant impact on a person's willingness to accept an idea, and especially if the idea is contrary to the norms of the group.[3]

Orientation toward the topic.   Your analysis of the interviewee must also include questions that assess the individual in relation to your topic. Of course, the basic question is, How much does the person know about the topic? Select subquestions that will focus your assessment. What is the person's involvement with the topic? Has the person experienced firsthand problems related to the topic? What are the problems experienced? How interested is the person in the topic? What is the person's position with respect to your proposal? Why does he or she take this stand?

Think also about the interviewee's orientation in relation to your goal. If the interviewee is likely to be for the proposal, then you probably won't need much effort to achieve your goal. If the interviewee is likely to be very much against your proposal, then you may hope to gain only a slight change in the direction of the proposal. However, if the interviewee is undecided about the proposal, you may have a good chance to achieve your goal with a carefully planned interview and proposal. Of course, some people are uncommitted because they do not want to take a stand or because doing so would violate some strongly held beliefs. In these cases, movement in the direction you plan will be difficult to achieve.

Psychological characteristics. Psychological characteristics includes such things as psychological orientation, values, and needs. A *psychological orientation* refers to the person's mental attitude or general frame of mind. Is the person generally optimistic or pessimistic? Is the person suspicious or trusting? Is the person open-minded or closed-minded? How has the person received past attempts at being persuaded?

Analyze the interviewee's value system. A *value* is a principle, standard, or quality considered to be worthwhile. As a guide in this analysis you might use the catalog of American values developed from research conducted by Edward Steele and W. Charles Redding.[4] These categories of values, along with those suggested by Milton Rokeach and Seymour Parker,[5] provide an excellent checklist from which to conduct an analysis. Which of these values are sources of motivation for your interviewee?

_____ 1. *Comfort, convenience* (the striving for comfort and the pleasant life)
_____ 2. *Health, safety, security* (for self, loved ones, friends, and others)
_____ 3. *Pride, social recognition, prestige* (for personal success and achievement)
_____ 4. *Affection, popularity* (among family, friends, and associates)
_____ 5. *Happiness* (by gaining pleasure from life)
_____ 6. *Ambition* (hard work and striving brings success)
_____ 7. *Cleanliness* (of self and surroundings)
_____ 8. *Companionship* (of friends and others)
_____ 9. *Competition* (winning, being number one)
_____ 10. *Conformity* (to be seen as fitting in, to be like others)
_____ 11. *Ownership, accumulation* (of material goods, achievements)
_____ 12. *Power, authority* (to control others)
_____ 13. *Freedom from authority/restraint* (independence)
_____ 14. *Sexual satisfaction* (from relationships)
_____ 15. *Accomplishment* (from personal contributions)
_____ 16. *Peace, tranquility* (in surrounding environment)
_____ 17. *Education, knowledge* (well educated and knowledgeable)
_____ 18. *Equality, value of individual* (equal worth and treatment of people)
_____ 19. *Change, progress* (movement toward goals, improvement of self and society)
_____ 20. *Efficiency, practicality, pragmatism* (in managing problems and proposing solutions)
_____ 21. *Consideration, generosity* (toward those who are less fortunate)
_____ 22. *Loyalty, patriotism* (in family, friends, coworkers, and others)

Of course, not all of these values will be relevant to a particular interview situation. The interviewer must analyze them based upon knowledge of the interviewee and the purpose. An interviewer who wanted his boss to purchase a new Zenith computer for his office found that ambition (6), competition (9), accomplishment (15), equality (18), change, progress (19), and efficiency, practicality, pragmatism (20) were all potential values upon which an appeal could be based. Once the values were identified, then the interviewer was ready to move to a consideration of needs.

A *need* is an urgent want. It is a desire to possess something that we don't have or don't have in sufficient quantity to satisfy us. A need, of course, is related to our value system because the urgency is created by the valuing of whatever it is. Therefore, look to your analysis of values to discover what might be unmet needs. Let us illustrate how this sort of analysis might work. Consider again the persuasive appeal for a new computer. The value represented by the category "competition" suggests a potentially unmet need to be number one—perhaps in terms of productivity. The computer may be seen as a solution in that it may allow achievement of greater productivity. The greater productivity then might lead to achievement of becoming number one and thus realization of the value.

Needs may not be recognized by the interviewee even though they are potentially there. The interviewer is not just in the business of discovering needs; they sometimes must be created and activated. Perhaps the boss hadn't thought about what a dramatic effect a sophisticated computer might have on productivity. Suddenly, though, the need is created because the employee presents the arguments and a plan that stimulates the boss's imagination and activates the need.

Attitude toward the interviewer.   The interviewee may be persuaded to accept a proposal because he or she is favorably disposed toward the interviewer and toward the proposal. The interviewee may even accept the proposal because he or she values the interviewer, rather than valuing the idea. This disposition toward the interviewer is often the result of source credibility. *Source credibility* is the favorability that the source of a message enjoys. It is derived from what is known about the person's reputation, attainments, personality, beliefs, and intent. Credibility is enhanced if the source appears to possess certain characteristics. Some of these are confidence, poise, restraint, even temper, energy, alertness, knowledge, sincerity, fairness, honesty, sympathy, and decisiveness.[6] Studies suggest also that the source will be trusted if that person is viewed as sharing important beliefs, attitudes, and values.[7]

Sometimes credibility is low because the interviewee dislikes or distrusts the interviewer. Perhaps, on the other hand, the distrust is not with the interviewer at all, but with the organization or department the person represents. Under either of these circumstances there is little chance of success unless the interviewee's opinion can be changed during the interview. It is possible to overcome this problem if the arguments and the interview are structured to enhance source credibility. We will address the structure of arguments and the interview shortly.

Analyzing the Interviewee's Position

At this point in the preparation, lay out your position on the proposition and view it in relation to that of the interviewee. This involves assembling a statement of specific purpose and the presumed position of the interviewee on the issue. Then, anticipate how far apart the two positions actually are. If they do not represent a nearly similar position, ask yourself what objections the interviewee might have that would differentiate his or her position from yours. Identify which of these are legitimate objections. You might acknowledge these as legitimate and suggest that the merits of the proposal outweigh these concerns. If you determine that these objections are not legitimate, consider what arguments or information will allow you to explain away or negate them.

Consider the proposal discussed above for the purchase of the new Zenith computer. The specific purpose might be stated as follows: "I wish to persuade Don to purchase a Zenith Eazy PC with a 20-megabit hard disk." The boss's position might be: "I am not sure that I should purchase a Zenith computer." But what might his objections be? Perhaps Don thinks it's too costly. Perhaps he doesn't think that it will prove to be useful enough to justify the expense. Perhaps he thinks that others will ask for a computer for their work and he will not be able to accommodate them all. Suppose the conclusion is that the boss will not believe that the purchase of this computer will be justified on the basis of usefulness and productivity. Then, data about anticipated usefulness and productivity would strengthen the proposal. You will want to be prepared to answer as many objections as possible.

Considering the Setting

You may have the opportunity to select a setting for the interview. Consider a location that will provide uninterrupted privacy. The persuasive interview is such that you will not be able to predict the exact amount of time necessary to complete it. Therefore, places that are private, and in which you will not be interrupted, are the best possible settings.

You might want to arrange the interview in your office if doing so will not be perceived as manipulative. This will allow provision for the interviewee's comfort and control of privacy. And perhaps the psychological advantage of being on your own turf, with all your materials at hand, is important to your purpose.

Sometimes you will prefer to meet in some area that is neutral space. You might believe that either your office or that of the interviewee will be perceived as providing unfair advantage or be inappropriate for some other reason. Sometimes lunch in a quiet restaurant provides this kind of setting.

On the other hand, you may wish to let the interviewee know that you want to accommodate by arranging the interview in his or her office or home. Meeting in the interviewee's space can give that person an advantage—it is easier to terminate an interview if you are on your own turf, for example. But it can be perceived as a gesture of politeness and consideration for the interviewee's time. You might consider meeting in the interviewee's home if your purpose would be best suited by that setting. Life insurance proposals and financial plans, for example, are often presented in the interviewee's home.

Consider also where you will want to sit to conduct the interview. Should the formality represented by staying behind your desk be maintained? Should a more informal sitting area be used? Perhaps a quiet lounge area is available if you do not have an informal sitting area available in your office. Will the direct face-to-face situation be too personal or too threatening? You will want to consider this issue if you have a choice about seating arrangements.

Think also about the timing of your interview. Have there been recent events that might influence the acceptance or rejection of your proposal? For example, it might be the wrong time to ask the boss for a new computer if you are at the end of the budget year and all the money is spent. On the other hand, if there is a surplus, the end of the year may be exactly the right time to ask.

Time of day can also be important. It may take a good deal of time to develop a proposal and answer any objections to it. Will you want to select a time when you will not have to rush through your presentation to make some other appointment? Is the morning or afternoon a better time for your interviewee? You may be able to know the answer to this question if you are familiar with the interviewee and his or her habits.

Planning the Interview

You are ready to plan the interview now that you have completed the research and analysis. We divide the planning process into consideration of the opening, the proposal, and the closing.

The opening. The opening has as its aims gaining the interest of the interviewee and establishing an appropriate relationship. There is no standard formula for doing these two things, but there are some important things to keep in mind. Begin by reviewing what we have said in Chapter 3 about opening an interview.

You will want to introduce yourself if the interviewee does not know you. This should include information about you, such as your name, position, and perhaps your relevant background, and something about your organization, such as its name, its location, the nature of the business, and sometimes its relevant history. You may also want to make polite inquiries about the interviewee. This sort of small talk must appear to be motivated by a sincere interest and not be overdone. It is important that the interviewee is involved in the talk. If he or she doesn't seem interested in participating, move on to the development of the proposal. The opening should also reveal the basic purpose of the interview.

The proposal.   Generally a persuasive interview is designed to make a proposal that is intended to solve some problem or satisfy some need. Sometimes the problem or need is already recognized by the interviewee. Sometimes the interviewer will have to uncover or even "create" it. In each case, what the interviewer does is develop a proposal that explores the need, develops evaluative criteria, and presents a solution. First, we consider the need.

The word *need* is used here to suggest the impelling force for the change you are advocating. A person does not usually make a decision to institute a change without recognizing some difficulty with the current circumstances. Something must be unsatisfactory. There must be some need to act or think differently. This is the part of the interview in which the interviewer works with the interviewee to explore and develop the need for change.

Begin the preparation by listing all the reasons you can think of for the change you will propose. Now analyze each of these. Which of these can you support with reasoning and evidence? Which of these will most likely appeal to the interviewee's values? When you know the answers to these two questions, use this information to pick your three or four most compelling need arguments. Pick more than one or two because the cumulative effect of having several arguments for the change is important to building your case.

Work on developing each need argument. Begin with the strongest and most compelling point and expect to present this one first. You want to be sure to make this point early in the interview so that you gain the interviewee's attention and interest. Prepare so that you can fully explain the point and provide evidence that is factual, documented, and recent. Present a variety of evidence that is designed to appeal to both the logical and the emotional side of the interviewee. Involve the interviewee by posing questions that will demonstrate how the need is a concern of the interviewee. For example, ask, "When was the last time you were pursuing a deadline for getting a report out and weren't sure you'd make it? How did this feel?" Gain agreement about the point you are making before going on to the next one. If the interviewee poses objections, they must be answered before going on. We will discuss the preparation of responses to possible objections shortly.

You should be prepared to move on to the criteria step if you seem to be gaining strong agreement to the points being made about the need. Overdoing the presentation of the need can bore and/or frustrate your interviewee and, if this person becomes angry because of your insensitivity, prejudice the results of the interview. When you sense that you have presented enough of your points to convince the interviewee of the need, summarize your points, gain the agreement of the interviewee, and move on to the criteria.

Criteria are the standards used for making a decision. Here you must imagine what features the interviewee will think are important. This analysis is needed because your planned solution will need to take these into account. Begin by listing all the general features that are important aspects of your proposal.

Return to the proposal for the computer. Imagine what features in a computer might be important if we were to support the values of competition, accomplishment, equality, change, progress, and efficiency. Perhaps these are speed, compatibility with other units already in use, enough memory to support the application programs that will be used, a modem device to connect to other computers through the telephone, and price. The interviewer would want to make sure each of these were taken into account in selecting the solution—a Zenith Eazy PC.

Of course, the important criteria are those of the interviewee. You will inquire of the interviewee what he or she sees as important features for meeting the need. The process of working with the interviewee in establishing the criteria shows this person that you are attempting to tailor the plan to his or her situation.

Secure agreement on the criteria. This will provide a set of statements that will allow you to evaluate your plan and any competing plans that you or the interviewee bring up. The statements can also help avoid objections to your solution.

A *solution* is the answer to a problem or need in that it seeks to remove or moderate the need. Of course, we can never know with certainty whether this will happen without implementing the solution and observing the results. So the task of the interviewer is to create a solution that seems to have a high probability of achieving this end. If the situation has been carefully researched and understood, the need is clearly present, the criteria are carefully drawn, and the plan meets the criteria and seems reasonably workable, then there is a good chance the solution will work and be accepted by the interviewee.

Present the solution in a positive, enthusiastic manner. It is important that you believe in the solution and convey that fact to the interviewee. Generally, emphasize the strengths and advantages of your proposal, rather than the weaknesses and disadvantages of counterproposals.

Evaluate the proposal according to each of the criteria—one at a time. If an objection is raised as your are presenting, stop to deal with it at that time. Show how your proposal satisfies the criteria better than any other. Gain the interviewee's agreement on matters such as quality, appropriateness, and workability.

Finally, use techniques that will involve the interviewee and help that person remember what you said. Use a number of different kinds of visual aids (if it seems sensible). Some of the more common visuals are booklets, brochures, drawings, diagrams, graphs, pictures, letters, slides, and computer printouts. Don't forget that an interviewee may be better able to visualize what you are describing by handling swatches of material, models, or the actual object. Repetition can be helpful in understanding and remembering. Repetition can also serve as a device to make the important ideas stand out.

The closing.   The *closing* is the part of the interview in which you ask for agreement to your proposal. As part of the closing, attempt to estimate where the interviewee stands. The answer to this speculation gives you information about how to proceed. The closing results in one of three outcomes: agreement to the proposal, discovery that no agreement can be reached, or knowledge that at least another interview will be necessary to secure agreement.

Understand that you must ask for agreement and know when to do so. Hesitation to ask for the sale has been recognized as a major reason for failure to make the sale.[8] But knowing precisely when to ask requires weighing the situation and making a judgment.

Close as soon as it appears that the interviewee has made a decision. You may be able to know this by observing the verbal and nonverbal cues. Any verbal indications of a positive attitude toward the proposal ("That makes sense." "Yes, I see that this will work."), or questions about how to get started with such a plan ("How soon could I get a delivery?" "How would this be financed?"), or anticipation of the benefits ("It will really be nice to get this problem settled.") may be indications that you should close. Look for nonverbal cues such as enthusiasm in the interviewee's voice, affirmative nods, and smiles. Sometimes an interviewee may physically take possession of brochures, models, or pictures. This may be a display of interest too.

Sometimes you can probe to see if the interviewee is at the point of making a decision. This kind of question is called a *trial closing*. For example, a question like, "You can see how this plan could allow you to [name an advantage of the plan for the person]?" Or perhaps you might say, "The cost of this [name the item] seems very reasonable, doesn't it?" If you get a no to a trial closing question, try to discover what the concern might be. If you get a yes, pause to allow the interviewee to gather his or her thoughts. If no further questions are asked, then you are ready to ask for the agreement. You are at the moment that you must ask for the agreement. You are ready to close.

Gerald Manning and Barry Reece suggest several closing techniques from which to choose.[9] You might use the *summary close,* in which you summarize the need, criteria, or agreements made earlier and then ask for agreement. Or you might choose the *assumptive close,* which uses a statement that begins with, "I assume that...." For example, you could say, "I assume that you would prefer a Zenith computer over a more expensive IBM?" If there is still an objection, you might select the *elimination of a single objection close*. This close acknowledges the reservation and counters with a contrasting advantage. For example, you could say, "I understand that spending $1500 on a computer represents a significant outlay, but think about the fact that I'll be able to get projects done 30 percent faster." The *either/or close* attempts to narrow the choices to two possibilities and persuade the interviewee to select the most desirable of the two (your plan, you hope). Sometimes, if the circumstances are just right, the *sense of urgency close* will be appropriate. Perhaps, for example, there is some sort of special incentive available that will disappear soon. Or there may be extra funds available for upgrading equipment. You might say, "We should act now on this because we can save $500 if we do so by the end of the month." Or, "This is an excellent opportunity. We have the funds available for upgrading, so that none of the rest of the budget will be affected by the expenditure." When the interviewee is clearly undecided, you might wish to employ the *I'll think it over close*. This close seeks to acknowledge the interviewee's wish to think about the proposal, while trying to discover the remaining area of concern and/or the interviewee's level of interest. In this case, you might say, "I'm pleased that you want to think about this plan. Is there a particular area that concerns you?" Or, perhaps, "I'm pleased that you want to think about the plan, as that suggests it interests you." Finally, you might employ a *price closing*, in which you stress your best offer and perhaps the savings it represents. For example, "The $999 price is my best offer. That will save you $500 over the regular price."

The outcome of your closing will help you know how you should take leave from the interviewee. If your proposal has been accepted, you will want to express your appreciation as sincerely as possible. If the interviewee wants to think about the proposal, you may want to arrange for an opportunity to meet again. On the other hand, if your proposal has been turned down, you will want to end on a pleasant note, leaving the possibility open for a future meeting. Whatever your decision, don't promise anything you cannot deliver and try to leave a positive impression with the interviewee.

MANAGING THE PERSUASIVE INTERVIEW

How successful you will be in a persuasive interview depends on how well you implement your preparation during the actual interview. The planning and preparation, of course, were quite important. But how you manage the interview—how you present yourself and the case, how you handle interviewee problems and objections—will have a dramatic impact on goal achievement.

Presenting Yourself

The presentation of self involves building rapport and credibility. *Rapport* is the cordiality and warmth that people experience toward each other in a relationship. You will want to pay attention to enhancing the rapport even if there is already a good deal of cordiality in the relationship.

One method of building rapport is to establish some common ground with the interviewee. Similarity is a basis for attraction, and so you may want to uncover some ways that you two are similar. There are many possibilities for similarities. Here are some of the more common sources:

Shared beliefs	Shared values
Shared reference groups	Shared goals
Shared friends	Shared interests
Shared experiences	Shared tastes

You may notice something in the interviewee's office that allows you to bring up the topic. Or the interviewee may open up the subject by commenting on one of these commonalties. Or, perhaps, you might bring up a mutual friend as you are greeting the interviewee in the opening. But be careful about overdoing this aspect of the interview, and especially if the item of conversation is only remotely related to the purpose of the interview.

There are two specific techniques for enhancing credibility during the interview. The first is to demonstrate your expertise. Of course, you would generally not want to brag directly about your knowledge. You can, however, show your expertise by demonstrating a thorough knowledge and understanding of the issue. You may also want to quote others who are known to be experts. You should be familiar with their work and have made use of it in doing your homework. (If you are not familiar with their work and have not used it, then the interviewee ought to be suspicious of your expertise.) You can call attention to this material and your use of it by saying something like, "When I was looking into how various computers compare, I found an article by David Bunnell, editor-in-chief of the *PC World* magazine, that was very helpful. He said,...."

The second way to build credibility is to show respect and consideration for the interviewee. This means showing respect for and interest in the person, that person's time, and that person's comfort. You might check to make sure the person still has the time to see you, "Is it still convenient to meet at three this afternoon?" You might make polite inquiry into how the day has been going, "How has it been going for you today, Don?" You could ask questions about some known area of commonality, "How is the golf game coming these days, Paula?" If the person is a stranger, inquiry about the person's experiences and interests will help you to know that person and allow you to demonstrate your interest in him or her.

Adapting to Problem Interviewee Temperaments

Temperament is something you may or may not be able to plan for in the interview. *Temperament* refers to the unique personal nature of the individual that affects the way he or she thinks, feels, and acts. The interviewee who is going to be indecisive may have a reputation for being so. On the other hand, it may be difficult to predict that the interviewee will be hostile. We present several of the usual problem temperaments with suggestions for managing them.

The interviewee may seem *apathetic or skeptical*. This may be an indication that the person does not fully understand the need for your proposal. If you have not presented this portion of your case, be sure, when you do so, to present your strongest need argument first. Draw attention to the extent of the harm being caused by the situation. Ask probing questions to discover how the person is feeling and why. Show how the harm is or is at least likely to affect the interviewee personally. Tell why there is some urgency to the problem. If the interviewee is uncertain about your plan, review your arguments and evidence. Present additional evidence if you have some.

The interviewee may be *closed-minded* and *authoritarian*. People with a disposition toward closed-mindedness and authoritarianism are often interested in who supports the idea. If people whom they believe in support it, this support will be viewed as important. Closed-minded, authoritarian people may also possess strong central beliefs and values. You might be able to use this fact in your effort to persuade. Plan arguments that allow you to identify yourself and your proposal with what the person seems to value.

The interviewee may have a *negative evaluation* of you or your organization. Approach the interview being positive about yourself and your organization. Be sure to employ the credibility-building techniques talked about above. Beyond these, you can develop some common ground through the approaches known as the "yes-yes" and "yes-but." Herbert Simons describes these:

> Two variants of this bridge-building process are the "yes-yes" technique and the "yes-but" technique. In both cases, little or no hint of any disagreement...is expressed until after a whole string of assertions is communicated about which agreement is sure. The object is to establish a habit of assent, to get receivers nodding "Yes," "That's right," "You said it," either aloud or to themselves. Once this is done, the audience will presumably be receptive to more controversial assertions.
>
> Using the "yes-but" approach, persuaders begin by noting those arguments of the opposition with which they can agree, and then having shown how fair minded they are, they offer a series of "buts" that constitute the heart of their case.[10]

Here is an example of the "yes-but" strategy used by the computer sales representative:

> We agree that your current computer has been serving you quite well. We also agree that both it and the new Mac have many of the same important features. And we agree that it is likely to serve you well for the next few years. But the one feature that it doesn't have is a sophisti-

cated graphics capability. And that one feature, alone, can make a considerable difference to you in terms of time and money saved. Do you see that?

When the difficulty is related to the interviewee's dislike for your organization, approach this situation by examining the source of the dislike. If the interviewee merely dislikes the organization and you are unsure of why this is the case, you might disassociate yourself from the organization. You can do this by withholding the name of the organization until it becomes necessary to reveal it. If the interviewee has not had recent contact with the organization, your approach might be to explain how the organization has changed since the person formed his or her objections. If, on the other hand, you think the dislike is based on misinformation or misjudgment, you might try to improve the image of the organization by presenting information and arguments.

If the interviewee is *hostile,* you may wish to attempt to counter the hostility. You might use some of the common-ground approaches we've already presented. You may also wish to pay special attention to the climate. In addition to maintaining supportive behavior, soften the impact of your counterarguments by giving the person credit for issues that are relatively minor in relation to your proposal. You might say, "That is a very good point, yet...." Or you might compliment the interviewee on a point raised, "That's a very good question. I'm glad you asked it, because...." Or you might counter with, "A number of people have raised this question. And I can understand why you are asking. Let me explain...." Hostility can most easily be defused if you are able to remain calm and polite, and are equipped with facts, figures, examples, and expert testimony.

Adapting to Special Interviewee Circumstances

There are two special interviewee circumstances that you will want to take into account. The first is the situation where the interviewee may be subject to *counterpersuasion.* Under this circumstance it is important to explore and explain whatever you believe may be the opposing view. Also be sure that the interviewee fully understands your arguments and evidence. Compare your case and the opposing one, showing the strengths and weaknesses of both sides. Do not dwell on the negative with regard to the opposition case; instead, take a positive approach that stresses the strengths of your position and proposal.[11] You can also strengthen your case by asking a series of questions that lead the interviewee to state the "negatives" of counterplans. Then reinforce what the interviewee said, by saying, "You're right about that."

The *highly intelligent* and/or *highly educated* interviewee also presents a special circumstance. This interviewee has a higher likelihood of having thought through the situation and of being aware that there are competing positions on the issue. It is important that you recognize there is a competing position and devote attention to that view. Rely on statistics, testimony, and reasoning to support your view. Avoid excessively emotional appeals, unless the interviewee is favorably disposed to your position. Ask questions and seek input that will allow the interviewee to be an active participant. On the other hand, if the case is reversed, if the interviewee is *not especially intelligent* or is *not well educated,* you should not be concerned with a careful presentation of the other side of the issue. Instead, concentrate on examples, illustrations, and emotional appeals. You can use evidence and reasoning to bolster the case.

Asking Questions

We have suggested throughout our presentation of the persuasive interview that you will want to ask questions. Here we present a brief summary of the kinds of questions you will find useful.

1. *Information gathering.* You will surely not know all you want to know about the interviewee. You may choose to ask for more information about his or her background, needs, attitudes, and knowledge level.

2. *Checking.* You will want to be sure you understand the important ideas the interviewee presents. Use reflective probes, mirror questions, and clearinghouse probes to check both your understanding of the interviewee and the interviewee's understanding of what you have said.

3. *Involvement.* You will wish to have the interviewee be actively involved in receiving and considering the proposal. You can achieve this involvement through asking questions. If the interviewee is not reacting very much to what you are saying, ask the person to tell you how he or she is receiving your proposal. Ask if he or she understands. Ask what he or she thinks. Ask what he or she might suppose would happen if....

4. *Agreement.* We have suggested that a series of small agreements can lead to the acceptance of a larger idea. You may plan to ask a series of questions that you believe the interviewee can agree to, with the aim of securing agreement to a larger idea. Timing is important in seeking agreement though. Be sure that you have presented enough of your arguments and evidence that there is a strong likelihood of gaining agreement when you ask these questions.

5. *Objections.* Finally, you will want to ask questions when an objection is sensed. Do not label these objections with the word *objection.* Call them *concerns* or some other word that minimizes the situation.

The questions to be asked can only be planned, of course. Thinking about them in advance will allow you to ask better-formulated questions. Be sure that the questions asked are adapted to the interviewee and the circumstances. Also, select carefully any leading questions you wish to use so that they will not be perceived as high pressure and, therefore, lead to hostility.

Managing the Interviewee's Objections

The interviewer must be prepared to answer the interviewee's objections. We've all heard comments like these when we are in meetings and when a proposal for change has been made:

PROCRASTINATION
"Let's worry about this later when we have more time."
"We've discussed this enough today. Let's meet again."

TRADITION
"We've tried this before, and it didn't work."
"We've always done it this way, and everything has worked out OK."

UNCERTAIN FUTURE
"We don't really know what is coming 'down the pike' in the next few months. This is not the time to change."
"With the economy the way it is, I think we should hold off."

FUNDING
"I'm not sure we can afford this right now."
"$1500 sure seems like a lot of money for a project like this."

NEED
"Things are just fine now. I don't see the need."
"We are facing problems, but they just aren't that bad."

WORKABILITY
"I just don't think this will work."
"This sounds good in theory, but...."

Review these major categories of objections in relation to your particular proposal and situation. Develop arguments that you can use to counter each if the issue is raised.

THE INTERVIEWEE IN A PERSUASIVE INTERVIEW

The interviewee has a number of important responsibilities as a participant in the interview. A central piece of advice is to be an active participant so that you will be able to give the interviewer a fair hearing. Beyond this,

Ethics and Responsibilities in Interviewing

A person considering a persuasive effort is always faced with questions of ethics. Sources might be available that are questionable. The proposal may be less impressive that others you know about. The interviewee may have racial or other prejudices that could be appealed to in order to gain acceptance of the proposal. Contrary evidence might be presented or omitted. Names of sources could be withheld because they would prejudice the case. Half-truths might be told.

There is some help available for making decisions about ethical behavior in the persuasive interview setting. But, ultimately, the decision rests with the interviewer, who will have to adopt or reject the advice in planning and managing the interview. Here are guidelines presented by Charles U. Larson that we believe are helpful in making ethical decisions[12]:

1 Do not use false, fabricated, misrepresented, distorted, or irrelevant evidence to support arguments or claims.
2 Do not intentionally use specious, unsupported, or illogical reasoning.
3 Do not represent yourself as informed or as an expert on a subject when you are not.
4 Do not distort, hide, or misrepresent the number, scope, intensity, or undesirable features of consequences or effects.
5 Do not use emotional appeals that lack a supporting basis of evidence or reasoning, or that would not be accepted if the interviewees had time and opportunity to examine the subject themselves.
6 Do not advocate something in which you do not believe yourself.

Joann Keyton[13] has offered some additional suggestions to help you in this role.

Be open to alternative views.   When a person is closed to the other's view, he or she will not give it a fair hearing. You can miss some very good ideas and opportunities if you are not open to considering the other's views.

Be a good listener.   A good listener makes a special effort to hear and understand the interviewer's message. This means that you ought to carefully receive and process the information provided. It also means that you should attempt to provide feedback about your understanding of the information being presented.

Ask questions when you don't understand. Sometimes people don't ask questions because they think they are asking about something they should already understand. Don't allow this kind of thinking to keep you from asking questions. There is no shame in admitting you don't understand; you have an obligation as an interviewee to understand as much as you can so that you can make an informed, intelligent decision.

Ask for evidence if you are unsure. If evidence is not provided to back up an idea, ask for it. Request more evidence if you need it. Ask for the sources of evidence too. Ask for information about the source if you are not sure of who the person or group making a statement actually is.

Don't let the personality of the interviewer cloud your judgment. Sometimes the "smooth talker" will make whatever he or she has to say sound so good that you may be tempted to accept the view without adequate support. On the other hand, the less polished presentation may be rejected even though it is a very good idea. And even the individual who is a little "brassy" and aggressive ought to be heard out for what he or she has to say. The personality or presentation style of the interviewer may have a greater positive or negative effect on your perception of the proposal than it ought to have.

Delay the decision if you need more time to think. Unless you have a tendency to procrastinate, you would not be considering the need for more time unless you had some reservations about the proposal. Allow yourself the opportunity to consider the proposal without the interviewer present if you have doubts.

SUMMARY

The persuasive interview provides a setting in which the interviewer consciously seeks to exert influence over the interviewee to think, feel, and/or act in a particular way. Preparing for such an interview involves a five-step process: preparing a statement of purpose, analyzing the interviewee, analyzing the interviewee's position, considering the setting, and planning the interview.

The purpose provides the guidance needed to carry out the remaining preparation and should be specifically tailored to the interviewee and the situation. Data must be gathered about the interviewee in order to analyze the person's personal characteristics, socioeconomic background, orientation toward the topic, psychological characteristics, and attitude toward the interviewer. Next, the interviewer's own position on the issue is considered and a setting planned for the interview. Finally, the opening, proposal, and closing are structured.

Issues with regard to managing the interview were presented. The interviewer must give consideration to building rapport and credibility. The presentation of the proposal must also be adapted to the unique temperament of the interviewee. Special circumstances such as the opportunity for counterpersuasion and intellect/education of the interviewee must also be considered. Attention was given to asking different kinds of questions and to managing interviewee objections to the proposal. Finally, the ethical responsibility of the interviewer was addressed.

The interviewee has certain responsibilities if he or she is to be a responsible participant. These involve participating actively, being open to alternative views, listening carefully, asking questions, asking for evidence, taking into account the personality of the interviewer, and delaying a decision when necessary.

NOTES

[1] Herbert W. Simons, *Persuasion* (New York: Random House, 1986), pp. 22–23.

[2] Eric William Skopec, *Situational Interviewing* (New York: Harper & Row, 1986), p. 111.

[3] Victoria O'Donnell and June Kable, *Persuasion: An Interactive-Dependency Approach* (New York: Random House, 1982), pp. 27–31.

[4] Edward D. Steele and W. Charles Redding, "The American Value System: Premises for Persuasion," *Western Speech, 26* (1962), 83–91.

[5] Milton Rokeach and Seymour Parker, "Values as Social Indicators of Poverty and Race in America," *Annals of the American Academy of Political and Social Sciences, 388* (1970), 101–102.

[6] Jack L. Whitehead, "Factors of Source Credibility," *Quarterly Journal of Speech, 54* (1968), 59–63; Charles U. Larson, *Persuasion: Reception and Responsibility,* 5th ed. (Belmont, CA: Wadsworth, 1989), 309–311.

[7] Ellen Berschied, "Opinion Change and Communicator-Communicatee Similarity and Dissimilarity," *Journal of Personality and Social Psychology, 4* (1966), 67–80.

[8] Gerald L. Manning and Barry L. Reece, *Selling Today: A Personal Approach* (Boston: Allyn and Bacon, 1987), p. 350.

[9] Manning and Reece, pp. 358–363.

[10] Simons, pp. 127–128.

[11] Manning and Reece.

[12] Larson, pp. 38–39.

[13] Joann Keyton, "Interviewee Behavior in the Persuasive Interview," unpublished manuscript, University of South Alabama, 1988.

SAMPLE PERSUASIVE INTERVIEW FOR ANALYSIS

This persuasive interview presents a proposal for reallocation of secretarial support in a communication department. Dawn Lee is the manager of the department; Jerry Garcia is one of five salaried employees in the department.

1. Jerry: Morning, Dawn. I wondered if you had a few minutes to talk about a problem that I've been experiencing.

2. Dawn: Sure, come on in. Do you need much time?

3. Jerry: Well, I think just a few minutes will do. Maybe five to ten minutes or so—just enough time to see if we can solve a problem that I and some others in the department have been experiencing. It concerns use of our secretarial pool. The pool concept works pretty well most of the time, but we've found that it doesn't seem to work too well for spur-of-the-moment situations. I think we all have spur-of-the-moment things that come up—we have to get something out right away, or we have to meet some sort of deadline that has been changed. I think you said last week that you were experiencing a crunch and sure could use some extra help to get some things out. Is that right, Dawn?

4. Dawn: Sure, I remember that.

5. Jerry: Well, then you understand what that feels like. I don't know how you handle it, but when I have situations like that, I end up pushing other things out of the way and doing much of the secretarial work connected with it myself. There's just not enough time to make arrangements for somebody else to do it. Has that been your experience, too?

6. Dawn: Well, I know what you mean. It's often just easier to sit down and work at the computer yourself than to arrange for someone else to do a job when you're in a hurry.

7. Jerry: Right! It makes me a lot less efficient when I have to sit down and do work that support people could be doing.

Another thing I've noticed, Dawn, at least for me, is how very difficult it is to plan certain kinds of activities. I may be working late at night on a report, and then it turns out that it goes a little longer than I expected it. Since it's too late to check whether the secretarial pool can squeeze it into the schedule the next day, I am stuck staying later, sometimes another hour or two, to get this work done.

There are all kinds of situations like that. Sometimes we are told that we have to wait a couple of days for a report to be typed that needs to go right out. So we end up sitting down and typing it ourselves. I know you work extra hours a lot and Hilda is not here to help because she leaves at five o'clock. And for us, it's hard to predict how the secretarial pool will work things like that into its schedule.

What it comes down to is this: We all are less efficient in getting things done. And sometimes we have difficulty meeting important deadlines.

I've been thinking that perhaps we can do something about this problem. I'd like you to help me think about a solution if you are willing.

8. Dawn: I'll help if I can.

9. Jerry: I know that sometimes you face unexpected deadlines. What do you do when you have priority secretarial work?

10. Dawn: When I have priority work I give it to Hilda and ask her to put it ahead of whatever she is doing.

11. Jerry: And when you've been working late at night and you have something that will need attention early in the morning, what do you do?

12. Dawn: I place it right on top of Hilda's desk so that she can get right to it in the morning.

13. Jerry: So you are able to short-circuit the everyday routine to gain control over the work flow?

14. Dawn: Yes, that's it.

15. Jerry: And Hilda is able to make her priorities your priorities. Isn't that pretty much how it goes?

16. Dawn: I think that's pretty much how it goes. But everybody cannot have a personal secretary.

17. Jerry: Oh, I understand that. But I don't think that's really the problem. I think the problem is allocating the time of the secretarial pool. We don't have the kind of control that you and others who have personal secretaries have over the time of the person who is doing your work. But we could have more control. Let me explain how this could work.

We could take a small portion of the time that each secretary in the pool works for each of us and assign that time directly to the person. This would mean that each of us would be able to count on, say, two hours a day—time in which we can take care of these special needs. That way when we have emergency things to be done, we can count on having time to get them done. What do you think about the possibility of taking the five of us and assigning each of us a two-hour block of time?

18. Dawn: Well, Jerry, frankly, I don't see a whole lot wrong with that idea. It does make me a little nervous to just out and out assign that time. I'm not sure how it would be used and sometimes, especially when we get really busy, it seems to me we might have to pull the secretaries off work that a person has counted on them doing. I'm just not quite sure that that would really work for us.

19. Jerry: Well, I thought about that some, Dawn, and I think that ways to deal with emergency situations could be built into the system. It seems to me that in emergency situations, we could agree to pick up time from people if we just have an out-and-out emergency. Beyond that, since this is something new, we might schedule some readjustment periods. We could try the plan for a week and see how it's going. If it seems to be going about right, we would keep the system as it is. If it seems like more time could actually be used, we might adjust it to give each person a little more time. And if it seems like it's too much, we might pull back on it. We might go ahead and try it again for two more weeks and have another adjustment period, and, then, beyond that, just check it at two-month intervals. We won't have to be married to the situation; we can provide for some adjustments to see how it will work. And it seems to me that might take care of the problem of emergencies. We just out and out say we will need time if we have emergencies and also adjust the time by building in the adjustment period. What do you think about that, Dawn?

20. Dawn: Well, Jerry, I think we might try that for a while, as long as people are willing to be flexible and build in some adjustment periods. Let me see if I understand this correctly. What we will be doing is assigning two hours per day to a particular individual and that person will have control over that time; that is, that person will have priority use at that time. But if the time is not being used, the secretary could work on somebody else's work. I think that's what you were proposing?

21. Jerry: That's right. Beyond that I suggest that we have some adjustment periods to adjust the time either up or down.

22. Dawn: Jerry, I think that sounds like it might solve the problem, and I'm certainly willing to try that if it will makes people's work more efficient and allows them to handle emergency situations better.

23. Jerry: You'll put the word out, then?

24. Dawn: I'll start the new schedule on Monday.

25. Jerry: I appreciate your help. This has been a difficult situation for some time.

ROLE-PLAYING CASES

A Proposal for Lighting

John Jacobs, the interviewer, represents Maryknoll Subdivision, one of the older sections in western Centerville. The subdivision includes about two hundred houses and five streets. Because of the age of the subdivision, the street lighting originally installed does not meet current standards of distance between lights. Consequently, the neighborhood is rather dimly lit. But Maryknoll is not alone with this problem, as there are approximately twenty-five other areas that suffer from the same problem. Residents of Maryknoll are concerned, nonetheless, as there is clearly a potential for increased crime in neighborhoods that are not well lit.

The interviewee, John George, Director of Public Works, is a fifty-five-year-old man who has been in his post for ten years. He understands the problem and is sympathetic, but has too many projects for the size of his budget. He must decide whether the circumstances regarding the lighting of this neighborhood warrant moving it up on the schedule for upgrading lighting in the city.

A Salary Increase

The interviewer, Jill Spiller, is a thirty-five-year-old single-again woman with two children. She has been through a divorce three years ago that left her stunned. She needed extra funds to meet her financial obligations, and so she turned to a neighbor who had just opened Gulf Coast Dive Shop for possible employment. Jill is an expert diver who holds instructor certification. She was hired by Gulf Coast as an instructor at a salary that was somewhat higher than minimum wage. Now that Gulf Coast is no longer struggling, Jill thinks that it is time she be paid a salary appropriate to her skill and position. She clearly excels above the other instructors both as a diver and as an instructor. She expects to ask for and receive a substantial raise.

The interviewee, Steve Orlando, is the owner of Gulf Coast Dive Shop. He is appreciative of Jill's loyalty in times when he was struggling to get the dive shop established. He would like to pay Jill more and has really intended to do so. He is particularly concerned, on the other hand, about the level of salary increase for Jill because he has two other instructors who might also demand a substantial increase if he gives her one. Steve is also concerned about meeting the loan payment he took on when he built the current shop and diving facility. If business should take a sudden slump, he might face financial trouble.

A New Home

Don Jones is a real estate representative for Martin Brothers Realty. He knows that the interviewees (a couple with two children) have been looking at a variety of homes, both used and new. Martin Brothers Realty has a 9-year-old home located on a lot that is 100- by 150-feet deep. The house has a large family room with a fireplace, a living room, a kitchen, four bedrooms, two baths, a laundry room, and a utility room. In addition to these features, there is a 2½-car carport and a 20- by 10-foot shop. The interview is taking place in the couple's small three-bedroom house.

The interviewees are both professional people. The wife, Cynthia, is a speech pathologist, and the husband, Kevin, is a high school principal. Their combined income is $65,000. Their children, Shawn, aged fourteen, and Ellen, aged ten, are active and need the extra space a larger house would provide. Kevin would like some space for his woodworking; Cynthia would like a work area for the calligraphy projects she does. They view the interviewer as a typical real estate representative, anxious to make a sale, as the market is slow due to rising interest rates.

A New Computer

Susan Keyton, the interviewer, is an assistant professor at Western University, a school of about ten thousand students. She teaches both graduate and undergraduate classes. A good portion of her work involves writing and research. She writes for both professional meetings and college textbooks. She also is an active researcher, having averaged more than two publications in scholarly journals for each of the three years she has been at the university. Because of a shortage of funds, a computer was not placed in her office when she joined the faculty. Thus, she has been forced to do much of her work in a computer laboratory in the building next to her office. She believes that she ought to have a computer in her office that will provide easy access to the mainframe computer and plans to schedule an interview with her department chair.

Dr. Pappas is the chair of Susan's department, having been in the position for five years. Pappas is an active teacher and scholar as well as an administrator. Keyton's request will fall on sympathetic ears, but must be weighed against other very pressing needs for equipment.

An Expanded Menu

The interviewer, Carlos Almada, is a twenty-five-year-old assistant manager at a thriving fast-food restaurant near Southern University. He is working at the restaurant as the night manager while attending classes during the day. Carlos worked his way up to assistant manager from a starting position as counter help. Patronage of the restaurant slows down in the evenings at about the time that most people have finished their evening meal. Carlos concludes that this is because their menu does not include some of the traditional evening snack food. He decides to meet with his boss to persuade her to try some new items on the menu. The interview takes place after the store closing at 11 P.M.

The interviewee, Missy Wilkins, is a forty-two-year-old who purchased the restaurant fifteen years ago. After five years of struggle with marginal profits, she quit her job as an accountant and took over the restaurant's management. Business did not turn around over night, but she worked hard and soon began to see a steady increase in business and profits. The restaurant is now at the point that it is making a nice profit. The interviewee likes Carlos because he is personable and a hard worker. He also seems to relate well to restaurant employees, most of whom are college students. Some of Carlos's suggestions have paid off in the past; others haven't. Missy is open to considering his suggestions.

EXPERIENCES

1. Interview a person who is a professional sales representative. Discover how this person prepares for a sale. Ask about what kinds of information this person attempts to get from the client during the interview. Find out also what part nonverbal characteristics of the interviewee play in the interview.
2. Plan an interview using one of the role-playing cases above. State the purpose. Analyze the interviewee and the context. Now plan the interview, including the opening, proposal, and closing.
3. Select a product that might sell to a particular person. Imagine what this person is like. Create a description of the person and then plan an interview to sell the product.

RECOMMENDED READINGS

Johannesen, Richard L., *Ethics and Persuasion: Selected Readings* (New York: Random House, 1967).

Larson, Charles U., *Persuasion: Reception and Responsibility,* 5th ed. (Belmont, CA: Wadsworth, 1989).

Manning, Gerald L., and Barry L. Reece, *Selling Today: A Personal Approach* (Boston: Allyn and Bacon, 1987).

Simons, Herbert W., *Persuasion: Understanding, Practice, and Analysis,* 2d. ed. (New York: Random House, 1986).

TROUBLESHOOTING THE INTERVIEW

Most professionals we know keep a library of reference works to help them resolve the problems they encounter in the world of work. Sooner or later they encounter communication problems. We want this book to be helpful as a tool for working with common communication problems that occur in interviews in a variety of organizational settings.

Many texts written for the college classroom do not lend themselves well to use as a reference for solutions to problems. For example, a typical index—like the one at the end of this book—presents a fairly thorough list of key words. But that kind of index is not a very helpful problem-solving reference because it is not problem-specific. Thus you have to sort through many sections of a book to find answers to specific questions. Our solution was to develop this troubleshooting guide.

The guide poses more than two hundred of the most common questions people in organizations ask about communication problems in interviews. We have indexed these problems in a way that refers you to the locations in the book where solutions are suggested.

HOW TO USE THIS PROBLEM-SOLUTION INDEX

1. Verbalize the problem you are experiencing.
2. Look for key words that describe the nature of the problem. Key words are listed alphabetically in the directory that follows.
3. Locate these key words in the problem-solution index (page 329).
4. Find a question close to the one you are asking, and turn to the indicated pages for the answer.
5. If the key words are not listed here, consult the index in the back of the book.

Problem Category and Questions(s)	Location of Solution
INTERVIEWING BASICS	
Approaches	
I'm often not sure if I am exercising too little or too much control in an interview. How can I decide about how much to control?	42–44
Communication Breakdown	
I experienced a breakdown in communication. Where can I look to discover what might be the problem?	5–10, 30–40
Context	
What are the important context aspects for me to consider in an interview?	13–15, 26–48
Ethics	
Ethics is becoming quite a concern. What factors might I consider in trying to be more ethical in interviews?	19–20
Images	
I don't think that I always have a good picture of who the other person in the interview is. Is there something to focus my thoughts?	29–30, 45–47
Listening	
I know I sometimes have trouble listening, but don't know why.	35–36
What does the listening process involve?	35–36
How can I improve my listening?	36–40
How can I improve my ability to remember what I've heard?	37–40
Messages	
Sometimes I experience misunderstandings, disagreements, and even conflict in interviews. What might be wrong?	30–31
I know that a good deal can be known about the other person in an interview by carefully observing the nonverbal behavior. What kinds of things should I look for?	31–34
Needs	
Sometimes I sense that those I interview want more from me than just the superficial interaction of the interview. What kinds of needs might I try to meet in the interview?	28–29

(Continued)

(Continued)

GLOSSARY

active listening Response in which the listener paraphrases the speaker's ideas and feelings.

affection need Desire to like and be liked by the other person in the interview.

Age Discrimination in Employment Act of 1967, 1978 Federal legislation that makes it unlawful to discriminate against applicants or employees who are between forty and sixty-five years old.

agreement/disagreement scale (Likert scale) Typical evaluative interval scale that asks the interviewee to make a judgment.

Amendments to Higher Education Act of 1972 Federal legislation that prohibits sexual discrimination in federally assisted educational programs and places educational institutions under the Equal Pay Act.

attitude A predisposition to respond for or against a position, an object, or a person.

bipolar question Question worded in such a way as to limit the respondent to one of two answers.

belief Statement about what a person thinks is true; a conviction. There are three categories: primitive beliefs, surface beliefs, and derived beliefs.

behaviorally anchored rating scale (BARS) Assessment scale developed to overcome some of the difficulties associated with the conventional rating scale.

BFOQ Bona fide occupational qualifications.

cause-to-effect pattern Pattern where the principle is to discuss causes before effects and then to link causes to effects.

certainty In logic, the position that what is being observed could not have occurred by chance. One hundred percent confidence level. Certainty also refers to a closed-minded attitude or to language that suggests such an attitude. The opposite of certainty, from this perspective, is provisionalism.

channel Medium through which the message is sent.

Civil Rights Act of 1866 Federal legislation giving all persons the same contractual rights as "white citizens." It was the first law that prohibited discrimination.

Civil Rights Act of 1964, 1972 Comprehensive federal legislation that addressed discrimination in such areas as education, federally assisted programs, and voting. Title VII of the act forbade employment discrimination or membership discrimination by employers, employment agencies, and unions on the basis of race, color, religion, sex, or national origin.

clarification probe Follow-up question that is asked in an attempt to gain further information regarding an unclear idea presented by the interviewee.

clearinghouse probe or question Question asked by an interviewer that allows the interviewee to tell anything that might remain unsaid about the topic of the interview.

climate Atmosphere present in a communication event such as an interview.

closed question Question that narrows the options for responding to an interviewer's question to a specific area.

closing That part of the interview in which the interviewer concludes the interview.

communication Any speech act, such as talking with a stranger, exchanging information in a group, making a public speech, or asking and answering questions in an interview.

communication process Any speech act that develops meanings over time and changes those meanings with the passage of time.

content analysis Line-by-line inspection of particular data to count the number of times certain ideas, themes, or trends are present.

context of communication Physical, social-psychological, and temporal environment in which communication takes place and which exerts influence on the form and content of communication.

control (noun) Defensive behavior characterized by manipulation in an attempt to impose an attitude or viewpoint on another. One of three interpersonal needs identified by William Schutz. The degree of desire to exercise power and authority. Behavioral opposite of problem orientation. (verb) To exercise restraint, dominance, or direction over; to command.

control need Desire to both exercise power and authority and have it exercised over us.

conventional rating form Assessment instrument generally consisting of a series of items—either employee characteristics or behaviors—with some type of a high-to-low rating scale.

criteria Standards for making a decision.

critical incident appraisal Assessment, provided in essay form, of behavior relating to particular situations where the assessor is asked to write a specific example of good and poor employee performance.

culture Integrated pattern of human behavior that includes thought, speech, action, and artifacts and depends upon the capacity of people for transmitting knowledge to succeeding generations.

decoder Person who interprets the meanings of the messages of the source.

defensive behavior Behavior that occurs when an individual perceives or anticipates threat.

defensiveness State of having assumed a position or attitude to protect against attack. In interpersonal communication, manifested in such behaviors as evaluation, superiority, certainty, control, neutrality, and strategy, each of which terms is defined in this glossary. Behavioral opposite of supportiveness.

demographic variables Characteristics of the people surveyed.

description Statement that represents another's behavior or a situation objectively. Behavioral opposite of evaluation.

directive approach Style of interview in which the interviewer establishes the purpose of the interview and generally continues to control the interview by structuring and asking nearly all the questions.

disciplinary interview Interview in which fact-finding takes place, with punishment being administered if the employee is found to be at fault and if the situation is serious enough that such action be taken.

double-barreled question Question that asks more than one question as if they were a single question.

dyad Two-person group.

either/or close Technique used to conclude a persuasive interview where the interviewer attempts to narrow the choices to two possibilities and persuade the interviewee to portray the most desirable of the two as the one he or she is advocating.

elaboration probe Follow-up question used to encourage the person to provide additional information that will amplify or extend an incomplete answer.

elimination of a single objection close Strategy used in a persuasive interview that acknowledges the reservation and counters with a contrasting advantage.

emotional interview Interview where the interviewee is displaying strong feelings due to intense identification with the subject of the interview.

empathy Supportive behavior characterized by identification with experiences, feelings, and problems of others and affirmation of another's self-worth.

employee-centered performance appraisal interview Interview that is designed to evaluate work behavior in which the employee is asked to provide analysis of his or her behavior and solutions to any performance problems encountered. This is in contrast to an interview where the boss does most of the analysis and problem solving.

encoder Person who initiates an interaction.

Equal Employment Opportunity Act of 1972 Federal legislation that amended Title VII of the Civil Rights Act of 1964 to broaden coverage to include state and governmental agencies and educational institutions and to give the EEOC authority to bring lawsuits.

Equal Employment Opportunity Commission (EEOC). Federal commission charged with overseeing the enforcement of the federal employment law.

Equal Pay Act of 1963, 1972 Federal legislation that made it unlawful to pay different hourly rates for the same work on the basis of sex.

equality Supportive behavior characterized by a show of respect for another, and efforts to minimize differences in ability, status, power, and intellectual ability. Behavioral opposite of superiority.

essay appraisal Performance evaluation that uses the narrative form to discuss the strengths and weaknesses of an employee.

evaluation The process of making a value judgment about some person, object, or event. A behavior identified as a potential stimulus of defensive behavior in another person, especially if the evaluation questions the other person's viewpoint or motive. Behavioral opposite of description.

evaluative interval scale Assessment instrument that may be used to seek an evaluation. It might include categories such as excellent, good, average, below average, and poor.

feedback Verbal and nonverbal behavior of a receiver directed back to the source in reaction to the content of the message; the perceivable response of a receiver to the message that has been communicated.

field of experience Sum of an individual's experiences, plus all connections drawn among them, that allows a person to talk about and interact with the world. Some theorists believe that people cannot interact unless their fields of experience overlap.

forced-choice rating Evaluation instrument that requires the assessor to select a description of a category from choices supplied.

formal roles Sets of behaviors that a person assumes because of his or her position within a group or organization.

frame of reference Sum of our past experiences that color the way we interpret whatever we are observing; our past experience with the topic, the other person, and even the particular context.

frequency count Number that refers to how many respondents selected each of the particular answers to a question.

frequency interval scale Instrument to report how often the respondent does something or uses something.

funnel sequence Ordering of questions in an interview that begins with a broad, open question and follows with questions that narrow the focus of the topic, becoming more specific and closed.

general situation Events that surround the interview in its given time in history.

goal-setting step Step in the problem/solution interview in which ways of solving the problem and commitment to a practical course of action are explored.

group interview Interview in which there are multiple interviewers or interviewees, or both.

highly closed question Question that supplies a short list of responses, or implies a very limited response, from which the interviewee is expected to select.

highly leading question Question that may compel the interviewee to give a desired answer.

highly open question Question that suggests a general topic area, but allows almost complete freedom of response.

highly scheduled interview Schedule of questions that contains all the questions to be asked during the interview, including those to be used for probing, ordered and worded as they will be asked.

hostile interviewee Person who displays defensive communication behavior.

I'll think it over close Conclusion of a persuasive interview that seeks to acknowledge the interviewee's wish to think about the proposal, while trying to discover the remaining area of concern and/or the interviewee's level of interest.

Immigration Reform and Control Act of 1987 Federal legislation that prohibits discrimination on the basis of citizenship, providing an alien has a work permit and appropriate visa.

inclusion need One of the interpersonal needs identified by William Schutz that includes an individual's desire to be accepted. to feel wanted, and to be a part of groups.

in-depth information gathering Communication where questions are asked that are designed to acquire information about a subject, process, or person.

indirect question Question that does not ask specifically for, but hopes to secure, the information the interviewer would like the interviewee to provide.

informal roles Sets of behaviors that develop as a function of a relationship that has emerged (friend) or has been assumed (colleague).

interact Exchange verbal and nonverbal messages.

interaction step Step in the problem-solving interview in which the problem that is discussed has been agreed upon and any emotions that may block successful attempts to manage a solution are brought out.

internal summary Condensed version of what an interviewee has said, which is provided for the interviewee's response in order to check if the interviewer's perception of what the interviewee has said is accurate.

interval scale Data collection instrument that gives the respondent an opportunity to indicate choices along a continuum that provides distances between measures.

interview Communication process in which two or more people interact within a relational context by asking and answering questions to achieve a specific purpose.

inverted funnel sequence Schedule of questions for an interview where the interviewer begins with a relatively closed question and moves progressively to more open questions.

leading question Question in which the interviewer, either directly or indirectly, signals or pushes an interviewee to a particular answer.

leaning question Question that asks the interviewee what direction his or her opinion might favor regarding some idea, issue, or candidate.

listening process Acts of receiving, interpreting, and remembering the message taken together.

loaded question Highly leading question that contains emotionally charged words, such as *jerk, cheating,* and *radical.*

management by objectives (MBO) Process in which the manager and subordinate, working together, to develop standards of performance by setting goals (objectives) rather than stipulating activities to be performed.

message Ideas conveyed by the verbal and nonverbal behavior of a source; the idea or combination of ideas expressed by the receiver (usually labeled *feedback* when expressed by the receiver).

mildly leading question Question that is worded to make it easier for the interviewee to answer in a given direction.

model Physical representation of something. A metaphor that allows examination of some object or process in a particular way but also limits what can be observed in that way.

moderately closed question Question that asks the interviewee to supply a particular piece of information.

moderately open question Question that produces a less lengthy and more focused response than an open question.

moderately scheduled interview Structure of questions for an interview that reflects the major topics of the interview along with possible probing questions under each.

mutually exclusive Not overlapping or lining up in some kind of continuum.

need Urgent want; can suggest the impelling force for the change you are advocating.

neutral question Question that does not influence the interviewee to answer in any special direction.

neutrality Impersonal communication response pattern that can create defensiveness in another person. Opposite of empathy.

noise Interference in channels that disrupts our ability to receive a message.

nominal scale Measurement instrument that uses categories (variables) that are considered to be mutually exclusive.

nondirective approach Style of interview in which the interviewer turns responsibility for (control of) the interview over to the interviewee.

nonscheduled interview Interview in which the list of questions to be asked is not preplanned. General topics of the interview might or might not be planned.

nonverbal message Information provided by a source that serves to communicate, but does not involve the use of verbal symbols.

numerical interval scale Measurement instrument used to collect information about age, income, educational level, rank in an organization, and the like.

open question Question that asks for information that is broad and general.

opinion poll Survey to collect data about some group's attitudes.

ordinal scale Measurement instrument that asks the respondent to rate or rank variables in relationship to one another.

organization goal As used in a performance appraisal interview, a standard of performance behavior that contributes to the purpose of the organization.

paraphrasing Casting what you have heard into your own words.

performance appraisal Method by which an employee's work is evaluated in an organization.

personal characteristics Physical and mental features of the individual.

persuasion Communication process of influencing attitudes and behaviors.

physical noise External interference in the communication process.

population Identifiable group of people that represent some set of ideas, attitudes, and beliefs.

price closing Conclusion of a persuasive interview in which the interviewer stresses the best offer and perhaps the savings it represents.

primary question Question that initiates a new line of questioning within the overall interview schedule.

probing question Question that illuminates and adds to the information that was received when the primary question was asked.

problem orientation Supportive behavior characterized by a desire to collaborate with another in defining and solving a problem. Behavioral opposite of control.

problem-solution interview Interview in which the goal is to help the interviewee overcome a specific problem by articulating its causes and effects.

problem step Step in the problem-solving interview in which the interviewer inquires into the nature of a problem from the interviewee's perspective.

process Phenomenon that occurs over time and changes with time as it occurs.

provisionalism Supportive behavior characterized by a willingness to be tentative, to share information, to suggest that additional information might change one's mind, and to work jointly with another. Behavioral opposite of certainty.

psychological characteristics Attributes of a person that include such things as psychological orientation, values, and needs.

psychological orientation Person's mental attitude or general frame of mind.

public Group of people who have a common interest and are capable of engaging in discussion of an issue in order to do something about it.

random sample Members of a population chosen in a way that allows every possible member to have an equal probability of being selected.

ranking system Measurement instrument that, when used in a performance appraisal system, forces the rater to compare each employee within a particular work unit of the organization.

rapport Cordiality and warmth that people experience toward each other in a relationship.

receiver Person who interprets the meanings of the messages of the source.

reflective probe (mirror question) Question that feeds back what the interviewee said.

Rehabilitation Act of 1973 Federal legislation that mandates affirmative action to employ and promote qualified handicapped people.

relational context Formal and informal roles that the participants perform.

relationship Formal or informal connection that people hold toward each other.

reliability In interviewing, quality that refers to the consistency of a question.

reluctant interviewee Person who has agreed to be interviewed but does not fully participate in the interview.

remembering Process of recalling by an effort of memory. Fourth component of the listening process.

sample point (start point) Method of choosing interviewees for a survey in which city blocks are selected by using a table of random numbers. The residents in these selected blocks serve as a sample of the population and are interviewed.

sampling error Problem that results when what we measure in the sample does not match what exists in the target population.

secondary question Question that follows up the primary question to explore deeper. Gives depth to an interview.

selection interview Interview that is conducted to make a decision about the interviewee's membership in some program, group, or organization.

selective attention Process of choosing one or more of the stimuli to which we are exposed.

selective exposure Process of choosing certain stimuli while disregarding or avoiding others.

self-development goal Outcome of an appraisal interview where the aim is to increase the ability of the employee to cope successfully with work-related problems.

self-disclosure Revealing one's thoughts, feelings, beliefs, and the like to another.

self-esteem Value of oneself. Self-love. Self-respect.

semantic differential questions Measurement scale between sets of bipolar adjectives to indicate a response.

sequence Series of interconnected questions that are organized around some overall plan.

social needs Interpersonal needs that can be fulfilled through the social relationship between the interviewer and interviewee.

social step Step in the problem-solving interview in which the interviewer and interviewee meet and greet each other, exchange pleasantries, and generally attempt to relax and feel comfortable.

solution Answer to a problem or need in that it seeks to remove or moderate it.

source Person who initiates the interaction.

source credibility Favorability that the source of a message enjoys; is derived from what is known about the person's reputation, attainments, personality, beliefs, and intent.

specific situation Immediate events and circumstances that surround the interview.

spontaneity Supportive behavior characterized by the candid, straightforward, and uncomplicated presentation of the self. Behavioral opposite of strategy.

standardized (highly scheduled) interview Schedule for an interview that provides questions worded as they will be stated and options to answers as they will be offered.

stratified random sample Group selected from a population that includes a minimum number of respondents from each of several groups or a percentage of the entire sample that represents that group's percentage in the actual population.

summary close Conclusion of a persuasive interview where the interviewer will summarize the need, criteria, or agreements made earlier and then ask for agreement.

superiority Defensive behavior characterized by suggestions that another is inadequate or inferior and thus unable to entertain feedback or share in problem solving. Behavioral opposite of equality.

supportiveness Interpersonal behavior characterized by description, problem orientation, spontaneity, empathy, equality, and provisionalism, each of which is defined in this glossary.

symbol Something that stands for something else when no natural relationship exists. In language, words, phrases, and sentences that stand for thoughts.

temperament Unique personal nature of the individual that affects the way he or she thinks, feels, and acts.

time pattern Pattern for an interview that allows the interviewer to organize topics and/or questions to be pursued according to corresponding dates.

topical pattern Pattern for an interview that is based on the assumption that an interviewer has more than one basic area of questioning that needs to be explored.

transactional Characterized by mutual negotiation of meaning or mutual influence.

trust Feeling of comfort that derives from the ability to predict another's behavior. A belief that the other can be relied on.

tunnel sequence Sequence that uses a series of questions that have a similar degree of closedness or openness.

understanding Third component of the listening process. Interpretation and evaluation of what is sensed.

validity Accuracy of the information elicited from a question.

verbal misunderstanding Failure to interpret a message correctly. This may result when one person's frame of reference doesn't coincide with the other's.

Vietnam Era Veterans Readjustment Assistance Act of 1974 Federal legislation that requires employers with government contracts of $10,000 or more to take affirmative action to employ and promote Vietnam era veterans.

NAME INDEX

SUBJECT INDEX

Active listening, 37, 194–195
Age Discrimination in
    Employment Act, 120
Amendments to Higher Education
    Act of 1965 (1972), 120
Appearance, as nonverbal
    message, 32
Approach to interviewing:
  directive, 42–44
  nondirective, 42–44

Behaviors:
  communication, 30–40
  of eyes, as nonverbal message,
    33
  of face, as nonverbal message,
    33
Bona fide occupational
    qualifications (BFOQs),
    118–119

Career path, 167–168
Career plan, 167–170
  implementation of, 168–170
Channels of communication, 6,
  9–10
Civil Rights Act:
  of 1866, 120
  of 1964, 117, 120, 182
    Title VII, 120, 182
  of 1972, 220
Climate of an interview, 40–41
Communication:
  and relationships, 41–42
  and tasks, 41

Communication process, 5–11
Content analysis, 263
Context, 12–15, 26–48
  communication, 13
  cultural, 13
  interviews in, 13–15
Cover letter, 143–146
Credibility of message source, 306
Culture, 13

Decoded meaning, 7
Disciplinary interview(s), 198–199
  managing, 199
  planning, 198–199
Dyad, 12

Employment Act of 1967 and
    1978, 120
Encoded meaning, 7
Endicott Report, Northwestern,
    156, 159
Environment, physical, 34
Equal Employment Opportunity
    Act of 1972, 120
Equal Employment Opportunity
    Commission (EEOC), 118,
    182
  guidelines, 117–119
Equal Pay Act of 1963 and 1972,
    120
Ethics, 19–20, 131, 166, 201,
    235–236, 265, 291, 318
  in in-depth information-
    gathering interviews, 235–
    236